TV licence
[illegible]
m Fuel
m TB
m [illegible]

OXFORD MONOGRAPHS ON LABOUR LAW
General Editors: PAUL DAVIES, KEITH EWING, MARK FREEDLAND

A Purposive Approach to Labour Law

OXFORD MONOGRAPHS ON LABOUR LAW

This series has come to represent a significant contribution to the literature of British, European, and international labour law. The series recognizes the arrival not only of a renewed interest in labour law generally, but also the need for fresh approaches to the study of labour law following a period of momentous change in the UK and Europe. The series is concerned with all aspects of labour law, including traditional subjects of study such as collective labour law and individual employment law. It also includes works that concentrate on the growing role of human rights and the combating of discrimination in employment, and others that examine the law and economics of the labour market and the impact of social security law and of national and supranational employment policies upon patterns of employment and the employment contract. Two of the contributing authors to the series, Lucy Vickers and Diamond Ashiagbor, have received awards from the Society of Legal Scholars in respect of their books.

TITLES PUBLISHED IN THE SERIES

Bullying and Behavioural Conflict at Work
The Duality of Individual Rights
Lizzie Barmes

The Concept of the Employer
Jeremias Prassl

The Labour Constitution
The Enduring Idea of Labour Law
Ruth Dukes

The Legal Construction of Personal Work Relations
Mark Freedland and Nicola Kountouris

A Right to Care?
Unpaid Work in European Employment Law
Nicole Busby

Regulating Flexible Work
Deirdre McCann

Welfare to Work
Conditional Rights in Social Policy
Amir Paz-Fuchs

EU Intervention in Domestic Labour Law
Phil Syrpis

Towards a Flexible Labour Market
Labour Legislation and Regulation since the 1990s
Paul Davies and Mark Freedland

The European Employment Strategy
Labour Market Regulation and New Governance
Diamond Ashiagbor

The Law of the Labour Market
Industrialization, Employment, and Legal Evolution
Simon Deakin and Frank Wilkinson

The Personal Employment Contract
Mark Freedland

International and European Protection of the Right to Strike
A Comparative Study of Standards Set by the International Labour Organization, the Council of Europe and the European Union
Tonia Novitz

A Purposive Approach to Labour Law

GUY DAVIDOV

Elias Lieberman Professor of Labour Law, Hebrew University of Jerusalem

OXFORD
UNIVERSITY PRESS

OXFORD
UNIVERSITY PRESS

Great Clarendon Street, Oxford, OX2 6DP,
United Kingdom

Oxford University Press is a department of the University of Oxford.
It furthers the University's objective of excellence in research, scholarship,
and education by publishing worldwide. Oxford is a registered trade mark of
Oxford University Press in the UK and in certain other countries

First Edition published in 2016

Impression: 1

Published in the United States of America by Oxford University Press
198 Madison Avenue, New York, NY 10016, United States of America

British Library Cataloguing in Publication Data
Data available

Library of Congress Control Number: 2016936871

ISBN 978–0–19–875903–4

Printed and bound by
CPI Group (UK) Ltd, Croydon, CR0 4YY

General Editors' Preface

In this volume Guy Davidov tackles what many have seen as the 'crisis' in labour law by proposing that it lies in the disjunction between the goals of labour law and the means which lie at its disposal to achieve its goals. In his view, whilst it is debatable whether this problem is in any way new for labour law, it is nevertheless a profound problem which constantly manifests itself in a new way as the social phenomena labour aims to regulate themselves change and develop.

Accordingly, the book is divided into two halves: the first aimed at articulating the goals of labour law and the second at analysing the means available to achieve those ends. The overall thesis is that a purposive approach to both law making and law interpretation can produce a coherent set of labour law rules, once its goals have been properly understood and the strengths and weaknesses of the mechanisms available to it taken on board.

It would be wrong, however, to view the first part ('goals') as pure theory and the second ('means') as pure practice. The goals, once articulated, are illustrated in relation to three very topical problems: minimum wage legislation, laws supporting collective bargaining and unfair dismissal laws. Equally, the 'means' part explores, for example, the boundaries between rules and standards and theories challenging the 'command and control' approach to rule enforcement.

Whilst this book is not systematically comparative, it draws on the author's considerable experience, not only of his native Israeli labour law, but also of UK and North American rules. It will be of interest, in fact, and value to anyone in any jurisdiction concerned with the perennially important questions, what is labour law for and how well does it do its job?

We warmly welcome this addition to the Oxford Monographs on Labour Law series.

Paul Davies, Keith Ewing, Mark Freedland

Preface

This book puts forward my views about the goals and means of labour law and the best path for the development of the field in light of new challenges. The term 'labour law' is used here in its meaning outside of North America, i.e. including all regulations of the employment relationship, at the individual and collective level. The basic idea—that we need to think about labour law *purposively*—may seem trivial; but working out the details of this general claim is far from simple. The book seeks to articulate the goals behind labour laws, at different levels of generality/abstraction, and to suggest the best legal means to advance these goals. I attempt to offer ways to reinvigorate labour law while resisting the current trend to retreat towards self-regulation (which necessarily involves some degree of *de*regulation).

This line of research started in my doctoral dissertation and continued in several articles I have published over the past decade and a half. Chapter 2 is based on 'Articulating Labour Law's Goals: Why and How' (2012) 3 Eur Lab LJ 130. Chapters 3 and 6 are based in part on 'The Three Axes of Employment Relationships: a Characterization of Workers in Need of Protection' (2002) 52 U Toronto LJ 357. Chapter 4 is based on 'The Goals of Regulating Work: Between Universalism and Selectivity' (2014) 64 U Toronto LJ 1. In a few other places I relied on previous publications and sometimes reproduced (smaller) parts from them, and have noted so in footnotes. All of these materials have been substantially updated and re-edited into the new framework. The structure and significant parts of the content are new.

Over the years I have been fortunate to enjoy encouragement and critique from many colleagues and friends. I owe special thanks to Brian Langille for his ongoing support and generosity from the very beginning of my academic career. At several junctures along the way this has made a great difference. My faith in the purposive approach was first shaped by the judgments and writings of Aharon Barak, before being cemented during my graduate studies at the University of Toronto, thanks to Brian as well as David Beatty, who supervised my LLM work with inspiring commitment. Patrick Macklem and Kerry Rittich have also been immensely helpful and supportive during those formative years.

In the years since then I have also benefited greatly from discussions with (and comments from) Einat Albin, Harry Arthurs, Pnina Alon-Shenker, Kevin Banks, Paul Benjamin, Adelle Blackett, Douglas Brodie, Hugh Collins, Nicola Countouris, Simon Deakin, Riccardo Del Punta, Matt Finkin, Mark Freedland, Judy Fudge, Frank Hendrickx, John Howe, Alan Hyde, Gillian Lester, Julia López, Lilach Lurie, Faina Milman-Sivan, Richard Mitchell, Guy Mundlak, Sharon Rabin-Margalioth, Kathy Stone, Gilles Trudeau, Eric Tucker, Evert Verhulp, Manfred Weiss, and Noah Zatz. I thank all of them for helping to shape different arguments that have reached the book. I have also learned a lot from my doctoral students Edo Eshet, Tammy Katsabian, and Reut Shemer-Begas. Different parts of the book have been presented over the last few years in conferences and workshops at the Hebrew University (my home institution), McGill University, Pompeu Fabra University, Osgoode Hall, UCL, the Universities of Oxford, Amsterdam, Haifa, Tel-Aviv, British Columbia, Tilburg, and Beijing, and at conferences of the LLRN, ILERA, ISLSSL, CRIMT, COSELL, IISL (Onati), and the LSA. I am thankful for many helpful comments from audiences on all of these occasions.

I acknowledge with gratitude financial support from the Hebrew University, from the Halbert Centre for Canadian Studies (for research leading to Chapter 7), and from the Israel Science Foundation (grant 1064/09, for research incorporated in Chapter 5). I have also enjoyed the gracious hospitality of the University of Toronto, Osgoode Hall Law School and UC Berkeley, where I spent time as a visiting scholar while writing parts of the book.

The book is dedicated to my beloved family: my wife Maayan, my children Noam and Aviv, my mother Nili, my father Amir (who practised labour law for almost four decades and gave me the love for the field and the understanding of its fundamentals), my sister Sigal (a judge at the Israeli National Labour Court, whose opinion I so deeply value when discussing labour law challenges), and my brother Itay. In different ways, you have all been a constant source of inspiration.

Table of Contents

List of Abbreviations

AJLL	Australian Journal of Labour Law
BJELL	Berkeley Journal of Employment and Labor Law
BJIR	British Journal of Industrial Relations
CLELJ	Canadian Labour and Employment Law Journal
CLLPJ	Comparative Labor Law & Policy Journal
CLP	Current Legal Problems
ELLJ	European Labour Law Journal
HUP	Harvard University Press
IJCLLIR	International Journal of Comparative Labour Law and Industrial Relations
ILJ	Industrial Law Journal
ILRR	Industrial and Labor Relations Review
ILO	International Labour Organisation
ILR	International Labour Review
JIR	Journal of Industrial Relations
JLR	Journal of Labor Research
JLS	Journal of Legal Studies
LQR	Law Quarterly Review
MLR	Modern Law Review
OJLS	Oxford Journal of Legal Studies
OUP	Oxford University Press
UTLJ	University of Toronto Law Journal

1
Introduction

Part I—The Crisis of Labour Law

It is almost a cliché to say that labour law is in crisis. It seems that labour law is *always* in crisis.[1] Perhaps this is not surprising; labour laws have clear and direct distributional effects, and as such they invite resistance and evasion, which lead to on-going problems of enforcement, calls for deregulation, and a perpetual need to re-assert the justification of regulations in this field. Moreover, labour markets are dynamic, so the laws regulating them require continuous adaptations; but given the background of resistance and evasion, such adaptations are often not politically feasible. Therefore the ingredients of a crisis are arguably an inherent part of labour law.

There is some debate about the nature of the current crisis. Some prominent labour law scholars believe that the field needs a new 'paradigm', or a new constituting narrative—in other words, that there is crisis at the level of *goals*.[2] According to this view, there is a need to come up with new justifications for labour market regulations—a new way to explain and justify labour law, which could also lead to changes in the regulations themselves. Others argue that the problem lies with the field's boundaries: its limited focus on paid work and employer–employee

[1] On the current crisis see, e.g., various chapters in Guy Davidov and Brian Langille (eds), *The Idea of Labour Law* (OUP 2011), especially by Alan Hyde and Brian Langille; Mark Freedland and Nicola Kountouris, *The Legal Construction of Personal Work Relations* (OUP 2011) 5; Michel Coutu, Martine Le Friant, and Gregor Murray, 'Broken Paradigms: Labor Law in the Wake of Globalization and the Economic Crisis' (2013) 34 CLLPJ 565 (opening a special issue on the topic). For previous discussions see Keith Ewing, 'The Death of Labour Law?' (1988) 8 OJLS 293; Dennis Davies, 'Death of a Labour Lawyer?' in Joanne Conaghan, Richard M Fischl, and Karl Klare (eds), *Labour Law in an Era of Globalization* (OUP 2002) 159; Paul O'Higgins, 'The End of Labour Law as We Have Known It?' in Catherine Barnard, Simon Deakin, and Gillian S Morris (eds), *The Future of Labour Law: Liber Amicorum Bob Hepple* (Hart 2004) 289. A much earlier discussion appeared in Hugo Sinzheimer, *Die Krisis des Arbeitsrechts* [The Crisis of Labour Law], published in 1933, and discussed in Michel Coutu, 'With Hugo Sinzheimer and Max Weber in Mind: The Current Crisis and the Future of Labor Law' (2013) 34 CLLPJ 605.

[2] Brian Langille is the most enthusiastic proponent of this view and has argued it explicitly and strongly in a series of articles; see mainly Brian Langille, 'Labour Law's Back Pages' in Guy Davidov and Brian Langille (eds), *Boundaries and Frontiers of Labour Law: Goals and Means in the Regulation of Work* (Hart 2006) 13; Brian Langille, 'Labour Law's Theory of Justice' in Davidov and Langille (n 1) 101. Others have also expressed similar views; see, e.g., Richard Mitchell, 'Where are We Going in Labour Law? Some Thoughts on a Field of Scholarship and Policy in Process of Change' (2011) 24 AJLL 45; Freedland and Kountouris (n 1) 371–82.

relations.[3] Yet others identify the problem in the realm of *means*: labour law's heavy reliance on substantive standards imposed by 'command-and-control' regulations. 'Reflexive law' and 'new governance' scholars believe that we should encourage self-regulation and focus on setting procedures and boundaries for it.[4]

My own view is that the goals of labour law have not changed; there is a need to clearly articulate them, and new articulations can be useful, but the basic problems that require legal intervention are the same as they have been in the past.[5] Similarly, while it is important to find legal solutions for problems associated with unpaid work and for those working without an employer, these are necessarily distinct from the solutions offered by labour law—so the traditional focus of the field is still justified.[6] As for means, while it is good to experiment with new techniques, it seems that even the strongest supporters of new governance and reflexive law would not argue that 'soft' regulations should replace labour legislation setting *basic* standards.[7] Whether or not we can rely on self-regulation in some contexts (which is a contested issue[8]), these contexts are bound to be relatively limited, not upending the basic structure of the system.

The main problem of labour law—the reason for the sense of crisis—lies elsewhere in my view: in the mismatch between goals and means.[9] The regulations that we use—the legal instruments and techniques—have lost their harmonization with the goals they are supposed to advance. This mismatch has two manifestations. The first is related to coverage: there is a growing discrepancy between the group of workers that need the protection of labour law and those who actually enjoy such protection.[10] This is sometimes based on deficiencies with the tests for

[3] See notably Marc Linder, *The Employment Relationship in Anglo-American Law: A Historical Perspective* (Greenwood Press 1989) 239–41; Judy Fudge, 'Labour as a "Fictive Commodity": Radically Reconceptualizing Labour Law' in Davidov and Langille (n 1) 120.

[4] On reflexive law see Ralf Rogowski, *Reflexive Labour Law in the World Society* (Edward Elgar 2013). On new governance see, e.g., Orly Lobel, 'The Renew Deal: The Fall of Regulation and the Rise of Governance in Contemporary Legal Thought' (2004) 89 Minn L Rev 342; Cynthia Estlund, *Regoverning the Workplace: From Self-Regulation to Co-Regulation* (Yale 2010).

[5] Guy Davidov, 'Re-Matching Labour Law with Their Purpose' in Davidov and Langille (n 1) 179. For other defences of 'traditional' ideas of labour law see, e.g., Karl Klare, 'Countervailing Workers' Power as a Regulatory Strategy' in Hugh Collins and others (eds), *Legal Regulation of the Employment Relation* (Kluwer 2000) 63; Manfred Weiss, 'Re-Inventing Labour Law?' in Davidov and Langille (n 1) 44; Ruth Dukes, *The Labour Constitution: The Enduring Idea of Labour Law* (OUP 2014).

[6] Guy Davidov, 'Setting Labour Law's Coverage: Between Universalism and Selectivity' (2014) 34 OJLS 543, 563–66.

[7] Proposals based on these theories have mostly focused on employment equality and health and safety. See, e.g., Susan P Sturm, 'Second Generation Employment Discrimination: A Structural Approach' (2001) 101 Colum L Rev 458; Lobel (n 4).

[8] For a recent sceptical evaluation see Diamond Ashiagbor, 'Evaluating the Reflexive Turn in Labour Law' in Alan Bogg and others (eds), *The Autonomy of Labour Law* (Hart 2015) 123.

[9] Davidov (n 5).

[10] See Noah Zatz, 'Working Beyond the Reach or Grasp of Employment Law' in Annette Bernhardt and others (eds), *The Gloves-Off Economy: Problems and Possibilities at the Bottom of America's Labor Market* (Cornell University Press 2008) 31; Mark Freedland, 'The Segmentation of Workers' Rights and the Legal Analysis of Personal Work Relations: Redefining a Problem' (2015) 36 CLLPJ 241.

'who is an employer' and 'who is an employee'—the 'building blocks' setting the scope of labour law. In other cases or contexts, the problem is not with the legal coverage but with the *actual* coverage, i.e. a problem of compliance and enforcement. Altogether there is a noticeable trend away from universal application of labour laws and towards what can be termed 'regressive' selectivity—labour laws do not cover the workers that need them the most.[11]

A second and separate manifestation of the mismatch problem can be termed 'obsoleteness': the fact that labour laws have not been sufficiently updated in light of dramatic changes in the labour market. As a result, the laws are often becoming irrelevant (in terms of their *substance*) to the actual problems faced by workers, or otherwise outdated. Sometimes there are new problems that have not been addressed by the legislature (e.g. privacy in the age of social media). At other times, there is a need to tailor regulations in order to address vulnerabilities specific to some group or sector.[12] Yet other times, labour laws have developed in a formalistic way (by judges) or incremental way (by legislatures) without due consideration to their overarching goals. In such cases as well, there is a need to bring goals and means together.[13]

The reasons for this double mismatch are complex. At one level, we can say that the coverage problem is the result of new and increased evasion attempts by employers, which the law failed to keep pace with. However, this begs the question of *why* have employers intensified their evasion attempts, and *why* has it been so difficult for the law to respond (both to the coverage problem and to changes in the labour market sometimes leading to obsoleteness). This surely has to do with globalisation (global competition creating more pressure); technological advancement (again leading to stronger competition, and also, changes are quicker and more frequent, requiring faster response); changing cultural and social norms (more individualism, less solidarity—arguably making evasion less abhorrent in the view of some people); political shift to neo-liberalism (less support among governments for labour law and less interest in responding to new problems); and probably many other reasons.[14] The dramatic changes that labour markets have experienced in recent years/decades have been documented elsewhere;[15] they are

[11] For further elaboration of this argument see Davidov (n 6). See also Freedland (n 10).

[12] On the need to balance between universalism and selectivity see Davidov (n 6). On regulations addressing sector-specific vulnerabilities see Guy Davidov, 'Special Protection for Cleaners: A Case of Justified Selectivity?' (2015) 36 CLLPJ 219.

[13] This is not to suggest that legislatures and courts have been idle. A recent study covering sixty-three countries shows an increase in protections afforded to part-time, fixed-term and agency workers in the last two decades (see Zoe Adams and others, 'Labour Regulation Over Time: New Leximetric Evidence' <http://www.rdw2015.org/uploads/submission/full_paper/382/labour_regulation_over_time_rdw.pdf> accessed 17 October 2015). However, these regulations have not kept pace with the magnitude of the changes.

[14] For a recent and illuminating discussion of the causes of the current crisis see David Weil, *The Fissured Workplace: Why Work Became So Bad for So Many and What Can Be Done to Improve It* (HUP 2014) ch 3.

[15] See, e.g., Katherine VW Stone, 'The Decline in the Standard Employment Contract: A Review of the Evidence' in Katherine VW Stone and Harry Arthurs (eds), *Rethinking Workplace Regulation: Beyond the Standard Contract of Employment* (Russell Sage Foundation 2013) 366.

not the subject of this book. I take the problem just described as a starting point, focusing on what can be done to address it.

Nonetheless, my arguments do not depend on any specific view regarding the nature of the crisis, or even on an agreement about the existence of a crisis. One could plausibly argue that the problems of coverage and obsoleteness have *always* plagued labour law, and there is nothing unique about the current time. This will not affect the arguments of this book. The approach offered here aims to deal with problems inherent in labour relations and thus perpetual for labour law. The methods of analysis, and the solutions offered, are therefore relevant and useful in 'regular' times just as well. Still, it seems that we do experience heightened levels of coverage and obsoleteness problems, creating together a 'mismatch' affecting numerous workers—so I find it useful to use the narrative of a 'crisis' in this introduction.

Part II—A Purposive Approach

The book attempts to address this crisis by taking a purposive approach. It starts from a very simple premise: labour laws (like all other laws) are means to an end; we need them, and use them, to advance societal goals. Given the mismatch just described, we have to restore the connection between labour laws and the goals behind them. To do so, we first have to understand, and articulate, the goals—to explain to ourselves (and to legislatures, courts, employees, and employers) the purpose of labour laws at the deepest possible level. The next step is then to reconsider our means—to ask what we need to change or improve in the laws themselves in order to better advance the goals. The book is accordingly divided into two general parts: the first dedicated to the goals of labour law, the second to the means. Together they aim to rectify the mismatch causing the crisis of labour law. To be sure, I do not purport to offer a *full* solution to the mismatch problem; that would be an impossible mission for one book. My hope is rather to offer several solutions and also provide a structure that can be useful for thinking about additional solutions.

Many have championed the purposive approach before me; I make no claim for originality when arguing that labour laws should be interpreted purposively. Nevertheless, I am not aware of any systematic and comprehensive attempt to actually perform such an analysis. The first goal of the book is to provide a 'toolbox' for performing purposive interpretation of labour laws in an optimal way, by analysing the goals of labour law and by showing how the goals can be put to work in solving practical interpretive questions. That includes a discussion of the *general* goals of labour law (Chapters 3 and 4), later followed by proposals for how to interpret the terms 'employer' and 'employee' (Chapter 6). It also includes discussions of several *specific* laws, starting by understanding their goals (Chapter 5) and later giving examples for several interpretive questions answered by way of purposive interpretation (Chapter 8). These examples can also provide guidance on how to perform such an analysis in additional cases and contexts. The second main contribution of the book is to identify legal mechanisms and institutions that have the capacity to advance the goals of labour law, including by way of allowing ongoing development and adaptation. That includes—alongside the 'building blocks' of employer and employee—open-ended standards (Chapter 7). It also includes various solutions that can be employed to address the compliance/enforcement problem which looms large over labour law throughout the world (Chapter 9).

I will use examples from several different countries, attempting to show that the conclusions and proposals are not limited to any specific legal system. Special attention is given to examples from Israeli labour law, not only because this is the system I am most familiar with, but also because it is a mixed jurisdiction[16] and thus has similarities to both common law and civil law systems. But additional examples are brought from other countries, especially Canada, the United Kingdom, and the United States. I am aware, of course, of the risks inherent in doing comparative labour law,[17] and I am not claiming sufficient familiarity with the context of every legal system—so the book is not intended to propose *specific* solutions that are universally applicable. Notwithstanding, most of the book is devoted to relatively general questions—a level of generalization at which the similarities between legal systems are great, and the differences small. The more concrete questions are considered (especially in Chapter 8) as examples, to show how purposive interpretation can be useful for solving concrete questions and how (in my view) it should be performed. I am not arguing that the specific conclusions adopted on such concrete questions are necessarily applicable in every legal system.

Adopting a purposive approach does not mean being naïve about the actual ability to translate goals into action. There are surely economic and political forces pushing in other directions; however they are beyond the scope of this book. There are several reasons for this choice. First, my discussion is normative and designed to aid anyone who is interested in thinking about reforming labour laws, answering interpretive questions about existing laws, or examining the constitutionality of such laws. It is important to have a clear view of what is the best solution normatively before starting to compromise in order to overcome barriers towards this goal. Second, the existing forms of regulations have been with us for more than a century; they are not likely to disappear any time soon. While I do not dispute the usefulness of thinking about additional kinds of regulations (such as 'new governance' ones), we must not neglect the study and further development of the existing labour law, which is for the most part of the 'command and control' type. The book focuses on the best ways to improve and interpret our

[16] Vernon Valentine Palmer, *Mixed Jurisdictions Worldwide: The Third Legal Family* (2nd edn, Cambridge UP 2012).

[17] Otto Kahn-Freund, 'On Uses and Misuses of Comparative Law' (1974) 37 MLR 1; Harry Arthurs, 'Cross-National Legal Learning: The Uses of Comparative Labor Knowledge, Law, and Policy' in Stone and Arthurs (n 15) 353.

existing labour laws. Third, one of the main reasons for the 'reflexive turn'[18] of some scholars is the disbelief in any ability to effect change by way of 'traditional' legislation against the will of employers. But, while the difficulties are surely real, they are not necessarily insurmountable. I discuss various possible solutions in Chapter 9 (including some 'softer' solutions). In any case, the enforcement crisis notwithstanding, most employers still follow the (traditional) laws. These laws *do* have an impact and we should not abandon them so easily.

Part III—The Purpose of What? Framing the Topic of Discussion

Before we articulate the goals of labour law (which is the task of the first part of this book), we have to decide what the term 'labour law' includes for this purpose. If, for example, one adopts the narrow sense of the term, referring only to collective labour laws (as used in North America), the goals are likely to be narrower than the goals of the entire body of employment-related regulations. This book uses the term 'labour law' in the meaning common in most of the world—including employment law and workplace discrimination law. This makes sense because of the shared characteristics of these laws, and particularly the fact that they address the same set of problems (as will become clear in Chapter 3).

More contentious is the question of where to put the line in terms of potential expansions of labour law. In recent years there is growing demand from scholars to go 'beyond employment', and one of the meanings of this call has been to broaden the legal 'field', in several ways.[19] First, there is a view that labour law should be understood as including regulations that affect workers even outside of the relationship with a specific employer, such as social security laws, tariff protections, and policies designed to create jobs.[20] Second, some scholars lament the exclusion of unpaid work (specifically unpaid care work) from the ambit of labour law.[21] Finally, there are calls to use labour law to extend protections to small vendors, i.e. workers in a relatively vulnerable situation but without any 'employer'.[22]

18 Ashiagbor (n 8).

19 This section relies on Davidov (n 6).

20 Mitchell (n 2); John Howe, 'The Broad Idea of Labour Law: Industrial Policy, Labour Market Regulation, and Decent Work' in Davidov and Langille (n 1) 295.

21 See, e.g., Sandra Fredman and Judy Fudge, 'The Legal Construction of Personal Work Relations and Gender' (2013) 7 Jerusalem Rev of Leg Stud 112; Brian Langille, 'A Question of Balance in The Legal Construction of Personal Work Relations' (2013) 7 Jerusalem Rev of Leg Stud 99.

22 See, e.g., Brian Langille, 'Labour Law's Theory of Justice' in Davidov and Langille (n 1) 101; Langille (n 21). For calls to abolish the distinction between 'employee' and independent contractor altogether—and extend protection to all those working for others—see Linder (n 3); Richard R Carlson, 'Why the Law Still Can't Tell an Employee When It Sees One and How It Ought to Stop Trying' (2001) 22 BJELL 295; Judy Fudge and others, 'Employee or Independent Contractor? Charting the Legal Significance of the Distinction in Canada' (2002) 10 CLELJ 193; Judy Fudge, 'Fragmenting Work and Fragmenting Organizations: The Contract of Employment and the Scope of Labour Regulation' (2006) 44 Osgoode Hall LJ 609; Fudge (n 3).

All of these proposals have good reasons behind them, but cannot justify the solution of broadening our understanding of 'what is labour law'. If we are defining the field of research and study, labour law would surely benefit from a closer inspection of other fields of law that indirectly affect workers, or affect workers outside of an employment relationship. Yet it is highly doubtful if a field of study and research has to be 'defined' at all. Scholars generally enjoy the academic freedom to structure their courses and choose their research topics. To the extent that the call to expand labour law is meant as a call for labour law scholars to engage more closely with related fields in their research and teaching, this is an important and useful point;[23] however, it is not related to the boundaries of labour law in the sense relevant to this book.

Admittedly, when we think about reforming welfare state programmes we have to be aware of changes in the labour market and take the rights and benefits secured by labour law (or *not* secured) into account. Thus, for example, if we are interested in achieving economic security, this can be done by a combination of labour laws and social security laws; so the two fields must be coordinated. However, this does not mean that the fields become one. At a high level of generality the goals may be the same, but there are also more specific, separate goals (such as those related to redressing the inequality of power between employer and employee), as well as very different structures and techniques. The same is true with regard to the inclusion of unpaid work and small vendors. Surely these kinds of work require protection, which at some level is similar to the protection required by employees. But absent an employer that can be required to take responsibility, and against which there is vulnerability, there are also important differences in terms of goals as well as techniques used.

At the end of the day, the calls to broaden what we see as labour law—or expand protection to other kinds of work—are not relevant for the current project. We have many different problems in the world and to bring them all together under one heading would hardly be a useful route towards a solution. The question is whether there is sufficient commonality to make such grouping useful. Perhaps for some purposes it is useful to bring the plight of tenants versus landlords (for example) together with the plight of employees versus employers. Such broadening could potentially be useful to forge solidarity between the two groups, and perhaps also draw inspiration from legal solutions used in the other context.[24] But most of the regulations will *have* to be different. Laws mandating minimum wages, maximum hours, parental leave, etc. are not relevant for tenants.

[23] I believe that this indeed was the intention of most of the 'law of the labour market' supporters. For this approach see Simon Deakin and Frank Wilkinson, *The Law of the Labour Market: Industrialization, Employment and Legal Evolution* (OUP 2005); Richard Mitchell and Christopher Arup, 'Labour Law and Labour Market Regulation' in Christopher Arup and others (eds), *Labour Law and Labour Market Regulation* (Federation Press 2006) 3; Harry Arthurs, 'Charting the Boundaries of Labour Law: Innis Christie and the Search for an Integrated Law of Labour Market Regulation' (2011) 34 Dalhousie LJ 1.

[24] Harry Arthurs, 'Labor Law as the Law of Economic Subordination and Resistance: A Thought Experiment' (2013) 34 CLLPJ 585.

Collective bargaining could perhaps be used in other contexts as well, but will need many adaptations. In short, whatever the political gains might be, for *legal* purposes conflating employees with tenants is untenable. The same is true for unpaid care work and for small vendors. Absent an employer, their plight is against the state—and regulations addressing their needs will have somewhat different ends, and certainly different means, compared with laws protecting employees.[25]

It is true that some social security programmes are directed only at employees, while in fact they should be extended in one way or another to others as well (including, notably, those performing unpaid care work and the small vendors). Nevertheless, such programmes are, again, substantially different from collective labour laws, employment standards and workplace discrimination laws (the components of 'labour law'). In some respects it could be convenient to group social security programmes together with labour law—indeed in some European countries the term 'social law' often covers both. It could be useful, for example, for general political discussions, or for delineating the jurisdiction of 'social courts'. Yet for purposes of interpreting, reforming, and adapting labour laws—which is what this book is concerned with—it is better not to lose focus. Accordingly, I will concentrate on employer–employee relations.

Part IV—The Structure of the Book

The first part of this book focuses on the purpose of labour laws. Chapter 2 opens this part by putting forward an explanation of why articulating the purpose (goals) is useful and indeed necessary. Whether we are confronted with the need to update (or reform) labour laws, interpret specific provisions, fill lacunas when new problems emerge without a solution in legislation, or ask whether a law is constitutional—the discussion must start with a clear understanding of what the law is trying to achieve (or *should* try to achieve). The chapter then moves to discuss a series of methodological questions related to the articulation of goals.

The actual exploration into the goals of labour law starts in Chapter 3 with an attempt to pinpoint the unique characteristics of employment relations, as opposed to other relations, and particularly to understand in what sense employer–employee relations can be said to be different from client–independent contractor relations. The identified *vulnerabilities* that characterize employment are then used to explain why labour laws are needed. This is one useful way to articulate the goals of labour law. The chapter proceeds to consider other articulations that share a similar structure, i.e. attempt to solve the 'problems' of labour markets or labour relations: the prevalence of market failures and inequality of bargaining power.

Chapter 4 complements this discussion—and completes the review of the *general* goals of labour law—by shifting to a higher level of abstraction. It includes

[25] See also Noah D Zatz, 'The Impossibility of Work Law' in Davidov and Langille (n 1) 234.

a list of various values and interests that labour laws are said to advance. I discuss many different articulations that can be found in the literature: democracy, redistribution, dignity, social inclusion, stability, efficiency, human freedom, capabilities, emancipation, and social equality. By explaining the meaning and importance of each goal, I hope to contribute to future purposive analyses of labour laws, including of issues not discussed in the current book. The chapter concludes with some words of caution against putting too much emphasis on goals that aim to be 'good for everyone', when this comes with rejection (even if only implicit) of the conflicts and power imbalance inherent in labour relations, and the resulting need for redistribution.

Chapter 5, the last chapter in the first part of the book, moves from the general to the more specific. As explained in Chapter 2, the purposive approach requires that we understand and articulate the goals of labour law as a whole, but also the more concrete goals of the specific law under discussion (the law that requires reform, or interpretation, or is being constitutionally challenged). It is not possible to perform this kind of analysis for every labour law here, but Chapter 5 does so for three key labour regulations, as examples: minimum wage laws, collective bargaining laws, and unjust dismissal laws. Obviously the specific arrangements vary from one legal system to another, so some additional country-specific discussion might be required before making concrete proposals. The chapter can nonetheless show how this kind of analysis can (and should) be performed, and also provides some useful starting points—at the very least—for further (more concrete) discussions.

After setting forth the goals of labour law, the second part of the book moves to put this discussion to practical use: analysing the means (legal techniques) of labour law—both existing and proposed—and examining how they can be used to better advance our goals. Chapter 6 begins this task in the most familiar setting—the concepts of 'employee' and 'employer' which are used around the world to set the scope/boundaries of labour laws. The chapter includes three separate discussions: one dealing with the age-old (and widely discussed) employee–independent contractor distinction; another considering the addition of a third (intermediate) category in-between them; the final concerning the question of who is the legal 'employer', especially in cases of triangular relations involving a temporary employment agency or a subcontractor. In all of these contexts, I offer purposive interpretations (based on the analyses of the previous part) that tie the scope of labour law to the identification of those who need the protection of labour law and those who should take responsibility for them. Along the way some concrete proposals are also made for legislative amendments that can aid in this task.

Chapter 7 suggests another legal technique for advancing the goals of labour law: using open-ended standards. In recent years the use of such standards—mostly 'good faith' and proportionality—has become widespread and important in many legal systems. Courts are using these legal tools to develop labour law and adapt it to new needs and new circumstances. Focusing on three standards—good faith, proportionality, and the managerial prerogative—I justify the new trend and support its further expansion by relying on the literature concerning rules versus standards and by showing how these standards have been applied in practice. The general idea is that standards allow ongoing adaptation and response to new problems in line with the goals of the law. Among other advantages, standards can be used to compensate for adaptations that were previously achieved through collective bargaining, a route which is surely preferred in theory but is much less available today for workers in practice.

Chapter 8 is dedicated to specific examples of purposive interpretation. I address a variety of timely legal questions that courts in several different countries have struggled with in recent years: whether tips should be seen as part of the minimum wage; which deductions can be made from the minimum wage for accommodation and related expenses; what are the rights of apprentices, trainees, interns, and volunteers; what are the rights for time spent being 'on call'; whether minimum wage obligations apply for activities done before and after the actual 'work'; whether cleaners working through contractors are entitled to severance pay when contractors change; what is the effective date of dismissals; whether freedom of association means that employers should be prohibited from voicing objection to unionization; and whether compulsory union agency fees are justified. The various examples show how purpose directs us to the optimal solution. They also show why context is crucial (as part of the purposive analysis), and that the same approach is needed in every legal question, from lofty constitutional interpretation to mundane procedural questions (and everything in between).

Chapter 9 addresses one of the main components of labour law's crisis—the compliance/enforcement problem. This is a crucial element of any attempt to advance the goals of the field. The chapter starts by explaining the reasons for enforcement problems and their intensification, then turns to consider several possible solutions that have been discussed or experimented with in recent years. Some of these techniques are designed to improve compliance: creating positive incentives for employers to comply; inducing compliance through pressure on 'lead companies' (that have power over contractors); and promoting unions because of their proven record in ensuring compliance. The other group of means that will be considered is focused on the enforcement stage: 'responsive' enforcement, based on a multitude of possible sanctions and gradual escalation; withholding privileges (licences and doing business with the government); and finally, different modalities of independent monitoring.

To a large extent the different chapters can be read independently from each other: every chapter has its own beginning and end, advancing some independent arguments. Hopefully it will become clear for the readers how the chapters are all woven into one coherent story, advancing the same idea of the purposive approach. In Chapter 10 which concludes the book, I summarize the main arguments and very briefly situate this work in relation to other contemporary labour law discourses.

I

GOALS

2

Articulating Labour Law's Goals: Why and How

It may seem obvious to most readers that before doing anything—let alone something as important as interpreting or reforming labour law—we must ask ourselves what exactly is the goal of what we do. This seems to be the only rational approach to such tasks. Yet quite often we do things automatically, without stopping to think about them.[1] The goal of this chapter is to explain *why* we need to articulate explicitly the goals of labour law, and *how* this should be done. This methodological inquiry is a necessary step before proceeding to discuss the goals themselves, in the following chapters.

The chapter proceeds in two parts. Part I addresses the question of 'why' (and 'when') is it necessary to explain (to ourselves and to others) the goals of labour law. Part II then discusses the 'how', going through a number of steps that can assist us in articulating goals, and attempting to resolve a number of issues that arise when starting to think about the best way to approach this problem.

Part I—Why

There are three main (practical) reasons for articulating labour law's goals. One is at the level of the legislature or otherwise the policy-making sphere (asking whether changes/additions to the law are needed). The second is at the level of the courts or otherwise the realm of applying the law (interpretation). The third is at the level of the constitution, in case the law is challenged as unconstitutional. I will discuss them in turn.

There is a rich scholarly debate on the goals/idea of labour law in recent years. It should be made clear that some do not think about the issue in the terms I am using here. For example, Brian Langille has been offering a new 'narrative' for

[1] Scholars who champion purposive examination often make reference to a powerful quote attributed to Friedrich Nietzsche: 'To forget one's purpose is the commonest form of stupidity.' See, e.g., LL Fuller and William R Perdue Jr, 'The Reliance Interest in Contract Damages: 1' (1936) 46 Yale LJ 52, 52; Brian Langille and Guy Davidov, 'Beyond Employee and Independent Contractors: A View from Canada' (1999) 21 CLLPJ 7, 9. In the current context it would be more correct to say that too often people *neglect to articulate*—even to themselves—the purpose of what they do.

labour law,[2] Richard Mitchell has talked about the need for a new 'paradigm',[3] and Alan Hyde asked whether the idea of labour law can still serve as a 'source of inspiration'.[4] My own starting point is different and more practical. Once we articulate the goals for legal purposes, they might also offer a new narrative, paradigm, and a source of inspiration. But this is not the immediate goal of the analysis. Below I explain the legal-practical reasons for articulating labour law's purposes in more detail.

The policy-making level

Labour laws are often under attack. They are seen by some as impediments to efficiency, flexibility, and growth; as a reason for unemployment; as creating inequality between different groups of workers and between those employed and the unemployed; and as an outdated form of regulation due to their mandatory ('command and control') type. These critiques can be debated on their own terms: for example, there is empirical evidence refuting the claim that labour laws (specifically, the minimum wage law) bring about unemployment.[5] However, it is fair to assume that there is at least *some* truth in these allegations. At least some labour laws, in some contexts, demonstrate the ills listed above (and probably a few others). Obviously, though, this should not in itself result in a conclusion that such laws should be repealed. Laws are usually a compromise between conflicting values and interests. There could certainly be justifications for labour laws that outweigh their drawbacks.

Any attempt to respond to attacks on labour law, from whatever direction, must therefore be based on a clear view and articulation of why such laws are needed. Otherwise put: faced with claims that a labour law X has a negative effect Y, one could respond by denying the Y effect, or by arguing that despite Y, there are other reasons that justify the law. Those other reasons—we can call them a positive effect Z—are the justifications that need to be articulated explicitly.

To be sure, policy-making in labour law is not only defensive (or at least *should not* be only defensive). It is not limited to 'attacks' or 'defence' of a given set of regulations. Reforms are often needed, for several reasons. First, responding to changes in labour market conditions. Thus, for example, macro changes such as the feminization of the workforce, or labour migration, required (or still require) changes in labour laws. Second, reforms are needed to address ongoing changes in employment practices. For example, the shift towards indirect, temporary,

[2] Brian Langille, 'Labour Law's Theory of Justice' in Guy Davidov and Brian Langille (eds), *The Idea of Labour Law* (OUP 2011) 101.

[3] Richard Mitchell, 'Where are we Going in Labour Law? Some Thoughts on a Field of Scholarship and Policy in Process of Change' (2011) 24 AJLL 45.

[4] Alan Hyde, 'The Idea of the Idea of Labour Law: A Parable' in Davidov and Langille (n 2) 88, 97. Hyde is too discouraged by the state of US labour law to believe that the idea of labour law can inspire people.

[5] See Chapter 5.

and part-time employment requires changes to protect workers in new forms of employment. Third, reforms could be needed to reflect developments in societal values. For example, the increased importance that society allocates to the work–family balance requires some rethinking of labour laws, to amend laws that are not sensitive to such needs. Finally, reforms are often needed to correct regulations which turned out to be failures in some respect, or just need improvement, after a period of examination. For example, when introducing the National Minimum Wage Act in 1998, the British legislature simultaneously set up an independent body (the Low Pay Commission) to advise it on the way the Act was actually working. The Commission produces yearly reports[6] and often recommends amendments to the Act, in light of experience accumulated 'on the ground' with the Act's impact, successes, and failures. Reflection on the actual working of labour laws is not always so well-structured, but it is certainly always needed.

These are only some examples of why policy-makers should always think about the need to reform labour law. When doing such re-thinking, it is necessary to have a clear view of what the law is supposed to achieve, i.e. what are its goals. If we suspect that current labour laws are not working, or need updating, for one of the reasons mentioned above, how do we know that they are not working? In what sense are they failing? What would amendments try to achieve? All of these crucial questions require an explicit articulation of goals. The goals of the law are the basic yardstick by which we have to examine whether it is working or not.[7] Too often, people tend to have automatic and simplistic opinions about labour law—for example, that it is always inefficient and must be deregulated, or in contrast, that it is always just and necessary and cannot be reformed.[8] A purposive approach goes against pre-conceived conclusions.

A similar reasoning can be used to explain the importance of articulating goals when courts have to fill gaps in the legislation. Regulating is not a task restricted to legislatures; courts also play a major role in making policy choices, in areas not covered by legislation. This is most obvious in common-law systems, where major parts of the private law are left for judicial development, but there are parallels in civil-law systems as well. Sometimes the rules developed by courts can be seen as flowing from interpretation of the (usually implied) contract of employment. But quite often judicially developed rules also place limits on what the parties can agree upon. Consider, for example, the question of whether an employer can log into e-mail accounts he has assigned to employees and read their correspondence. In some countries there are explicit answers in legislation to this question, but other legislatures have refrained from any discussion of this issue. The Israeli

[6] See Low Pay Commission <http://www.lowpay.gov.uk/> accessed 10 October 2015.

[7] For a similar point see Stephen F Befort and John W Budd, *Invisible Hands, Invisible Objectives: Bringing Workplace Law and Public Policy Into Focus* (Stanford UP 2009) ch 1. See also Langille (n 2) 101 (arguing that it is necessary to provide labour law with a theory of justice—an ethical account). See also Mark Freedland and Nicola Kountouris, *The Legal Construction of Personal Work Relations* (OUP 2011) 317.

[8] And see Bruno Caruso, 'New Trajectories of Labor Law in the European Crisis: The Italian Case' (2015) 36 CLLPJ 181, 184 (describing this as a 'double obsession').

National Labour Court recently had to develop rules for such problems, brought before it by employees contending violation of their privacy.[9] One could search for solutions in contract law or property law for such questions, but these provide very limited guidance. At the end of the day there is no way (and no reason) to avoid an examination of a policy-making nature. When legal questions arise without any solution in legislation, judges have to look for the best solution, in light of the *purpose* of (possible) regulations in this field, and in line with the general purposes of labour law as a whole.

Purposive interpretation

We have seen that articulation of goals is needed when legislating or rethinking legislation, and in filling lacunas. The same is true at the stage of *applying* the law. It is well-known that there is no law without interpretation. Very often judges need to decide on the meaning of legal provisions or even just single words in a particular context. Sometimes the legislature intentionally leaves a broad room for judicial discretion—for example, when labour laws apply only to 'employees', and the legislature refrains from any definition of this term. Given that disputes about whether one is an employee or an independent contractor are very common, the lack of any definition in the law means that courts were entrusted with the task of developing tests and applying them, to give meaning to this term. But even if the legislature *does* include a detailed definition, there is still (always) some debate about what the definition means and whether specific cases are covered by it or not. It is impossible to anticipate in advance every possible contingency and provide solutions in advance to every problem.

What should courts rely on when interpreting legislation? It would be naïve to suggest that they must simply rely on the 'literal' meaning of words, as found in the dictionary. Quite often there is more than one possible meaning to choose from, and furthermore, the meaning of words often depends on their context and can change over time.[10] On the other extreme, it is difficult to accept the view that judges should simply be looking at the expected results, choosing the interpretation that would bring about the best consequences in their (own) view, without any other frame of reference.[11]

There seems to be broad agreement that laws should be interpreted in light of what they try to achieve.[12] In Britain this is sometimes called the 'mischief rule',[13] meaning that laws should be interpreted in light of the 'mischief' they

[9] *Tali Issakov v The State of Israel*, judgment of 8 February 2011 (National Labour Court).

[10] Cass R Sunstein, 'Interpreting Statutes in the Regulation State' (1989) 103 Harv L Rev 405, 422–23; A Raymond Randolph, 'Dictionaries, Plain Meaning, and Context in Statutory Interpretation' (1994) 17 Harv J L & Pub Pol'y 71, 73–74.

[11] Richard A Posner, 'Legal Formalism, Legal Realism, and the Interpretation of Statutes and the Constitution' (1986–87) 7 Case W Res L Rev 179, 200.

[12] See, e.g., Fuller and Perdue (n 1).

[13] *Heydon's Case* (1584) 3 Co Rep 7a, 76 ER 637. For a contemporary application of this approach see, e.g. *R v Secretary of State for the Environment, Ex Parte Spath Holme Limited* [2000] UKHL 61, [2001] 1 All ER 195 (opinion of Lord Nicholls).

aim to cure. In Continental Europe it is usually referred to as the 'teleological approach'.[14] There are disagreements on whether courts could go so far as to adopt interpretations that do not conform to the language of the law, but these are not important for current purposes. We can assume that judges are limited to what the semantic possibilities allow. This still leaves a broad range of options in many cases, which raises the question of how to choose among those options.

How would we know what a piece of legislation is trying to achieve? One option is to decipher or try to assess what the intention of the legislature was.[15] But legislation is usually based on political compromise, so different members of the legislative body may have somewhat different views about what it means and why it is needed.[16] Furthermore, since the legislature cannot foresee every contingency, it will not always have an 'intention' with regard to the interpretive problem at hand.[17] Finally, and more fundamentally, the meaning of a law is not 'frozen' in time. The legislature can have specific reasons for enacting a piece of legislation, but a future legislature might have different reasons for choosing not to repeal it.[18] Seen in this light, legislative documents can be helpful when trying to understand the reasons behind the law, but they are only the beginning of the enquiry and not the end.

However important text and legislators' intent may be they are not sufficient for the task of judicial interpretation. They must be supplemented by *purpose*. This view was formulated in the influential work of Hart and Sacks as follows:

> In interpreting a statute a court should: (1) Decide what purpose ought to be attributed to the statute and to any subordinate provision of it which may be involved; and then (2) Interpret the words of the statute immediately in question so as to carry out the purpose as best it can, making sure, however, that it does not give the words either—(a) a meaning they will not bear, or (b) a meaning which would violate any established policy or clear statement.[19]

[14] It is often maintained that judges only turn to the teleological (purposive) approach when the language is unclear or when there is a lacuna in the law. But this is still quite common, especially in labour law. See, e.g., Nigel Foster and Satish Sule, *German Legal System and Laws* (4th edn, OUP 2010) 75–76; Massimo La Torre, Enrico Pattaro, and Michele Taruffo, 'Statutory Interpretation in Italy' in Neil MacCormick and Robert Summers (eds), *Interpreting Statutes: A Comparative Study* (Dartmouth 1991) 213, 222; Claire M Germain, 'Approaches to Statutory Interpretation and Legislative History in France' (2003) 13 Duke J Comp & Int'l L 195, 201. On the prevalence of judicial law-making in the labour law context see, e.g., Manfred Weiss, 'Industrial Action, Collective Bargaining and Trade Union Rights: Examples of Judge-made Law in Germany' (2011), paper presented at the Hebrew University.

[15] See, e.g. Joseph Raz, *Between Authority and Interpretation* (OUP 2009) ch 11.

[16] Ronald Dworkin, *Law's Empire* (HUP 1986) 318–21; Kent Greenawalt, 'Constitutional and Statutory Interpretation' in Jules Coleman and Scott Shapiro (eds), *The Oxford Handbook of Jurisprudence and Philosophy of Law* (OUP 2002) 268, 288.

[17] Dworkin ibid 325.

[18] Another way of saying this is by pointing to the preferred understanding of a given section. Perhaps the original legislature preferred a given interpretation, but the current legislature prefers a different one (to the same text of the law). It is difficult to justify giving preference to the views of the original legislature. See Andrei Marmor, *Interpretation and Legal Theory* (2nd edn, Hart 2005) 133.

[19] Henry M Hart Jr and Albert M Sacks, *The Legal Process: Basic Problems in the Making and Application of Law* (Foundation Press 1994) 1169.

Another useful formulation can be found in the Spanish Civil Code, which states: 'Norms are to be interpreted in accordance with the proper meaning of their words, in relation to the context, the historical and legislative background, and the social reality of the time in which they are to be applied, bearing in mind, fundamentally, the spirit and purpose of the former.'[20]

Otherwise put, when interpreters ask what the law is trying to achieve, rather than focus on the intent of its drafters or look for hidden meanings in the words themselves, they should place most emphasis on trying to understand the *purpose* behind it. Others have added that laws should not be read in isolation, but as part of a broader system. Ronald Dworkin has argued that judges should interpret the law in light of its surrounding political history, and consider the 'abstract intent' of the legislature, which is to fulfil fundamental principles of justice, fairness, and procedural due process.[21] Aharon Barak also believes that interpretation should take into account fundamental values and principles of the legal system, although not necessarily limited to those three. He has offered a set of rules to structure and limit judicial discretion in performing the interpretive task. Judges should consider 'subjective' alongside 'objective' purposes, and there are various techniques and presumptions that Barak has developed for this purpose. But at the end of the day he leaves the balance and choice between competing views to judicial discretion.[22]

Such approaches are still fiercely objected by some, notably by American judges who define themselves as 'textualists'. Justice Scalia of the US Supreme Court, for example, argues that judges should focus on the text and ask how a reasonable person would have understood it at the time of the enactment.[23] His claim is that if judges use more abstract notions such as purpose or fundamental values in aid of interpretation, it will result in them interpreting the law *as they want it to be*, rather than as it is.[24] But it is known that reasonable people often disagree about the meaning of a text; we should therefore acknowledge the fact that there is room for judicial discretion in interpretation, and offer tools to perform this role (e.g. by looking for purpose), rather than deny it and end up with 'subjective' considerations entering in a less structured, principled, and transparent way.[25] Moreover, even if we assume that textualism *does* provide more certainty and lessens the risk of judicial encroachment, this comes with a hefty price: we can end up with results that frustrate, rather than promote, the goals of the law.

20 Art 3.1 (as quoted in Lawrence M Solan, 'Linguistic Issues in Statutory Interpretation' in Peter M Tiersma and Lawrence M Solan (eds), *Oxford Handbook of Language and Law* (OUP 2012) 88).

21 Dworkin (n 16) chs 7 and 9.

22 Aharon Barak, *Purposive Interpretation in Law* (Princeton UP 2005).

23 Antonin Scalia, *A Matter of Interpretation: Federal Courts and the Law* (Princeton UP 1997).

24 This is by no means the only view on the US Supreme Court. Some of the other judges support the purposive approach; see, e.g., Stephen Breyer, *Active Liberty* (OUP 2008) 108.

25 'Indeed, new textualism may very well expand judicial discretion...outside any normative framework' (Barak (n 22) 282). See also William N Eskridge Jr, 'The New Textualism' (1990) 37 UCLA L Rev 621, 674–75.

Admittedly, the more judges rely on abstract 'fundamental values' of the system, the higher the risk of losing touch with what the specific law was actually trying to achieve, and the easier it is to replace legislative purpose with the judges' own purposes. Nonetheless, it is important to remember that the legislature can always correct judicial mistakes in future legislation.[26] In addition, the fear of purposive interpretation creating democratic/legitimacy problems is significantly reduced once we focus more on finding *justifications* that can explain the law,[27] rather than making assumptions about the goals of the law based on presumed 'fundamental values' of the system.

It is important to clarify that a purposive approach is *not* synonymous to case-by-case decision-making based on the expected outcome of a specific case. Taking the term 'employee' as an example, it is not suggested that courts should eschew all tests and decide who is an 'employee' in each case simply by asking what the purpose of the law requires. Purposive interpretation does not come instead of adopting interpretation that can be used in other cases (including by way of devising tests); rather, it means that the interpretation (and tests) have to be in line with the purpose. Obviously courts do not need to repeat this inquiry in every case, but it would be good to rethink the tests (or otherwise the accepted interpretation) when circumstances change or every few years.

The purpose of the law therefore plays a significant role in the everyday task of legislative interpretation.[28] This requires us to articulate (and re-articulate every once in a while) the goals of every piece of labour legislation. It also requires us to articulate the more general goals coming out of the labour law system as a whole. This general articulation is important for placing the specific legislation in context, and it is useful because different laws are usually based on the same basic assumptions about the vulnerability of workers and the need to protect them. I discuss the distinction between general and specific goals further in part II of this chapter below.

Constitutional challenges

Many legal systems are based on written constitutions and offer the option of challenging legislation as unconstitutional.[29] In the UK a similar challenge is now possible when legislation is claimed to contradict the European Convention on Human Rights.[30] Labour laws could be the target of such challenges, because

[26] As Eskridge and Frickey note, interpretation is a 'dynamic enterprise', and the 'counter-majoritarian anxiety' is often exaggerated (William N Eskridge Jr and Philip P Frickey, 'Statutory Interpretation as Practical Reasoning' (1990) 43 Stan LR 321, 378–81).

[27] Dworkin (n 16) 338.

[28] For a recent example from the UK Supreme Court see *Autoclenz Limited v Belcher and others* [2011] UKSC 41 para 35.

[29] Usually this option is offered explicitly in the Constitution; at other times (as in the US or in Israel, for example) it is assumed by the courts.

[30] Unlike the situation in most constitutional democracies, UK courts cannot declare a statute unconstitutional and therefore void, they can only declare its incompatibility with the Convention and refer the issue to the legislature. See Human Rights Act 1998 s 4.

by their very nature they are designed to intervene in the contractual relationship between employer and employee, and often to redistribute resources from one to the other. Accordingly they can be seen as infringing the right to property, the freedom of contract, and the freedom to conduct a business (protected, all or in part, at least in some constitutions).[31]

It is not only employers that can use the Constitution to put labour laws into question. Some laws could also infringe employee rights; for example, a law regulating surveillance over employees (and allowing it in some circumstances) could be challenged as violating the right to privacy, and a law regulating collective bargaining but excluding some groups of workers from its scope is arguably violating their freedom of association.[32] Exemptions in labour laws that exclude some workers are quite common; they can also be seen as infringing the right to equality. Finally, in some countries where *social* rights are entrenched constitutionally, whether explicitly or by way of interpretation, labour legislation can be challenged for infringing (or even failing to positively protect) the right to strike, the right to work, or the right to fair work conditions.[33]

Of course, constitutional rights are not absolute. Once a piece of legislation is constitutionally challenged, the State (and the other party to the dispute) can defend it in courts by showing that the infringement is justified. This is usually examined through the tests of proportionality.[34] The courts will have to examine whether there was a legitimate purpose behind the infringement of rights, and whether—given this purpose—the infringement was necessary. This obviously requires an articulation of purpose, both to examine the legitimacy of the purpose itself and to examine the means–end relationship.[35]

Usually it is not an entire legislation that is challenged, but rather a specific section of it. This means that both the goals of the specific section under dispute and the goals of the legislation as a whole have to be examined as part of the constitutional analysis. Once again, then, we see that articulating the *purpose* (i.e. goals) of labour laws is crucial. We need it for making new laws or improving old ones; for interpreting pieces of legislation; and for examining their constitutionality.

[31] See, e.g. US Const amend XIV; Charter of Fundamental Rights of the European Union [2012] OJ C 326/391 arts 16–17 (Charter of Fundamental Rights).

[32] On the latter example see *Dunmore v Ontario (Attorney General)*, 2001 SCC 94, [2001] 3 SCR 1016 (Supreme Court of Canada); *Ontario (Attorney General) v Fraser*, 2011 SCC 20, [2011] 2 SCR 3.

[33] For explicit constitutional social rights see, e.g., Constitution of the Republic of South Africa, 1996, section 23; Charter of Fundamental Rights, arts 27–34. For social rights derived from civil rights see, e.g. *Health Services and Support-Facilities Subsector Bargaining Association v British Columbia*, 2007 SCC 27, [2007] 2 SCR 391 (Supreme Court of Canada deriving the right to collective bargaining from freedom of association); *Saskatchewan Federation of Labour v Saskatchewan*, 2015 SCC 4 (Supreme Court of Canada deriving the right to strike from freedom of association).

[34] David Beatty, *The Ultimate Rule of Law* (OUP 2004).

[35] In many legal systems, the means–end examination includes three steps: Is there a rational relation between the two (i.e. the means can rationally lead to the end)? Are the means chosen minimally impairing the right (i.e. are there any other means that can achieve the goal with a lesser impairment)? And finally, is there proportionality between the harm caused and the benefit achieved by the legislation? See, e.g. *R v Oakes*, [1986] 1 SCR 10 (Supreme Court of Canada).

Part II—How

This part is dedicated to offering some suggestions on how to articulate the goals of labour law. It proceeds by examining the following questions: Should we accept a presumption in favour of the 'free' market? Should we articulate the goals of each labour law separately, or rather the entire body of labour laws as a whole? Should we look for explanations (which might include hidden or unjustified goals) or rather focus on normative justifications? Is it possible to articulate goals without reference to a specific time and place? Should we distinguish between main goals and ancillary ones? Can we find the goals within legal texts or are we required to perform a multi-disciplinary search? Finally, how do we choose the appropriate level of abstraction? What follows is a brief discussion of all of these issues in turn.

A presumption in favour of private law rules?

The discourse on the goals of labour law—at the political as well as the academic level—usually takes the basic rules of private law as a background. That is, the laws of contract, property, corporations, etc. are taken for granted—they are assumed to exist without question and, in effect, are given priority. These private law rules are seen as structuring and protecting the 'free market', which in turn is seen as a necessary and important component of democratic societies. Labour laws, in contrast, are conceptualized as 'interventions' in the free market—and special justifications are needed for such impediments to be accepted.

This view is so entrenched in the way we think about labour law that it is difficult to conceive of an alternative view;[36] but it creates an unfair default in favour of employers. Contract law gives force to agreements without inquiring into the power disparities between the parties, thus favouring in effect the more powerful (in most cases, the employers) who can impose terms preferable to them. Property law gives employers full ownership and control over the workspace, the equipment, and everything produced in the workplace, ignoring the interests of workers who arguably could have been seen as equal partners in this production. Company law limits the liability of employers incorporated as companies, thus allowing them to enjoy rewards while in effect shifting risks to others (including

[36] Simon Deakin argues that labour law is an inseparable, necessary part of the market, 'constituting' it rather than 'limiting' or 'correcting' it (Simon Deakin, 'The Contribution of Labour Law to Economic and Human Development' in Davidov and Langille, *The Idea of Labour Law* (n 2) 162). Brian Langille argues even more broadly that 'markets are just an aspect and means of human freedom' and labour law on this view is also an inseparable aspect of markets necessary to achieve the broad goal (Brian Langille, '"Take These Chains From My Heart and Set Me Free": How Labor Law Theory Drives Segmentation of Workers' Rights' (2015) 36 CLLPJ 257, 274). Both Deakin and Langille can thus be seen as offering an alternative to the entrenched view. However, they will surely not object to the idea of freedom of contract in general, only in the specific context of labour relations (and perhaps some other specific contexts). So we are still left with the need to explain, and justify, why the law should treat some specific relations (or contexts) differently.

employees). These pillars of private law could all be restructured in a way that gives more weight to the interests of those without bargaining power, without property, and without access to the benefits of limited liability. So there is something unfair about giving these laws default status, while requiring special justifications from any changes to this default. Otherwise put, it is misleading to view private law rules as a given and any deviation from the 'free market' which they create as an 'intervention' which is by definition suspicious. The 'free market' is not the 'natural' state of affairs. It is created by regulation (contract, property, company law, etc.) and enforced with the mechanism of the State (courts, police, etc.). In principle, private law rules are not different from other laws regulating the market (such as labour law) and accordingly, should not enjoy a superior default position.

It is important to have these reservations in mind. However in this book I will accept the common capitalistic structure and offer justifications for labour laws as interventions in the 'free' market. Private law rules have their own justifications, of course. Whether they are justified in the forms currently existing or should be modified to give more weight to workers' interests is an interesting and important question, but out of the scope of this book.[37] Moreover, given that (as an historical matter) the basic rules of private law were developed *before* the advent of modern labour law, presumably legislatures accepted them as a background. Reluctantly, then, I accept a presumption in favour of the market. Usually this is assumed implicitly; acknowledging it explicitly is important, to remind ourselves that background rules can (and should) be questioned as well.

A related question is whether our articulation of the goals of labour law should include the interests of employers, which obviously are taken (and must be taken) into account when structuring the law. For example, the law usually recognizes an employer's prerogative to make managerial decisions, in the interest of efficiently running the business. This is undoubtedly part of labour law. But are the efficiency interests of the employer among the *goals of labour law*, or is the legal rule a result of a compromise between the goals of labour law and other interests? Both models are possible. Stephen Befort and John Budd, for example, prefer the former: they identify efficiency (in the sense just described), equity, and voice as the three objectives of labour law, and argue that the goal of labour law is to balance these three objectives.[38] Nonetheless, most labour law scholars seem to prefer the latter model, focusing on the goals of deviating from the private law background rules.[39] This is the approach I take here as well. The managerial

[37] For a convincing progressive reorientation of private law doctrines, see Edo Eshet, *The Social Dimension of Contract, Property and Corporate Law in Business Transfers* (PhD dissertation, Hebrew University, 2013) [in Hebrew].

[38] Befort and Budd (n 7). See also John W Budd, *Employment With a Human Face: Balancing Efficiency, Equity and Voice* (Cornell UP 2004).

[39] See, e.g. Hugh Collins, 'Justifications and Techniques of Legal Regulation of the Employment Relation' in Hugh Collins, Paul Davies and Roger Rideout (eds), *Legal Regulation of the Employment Relation* (Kluwer 2000) 3 (discussing market failure justifications and distributive justifications for labour law); KD Ewing, 'Democratic Socialism and Labour Law' (1995) 24 ILJ 103, 111 (listing a social justice purpose and democratic purpose).

prerogative is based on the laws of contract and property; labour law places *limitations* on this prerogative based on its protective goals. Various other labour laws surely take the employers' interests into account, but it is useful to understand these interests as based on private law background rules, and the labour laws as intervening in these rules. The goals are articulated accordingly.

General and specific goals

Assume a labour law system with ten different pieces of legislation regulating different employment standards (such as minimum wage, maximum hours, etc.) as well as a law regulating collective bargaining and strikes and a law designed to ensure equal opportunities at work. They may come separately or in one Labour Law Code with several chapters. Either way, it is quite obvious that each piece of legislation (or chapter) has its own goals. If we ask ourselves what are the goals of setting a minimum wage, and what are the goals of allowing and promoting collective bargaining (for example), we will come up with different answers, albeit with some overlap. We can say that the minimum wage law is designed to protect the dignity of employees and redistribute resources from employers to employees, and that collective bargaining laws are designed to promote workplace democracy, redistribute resources from employers to employees, and enhance efficiency.[40] Of course, there can be other views about the goals of these laws, and also one could argue that their goals should be articulated at a different level of abstraction (an issue which I discuss separately below). But it would be difficult to deny the claim that different laws regulating labour relations can have different goals. At the same time, it is quite obvious that they also have something in common—that they share some basic reasoning.[41] Therefore, should we articulate the goals of each labour law separately, or the goals of the entire enterprise as a whole?

The answer is both. When thinking about a specific law (the minimum wage, for example)—whether it requires changes, or how to interpret it, or whether it is constitutional—one must articulate the goals of the *specific* law (and sometimes even the goals of the specific section under discussion).[42] At the same time it is useful in such cases to have a *general* understanding of why labour laws are needed, using it as a starting point to examine the purpose of the specific regulation.[43] In most cases this is simply a practical solution: given that different labour laws are often needed for similar reasons, which flow from the very nature of the

[40] See Chapter 5.

[41] Matthew Finkin has argued that labour law developed as a series of responses to specific social problems (Matthew W Finkin, 'The Death and Transfiguration of Labor Law' (2011) 33 CLLPJ 171, 181). But this does not mean that these problems and/or responses do not have something in common, that distinguishes them from other sets of problems/responses.

[42] For an excellent recent example see Brian Langille and Pnina Alon-Shenker, 'Law Firm Partners and the Scope of Labour Law' (2015) 4 Can J of Human Rights 211.

[43] On the need to articulate a general purpose see also Langille (n 36) 262. Langille believes that the specific purposes sometimes 'stand in the way' of the general purpose. My own view is that they are for the most part compatible.

employer–employee relationship, there is no reason to 'invent the wheel' again every time. Relying on the general understanding of labour law—at least as a starting point—will also ensure some coherence and consistency in the system (e.g. regarding the interpretation of similar terms in different labour laws).

Consider the following example: the term 'employee' appears in different labour laws. It is used—without being defined in the laws themselves—to set the scope of these laws. Courts need to give meaning to this term—to interpret it. Assume that a worker is suing for a minimum wage, but the defendant is arguing that the worker is in fact performing the work as an independent contractor and the minimum wage law does not apply. In order to decide whether the plaintiff is an employee or not, courts will usually use a number of tests and indicia which they have developed. Indeed, there is no need to develop new tests in every case. However, in difficult cases, when applying these tests it is helpful to have in mind the purpose behind them. Moreover, every once in a while it is important to ask whether the tests still serve their purpose.[44] To re-examine the tests and perhaps develop new ones, we need to ask why the distinction between employees and independent contractors is needed. To make sense of this distinction we need to ask why labour laws are needed. Then we can come up with tests that could help us distinguish those who need to be covered by such laws from those who do not. The term 'employee' can then be interpreted accordingly.

In principle, from a purposive point of view, one could be an employee for minimum wage purposes, and an independent contractor for collective bargaining purposes, or vice versa. However, there is an obvious advantage in maintaining a degree of uniformity in the system, to allow workers to know their rights and employers to know their obligations.[45] So this particular example gives another reason for articulating the *general* goals of labour law before looking into the more specific ones. It is useful to create a general test for 'who is an employee', and a presumption that this test will apply in different labour law contexts, unless there is a strong reason—given the *specific* goals of some law—to deviate from this default.[46]

Justifications or explanations?

In an important analysis of American labour law, James Atleson uncovered five hidden assumptions that can explain the attitude of judges and their decisions: continuity of production must be maintained; employees, unless controlled,

[44] In the specific context one can also ask whether these tests were developed in line with some clear purpose in the first place. In some legal systems the tests used to decide whether one is an employee or not have in fact been developed (at least according to one view) in a different context altogether: to decide whether the employer should bear vicarious liability for workers' actions. See PS Atiyah, *Vicarious Liability in the Law of Torts* (Butterworths 1967) ch 5. These tests have then been adopted in the labour context as well. But obviously the purpose of the 'employee' definition in tort law is entirely different (or at least *could* be entirely different) from the purpose of applying labour laws to some people who work for pay but not others.

[45] See Chapter 6. [46] See Chapter 6.

will act irresponsibly; employees owe a measure of respect and deference to their employers; the workplace is the property of the employer and primarily under management's control; employees cannot be full partners in the enterprise because that would interfere with inherent, exclusive managerial rights of employers.[47] These assumptions seem to be based on the basic legal concepts of private property and freedom of contract, which in themselves are difficult to deny. In some countries the right to property and freedom of contract appear in constitutions, in others in legislation; but even where they were developed by courts as part of the common law, it should be acknowledged that these principles are important pillars not only of the 'free' market but of the legal system. There are obviously strong justifications for having a right to private property and to freedom of contract—generally, to protect autonomy and maximize efficiency.[48] So in principle, judges cannot be faulted for interpreting labour laws in line with those basic principles of the legal system. Indeed, as already noted, it is fair to assume that labour laws themselves were legislated with the background assumption of a system based on property and contract rights.

Nonetheless, the fact that property and contract rights are present in the background does not mean that such rights should only support the employer. Here judicial assumptions about what constitutes 'property' and what the parties have implicitly agreed upon in the contract indeed play a major role.[49] Which raises two important questions: when articulating the goals of the labour law system as a whole, should we take into account the laws developed by courts, alongside legislation? And assuming we do, should we look for the 'real' goals even if they are hidden and unjustified, or rather search only for normative justifications?

I would answer the first question positively. Judges are obviously partners in the enterprise of law-making. Through case-by-case advancement they give meaning to open-ended concepts in legislation. Their interpretation completes the legislation by connecting it to real-life problems as they arise. They fill gaps in pieces of legislation that cannot provide solutions to every legal problem. All of this is an important part of labour law—of our understanding of what labour law is all about. Assuming, of course, that it does not contradict (but only completes) the spirit of the legislation itself. As for uncovering the hidden assumptions and political preferences of judges, this is a highly important task as part of critically analyzing the case law. Nevertheless, these are not 'goals' in the same sense discussed in this book. For purposes of reforming/improving the law, and for purposes

[47] James B Atleson, *Values and Assumptions in American Labor Law* (U of Massachusetts Press 1983) 7–9. For a descriptive-positive analysis of goals, see also Hyde (n 4) (listing 22 different 'ideas' of labour law, many of them descriptive); Michael Quinlan, 'Contextual Factors Shaping the Purpose of Labour Law: A Comparative Historical Perspective' in Christopher Arup and others (eds), *Labour Law and Labour Market Regulation* (Federation Press 2006) 22; Arianne Renan Barzilay, 'Labor Regulation as Family Regulation: Decent Work and Decent Families' (2012) 33 BJELL 119.

[48] See, e.g. Michael J Trebilcock, *The Limits of Freedom of Contract* (HUP 1993).

[49] Philip Selznick, *Law, Society and Industrial Justice* (Russell Sage Foundation 1969); Alan Fox, *Beyond Contract: Work, Power and Trust Relations* (Faber and Faber 1974); Atleson (n 47).

of interpreting it, we are interested in the *normative* level—in goals that can be defended.[50] So judicial attitudes towards the law (that could sometimes be negative and constricting) should not constitute part of our understanding of what the law is about; but the general approach of the court, to the extent that it conforms to the ideas behind the legislation, should be taken into account.

This might seem confusing. Are we looking for *justifications* or rather for *explanations* of the law? In my view, the answer should be both. Adopting the influential methodology of Ronald Dworkin, I would argue that we should give the law the best possible reading. This can be done by thinking about normative justifications, but at the same time making sure that there is a reasonable degree of 'fit' with actual law.[51] In other words, we are looking for justifications that can best explain the law as it is.

To avoid an inherently conservative bias, one should be careful not to require 'fit' with specific solutions or details. That would lead to interpretations that cannot break away from previous precedents when they are no longer appropriate, and to difficulties in suggesting legislative reforms. The idea of 'fit' in interpreting legislation is simply to ensure that the interpretation chosen (based on justifications) conforms to the text of the law, and, as much as possible, to other relevant pieces of legislation. In the context of common-law judicial development of the law, 'fit' means ensuring some continuity—in Dworkin's terms, the idea is to write another chapter in a chain-novel,[52] so you can certainly add something new, but it cannot be detached from previous chapters. The same is true if we think that a piece of legislation needs to be improved—for example, that a specific section needs to be changed. The new proposal has to be justified normatively, but also to have some degree of 'fit' with the existing structure of the law and the ideas

[50] The case of constitutional challenges is a bit more complicated. Sometimes (even if rarely) a legislature might have hidden goals that cannot be defended and because of that are not explicit. For example, an Israeli law prohibiting family unification of Palestinians in Israel cited security concerns, but it has been argued that in fact the reasons behind it were demographic (preserving the Jewish majority in Israel). See HCJ 7052/03 *Adalah v The Minister of Interior*, PD 61(2) 202 (2006) (Supreme Court of Israel), English version available at <http://elyon1.court.gov.il/files_eng/03/520/070/a47/03070520.a47.pdf> accessed 10 October 2015. Arguably, hidden goals should be uncovered as part of the constitutional analysis—and if they are illegitimate, the legislature should not be able to enjoy the mask of other (explicit) goals. However, the analysis of proportionality itself will be conducted in light of the explicit goals—assuming there are any (see Guy Davidov, Jonathan Yovel, Ilan Saban and Amnon Reichman, 'State or Family? The 2003 Amendment to the Citizenship and Entrance to Israel Law' (2005) 8 Mishpat Umimshal 643 (Hebrew)). The task of articulating goals is thus still concerned with *goals that can be justified*—for the purpose of constitutional challenges as well.

[51] Dworkin (n 16). Dworkin's theories in general have been the subject of much debate and critique, but this particular methodology is, as far as I am aware, relatively uncontroversial. There were objections concerning the subjectivity which is unavoidable when a judge decides what would be the best reading of a statute (or how to view it in the 'best light'). But a degree of judicial discretion—which includes some subjectivity—is a necessary part of interpretation either way. Moreover, for current purposes, we do not need to accept Dworkin's views that the fit-justification methodology is also a correct *description* of how judges actually operate, or his view that there is only one 'right' interpretation (both of which have been strongly challenged).

[52] Dworkin (n 16) 228.

behind it. Unless, of course, one wants to start something entirely new, whether in legislation or in common law. In such cases there are fewer constraints in terms of 'fit'. That is certainly possible and *should* be possible, but it is much less common.

Goals specific to time and place?

Given the assumption that we aim to articulate goals that will have some 'fit' with existing labour laws, the question arises whether it is possible to articulate goals that are not specific (or 'contextual') in terms of time and place. In the UK, for example, there have been some interesting discussions regarding changes in the goals of labour law as a result of changes in government.[53] It appears, though, that at least in developed economies (and perhaps in other legal systems as well) the basic goals are very similar across time and place. The situation may be different if one is trying to articulate the goals as a purely positive-descriptive matter.[54] Nonetheless, the current project is, first and foremost, normative and it seems that the basic idea behind labour law does not change much as a result of government changes, or between countries.[55]

Consider, for example, the minimum wage. Obviously a lot has changed between the time it was first adopted more than a century ago and the present, but it still exists throughout the world. Notwithstanding the dramatic shift from an industrial economy to a service economy, from Fordism to post-Fordism, the feminization of the workforce, the increasing precariousness of employment, the impact of globalization, etc.—the minimum wage is still here, and it is needed for very similar reasons as before. The level of the minimum wage, and its scope, could be different under different regimes, and this has crucial implications for workers and employers. But the normative justifications for enacting a minimum wage law are similar. The same is true for other major components of the body of labour laws.

To be sure, in some countries and at some times, employment relations are less heavily regulated, but that does not mean that the goals are different. It is also quite possible that there are differences in terms of emphasis on some goals and not others, depending on the time and place. So there should certainly be sensitivity to context, and one should be mindful to variations. However, given that

[53] Sandra Fredman, 'The New Rights: Labour Law and Ideology in the Thatcher Years' (1992) 12 OJLS 244; Hugh Collins, 'Regulating the Employment Relationship for Competitiveness' (2001) 31 ILJ 17; Hugh Collins, 'Is There a Third Way in Labour Law?' in Joanne Conaghan, Richard Michael Fischl and Karl Klare (eds), *Labour Law in an Era of Globalization: Transformative Practices and Possibilities* (OUP 2002) 449; Sandra Fredman, 'The Ideology of New Labour Law' in Catherine Barnard, Simon Deakin and Gillian S Morris (eds), *The Future of Labour Law: Liber Amicorum Bob Hepple* (Hart 2004) 9.

[54] See sources in n 47 above.

[55] And see Simon Deakin, 'Conceptions of the Market in Labour Law' in Ann Numhauser-Henning and Mia Rönnmar (eds), *Normative Patterns and Legal Developments in the Social Dimension of the EU* (Hart 2013) 141 (discussing aspects of labour law that vary across national contexts, and in some cases result from local political and industrial factors, but adding that labour law systems also have 'universal features').

labour law has developed as a set of solutions to 'labour problems'[56]—and the problems are virtually the same across countries—there are sufficient similarities across legal systems to make it possible to pursue a general analysis of goals.[57]

Main and ancillary goals

The next issue we should consider is whether there needs to be some hierarchy among goals. Are some goals more important than others, and should receive priority in case of conflict? Consider, for example, the issue of efficiency. Some could say that maximizing efficiency is one of the main goals of labour law.[58] Others would argue that labour laws are by their very nature—because of their intervention in the 'free' market—*impediments* to efficiency. From here the argument could take two opposing directions. Neo-classical economists would argue that because of their inefficiency labour laws are unjustified (and thus would favour in most cases deregulation). The 'traditional' view of labour lawyers, on the other hand, has been to accept (at least implicitly) the charge of inefficiency, but argue that labour laws are justified because they are designed to achieve other goals (say, protect the dignity of workers) that *trump* efficiency concerns. With this basic approach in the background, presumably labour lawyers would accept efficiency at least as an ancillary goal, meaning that, if there are two equally valid ways to achieve the goals of labour law, one should prefer (all other things being equal) the law that is more efficient (or less *in*efficient).

Most scholars today probably hold a more nuanced view towards efficiency: labour laws sometimes enhance it, sometimes they are neutral in this respect, and at other times they can be inefficient and still justified for other reasons.[59] In the first group of cases, efficiency is one of our goals, and obviously should not be relegated to some lower status compared with other goals. However, in the second and third groups of cases, when the law is *not* designed to promote efficiency, arguably it is still justified to add it as an ancillary goal, in the sense noted above.

Another possible example is fair distribution of resources or opportunities among workers.[60] In some labour laws—notably employment equal opportunities

[56] See Finkin (n 41) 181.

[57] And see Adrián Goldin, 'Global Conceptualizations and Local Constructions of the Idea of Labour Law' in Davidov and Langille (n 2) 69. Goldin argues that there is a global 'basic idea' of labour law, which is still dominant in European and Latin American systems. He notes that in common-law countries, scholars are more inclined to revise this basic idea. Yet, he does not bring any evidence to show that this has actually happened as a matter of law.

[58] Alan Hyde goes some way towards this view when he argues that the main goal of labour law is to correct market failures. See Alan Hyde, 'What is Labour Law?' in Guy Davidov and Brian Langille (eds), *Boundaries and Frontiers of Labour Law: Goals and Means in the Regulation of Work* (Hart 2006) 37.

[59] For the view that labour laws are *sometimes* efficient see, e.g. Collins (n 39) 3; Simon Deakin and Frank Wilkinson, 'Labour Law and Economic Theory: A Reappraisal' in Collins, Davies and Rideout (n 39) 29. See also Guy Davidov, 'The (Changing?) Idea of Labour Law' (2007) 146 ILR 311.

[60] See Guy Mundlak, 'The Third Function of Labour Law: Distributing Labour Market Opportunities among Workers' in Davidov and Langille (n 2) 315; ACL Davies, 'Identifying

laws—this is one of the main (and explicit) goals. But in other cases, the law might appear to be oblivious to this issue. In such cases, one could argue that fair 'horizontal' distribution (between workers, as opposed to redistribution from employers to employees) should still be taken into account as an ancillary goal. That is, even if the law aims to achieve other goals, all else being equal it is better to structure or interpret the law so as to promote equality (or fair distribution) among different workers. It appears, then, that there is some room for a distinction between main and ancillary goals in labour law.

Thinking about goals: A multi-disciplinary endeavour

I have suggested some ground rules for articulating labour law's goals. But we are still left with a fundamental question: how (or where) do we 'find' the goals? Think about a specific labour law first. One answer would be to search in the legislation itself, perhaps there is a 'purpose statement' at the beginning explaining what the law is aimed at, or perhaps the goals can be understood from the language of the law. Then there are legislative documents: the proposed bill (presumably with explanatory notes), background papers prepared at the relevant Ministry, protocols of discussions at the legislature and at committees preparing the bill, and so on. Finally, still within the 'internal' confines of the law, one could look for insights in the case-law, and perhaps in other (relevant) pieces of legislation.

These are all useful and important sources, but as noted above in the discussion of purposive interpretation, not sufficient. These sources are often not up-to-date, and are sometimes based on unstated assumptions. If our aim is to provide the law with the best possible reading (in interpretation), or to suggest well-informed reforms (in policy-making), we will benefit most from theoretical and empirical explorations of this law (or the problems that the law addresses). We know that a piece of legislation aims to achieve certain social goals. To best understand and articulate these goals, one should look for academic discussions, especially *outside* the confines of doctrinal law—in economics, sociology, psychology, philosophy, political science and more. Obviously this is not an easy task for judges and legislatures. It is the role of academics (and a goal of this book) to assist in this task.

Consider, for example, a minimum wage law. Looking at legislative documents in Israel (for example), one would find references especially to the goal of alleviating poverty. This was also cited in the Israeli case-law as one of the main goals of the minimum wage legislation.[61] However, while it might make sense for politicians to discuss the law in these terms, it is a very imprecise and rough articulation of goals, and as a result will be of little help for our purposes. If the goal was to

"Exploitative Compromises": The Role of Labour Law in Resolving Disputes Between Workers' (2012) 65 CLP 269.

[61] See, e.g. *Paltours Traveling and Tourism Ltd v Judah Padan* 22 PDA 356, 361 (1990) (National Labour Court); *Sadot v Israel Prison Service* 58(4) PD 817, 835 (2001) (Supreme Court); *Yaacov Roth v Ram Building Ltd*, judgment of 1 October 2009 (National Labour Court).

alleviate poverty, one would expect to see a law that targets those most in poverty. But in fact the unemployed who are presumably poorer than low-wage employees are not covered by minimum wage laws. Based on academic sources from different disciplines I will argue that the goals of the minimum wage are redistribution of resources to the lowest-paid employees and protection of employees' dignity.[62] Obviously other views about the goals of this law can be just as valid. My point here is simply about the importance of relying on a careful reading of extra-legal sources, both theoretical and empirical.

A related question is whether we should consider critiques as part of this analysis. To continue with the minimum wage example, there is a fierce debate among economists about the desirability of this law—with the traditional/conservative view being that an imposed minimum wage is not only inefficient but also harms the most vulnerable workers (who will lose their jobs). According to this view, the group of low-wage workers who will get a raise as a result of the law will do so on the back of workers who are even weaker. Employers will shift the cost of the law to this group, leading to regressive—rather than progressive—redistribution. To be sure, this is by no means the accepted view. There are recent studies that show that a minimum wage set at a reasonable level does not lead to unemployment, and that the costs of the minimum wage are borne to a large extent by employers themselves.[63] The empirical debate is on-going, and different people could make different conclusions from it. However, an informed view about what the law aims to achieve should take this debate—or more generally, critiques of the law—into account. Critiques can obviously support reforms, and they can also be used as part of the process of interpretation: to give a law the best possible reading, its potential negative consequences should be taken into account. For example, when interpreting sections dealing with exemptions in the legislation—such as a lower level of minimum wage for young workers or workers with disabilities—we should consider the context which includes the concern of harming employment prospects for these groups. The best way to understand such concerns is by reading the critiques of the minimum wage law.

So far our focus has been on a specific labour law. But the same ideas (the multi-disciplinary nature of goal-searching and the need to consider critiques) apply when articulating the *general* goals of labour law as well. To understand why we need labour laws, we need to start from understanding what is unique about the employment relationship. Then it will become clear why we need to regulate this relationship in certain ways. The unique nature of the employment relationship has been studied extensively by economists, sociologists, psychologists, and others. Such studies are most informative for understanding and articulating the general goals of labour law.

[62] See Chapter 5. [63] See discussion and references in Chapter 5.

Choosing the level of abstraction

The final issue that needs to be addressed concerning the 'how' question is, in my view, the most elusive and difficult one: how to choose the appropriate level of abstraction or generalization. One could say that the goal of the minimum wage law (for example) is simply to ensure that every worker is paid at least X Euros per hour of work. This is obviously correct, but too specific and as a result not very useful for the purposes discussed above. On the other extreme, one could say that the goal of the minimum wage is to protect workers, which is also correct, but this time too general and again not useful. The point of the exercise, as we have seen in the previous part, is to assist us when suggesting reforms, or interpreting the law, etc. It is difficult to see how any of these articulations—ones that are very specific or very general—can help us when attempting to make informed choices about reforms or the best interpretation.

Thinking about the *general* goals of labour law, one could find at least three levels in the literature.[64] At the highest (first) level we can refer to abstract values that labour laws aim to protect or promote, such as autonomy, equality, democracy (or 'voice'), human dignity, social inclusion, distributive justice, or capabilities. Somewhat more specifically (second level), we can point to some broad characteristics of labour markets that explain/justify the need to regulate them, such as inequality of bargaining power, the prevalence of market failures, the commodification of labour, or the existence of obstacles to the realization of human capital. The goal of labour law is then understood (sometimes implicitly) as addressing this problem. Finally, a yet more specific (third) level is focused on the unique characteristics of employment relationships that put the employee in a vulnerable position, for example, subordination and dependency. On this view, the general goals of labour law would be minimizing these vulnerabilities and preventing unwanted outcomes resulting from them.

The different levels do not contradict each other, indeed they are perfectly compatible. One can agree with all of the above articulations at the same time. So the question becomes which one is more relevant (or useful) for given purposes. Otherwise put: to choose the appropriate level of abstraction, we should ask what the goal of the enquiry is—i.e. use a purposive approach to the question of how to perform the purposive analysis. The answer depends on the context: if we are looking into proposed reforms, perhaps we should articulate the goals differently than when interpreting the law. Also, when interpreting a specific section we might have to use a different level of abstraction than the one used for more general problems (such as 'who is an employee').

I do not have a general formula that can point to the best level of abstraction in each context. It is, first and foremost, important to be mindful of the issue—to realize that this is a critical part of the goals-articulation process and then one should make an effort to find a level that is useful for the purpose of the enquiry.

[64] For a full discussion of the various goals mentioned below see Chapters 3 and 4.

I would, though, argue that too much emphasis has been given over the years to the second level, while in fact the third one turns out to be much more useful in most cases. Ideas like 'inequality of bargaining power' are perhaps important in terms of putting forward a narrative to support labour laws. But such articulations are not easy to translate into concrete interpretations or legislative improvements. As noted in Chapter 1, there is a crucial problem of mismatch between labour laws and their purpose; addressing this problem would usually require that we focus on the specific vulnerabilities of employees as mentioned above.[65] This is true whether we are suggesting solutions by way of legislative reforms or by way of judicial interpretation. Just to give one example, it is difficult to interpret the important concepts of 'employee' and 'employer'—setting the scope of labour law—by reference to inequality of bargaining power. But these concepts can certainly be given meaning by reference to the vulnerabilities that characterize employment relationships.

So far we have discussed the level of abstraction when articulating the general goals of labour laws. What about the goals of *specific* regulations? Here one might continue to an even more concrete (fourth) level, and focus on concrete results that society finds unacceptable (e.g. wages that are below a certain level). The goal of the law would then be to prevent such unwanted results. However, this will simply raise the question of *why* these results are unacceptable, and perhaps the best way to explain that would be by going back to the most general level of values. I try to show later (in Chapter 8) that broad goals such as achieving redistributive justice and protecting human dignity can be useful in interpreting specific sections of a minimum wage law.

Conclusion

We have seen in the first part of this chapter *why* it is necessary to explicitly articulate the goals of labour law: for purposes of improving/changing the law, or filling gaps in it; for purposes of interpreting the law; and to examine constitutional challenges. I have argued in Chapter 1 that there is a mismatch between goals and means, which creates a crisis in the field. Addressing this problem requires changes to the law itself or to prevailing interpretations, so the solution must start with an articulation of goals.

I then discussed in the second part several methodological questions about *how* to articulate the goals: I (reluctantly) accepted a presumption in favour of the 'free' market; argued that we should articulate the goals of each labour law separately, and at the same time the *general* goals of labour law as a whole; explained that we should be looking for *justifications* that can also *explain* the law; argued that it is possible (although requires caution) to articulate goals that are not 'contextual';

[65] For examples see Guy Davidov, 'Re-Matching Labour Law With Their Purpose' in Davidov and Langille (n 2) 179.

argued that there could be some ancillary goals distinguished from our main goals; showed that the goals cannot be found only within legal texts, but rather require a multi-disciplinary search; and pointed attention to the importance of choosing the right level of abstraction.

Armed with these insights, we can move on to consider some possible articulations of goals. This is the task of the next three chapters.

3

The Idea of Labour Law as Addressing Vulnerabilities or Labour Market 'Problems'

In Chapter 2 we have seen that we need to articulate the goals of labour law for several important reasons. Specifically, this is a necessary step for any reform in legislation and/or judicial interpretations, which are needed to address the crisis in this field. We have seen that there is a need to articulate the goals both in general—the goals of the labour law system as a whole—and at the level of specific regulations. The current chapter and the next one are dedicated to the first task.

As explained in the previous chapter, the goals of labour law can be articulated at different levels of abstraction. This chapter starts with the most specific level: understanding the unique characteristics of employment relations—which translate to specific vulnerabilities—and explaining the goal of labour law as addressing these vulnerabilities (Part I). I then move to consider two characteristics of labour relations or labour markets that are somewhat more abstract and less concrete: inequality of bargaining power and market failures (Part II). Labour law has been explained based on these concepts as well. The different articulations of the idea of labour law discussed in this chapter are brought here together because they share a basic structure: seeing labour law as a solution to a 'labour problem'.[1] The next chapter then moves to add the more 'positive' view of the idea of labour law, listing (and discussing) the various values that labour laws are trying to advance.[2]

Matthew Finkin has recently argued that labour law does not have one goal, but rather it should be understood as a set of solutions to various labour 'problems'—whether it is wages that are too low, working hours that are too long, and so on.[3] I agree with the basic 'problem-solving' view but believe that alongside

[1] The term 'labour problems' was commonly invoked by early institutional economists; see Bruce E Kaufman, 'Economic Analysis of Labor Markets and Labor Law: An Institutional/Industrial Relations Perspective' in Cynthia L Estlund and Michael L Wachter (eds), *Research Handbook on the Economics of Labor and Employment Law* (Edward Elgar 2012) 52, 64.

[2] Christopher McCrudden, 'Two Views of Subordination: The Personal Scope of Employment Discrimination Law in *Jivraj v Hashwani*' (2012) 41 ILJ 30, 46 describes these as alternative/opposing theories of employment law: the 'vulnerability' approach versus the 'rights' approach. I argue that they are complementary, offering explanations of labour law that live side by side, at different levels of abstraction.

[3] See Matthew W Finkin, 'The Death and Transfiguration of Labor Law' (2011) 33 CLLPJ 171; Matthew W Finkin, 'Introduction: The Past and Future of Labor Law in Comparative Perspective'

the various specific problems it is also possible, and useful, to identify a larger overarching problem that explains the emergence and persistence of the specific problems. This chapter is devoted to articulating this overarching 'problem', that can explain why we need labour law at the level of the project as a whole.

Debates on the idea of labour law in recent years have focused on a high level of abstraction—the advancement of lofty values—and especially on finding 'new' goals. This level of analysis is certainly useful and I engage with it in detail in the next chapter. However, scholars who champion new goals usually admit that the 'old' justifications for labour law are still relevant;[4] indeed they are the ones more relevant in most cases. Hence, even those who prefer to turn their attention to 'new' goals will likely admit that it is crucially important to improve our understanding of 'old' goals as well—and to examine the compatibility of our labour laws with these goals.

Part I—Addressing Concrete Vulnerabilities

One possible way to explain and justify labour law is by reference to the vulnerabilities of employees—as opposed to independent contractors—that explain the need for protective labour laws. This approach starts from asking: What are the unique characteristics of employment relationships? What makes them different from other relations? Specifically, why does the law heavily regulate some work relations (employer–employee) but not others (client–independent contractor)? Once we pinpoint the characteristics of the former relations that distinguish them from the latter, it will also become clear why labour law is needed (for the former).

In this part I argue that employment is characterized by a set of unique vulnerabilities, which can best be described from three separate viewpoints: organizational, social/psychological, and economic. The first viewpoint directs attention to *democratic deficits* within the relationship (or: subordination, broadly conceived). The other two reveal the *dependency* of employees on the relationship with a specific employer. At the end of the day, then, I conclude with two familiar notions. Since courts in many countries already refer to subordination and dependency when discussing the employment relationship (at least in the context of identifying 'who is an employee'), one might question the ability of this articulation to bring about any change.

Nonetheless there are several important contributions to the analysis offered here. First, it provides a theoretical explanation and justification for some existing

in Bob A Hepple and Otto Kahn-Freund (eds), *XV International Encyclopedia of Comparative Law* (Mohr Siebeck 2014) 3. Finkin therefore prefers a lower level of abstraction/generality than the one I pursue here.

[4] Mark Freedland and Nicola Kountouris, *The Legal Construction of Personal Work Relations* (OUP 2011) 370; Brian Langille, 'Labour Law's Theory of Justice' in Guy Davidov and Brian Langille (eds), *The Idea of Labour Law* (OUP 2011) 101.

practices that have been questioned, suggesting that the solution is not in abandoning old concepts but in better applying them. Chapter 6 will explain how the law concerning 'who is an employee' should change to better give effect to the justifications offered here. Second, this part explains the difference between subordination and dependency, concepts that are often used interchangeably. Third, it gives a new and deeper meaning to the concepts of subordination and dependency, based on economic, sociological, and organizational understandings of the vulnerabilities of employees, instead of the narrow 'legal' meaning usually given to these concepts. Discussions of subordination and dependency in the literature are often doctrinal, focusing on the meaning given to these terms by the judiciary. Below I try to give these concepts a much richer meaning.

As is well known, in the last few decades employment relations have gone through dramatic transformations; atypical, precarious arrangements have often replaced the 'standard' employment relationship.[5] These changes obviously pose new challenges for labour law, and these are addressed at different parts of this book. However, as far as the basic characteristics of employment are concerned—the characteristics that require the protection of labour law and explain the need for labour law—the situation has not changed. The 'standard employment relationship'—based on long-term, bilateral, full time, relatively secure employment—has not dissolved; many workers are still employed in this arrangement or some variation of it.[6] Moreover, those engaged in alternative, precarious arrangements suffer from the same vulnerabilities discussed below—only, usually, to an even larger extent. The characteristics of work relations are described here at a level of generalization that is true for all kinds of workplaces: large and small, in manufacturing or services, with or without an internal labour market. The dramatic shifts in labour markets and labour relations have not changed these basic characteristics.

The organizational viewpoint

Employment represents one possible framework in which people perform work for remuneration. What makes it different from other frameworks, most notably that between firms and independent contractors? Organizationally, an employment relationship is best described as a *structure of governance with democratic deficits*. To support this claim, this section proceeds as follows. First, I briefly explain why a structure of governance other than the market is a necessary part of employment relationships. The existence of democratic deficits as part of this governance structure is then explained from two viewpoints: power and efficiency. Together

[5] For recent discussions see Katherine VW Stone and Harry Arthurs (eds), *Rethinking Workplace Regulation: Beyond the Standard Contract of Employment* (Russell Sage Foundation 2013); David Weil, *The Fissured Workplace: Why Work Became So Bad for So Many and What Can Be Done to Improve It* (HUP 2014).

[6] Zoe Adams and Simon Deakin, 'Institutional Solutions to Inequality and Precariousness in Labour Markets' (2014) 52 BJIR 779.

these viewpoints explain why—absent any dramatic changes to current market and legal structures—democratic deficits are an inseparable part of the employment relationship.

Why governance?

People tend to work together with others, for efficiency reasons,[7] and probably also for social reasons. Since people usually work together, their work must be coordinated. Consider a car assembly plant for example. There are thousands of workers in such a plant. If each person were able to do whatever he wants or thinks fit, they would never manufacture a single car. Even if they were somehow able to reach a preliminary agreement on the allocation of tasks, the production process inevitably requires numerous decisions, many of them on questions not known in advance. Work relations are continuous, and involve much more than a one-time transaction. Circumstances inevitably change all the time, and it is not possible to know in advance—not to mention specify in advance—what each worker will have to do.[8] There must be continuous coordination with regard to various aspects of the work, involving complexity which cannot be dealt with through discrete market transactions.[9]

When a small number of people are involved, coordination can presumably be achieved by some cooperative structure of governance, in which all the workers can take part in any decision. When two or three people are working together, they might be able to reach decisions on every matter mutually, in a peaceful and efficient way. But in a larger enterprise, the existence of managers is inevitable.[10] There are too many decisions to take, and they have to be taken too quickly, for all the workers to be able to participate directly in any decision. Organizations involving a substantial number of people working together therefore require managers, at the very least, to mediate between the different ideas and interests involved and coordinate the activities of different workers.[11] This is not unique to

[7] Efficiency gains can result from a division of labour (see Adam Smith, *An Inquiry into the Nature and Causes of the Wealth of Nations* (Kathryn Sutherland ed, first published 1776, OUP 1993) 12–20); the efficient use of resources and greater specialization (see Charles Babbage, *On the Economy of Machinery and Manufacturers* (first published 1832, 4th edn, Augustus M Kelley 1963) 175–76); or the minimizing of transaction costs (see Ronald H Coase, 'The Nature of the Firm' (1937) 4 Economica 386).

[8] See Alan Fox, *Beyond Contract: Work, Power and Trust Relations* (Faber and Faber 1974) 183.

[9] Paul Milgrom and John Roberts, *Economics, Organization, and Management* (Prentice-Hall 1992) ch 4.

[10] See Max Weber, *The Theory of Social and Economic Organization* (A M Henderson and Talcott Parsons trs, Talcott Parsons ed, Free Press 1964) 328.

[11] As Marx explained, 'all directly social or communal labour on a large scale requires, to a greater or lesser degree, a directing authority, in order to secure the harmonious co-operation of the activities of individuals, and to perform the general functions that have their origin in the motion of the total productive organism, as distinguished from the motion of its separate organs. A single violin player is his own conductor: an orchestra requires a separate one.' (Karl Marx, *Capital: A Critique of Political Economy*, vol I (first published 1867, Penguin 1976) 448–49). See also Friedrich Engels, 'On Authority' in Karl Marx and Friedrich Engels (eds), *Basic Writings on Politics and Philosophy* (Lewis S Feuer ed, Doubleday 1959) 481, 483.

workplaces; 'virtually universally, in organizations of any size, decisions are made by some individuals and carried out by others'.[12] Yet governance within employment relationships is somewhat uniquely characterized by its democratic deficits.

The existence of democratic deficits

One of the basic principles of democracy maintains that every person affected by the decisions of a government should have the right to participate in that government.[13] Workplace decisions have a direct and tremendous impact on employees, affecting their daily lives as well as their long-term aspirations. Considerations of competence (expertise) and economy (efficiency) have been recognized as justifying limitations on democratic decision-making,[14] and this can justify the existence of professional managers. But while managers are necessary to the functioning of the workplace, it cannot explain why these managers are not democratically elected by the workers. Nonetheless, democratic deficits exist (to different extents) in any employment relationship.[15] Employers always retain a position of *power* over their employees; to one extent or another, they *control* them.[16] This characterization is not specific to 'traditional' forms of employment in manufacturing firms or large bureaucratic service firms. Control is equally present in small workplaces, in high-tech companies, and often in the 'on demand' (so-called 'sharing') economy. The level of control varies from one employment relationship to another, from employees who do (almost) as they wish to those who are not very far from being slaves.[17] But *some* control—an 'ability of capitalists and/or managers to obtain desired work behaviour from workers'[18]—is always there.

[12] See Kenneth J Arrow, *The Limits of Organization* (W W Norton 1974) 63. And see Arnold S Tannenbaum, *Control in Organizations* (McGraw-Hill 1968) 3 ('Organization implies control. A social organization is an ordered arrangement of individual human interactions. Control processes help circumscribe idiosyncratic behaviors and keep them conformant with the rational plan of the organization').

[13] Robert Allan Dahl, *After the Revolution? Authority In a Good Society* (Yale University Press 1970) 641; Karl E Klare, 'Workplace Democracy and Market Reconstruction: An Agenda for Legal Reform' (1988) 38 Cath U LR 1, 7; Robert E Goodin, 'Enfranchising All Affected Interests, and Its Alternatives' (2007) 35 Phil & Pub Aff 41.

[14] Robert Allan Dahl, *A Preface to Economic Democracy* (U of California Press 1985) ch 4.

[15] 'The organization of work in our society carries with it a structure of authority relations which is incorrigibly *undemocratic*' (Richard Hyman, 'A Critical View of Industrial Democracy Schemes' in Geoffrey England and George Lerner (eds), *Essays in Collective Bargaining and Industrial Democracy: Papers presented at the Conference on Collective Bargaining, School of Management, University of Lethbridge, September 9–23 1982* (CCH Canadian 1983) 107). As Alain Supiot has put it, 'the distinctiveness of wage employment lies in the fact that it necessarily implies some impairment of personal freedom' (Alain Supiot, 'Perspectives on Work: Introduction' (1996) 135 ILR 603, 612).

[16] See Marx (n 11) 291.

[17] The level of control, and changing methods of control, are influenced (among other things) by workers' resistance. See Andrew L Friedman, *Industry and Labour: Class Struggle at Work and Monopoly Capitalism* (Macmillan 1977) 82; Michael I Reed, *The Sociology of Management* (Harvester Wheatsheaf 1989) 42.

[18] Richard Edwards, *Contested Terrain: The Transformation of the Workplace in the Twentieth Century* (Basic Books 1979) 17.

By using different methods of direction, evaluation, and discipline, employers are able to control employees' actions.[19] They are thus able to resolve, in effect, the 'contested exchange'[20]—the problem of the 'incomplete contract'[21]—by forcing employees to work according to their commands.[22]

Control and subordination are thus the concepts most central to the understanding of the organizational aspect of employment relationships. But they must be understood very broadly. It does not necessarily mean control of the employer over every aspect of the production process. Nor does it mean 'bureaucratic' or 'organizational' control (which is what courts in some countries are looking for when determining employee status). The concept of control is used here in a broader sense, pointing generally to the superior power of the employer vis-à-vis the employee within their relationship, and the ensuing inability of the employee to control her own (working) life—in other words, the *subordination* of the employee. Both concepts (control and subordination) are thus useful but should be given a broad meaning that refers to the existence of democratic deficits.

Another articulation of the same idea is based on the concept of freedom as 'non-domination'.[23] In recent contributions, Virginia Mantouvalou relied on this concept to justify privacy protections in the workplace;[24] Alan Bogg and Cynthia Estlund have used the same concept when discussing the normative foundation of freedom of association.[25] The description of work relations as characterized by a degree of *domination* seems very similar to saying that work relations are characterized by subordination, in the broad sense given here. Just as regulations of privacy can be justified by the need to confront domination, and freedom of association can be justified on similar grounds, so could many other labour regulations. The same basic problem—which I call here subordination, preferring

[19] ibid 18.

[20] Samuel Bowles and Herbert Gintis, 'Is the Demand for Workplace Democracy Redundant in a Liberal Economy?' in Ugo Pagano and Robert Rowthorn (eds), *Democracy and Efficiency in the Economic Enterprise* (Routledge 1996) 64, 69.

[21] Oliver E Williamson, *The Economic Institutions of Capitalism* (Free Press 1985). And see Ian R Macneil, *The New Social Contract: An Inquiry into Modern Contractual Relations* (Yale UP 1980) 50; Claus Offe, 'The Political Economy of the Labour Market' in Claus Offe, *Disorganized Capitalism: Contemporary Transformations of Work and Politics* (John Keane ed, MIT Press 1985) 10, 20–25; Simon Deakin and Frank Wilkinson, 'Labour Law and Economic Theory: A Reappraisal' in Hugh Collins, Paul Davies, and Roger Rideout (eds), *Legal Regulation of the Employment Relation* (Kluwer 2000) 45.

[22] There are some who deny the existence of democratic deficits in employment relations, whether because they refuse to see any 'control' in these relations, or because they see a contract in which employees agree to relinquish control as perfectly democratic. I discuss these claims in Guy Davidov, 'The Three Axes of Employment Relationships: A Characterization of Workers in Need of Protection' (2002) 52 UTLJ 357, 385.

[23] See generally Ian Shapiro, *The State of Democratic Theory* (Princeton UP 2003).

[24] Virginia Mantouvalou, 'Human Rights and Unfair Dismissal: Private Acts in Public Spaces' (2008) 71 MLR 912, 925.

[25] Alan Bogg and Cynthia Estlund, 'Freedom of Association and the Right to Contest: Getting Back to Basics' in Tonia Novitz and Alan Bogg (eds), *Voices at Work: Continuity and Change in the Common Law World* (OUP 2014) 141.

the term commonly used in labour law—explains the need for labour law more generally.[26]

Power and efficiency explanations

There are two major lines of explanations for the existence of control over employees in virtually any employment relationship. One is concerned with power; the other with efficiency.[27] Power theories point attention to the inherent conflict of interests between capital and labour, in terms of the intensity of the work performed, wages, work conditions, and control over the content of the work.[28] These conflicts create an ongoing power struggle.[29] And because of inequality of bargaining power (explained separately in Part II below) employers are able to 'win' this struggle and gain control. Even in the relatively rare cases when a specific employee enjoys equal or superior bargaining power over the employer, the existence of an organization, in itself, gives the employer some power to control the employee. In such cases democratic deficits result from *bureaucratic* power—derived from the rules of the organization and the roles assigned to each party by these rules—rather than *market* power.[30]

It has been argued by scholars focusing on power struggles that employers look for control not in order to maximize general efficiency, but simply to maximize their own profit—their own share of the pie.[31] In contrast, efficiency theories insist that the hierarchical structure of the firm is preferred because it is efficient.

[26] See also Samuel R Bagenstos, 'Employment Law and Social Equality' (2013) 112 Mich LR 225 (arguing that 'social equality' can serve as justification for employment law, and defining this term by reference to non-domination and minimizing subordination). Bagenstos refers also to social hierarchies *outside* of the employment relationship; I discuss these aspects in the next chapter.

[27] See generally Paul Marginson, 'Power and Efficiency in the Firm: Understanding the Employment Relationship' in Christos Pitelis (ed), *Transaction Costs, Markets and Hierarchies* (Blackwell 1993) 133.

[28] See generally Marx (n 11). To be sure, these conflicts are not limited to capitalist enterprises. Governments, workers' cooperatives and employee-owned firms also prove to have the same conflicts, if only because of the unavoidable gap between the interests of any individual employee and those of the collective.

[29] This does not mean that there are no spheres of cooperation and collaboration as well. But one does not have to assume that people are interested only and always in themselves to accept the existence of the above-mentioned conflicts. Power struggles can be more dominant and vocal, or just in the background. But to some extent, they are always there.

[30] See Hugh Collins, 'Market Power, Bureaucratic Power, and the Contract of Employment' (1986) 15 ILJ 1.

[31] See Karl Marx, *Capital: A Critical Analysis of Capitalist Production* (14th edn, William Glaisher 1912) 321 ('The work of directing, superintending, and adjusting, becomes one of the functions of capital, from the moment that the labour under the control of capital, becomes co-operative...The directing motive, the end and aim of capitalistic production, is to extract the greatest possible amount of surplus-value, and consequently to exploit labour-power to the greatest possible extent'). See also Stephen A Marglin, 'What Do Bosses Do? The Origins and Functions of Hierarchy in Capitalist Production' (1974) 6(2) Review of Radical Political Economics 60; Edwards (n 18); Samuel Bowles, 'The Production Process in a Competitive Economy: Walrasian, Neo-Hobbesian, and Marxian Models' (1985) 75(1) Amer Econ Rev 16; Hugh Collins, *Regulating Contracts* (OUP 1999) 240.

The basic approach of economic analysis is that control (decision-making power) should be given to those who have the strongest incentive to work towards maximizing efficiency. The accompanying assumption is that employers/shareholders assume the higher risk of loss and chance of profit, and therefore have the stronger interest in promoting efficiency.[32] It is not clear, however, that the risks assumed by workers are smaller; and it is certainly doubtful that employers' and managers' strongest incentive is to maximize overall efficiency rather than their own share of the pie.

A more sophisticated analysis is offered by transaction costs economists. According to this school of thought, control is the most important characteristic of employment relationships. In fact, it explains the existence of the firm itself. The foundations to this approach were laid by Ronald Coase, who first focused attention to the costs involved in organizing production, including the costs of negotiating and concluding a separate contract for each exchange transaction. These 'transaction costs' are substantially reduced by organizing the production within a 'firm', in which employees agree 'for certain remuneration ... to obey the directions of an entrepreneur within certain limits'.[33] The operation of a market costs something, explained Coase, and 'by forming an organization and allowing some authority (an "entrepreneur") to direct the resources, certain marketing costs are saved'.[34]

These ideas were developed years later by Alchian and Demsetz, who argued that hierarchy is efficient because the costs of detecting shirking are reduced and discipline is made more economic. Efficiency is expected because the owner would specialize in monitoring, and even more important, because the right to residual earnings would make sure that the owner does not shirk herself.[35] The analysis of the shirking problem was significantly developed, in turn, by Oliver Williamson, who recognized that transaction costs assume particular importance when people make relationship-specific investments.[36] Williamson explains that governance structures are used to avoid opportunism and minimize costs. The appropriate structure depends on the frequency and the characteristics of the investment. While market governance is suitable for discrete (occasional and nonspecific) transactions, internal organization is needed to govern relations like employment that are recurrent and idiosyncratic. Comparing different forms of work organization, Williamson concluded that the hierarchical capitalist firm is the most efficient in minimizing transaction costs.[37] He went on to argue that shareholders alone should have the control of the firm. While admitting that employees (or at

[32] Milgrom and Roberts (n 9). [33] Coase (n 7) 391.

[34] ibid 392. The organization and governance/management within a firm costs something too, of course. The idea is that firms are preferred when these costs are lower than transaction costs.

[35] Armen A Alchian and Harold Demsetz, 'Production, Information Costs, and Economic Organization' (1972) 62 Amer Econ Rev 777.

[36] See Oliver E Williamson, *Markets and Hierarchies: Analysis and Antitrust Implications* (Free Press 1975) ch 4; Williamson (n 21); Oliver E Williamson, 'Transaction-Cost Economics: The Governance of Contractual Relations' (1979) 22 J of Law and Economics 233.

[37] Williamson (n 21).

least some of them), like shareholders, make significant firm-specific investments, he argued that only shareholders need representation on the board of directors to protect these investments, since employees can sufficiently protect themselves by way of collective bargaining.[38]

This last assumption is highly doubtful, especially today (a few decades after Williamson made this argument).[39] But the efficiency explanation (or justification) of democratic deficits is still valuable. Whether one agrees with power theories or with efficiency ones, for the purpose of this chapter they can coexist. Both provide useful explanations for the continued existence of democratic deficits in employment relationships. Such deficits can be seen as a result of power struggles between labour and capital, in which the latter has the upper hand, and/or as an efficient structure designed to minimize transaction costs and opportunism.

Obviously there are no clear lines between democratic governance structures and democratically deficient structures. Far from it; there are infinite degrees of control in work relations, and it would be impossible to draw any rigid lines. The level of control is changing over time.[40] It is also different from case to case and from time to time within the same relationship.[41] And a certain degree of control often exists in commercial relations as well.[42] But while clear lines cannot be drawn, the asymmetry created by democratic deficits, and the ensuing inability of workers to control their own (working) lives, put these workers in a position of vulnerability that justifies regulatory intervention to protect them. A substantial

[38] Oliver Williamson, 'Corporate Governance' (1984) 93 Yale LJ 1197; Williamson (n 21). See also Henry Hansmann, 'When Does Worker Ownership Work? ESOPs, Law Firms, Codetermination, and Economic Democracy' (1990) 99 Yale LJ 1749 (arguing that workers should be excluded from the governance of the firm because their interests are heterogeneous, which will raise governance costs, causing inefficiency).

[39] Collective bargaining has significant limitations. First, employers currently enjoy a legal *right* to control their employees, while employees only have the 'right' to fight together. Second, the vast majority of employees are currently not unionized. The power of unions has been declining and their role diminishing. Collective power is thus simply non-existent for most workers. Third, at least in some countries, many important subjects are not at all open to negotiation by way of collective bargaining. Lastly, in extreme circumstances like plant closure—when collective power is most needed—it is virtually non-existent. When an employer decides to close a plant and move it elsewhere, or even to close the business altogether, there is not much that the workers (even united) can do. For critiques of Williamson's argument see also Katharine VW Stone, 'Labor and the Corporate Structure: Changing Conceptions and Emerging Possibilities' (1988) 55 U Chi LR 73, 157–58; David Kershaw, 'No End in Sight for the History of Corporate Law: The Case of Employee Participation in Corporate Governance' (2002) 2 J Corporate Law Studies 34.

[40] For example, in the past employers could control the number of hours that employees had to work every day; see B Veneziani, 'The Evolution of the Contract of Employment' in B Hepple (ed), *The Making of Labour Law in Europe: A Comparative Study of Nine Countries up to 1945* (Mansell 1986) 65.

[41] See John Storey, 'The Means of Management Control' (1985) 19 Sociology 193.

[42] Indeed, long-term relations between cooperating firms/contractors are often more accurately described as being in between markets and hierarchies. See Stewart Macaulay, 'Non-Contractual Relations in Business: A Preliminary Study' (1963) 28 Am Soc Rev 55; Walter W Powell, 'Neither Market Nor Hierarchy: Network Forms of Organization' (1990) 12 Research in Organizational Behavior 295; Collins (n 31) 248–52.

degree of democratic deficits is one of the main characteristics of employment relationships. In the rest of the book I will use the term subordination, for convenience reasons—but the meaning of subordination for current purposes is the existence of democratic deficits as discussed above—and not the much narrower meaning adopted by some courts.

The social/psychological viewpoint

The next two viewpoints—which can be termed social/psychological and economic—are closely related. Both describe aspects of workers' dependency on the relationship with a specific employer. Such dependency can be for the fulfilment of certain social and psychological needs, and it can be economic. Although these two vulnerabilities usually intersect, this is not necessarily the case, and since each can justify different regulations, it is important to keep them theoretically separated.

Research on the meaning of work has shown that, broadly speaking, work has four distinct functions.[43] One is, of course, economic. The other three functions—which are the focus of the current section—are social and psychological in nature: first, work enables people to interact, meet, and be with one another; second, work has an intrinsic meaning for the individual as a source of identity, self-realization, and fulfilment; and third, work plays an important role in the achievement of social status and prestige.[44]

There is a wealth of empirical research on these social/psychological aspects of the importance of work.[45] It is widely accepted that work is essential in imparting meaning to our lives. Work gives us opportunities for personal expression and creativity. It is a source of intellectual progress and individual advancement.[46] It shapes our personal identities, facilitating self-development and self-realization.[47]

[43] See, e.g., Branimir Sverko and Vlasta Vizek-Vidovic, 'Studies of the Meaning of Work: Approaches, Models, and Some of the Findings' in Donald E Super and Branimir Sverko, *Life Roles, Values, and Careers: International Findings of the Work Importance Study* (Jossey-Bass 1995) 3. For various additional functions see Brent D Rosso, Kathryn H Dekas, and Amy Wrzesniewski, 'On The Meaning of Work: A Theoretical Integration and Review' (2010) 30 Research in Organizational Behavior 91.

[44] This is not to deny the existence, and importance, of *negative* aspects to work. But for current purposes, my focus is limited to the positive aspects. Negative aspects are usually the result of democratic deficits and are thus included to a large extent within this viewpoint. For distinctions between positive and negative experiences at work see Fox (n 8) 221–25; Curt Tausky, 'Work is Desirable/Loathsome: Marx versus Freud' (1992) 19 Work and Occupations 3. And see more generally the extensive reviews in Adriano Tilgher, *Work: What it has Meant to Men Through the Ages* (first published 1930, Arno Press 1977) and Herbert Applebaum, *The Concept of Work: Ancient, Medieval, and Modern* (State U of New York Press 1992).

[45] See generally MOW International Research Team, *The Meaning of Working* (Academic Press 1987). For useful summaries of the research see Robert E Lane, *The Market Experience* (Cambridge UP 1991) ch 13; Itzhak Harpaz, *The Meaning of Work in Israel: Its Nature and Consequences* (Praeger 1990) 2.

[46] See, e.g., John Goodman, *Employment Relations in Industrial Society* (Philip Allan 1984) 2–3.

[47] On self-realization see recently Hugh Collins, 'Is There a Human Right to Work?' in Virginia Mantouvalou (ed), *The Right to Work: Legal and Philosophical Perspectives* (Hart 2015) 32.

It is a venue for individual contribution and self-expression.[48] Work provides the means to dignity, self-respect, and self-esteem;[49] it is part of our conception of human flourishing.[50] It is a major framework for social interactions; indeed, many employed people spend more time interacting with colleagues at work than with friends or members of their families.[51] Work provides opportunities to meet our basic need as social beings to belong.[52] It influences one's social standing and is necessary to maintain a feeling of 'usefulness to the world'.[53] It is an important aspect of being part of a community, of feeling a citizen, of feeling that your service is wanted and having an interest in being involved.[54] It has been described as a pathway to 'citizenship'.[55] It gives us structure that is necessary for using and enjoying our leisure time as well.[56] With all this in mind it is hardly surprising that, according to consistent evidence, most people would work even without economic necessity.[57]

All this is true for any kind of work, not only wage work. It is true for the plumber working as an independent contractor, and to some extent for the homemaker working without pay at home. But for most people, in any modern society, employment is the main institution in which work is performed. Although wage employment is a relatively recent innovation in historical terms, it has quickly become the way in which most of us exert our productive energies.[58] It is therefore hardly surprising that people have come to expect the employment relationship to satisfy their social and psychological needs from work.[59] Obviously this cannot be true for *every* employee. Some do not find any fulfilment or satisfaction in their job and have no expectations other than monetary.[60] But for many (if not most) of us, employment relationships are characterized by the dependency on the relationship for the social and psychological needs described above. We rely on the relationship with a specific employer for the fulfilment of those needs. Independent

[48] Edward J O'Boyle, 'The Need for Work as Such: Self-Expression and Belonging' in John B Davis and Edward J O'Boyle (eds), *The Social Economics of Human Material Need* (Southern Illinois UP 1994) 116.

[49] David M Beatty, 'Labour is Not a Commodity' in Barry J Reiter and John Swan (eds), *Studies in Contract Law* (Butterworths 1980) 313, 324; Vicky Schultz, 'Life's Work' (2000) 100 Colum LR 1881 pt I.

[50] Margaret Jane Radin, *Contested Commodities* (HUP 1996) 108.

[51] Sverko and Vizek-Vidovic (n 43) 4.

[52] O'Boyle (n 48).

[53] Robert Castel, 'Work and Usefulness to the World' (1996) 135 ILR 615.

[54] TH Marshall, 'Work and Wealth' in TH Marshall, *Class, Citizenship, and Social Development* (Anchor Books 1965) 230, 234–35.

[55] Jennifer Gordon and RA Lenhardt, 'Rethinking Work and Citizenship' (2008) 55 UCLA LR 1161.

[56] See Joanne B Ciulla, *The Working Life: The Promise and Betrayal of Modern Work* (Times Books 2000) ch 1.

[57] See Gordon E O'Brien, 'Changing Meaning of Work' in Jean F Hartley and Geoffrey M Stephenson (eds), *Employment Relations: The Psychology of Influence and Control at Work* (Blackwell 1992) 44, 55, 59.

[58] Beatty (n 49) 315.

[59] ibid.

[60] Indeed, work that lacks substantive complexity and is performed under close supervision is more likely to lead to alienation (see Melvin L Kohn and Carmi Schooler, *Work and Personality: An Inquiry Into the Impact of Social Stratification* (Ablex Pub Corp 1983) especially chs 4 and 6).

contractors, on the other hand, generally do not depend on their relationship with any *specific* client for those purposes. While they have similar social/psychological needs, independent contractors will be able to fulfil those needs through their relationships with a number of different clients.[61]

This is not to say that a clear dichotomy can be observed between employees and independent contractors. Employees sometimes have additional venues to fulfil work-related social and psychological needs, for example when they have an additional job. Independent contractors, on the other hand, may rely on a single relationship for a given period of time. There is unavoidably a grey area in which specific cases will be more difficult to analyse. But while clear-cut and easy answers should not be expected, there is nonetheless an observable difference between workers in terms of their social/psychological dependency. Workers with a stronger dependency on the relationship with a specific employer are workers in need of protection—which explains the need for labour laws.

The economic viewpoint

The third and last viewpoint describing the vulnerabilities that characterize employment relationships concerns the economic reliance of the employee on this relationship. Generally speaking, on this viewpoint the employment relationship is characterized by the employee having to take the risks of the relationship itself, thus relying and depending on it, while independent contractors spread their risks in the market (whether it is the products/services or labour market).

Relationships always involve risks. According to the standard contractual conception of the firm, capital is regarded as the only risk-bearing party. It is assumed that employees are paid a fixed price compensating them for all the risks they take. Shareholders, on the other hand, are assumed to be the ones bearing all the risks and then enjoying all the residual profits. In practice, nevertheless, employees regularly assume some of the risks without being compensated for them.[62] Most employees work without job security, thus bearing the risk of losing the job altogether at any given moment.[63] This entails significant transition costs to another job, if at all available, loss of income resulting from the loss of position within an internal labour market, and otherwise loss of job-specific investments. Most employees also bear the risk of damaging their health while working. And contrary to economic assumptions, employees are usually not compensated for these risks. Employees with less job security are often those with lower wages as

[61] For another interesting attempt to explain the goal of labour law on the basis of the importance of work for individuals, see Glenn Patmore, 'Happiness as an Objective of Labour Law' (2010) CELRL working paper 48. Patmore argues that 'happiness' is a major goal of labour law. By happiness he refers to workers' enjoyment at work, and more specifically, job satisfaction, less stress, more participation in decision making (and thus control over the work environment), a good work-life balance, etc.

[62] See Ernst Jonsson, 'Labour as Risk-Bearer' (1978) 2 Camb J Econ 373, 375.

[63] See Marc Linder, *Farewell to the Self-Employed: Deconstructing a Socioeconomic and Legal Solipsism* (Greenwood Press 1992) 38.

well; and although employees sometimes receive higher wages when they assume higher health risks,[64] this is far from being a full and realistic compensation.[65] In recent years, the proliferation of precarious employment has meant that employees have been forced to endure even greater risks.[66]

Both parties to the employment relationship thus bear some risks, and one might speculate that a specific allocation of risks characterizes employment relationships. This is *not* the case, however, as Hugh Collins eloquently shows. The standard risks in a contract involving the performance of services, according to Collins, are 'that the employee will not work diligently or carefully, the risk of unforeseen contingencies which hamper completion of designated tasks, and the risk of the unavailability of work'.[67] Collins explains that there is a spectrum of possibilities regarding the allocation of those risks. At one pole, the firm assumes all risks, and the contract established can be called a 'time service' one. (Needless to say, in such cases the firm will do anything possible to minimize such risks, e.g. by adopting bureaucratic controls over workers.) At the other pole, the worker assumes all the risks, and the contract selected is best termed a 'task performance' one. Yet this distinction cannot help in answering the question of who is (or should be) subject to labour laws. Most employees are considered to be somewhat closer to the 'time service' pole, because they receive a fixed wage (although without job security). However, many others work under arrangements closer to the 'task performance' pole, such as piecework or sales by commission. If two workers are doing the same job and generally have the same relationship with the firm, except that one is paid by the hour and the other by piece-rate, the difference between them hardly seems important or relevant for our purposes. Most significantly, this difference has nothing to do with their need of protection. If at all, the piece-rate worker should get *more* protection, as she is the one assuming more (apparently uncompensated) risks.

There is yet another reason—and a much more fundamental one—why the time service to task performance spectrum is unhelpful here. The place of any specific relationship on this spectrum is based on the firm's choice. We have already noted the superior power position of the firm vis-à-vis its workers. Thanks to this power, the firm can usually dictate to the people working for it how the

[64] See Morley Gunderson and Douglas Hyatt, 'Workplace Risks and Wages: Canadian Evidence from Alternative Models' (2001) 34 Canadian J of Economics 377.

[65] As Jonsson (n 62) notes, even with insurance organized by the state (and paid by employers), there is always some loss of income as a result of health-related inability to work. And see Jason R Bent, 'An Incentive-Based Approach to Regulating Workplace Chemicals' (2012) 73 Ohio St LJ 1389, 1407–8.

[66] See, e.g., Richard Breen, 'Risk, Recommodification and Stratification' (1997) 31 Sociology 473, 477; Peter Cappelli and others, *Change at Work* (OUP 1997); Sanford M Jacoby, 'Are Career Jobs Headed for Distinction?' (1999) 42(1) California Management Rev 123; Duncan Gallie and others, *Restructuring the Employment Relationship* (Clarendon 1998) 300; Ulrich Beck, *Risk Society: Towards a New Modernity* (Sage 1992) ch 6; Harry Arthurs, *Fairness at Work: Federal Labour Standards for the 21st Century* (Federal Labour Standards Review 2006) ch 2.

[67] Hugh Collins, 'Independent Contractors and the Challenge of Vertical Disintegration to Employment Protection Laws' (1990) 10 OJLS 353, 362.

work will be organized, including the way the risks will be allocated. The firm will thus choose the organization which it deems to be more efficient, or otherwise preferable, in the specific legal and economic circumstances. And often, one of the main reasons for this choice is the desire to avoid employers' responsibilities. Obviously this cannot be used as a relevant consideration when deciding whether (and when) labour law is needed.[68] Moreover, as noted, in recent years many employers have shifted more risks onto employees. Needless to say, the additional risks that employees now bear have not lessened their need for labour law protection; to the contrary.

So what are the economic characteristics of employment relations that explain and justify the need to heavily regulate these relations? Other relations for the performance of work, those involving independent contractors, are not subject to labour laws, apparently because independent contractors are presumed to be able to protect themselves, to some extent, from work-related risks. It seems that independent contractors are able to do this because they *self-insure* themselves to some extent by *spreading* their risks. Employees, on the other hand, find themselves in a position of *inability* to spread their risks.[69] Different employees bear different risks—some have job security and some don't, some are entitled to fixed wages and others are not, and so on. But all employees rely on their employer for their livelihood. On the other hand, employers—and independent contractors—are generally in a position to spread their risks and thus self-insure themselves to one extent or another. The labour market and the products/services markets enable the employer and the independent contractor to work with a number of clients, a number of workers, a number of products, and a number of suppliers—thus spreading all risks and in effect minimizing them. The employee, on the other hand, generally has no choice but to depend and rely on the employer, on its solvency and on the continued payment of wages. At any given time the employee must 'place all his eggs in one basket'.[70] An employing firm may assume some of the risks of the relationship with the employee, but it will protect itself by spreading its risks outside of this relationship. An independent contractor will similarly spread her risks among different clients. The reliance of the employee on the relationship with the employer—the inability to spread risks—is another major characteristic of employment relationships.

Here as well, there is no clear-cut dichotomy between ability and inability to spread risks. Thus, for example, employees who take on more than one job have

[68] 'It makes little sense to judge employees' need for employment protection rights by reference to managers' decisions which may have been calculated to limit those rights' (ibid 373).

[69] See Jonsson (n 62) 375; Branko Horvart, *The Political Economy of Socialism: A Marxist Social Theory* (ME Sharpe 1982) 447. Jonsson and Horvart both contrast the situation of employees with that of shareholders, who can spread their risks by diversifying their investment among different firms. My own focus is on the difference between employees and independent contractors.

[70] Paul C Weiler, *Governing the Workplace: The Future of Labour and Employment Law* (HUP 1990) 142. See also Richard A Epstein, 'Agency Costs, Employment Contracts, and Labor Unions' in John W Pratt and Richard J Zeckhauser (eds), *Principles and Agents: The Structure of Business* (Harvard Business School Press 1985) 127, 133.

some (albeit minimal) spreading of risks. The point is that work relations that involve a relatively high level of economic dependency, in the sense of inability to spread risks, require regulatory intervention and protection.

Conclusion

We have seen that employment relations are characterized by democratic deficits (subordination), dependency on the relationship with the specific employer for the fulfilment of certain social and psychological needs, and economic dependency (in the sense of inability to spread risks). This analysis pointed to some inherent vulnerabilities in the employment relationship. The general goal of labour law can be understood as addressing these vulnerabilities: minimizing them and preventing unwanted outcomes resulting from them. Otherwise put, the inherent vulnerabilities described and explained in this part are the overarching 'labour problem' that labour laws are designed to address.

Part II—Addressing Labour Market Problems

The previous part offered an articulation of the purpose of labour law at a low level of abstraction: based on identifying the concrete vulnerabilities that characterize employment relations. This part examines two articulations that are somewhat more abstract, yet still focus on specific problems that require redress (as opposed to abstract values, discussed in the next chapter). The first is the prevalence of market failures that characterizes labour markets. In recent years it has been suggested that the goal of labour law is (or should be) to correct these market failures. I explain this view, while also showing its limitations, below. The second problem discussed in this part, inequality of bargaining power, is the most common and often-cited rationale for labour law. While it still offers a useful narrative, I will argue below that it is not the most useful articulation of the idea of labour law for the more practical tasks that are the subject of this book.[71]

Systematic market failures

Standard economic analysis relies on the 'invisible hand' of the market to ensure that the wage will be set based on supply and demand. Thanks to competition from other employers, an employee is expected to get a wage equal to his marginal productive output. So, if his worth to the employer is £10 per hour, this is what he is getting (and should be getting) according to neo-classical economists. The

[71] This part is based partly on Guy Davidov, 'The Reports of My Death are Greatly Exaggerated: "Employee" as a Viable (Though Overly-Used) Legal Concept' in Guy Davidov and Brian Langille (eds), *Boundaries and Frontiers of Labour Law: Goals and Means in the Regulation of Work* (Hart 2006) 133. Parts of this chapter are reproduced here, and updated.

same applies to any other term of the contract; the entire package of employment conditions and benefits can be translated, according to economic analysis, into monetary values. In real life, though, the employee could be getting less, due to market failures. Whenever employers' competition for labour is limited—that is, there are impediments on the ability of workers to take other, comparable jobs—employers have the power to lower wages and working conditions below those that employees would have accepted in a perfectly competitive full-employment market.[72]

For example, monopsony conditions (few buyers of labour) in local labour markets and collusive agreements among employers leave workers with little choice but to accept the terms dictated to them.[73] Information asymmetries mean that employees are often unaware of the terms that they can achieve and thus are willing to work for less.[74] Bounded rationality, together with information deficiencies, also mean that many employees do not fully understand the terms of their engagement, particularly with regard to pensions or other complex benefits. The costs of searching and moving between jobs are often significant, similarly impairing workers' ability to enter and exit employment freely.[75] Firm-specific training, pension rights and benefits based on tenure all tie workers to the specific firm and limit their ability to find a suitable substitute elsewhere, thus also allowing the employer to pay less than the fully competitive wage rate. There are also externalities resulting from the fact that firms' actions often ignore their impact on society at large.[76] Finally, the existence of unemployment (due to these or other failures) gives employers—who no longer face unlimited competition for labour—further powers to lower wages and degrade working conditions.[77] All of these discrepancies between the perfectly competitive full-employment market and real life explain why employers often enjoy a superior market position over employees. Market failures in labour markets appear to be systematically tilted in favour of the employer, resulting in the employer having more ability than the employee to influence the terms of the contract.

[72] See generally Alan Manning, *Monopsony in Motion: Imperfect Competition in Labor Markets* (Princeton UP 2003).

[73] Monopsony has traditionally been considered by economists to be extremely rare, if not merely theoretical. But many economists are now willing to relax the definition and consider it more common. See David Card and Alan B Krueger, *Myth and Measurement: The New Economics of the Minimum Wage* (Princeton UP 1995) ch 11; William M Boal and Michael R Ransom, 'Monopsony in the Labor Market' (1997) 35 J of Economic Literature 86; Manning (n 72) 3.

[74] See Steven L Willborn, 'Individual Employment Rights and the Standard Economic Objection: Theory and Empiricism' (1988) 67 Neb LR 101.

[75] See Manning (n 72); Joseph Stiglitz, Democratic Development as the Fruits of Labor (Keynote Address, IRRA Conference, Boston, January 2000) <http://www0.gsb.columbia.edu/faculty/jstiglitz/download/2000_Democratic_Development_KEYNOTE.pdf> accessed 11 October 2015.

[76] Werner Sengenberger, 'Labour Standards: An Institutional Framework for Restructuring and Development' in Werner Sengenberger and Duncan Campbell (eds), *Creating Economic Opportunities: The Role of Labour Standards in Industrial Restructuring* (International Institute for Labour Studies Geneva 1994) 5; Weil (n 5) 19, 92.

[77] See Bruce E. Kaufman, 'Labor's Inequality of Bargaining Power: Myth or Reality?' (1991) 12 JLR 151.

Over the last two decades economic analysis has become an important tool of labour law scholars. In the past, the prevailing view was that labour law requires a balance between equity and efficiency considerations, and it was assumed that labour laws are inefficient. One had to show other justifications that outweigh the inefficiencies to support labour laws. Economists then tended to be suspicious of the claimed benefits/justifications, while labour lawyers perhaps tended to be dismissive of the importance of efficiency. In contrast, the more recent labour law literature recognizes the importance of efficiency, but at the same time argues that labour laws are not necessarily inefficient. The most common claim in this regard is that labour laws could prove efficient because they correct market failures.[78] Thus, for example, if lack of information leads to suboptimal inefficient results, a law could correct that by ensuring full disclosure of information. This could lead towards more efficient results because decisions by the parties will be based on fuller information.

There is little doubt that some specific parts of labour law can be seen as correcting market failures. It is much more doubtful, though, that this is a significant part of labour law. Would it be reasonable to say, in those instances, that the *goal* of the law is to correct market failures? Perhaps it is just a positive side effect but the law has other goals? Even if we can say in specific circumstances that one of the goals is to correct market failures, is it the *main* goal? Moreover, even if we assume that this is indeed the main goal of some specific labour regulations, could it seriously be argued that this is one of the main goals of labour law as a whole?

The answer probably depends on how broadly we define 'market failures'. Take the issue of externalities, for example. In a perfectly competitive market, each actor assumes the full costs of his or her activities. Thus, for example, if a factory creates pollution, which imposes some damage (cost) on the neighbours, the factory owners should pay the full cost. Otherwise, if they fail to internalize this cost, they are likely to produce more than they should in an efficient market. Their decision on how much to produce (and pollute) is not based on the *real* costs and benefits of the activity, but on a partial view that does not include the costs they 'externalize' to unwilling others. In theory, we can conceptualize many labour market problems as externalities. For example, if the employment contract requires the worker to work very long hours, or does not allow her to take vacations, there is a 'cost' on personal well-being and the family, and in the long term probably also on the public health system. Nevertheless, there is a normative question of how far can we claim that an actor is responsible for indirect costs. If because I contracted with you to do X, I am not able to do Y at the same time, is the cost of not doing Y your responsibility? Usually it is not. If I chose X over Y, this is my preference for how to spend my scarce time. So it is difficult to decide

[78] Hugh Collins, 'Justifications and Techniques of Legal Regulation of the Employment Relation' in Collins, Davies, and Rideout (n 21) at 7–11; Deakin and Wilkinson (n 21); Willborn (n 74); Alan Hyde, 'What is Labour Law?' in Guy Davidov and Brian Langille (eds), *Boundaries and Frontiers of Labour Law: Goals and Means in the Regulation of Work* (Hart 2006) 37.

what should be considered an externality. Furthermore, even if we assume that the employer should internalize this cost, how do we know that this has not already happened as part of the employment contract, i.e. that it is not already included in the salary? Because it is so difficult to quantify such costs, it would be very difficult to answer this question as well.

Similar difficulties arise with regard to transaction costs. Coase taught us that a firm has a reason to be formed because this will allow it to 'make' things internally and not only 'buy'—which could be efficient when hiring people as employees is cheaper than contracting with them.[79] This is the case when the costs of contracting, and especially the costs of changing the contract as demands change, are high. So the very existence of a labour market suggests the prevalence of transaction costs. Bruce Kaufman relied on this highly influential analysis by Coase to argue that a perfectly competitive labour market is simply impossible.[80] Others perhaps adopt a narrower understanding of what it means to have transaction costs or what level of such costs should count as a market failure justifying regulatory intervention.

If we adopt broad definitions of externalities, transaction costs and perhaps other market failures, it becomes plausible to suggest that the goal of labour law is to address market failures. But this makes sense only at a very abstract and general level: as support for the argument that labour markets are never perfect, market failures are prevalent, and regulatory intervention is justified. This can help justify labour law only in the very general sense that regulations in the labour market are needed. It would be very difficult to make a more concrete connection between existing labour laws and concrete market failures. Can we really say, for example, that a law giving all employees a right to ten vacation days per year represents the result expected in a perfectly competitive market? Or that limiting the regular workday to nine hours is justified because this specific solution was prevented by a market failure? This seems highly unlikely. Such claims are plausible perhaps with regard to procedural employment rights, requiring disclosure of information and perhaps even entrenching the right to organize, but not with regard to most employment standards.

Put differently: there has to be another reason for the legislature's decision to give employees a right to ten vacation days per year (for example). Even if the market works perfectly, it could still lead the employee to agree to work without any vacation. This could be the efficient result, but society still finds it unacceptable. The same is true for many other labour laws. The concept of 'market failure' thus has a very limited explanatory or justificatory power in the current context of looking for the *general* goals of labour law. It is still, to be sure, a very helpful concept at the very abstract level, as noted above, and also at a more concrete level with regard to some specific (usually procedural) labour regulations.

[79] Coase (n 7).

[80] Bruce E Kaufman, 'The Impossibility of a Perfectly Competitive Labour Market' (2007) 31 Camb J Econ 775.

Inequality of bargaining power

While the language of market failures is gaining some ground in recent years (for reasons I discuss in the next chapter), the view that is still by far the most widely accepted, throughout the world, is that which explains labour law by reference to 'inequality of bargaining power'. In recent years it became associated with Otto Kahn-Freund, who maintained that '[t]he main object of labour law has always been, and we venture to say will always be, to be a countervailing force to counteract the inequality of bargaining power which is inherent and must be inherent in the employment relationship'.[81] This has been the accepted wisdom among labour lawyers for many years. Even scholars who have suggested new rationales for labour law in recent years have not rejected this 'old' rational, at least not explicitly.[82] Nonetheless, the idea has always been contested. Neo-classical economists have challenged it because they refuse to accept the relevance of 'power' in market transactions. It is therefore worth trying to explain what inequality of bargaining power means, and ask whether it is useful to consider counteracting this inequality as a (or perhaps even *the*) goal of labour law.

Inequality of bargaining power can be understood to exist at two different levels (or stages): setting the terms of the employment contract (or changing those terms); and the existence of control/subordination as an inseparable part of the relationship.

Consider the terms of the contract first. The term 'inequality of bargaining power' seems to suggest that even though an employee should get a certain wage, she is willing to work for less. Or otherwise accept terms and conditions that she would not have accepted if she had more bargaining power. Otherwise put: this concept suggests that the employer usually has the power to determine the wage and the terms of employment, while the employee usually faces a 'take it or leave it' choice, and often has to take an unfavourable offer to make a living. But in what sense can we say that the employee 'should' have received more?

There are several possible explanations. One goes back to the idea of market failures. It assumes that the 'correct' wage is the wage determined by the market. However, while in a perfectly competitive market neither party has any 'power'—the wage is determined only by supply and demand—this is hardly a realistic description of labour markets. Employers usually *do* have some power—some leverage to offer less than the market dictates—without immediately losing the employee to another employer. If we remain within the confines of economic theory, this is possible because of the market failures discussed above. So one possible meaning for 'inequality of bargaining power' is as shorthand for the existence and prevalence of market failures (which are usually tilted in favour of the employer) in the employment relationship.[83]

[81] Paul Davies and Mark Freedland, *Kahn-Freund's Labour and the Law* (3rd edn, Stevens 1983) 18.

[82] Freedland and Kountouris (n 4) 370; Langille (n 4).

[83] See Fritz Machlup, *The Political Economy of Monopoly: Business, Labor and Government Policies* (The Johns Hopkins Press 1952) 369–70; Bruce E Kaufman, 'Labor's Inequality of Bargaining

There are also two other reasons that might cause an employee to accept the lower wage. The first is that due to the previous allocation of resources in society, she has to accept the first offer made to her—unlike the employer, she does not have the ability to wait (or 'hold out' of the market) for any significant period.[84] The acceptance of an unreasonable offer due to lack of freedom to choose otherwise can also be seen as inequality of bargaining power.[85] The second reason is that productivity could be lower than the optimum because the employer refuses to invest in equipment or training. So, perhaps the low wage represents the employee's worth to the employer, but only because the employer does not make investments that could raise productivity. In both cases, one has to accept a low wage—assume that the level is below what we find acceptable as a society—even though it is entirely possible for the employer to pay more. Both of these reasons can be seen as additional market failures, if this concept is given a broad understanding,[86] or they can be seen as another meaning of unequal bargaining power, outside of economic theory.[87]

An entirely different meaning does not concern bargaining over the terms of the contract, but rather refers to the existence of subordination—the agreement of the employee to submit herself (to some degree) to the control of the employer. This is actually what Kahn-Freund himself meant when he talked about inequality of bargaining power.[88] A few years later Hugh Collins termed this 'bureaucratic power'.[89] Here as well, neo-classical economists object, arguing that there is no

Power: Changes over Time and Implications for Public Policy' (1989) 10 JLR 285; Bruce E Kaufman, 'Labor's Inequality of Bargaining Power: Myth or Reality?' (1991) 12 JLR 151; Brian A Langille, 'General Reflections on the Relationship of Trade and Labor (Or: Fair Trade is Free Trade's Destiny)' in Jagdish Bhagwati and Robert E Hudec (eds), *Fair Trade and Harmonization (Vol. 2): Legal Analysis* (MIT Press 1996) 231, 243; Davidov (n 71).

84 As Adam Smith famously noted, 'it is not... difficult to foresee which of the two parties must, upon all ordinary occasions, have the advantage in the dispute, and force the other into a compliance with their terms... The masters can hold out much longer... Many workmen could not subsist a week, few could subsist a month, and scarce any a year without employment' (Adam Smith, *The Wealth of Nations* (Penguin Books) 169. See also Max Weber, *Economy and Society* (Guenther Roth and Claus Wittich (eds), U of California Press 1978) 730. The length of time and the severity of the situation may be somewhat different in a modern welfare state (particularly thanks to unemployment insurance), but the basic inequality of power is still obvious. Another way to put this, which is perhaps more 'internal' to economic theory, is to say that since employees are normally less wealthy than their employers, they are more risk averse to the possibility of unemployment, and will thus accept terms which they would not have accepted as risk-neutral (see Melvin W Reder, 'On Labor's Bargaining Disadvantage' in Clark Kerr and Paul D Staudohar (eds), *Labor Economics and Industrial Relations: Markets and Institutions* (H UP 1994) 237).

85 See Beatty (n 49) at 334–35.

86 See, e.g., Hyde (n 78) 54.

87 Langille (n 83); Davidov (n 71).

88 'Except in a one man undertaking, economic purposes cannot be achieved without a hierarchical order within the economic unit. There can be no employment relationship without a power to command and a duty to obey, that is without this element of subordination...' (Davies and Freedland (n 81) 18).

89 Collins (n 30) 1–2. See also Hugh Collins, 'Labour Law as a Vocation' (1989) 105 LQR 468, 479–81 (arguing that subordination is inherent in the way work relations are organized). And see Orsola Razzolini, 'The Need to Go Beyond the Contract: "Economic" and "Bureaucratic" Dependence in Personal Work Relations' (2010) 31 CLLPJ 267.

inequality: the employee agrees to submit herself to the control of the employer just as the employer agrees to pay her wages. It is an agreement like any other, they argue;[90] but this is misleading. The employer agrees to pay a sum known in advance; the employee has no power to change the wage later as she sees fit. The employee, on the other hand, agrees to an open-ended clause, giving the employer the right to issue commands which will change from time to time—as he sees fit. This part is unequal.

Like Kahn-Freund I believe that this submission is necessary; there is nothing inherently unjust about it. It is impossible to conduct any business or organization without giving someone the power to coordinate the work and make decisions that are binding for others—as explained in Part I of this chapter. Yet, this also means that inequality of power is inherent in the employment relationship—which explains the need to regulate this relationship and prevent abuse of power by employers.

It now becomes clear why 'inequality of bargaining power' has been such a useful concept over the last century. It points attention to two very basic characteristics of labour relations that explain the need to regulate them: first, the prevalence of market failures that give some power to the employer to set the terms of the employment contract unilaterally; and second, the existence of subordination as an inherent part of that contract. Is there, however, any advantage in using this shorthand term instead of referring directly to market failures and subordination when considering the goals of labour law? Perhaps the answer is positive if one is looking for a powerful catch-phrase; a narrative that is intuitively understood by the public at large. But for the more mundane purposes of legal analysis which are the concern of this book, it is better to refer to market failures and subordination *directly* when considering the goals of labour law.

[90] Alchian and Demsetz (n 35) 783; WH Hutt, *The Strike-Threat System: The Economic Consequences of Collective Bargaining* (Arlington House 1973) 67; Mayer G Freed and Daniel D Polsby, 'Just Cause For Termination Rules and Economic Efficiency' (1989) 38 Emory LJ 1097, 1100.

4

The Values and Interests Advanced by Labour Law

The previous chapter offered several ways to understand the goal (idea) of labour law. They all shared the view of labour law as a solution to a labour 'problem'—whether it is the inherent vulnerabilities characterizing employment relations, or systematic market failures, or inequality of bargaining power. Labour law was explained as a solution to these problems—a system that offers redress. The current chapter shifts to a more 'positive' viewpoint: discussing the various values and interests that labour laws are aimed to promote. Most of the chapter is dedicated to listing and analysing these values; I offer a comprehensive review, as much as possible, because different values/articulations can prove more useful in future analyses for different labour laws (Part I). After completing this review, I conclude with some observations about recent trends, and specifically caution against the shift to goals that appear to be good for everyone (workers, employers, society at large), instead of goals that explicitly acknowledge the distributive questions and promote the interests of employees (Part II).

There is some overlap between different articulations discussed in this chapter (and the previous one); I do not claim that they are entirely separable. However, the articulations discussed separately below are different at least to *some* extent (and not only by name), which justifies separate treatment. It should also be made clear that, for the most part, the different articulations have no claim for exclusivity, i.e. in most cases different goals (or articulations) can live side by side with each other.[1]

Part I—A Review of Labour Law Goals

The goals listed below are based on a review of the labour law literature. The literature in turn is based in some cases on a review of legislation and legislative background, but for the most part it is based on attempts to explain and justify labour

[1] As rightly noted by Matt Finkin, labour law 'is too all-encompassing for its purpose to be captured by a single catchphrase' (Matthew W Finkin, 'The Death and Transfiguration of Labor Law' (2011) 33 CLLPJ 171, 183).

laws at a normative level. Some of the contributions I rely upon here have focused on specific aspects of labour law and not the entire project; notwithstanding, the articulations I chose to include here are ones that are broad enough to potentially apply to labour law as a whole. I start with 'older' rationales and then move to newer ideas.

Democracy

We have seen that employment relationships are characterized by democratic deficits, and accordingly I have argued in the previous chapter that one of the goals of labour law is to minimize such deficits. While this articulation takes the point of view of employees—the problem they experience and their need of protection/intervention as a result—another approach is to focus on workplace democracy itself as a goal. This is quite common especially when describing collective labour law: without relying on (or referring to) any claimed vulnerability of employees, we can say that labour law (at least its collective part) is designed to create a degree of democracy in the workplace.

As noted in the previous chapter, general theories of democracy support the idea that, given the importance of work to our lives, people should have the right to participate in the government of the workplace (in one way or another). There is obviously a big difference between government of a private company and the government of a city or a state, and I do not mean to suggest that democratic ideals apply in the exact same way. At the same time, however, it is important to acknowledge that daily decisions taken at the workplace level are often much more important to us than decisions taken at higher levels. Such decisions affect important aspects of our lives and they do so directly. So it is not surprising that we see a value (as a society) in injecting some degree of democracy into the workplace. Of course, this will have to be balanced with conflicting values (such as the autonomy of controlling private property).

Workplace democracy can be understood at two different ways. One places emphasis on *voice*—the meaningful ability of workers to present their views and opinions regarding the governance of the workplace. This is important because the individual employee is often afraid of voicing concerns, or otherwise feels powerless to do so. This could lead to exit (as an alternative to voice)[2]—resulting in an unnecessary loss for both parties in terms of their investment in the relationship. Alternatively, when leaving is not an option due to lack of comparable alternatives, the employee is prevented from both exit and voice. This explains the importance of creating safe mechanisms for voice, both directly and through representatives.[3] Moreover, voice is important not only for airing concerns and

[2] The well-known exit–voice distinction from Albert O Hirschman, *Exit, Voice, and Loyalty* (HUP 1971) has been applied to this context by Richard B Freeman and James L Medoff, *What Do Unions Do?* (Basic Books 1984) ch 1. See also Paul C Weiler, *Governing the Workplace: The Future of Labour and Employment Law* (HUP 1990) 181.

[3] This understanding of voice is closely related to the idea of procedural justice. It has been shown empirically that procedural justice is highly important to employees (for a review of the

letting the employer know your views, but also because of an expectation for better (and more democratic) decisions after all the views have been heard. These ideas are supported by theories of deliberative democracy.[4]

A related view highlights the fact that participating in self-government (to some extent) at work can be instrumental in educating people to the value of democracy and improving their participation in the larger-sphere democratic process.[5] The workplace can be seen as a site of civil society, and one of the goals of labour law, on this view, is to encourage and support civic engagement through worksites.[6]

A second and different understanding of workplace democracy focuses on the *results* that collective bargaining (for example) produces. Instead of the *process* which gives employees voice, this view puts emphasis on the power that they have to negotiate with the employer on equal grounds—and make joint decisions concerning the workplace (and the distribution of profits).[7] The fact that decisions are based on a compromise between competing interests, rather than made unilaterally by the employer, is seen as crucial for ensuring the fairness of such decisions. This could also be framed as a democratic goal.

Redistribution

Another objective often mentioned as a major goal of labour law is redistribution—of resources, power, and risks.[8] The call for redistribution assumes that the ultimate goal is to advance distributive justice; it is assumed that employers are generally better off and therefore shifting resources to employees would serve this goal.

In terms of 'fit' with existing labour laws, redistribution seems like a good way to describe and explain what at least some laws are doing. For example, minimum

relevant literature see Katherine VW Stone, *From Widgets to Digits: Employment Regulation for the Changing Workplace* (Cambridge UP 2004) ch 5). Having an effective mechanism to voice your concerns—especially before the employer takes decisions that affect you—is an important aspect of procedural justice.

[4] Alan Bogg, *The Democratic Aspects of Trade Union Recognition* (Hart 2009). Bogg refers to the importance of democratic deliberations as part of the idea of collective self-government, which he puts forward together with community and non-domination as three values of civic republicanism (ch 4). He argues in favour of this view as a basis for collective labour law. I refer to community in a following section, as part of the goal of social inclusion. On non-domination see Chapter 3 at n 23 and the accompanying paragraph.

[5] Karl E Klare, 'Workplace Democracy and Market Reconstruction: An Agenda for Legal Reform' (1988) 38 Cath U LR 1, 4; Marion Crain, 'Building Solidarity Through Expansion of NLRA Coverage: A Blueprint for Worker Empowerment' (1990) 74 Minn LR 953, 968.

[6] Cynthia Estlund, *Working Together: How Workplace Bonds Strengthen a Diverse Democracy* (OUP 2003); Peter Levine, 'The Legitimacy of Labor Unions' (2001) 18 Hofstra Lab & Emp LJ 529, 567–68.

[7] See Stephen F Befort and John W Budd, *Invisible Hands, Invisible Objectives: Bringing Workplace Law and Public Policy Into Focus* (Stanford UP 2009) 106.

[8] On risks, see recently Mark Freedland and Nicola Kountouris, *The Legal Construction of Personal Work Relations* (OUP 2011) 439–46 (arguing that the 'mutualization of risks' is one of the goals of labour law).

wage laws and collective bargaining laws—both discussed in the next chapter—can be seen as designed to redistribute. Many other labour laws can similarly be understood as redistributing resources or power. Moreover, while my focus so far has been on redistribution from employers to employees, labour laws also strive towards a fair distribution between different groups of workers.[9] This purpose is most obvious in workplace equality laws, but in fact it is a relevant consideration (and *should* be a relevant consideration) in many other parts of labour law. This somewhat neglected function has recently started to receive increased attention, and rightly so, given the growing inequality between different groups of workers, which labour laws themselves are sometimes blamed for. The goal of labour law can thus be understood as redistributing resources, power, and risks to achieve a fairer distribution between employers and workers (in the first instance) but also among workers.

Is this justified? Let us first put aside two preliminary objections. One is the extreme libertarian position that governments should never engage in redistribution (i.e. not even by using taxation).[10] This would mean absolute protection for the existing distribution of resources, which is often arbitrary and unjust.[11] The second objection is that redistribution should be done only through the tax and welfare systems, which are presumably more efficient because they take only from those who really have more and give only to those who really need it.[12] However, the tax and welfare administrations are themselves very costly, and not always successful in extracting taxes from the rich and preventing false welfare claims by those who are not really poor.[13] Legal rules such as the minimum wage are admittedly less precise, but are very cheap to administer (because transfers are direct rather than through the state). They also have other advantages, such as avoiding the stigma associated with being a welfare recipient.[14]

So let us assume that redistribution through labour law is a possible, legitimate goal. But why should we pursue it? There are different theories about just

[9] See Guy Mundlak, 'The Third Function of Labour Law: Distributing Labour Market Opportunities among Workers' in Guy Davidov and Brian Langille (eds), *The Idea of Labour Law* (OUP 2011) 315; ACL Davies, 'Identifying "Exploitative Compromises": The Role of Labour Law in Resolving Disputes Between Workers' (2012) 65 CLP 269.

[10] Robert Nozick, *Anarchy, State, and Utopia* (Basic Books 1974).

[11] For critiques of Nozick see, e.g., GA Cohen, *Self-Ownership, Freedom, and Equality* (Cambridge UP 1995); Will Kymlicka, *Contemporary Political Philosophy: An Introduction* (OUP 1990) ch 4.

[12] Louis Kaplow and Steven Shavell, 'Why the Legal System is Less Efficient Than the Income Tax in Redistributing Income' (1994) 23 JLS 667.

[13] See, e.g., Anthony B Atkinson, 'On Targeting Social Security: Theory and Western Experience with Family Benefits' in Dominique van de Walle and Kimberly Nead (eds), *Public Spending and the Poor: Theory and Evidence* (Johns Hopkins University 1995) 25.

[14] For arguments supporting the use of law (other than tax and welfare law) to achieve redistributive goals see Anthony T Kronman, 'Contract Law and Distributive Justice' (1980) 89 Yale LJ 472 (and see specifically 499 for a labour law example); Chris W Sanchirico, 'Taxes versus Legal Rules as Instruments for Equity: A More Equitable View' (2000) 29 JLS 797; Daphna Lewinson-Zamir, 'In Defense of Redistribution Through Private Law' (2006) 91 Minn LR 326. For further discussion on the relationship between employment standards and welfare, see Brishen Rogers, 'Justice at Work: Minimum Wage Laws and Social Equality' (2014) 92 Texas LR 1543.

distribution. John Rawls' 'difference principle' supports redistribution in of the least-advantaged members of society.[15] Ronald Dworkin's resource-based theory would attempt to put people in the same starting point (equal resources), then giving them freedom to make their own choices.[16] Others advocate equality of opportunities.[17] Yet others argue that a just distribution must be based on desert—people should get the share of the pie that they deserve.[18] This is obviously not the place to choose among those competing theories, although this might be required in the context of specific regulations. For current purposes I think it is sufficient to rely on the (reasonable) assumption that private law rules (which constitute the 'free market') have unfair distributional outcomes, without explaining in what sense exactly these outcomes are not fair. We can say that the reasons for such unfair distribution are market failures or the previous unequal allocation of resources. This could present itself in low wages—below the level that society finds acceptable—or in other detrimental terms (long hours of work, etc.), which can be seen as resulting from an unfair distribution of power.[19]

Another way to explain this is by pointing attention to the inherent conflict of interests in employment relationships. This is not to ignore the importance of trust and cooperation between the parties, and the existence of joint interests within the relationship as well. But there are also some significant areas of conflict, which cannot be avoided—in terms of the wage and benefits package; the degree of effort or work load; and sometimes also the content of the work (the level of interest, responsibility, repetition, etc.).[20] In most cases, the employer can 'win' this conflict thanks to superior bargaining power, and impose the terms that he sees fit. It is here that regulation is required, to give employees more power in this conflict (via collective bargaining) and to put limits on what an employer can impose (minimum rights). So redistribution is strongly connected with the idea of inequality of bargaining power discussed in the previous chapter; we redistribute in order to offset this inequality.

Human rights/dignity

Recent years have seen an increased interest in conceptualizing labour rights as *human* rights.[21] For current purposes, we can leave aside the strategic question

[15] John Rawls, *A Theory of Justice* (Belknap Press of HUP 1971).

[16] Ronald Dworkin, *Sovereign Virtue: The Theory and Practice of Equality* (HUP 2000).

[17] See, e.g., Richard J Arneson, 'Equality and Equal Opportunity for Welfare' (1989) 56 Philosophical Studies 77.

[18] For a discussion see, e.g., Julian Lamont, 'The Concept of Desert in Distributive Justice' (1994) 44 The Philosophical Quarterly 45.

[19] And see Noah Zatz, 'The Minimum Wage as a Civil Rights Protection: An Alternative to Antipoverty Arguments?' (2009) U Chi Legal F 1 (arguing that wages below the minimum wage can be presumed to result—even if indirectly—from morally arbitrary factors such as race and sex).

[20] See Chapter 3, at n 28 and the accompanying paragraph. For a description of inherent conflicts as questions of distribution see also Simon Deakin and Frank Wilkinson, *The Law of the Labour Market: Industrialization, Employment and Legal Evolution* (OUP 2005) 349.

[21] See, e.g., Colin Fenwick and Tonia Novitz (eds), *Human Rights at Work: Perspectives on Law and Regulation* (Hart 2010); Guy Mundlak, 'Human Rights and the Employment Relationship: A Look

of whether resorting to constitutional litigation (or otherwise human rights' litigation) would help labour's cause or not.[22] What interests us here is whether a human rights discourse can offer a normative ground for labour law—i.e. whether some human rights can be seen as *justifying* labour law, thus providing assistance in thinking about labour law reforms, interpreting labour laws, and so on.

This is obviously so with regard to *specific* labour laws. A law supporting labour unions, for example, is justified by freedom of association. A law prohibiting workplace discrimination is justified by the right to equal treatment. A law limiting the power of employers to spy on their employees is justified by the right to privacy.[23] Is there some *broader* justification emanating from the idea of human rights? In a recent contribution, Hugh Collins takes up the challenge and examines the question directly. He argues that labour rights cannot be conceived as human rights in the traditional (strong) sense of this term, which would require them to be 'universal, natural, inalienable, and possessed by human beings simply by virtue of their humanity or "personhood"'.[24] He nonetheless examines whether there is normative basis to consider them 'fundamental' rights, still with some power to override other considerations. He argues that behind a 'veil of ignorance' (following Rawls[25]) people are likely to agree on some social and economic rights, and ideas of autonomy and dignity which include (and *should* include) some positive obligation on the State lead to similar conclusions. Nonetheless, he concludes that this can only support limited parts of labour law, given the fact the governments might sometimes prefer to satisfy basic needs by other welfare state mechanisms.[26]

Note, however, that there is no clear-cut line between rights that always trump other considerations and rights that never do. There are no absolute rights; strong justifications can always justify infringements. So if we recognize a right to a minimum wage (for example), the fact that a legislature might be justified in infringing this right by ensuring minimum income through alternative social policies does not negate the possibility of seeing this as a fundamental right. 'Traditional'

Through the Prism of Juridification' in Daniel Friedmann and Daphne Barak-Erez (eds), *Human Rights In Private Law* (Hart 2001) 297; Philip Alston (ed), *Labour Rights as Human Rights* (OUP 2005); Judy Fudge, 'The New Discourse of Labor Rights: From Social to Fundamental Rights?' (2007) 29 CLLPJ 29; Kevin Kolben, 'Labor Rights as Human Rights?' (2010) 50 Va J Int'l L 449.

22 This is the focus of many of the above-mentioned contributions. On the different issues discussed under the 'labour rights as human rights' heading, see Virginia Mantouvalou, 'Are Labour Rights Human Rights?' (2012) 3 ELLJ 151.

23 In some legal systems, human rights apply (to some extent at least) in private relations as well, in the sense that employers have to respect this human right. In other systems one might be able to demand that the State actively protect employees' right to privacy by introducing a law limiting employers' powers. For current purposes neither route is necessary, it is sufficient that society recognizes privacy as an interest of paramount importance for it to provide justification for relevant labour laws.

24 Hugh Collins, 'Theories of Rights as Justifications for Labour Law' in Davidov and Langille (n 9) 144. For a different view see Mantouvalou (n 22). For additional discussion see Tonia Novitz and Colin Fenwick, 'The Application of Human Rights Discourse to Labour Relations: Translation of Theory into Practice' in Fenwick and Novitz (n 21) 5–19.

25 Rawls (n 15).

26 Collins (n 24) 144–53.

rights can (legally) be infringed in very similar ways. Furthermore, whether or not we accept labour rights as 'fundamental' to the same extent as other rights or not, the important part for current purposes is their normative foundations and the idea of *dignity* certainly seems to offer a strong foundation.[27] Given the importance of work for the individual, not only in economic terms but also in social and psychological terms,[28] respect for one's dignity supports a right to earn a minimum wage through work, rather than by being dependent on social assistance.[29] The idea of respect for workers' dignity can similarly support laws preventing unfair dismissals,[30] laws prohibiting workplace discrimination,[31] laws limiting the number of work hours, and more.[32]

Strong support for this view is found in the *Charter of Fundamental Rights of the European Union*, which states explicitly that 'every worker has the right to working conditions which respect his or her health, safety and *dignity*'.[33] The connection that EU members have made between labour rights and dignity is reinforced by the exceptional importance they have placed on the value of dignity: the very first Article of the Charter exclaims that '[h]uman dignity is inviolable. It must be respected and protected'.[34] Also, there appears to be a strong connection between dignity and the idea that 'labour is not a commodity' (or, as more correctly phrased, that 'labour should not be regarded merely as a commodity').[35] The call to minimize the commodification of labour seems to be directly related to protecting the dignity of labourers.[36] A justification for labour law based on Kantian

[27] For a recent in-depth exploration of dignity as a legal and philosophical concept see Christopher McCrudden (ed), *Understanding Human Dignity* (OUP 2013).

[28] See Chapter 3. [29] See Chapter 5.

[30] See Chapter 5; and see Hugh Collins, *Justice in Dismissal* (Clarendon 1992) 16–18.

[31] See Sandra Fredman, 'Equality: A New Generation?' (2001) 30 ILJ 145, 155–56.

[32] For an argument that employment law should be based (and to some extent, *is* based) on the idea of dignity, see David C Yamada, 'Human Dignity and American Employment Law' (2009) 43 U Rich LR 523. Yamada argues that, among other things, the concept of dignity should be linked to psychological theories—specifically, the importance of relationships, and how relationships can become a 'good' or 'bad' experience.

[33] Charter of Fundamental Rights of the European Union [2012] OJ C 326/391 art 31 (Charter of Fundamental Rights) (my emphasis).

[34] ibid art 1. This echoes the earlier Universal Declaration of Human Rights, in which Article 1 ('All human beings are born free and equal in dignity and rights…'), is followed by work-related rights in Article 23, including: 'Everyone who works has the right to just and favourable remuneration ensuring for himself and his family an existence worthy of human dignity.' See also the Philadelphia Declaration (annexed to the International Labour Organization Constitution) art II(a). The concept of dignity is also considered to be the most fundamental and central idea in various national constitutions (e.g. in Germany, Israel, South Africa).

[35] See generally David M Beatty, 'Labour is Not a Commodity' in Barry J Reiter and John Swan (eds), *Studies in Contract Law* (Butterworths 1980) 313; Paul O'Higgins, 'Labour is Not a Commodity—An Irish Contribution to International Labour Law' (1997) 26 ILJ 225. The first articulation appears in the Clayton Act, 15 USC §§ 12–27, 29 USC §§ 52–53 and in the Declaration of Philadelphia art I(a). The second (more correct, albeit less catchy) articulation appears in Article 427 of the Treaty of Versailles (1919), in which the International Labour Organization was established (Treaty of Peace between the Allied and Associated Powers and Germany, and Protocol (signed 28 July 1919) [1920] ATS 1 (Versailles Treaty) art 427).

[36] On non-commodification as one of the goals of labour law, see Hugh Collins, *Employment Law* (2nd edn, OUP 2010) ch 1. And see Margaret Jane Radin, *Contested Commodities* (HUP 1996) ch 7. Radin describes work relations as 'incomplete commodification' created by regulations.

principles can also be seen as relying on the concept of dignity.[37] Moreover, it has been argued that dignity is an important element of the International Labour Organization's 'decent work' ideal.[38]

Protecting human dignity was one of the main goals of labour law articulated by Hugo Sinzheimer, widely considered to be among the founding fathers of the field.[39] It is perhaps part of a broader 'conception of the employee as a person' adopted in German law.[40] Dignity was also recently picked up by Mark Freedland and Nicola Kountouris as one of the three values underpinning labour law (together with capability and stability, discussed separately below). They espouse a broad understanding of dignity, by their own admission 'ultimately amounting to a conceptual amalgam of the concepts of personal autonomy and equality'.[41] This vision encompasses the ability of the person (here, the worker) to take decisions about the life to pursue (here, working life), in the absence of 'undue constraints' on this ability; as well as the idea of correcting 'all unchosen disadvantages' to ensure equality of opportunities.[42] Such a broad view obviously cannot lead directly to concrete solutions. But it does help to explain, and justify, labour laws with the same ultimate ideas behind fundamental rights.

Social inclusion/citizenship

Hugh Collins argues that one of the main goals of labour law is 'to reduce or minimize social exclusion'.[43] He points attention, in this context, to the importance of work for individuals, especially in terms of being part of the community. Various other laws and policies are designed to counter the social exclusion that results from not having a job, but labour law also plays an important part—by preventing discrimination, limiting dismissals, requiring hours of work (and other aspects of work organization) to be compatible with family obligations, improving

She does not refer to dignity, but justifies such regulations because of their connection to 'human flourishing', referring to the importance of work to the individual, control over one's own work etc.

[37] Horacio Spector, 'Philosophical Foundations of Labor Law' (2006) 33 Fla St U LR 1119, 1145 argues that labour law can be justified based on the idea of equal autonomy, which 'endorses Kant's ideal of an unconditional duty to respect one's own and others' autonomy and dignity'. See also Frank Hendrickx, 'Foundations and Functions of Contemporary Labour Law' (2012) 3 ELLJ 108. For a different attempt to rely on Kant as a justification for labour law—focusing on his citizenship theory—see Lisa Rodgers, 'Labour Law and Kantian Ideas of Legality and Citizenship' (2014) University of Leicester School of Law Research Paper No 14-07 <http://papers.ssrn.com/sol3/papers.cfm?abstract_id=2403498> accessed 15 October 2015.

[38] Adelle Blackett, 'Situated Reflections on International Labour Law, Capabilities, and Decent Work' (2007) 20(suppl) hors série RQDI 223, 242; Freedland and Kountouris (n 8) 373.

[39] Manfred Weiss, 'Re-Inventing Labour Law?' in Davidov and Langille (n 9) 44; Ruth Dukes, 'Constitutionalizing Employment Relations: Sinzheimer, Kahn-Freund, and the Role of Labour Law' (2008) 35 J L Soc'y 341, 345.

[40] See the broad historical account provided by Matthew W Finkin, 'Menschenbild: The Conception of the Employee as a Person in Western Law' (2002) 23 CLLPJ 577.

[41] Freedland and Kountouris (n 8) 373.

[42] ibid 374–75.

[43] Collins (n 36) 22.

employability (by requiring training for example), and also by indirectly controlling the size of the labour market. This is a strong and useful articulation, especially given the prevalence of this concept in political discourse, at least in Europe.[44] It can also be used to support various reforms. Although not referring specifically to social inclusion, Vicky Schultz has argued in a very similar vein that 'paid work has the potential to become the universal platform for equal citizenship'—and has made various proposals to better achieve this ideal.[45]

A related articulation focuses on *solidarity*. Catherine Barnard argues that although the concepts of solidarity and social inclusion overlap significantly, the former is preferable because it is more positive.[46] She puts emphasis on social ties as a justification for regulations: 'Underpinning the idea of solidarity is the notion that the ties which exist between the individuals of a relevant group justify decision-makers taking steps, both negative and positive, to ensure that all individuals are integrated into the community, thereby enabling them to have the chance to participate and contribute fully.'[47] And she shows how the concept of solidarity plays an important part in Europe, lying at the heart of the idea of citizenship.[48]

Cynthia Estlund has added that the workplace is a major forum of civil society.[49] It is at work—more than anywhere else—that we talk to people, creating bonds, including with people that are different from us. Work is an important site of integration—people from different backgrounds, races, and genders work side by side and interact with each other. Estlund sees here great potential for civic engagement and renewal, and she argues that labour law plays (and should play, even more) a role in supporting this aspect of work. The role of law is most obvious with regard to laws ensuring diversity in the workplace, not only by preventing discrimination but also by actively promoting diversity, and by preventing harassment of any kind. Workplace bonds are also supported by freedom of association and the laws regulating collective bargaining. Estlund has argued that minimum employment standards are also necessary for this goal, because without them, some workplaces are occupied mostly with minority and migrant workers (i.e. they are highly segregated). Detrimental work conditions also leave little time and space for informal interactions and make 'working together' in the way she envisions impossible. This view supports the idea that one of the main goals of

[44] Collins shows that the idea of social inclusion, as well as the ideas of competitiveness and citizenship, are found in the Treaty on the Functioning of the European Union (Consolidated version of the Treaty on the Functioning of the European Union [2012] OJ C326 art 151).

[45] Vicky Schultz, 'Life's Work' (2000) 100 Colum LR 1881, 1885. For further development of the idea that work is a pathway to citizenship see Jennifer Gordon and RA Lenhardt, 'Rethinking Work and Citizenship' (2008) 55 UCLA LR 1161.

[46] Catherine Barnard, 'The Future of Equality Law: Equality and Beyond' in Catherine Barnard, Simon Deakin, and Gillian S Morris (eds), *The Future of Labour Law: Liber Amicorum Bob Hepple* (Hart 2004) 214.

[47] ibid.

[48] ibid. See also Sandra Fredman, 'The Ideology of New Labour Law' in Barnard, Deakin, and Morris (n 46) 29.

[49] Estlund (n 6).

labour law is to achieve social inclusion, but adds a broader societal aspect. It is not only social inclusion within the workplace that we are after, but also making the workplace a site of civil society that can support integration and civic engagement *beyond* the workplace.

Stability/security

In a recent important contribution, Mark Freedland and Nicola Kountouris list 'stability' as one of the values underpinning labour law.[50] They describe the dramatic loss of stability in recent years to explain why they see this as a 'policy compass for labour law reform'.[51] They argue that stability has economic benefits, in the sense of the ability of the economic system to weather downturns; but also, and more importantly, stability should be promoted because of its importance to workers as individuals. This is most obviously fitting in the context of regulations limiting dismissals. Another way to articulate this goal is by reference to 'security'—which seems very similar in its intended meaning and perhaps better captures the needs of workers in this respect.[52] But Freedland and Kountouris rightly note that this idea is not limited to justifying job security laws; it is also directly related to the regulation of fixed-term and personal task contracts, as well as various other arrangements that render the life of workers unstable (or insecure).

Efficiency

As noted in the previous chapter—when the idea of market failures was presented—in recent years it has become common to portray labour laws as (at least in some cases) efficiency-enhancing. This view relies on developments in the economic literature—theoretical as well as empirical—especially over the last couple of decades. Labour markets are rarely competitive; transaction costs are widespread; and employers often have monopsony powers.[53] None of this is new, but under the influence of the Chicago School, for a few decades it seems that many economists have chosen to ignore these truisms. The regained recognition that labour markets do not follow the rules of supply and demand as the 'invisible hand' would predict, obviously has the advantage of rejecting economic arguments on their own turf and avoiding the need for equity-efficiency 'trade-off'. So there is an increasing tendency to argue that the goal of labour law is to maximize efficiency. Usually it is seen as one goal alongside others, and scholars are careful to note that not *all* labour laws are efficient (thus avoiding the implication that inefficient labour laws should be repealed).[54] But the view

[50] Freedland and Kountouris (n 8) 379–82. [51] ibid 381.

[52] See Chapter 5, and see Guy Davidov, 'In Defence of (Efficiently Administered) "Just Cause" Dismissal Laws' (2007) 23 IJCLLIR 117.

[53] See Chapter 3.

[54] Hugh Collins, 'Justifications and Techniques of Legal Regulation of the Employment Relation' in Hugh Collins, Paul Davies, and Roger W Rideout (eds), *Legal Regulation of the*

that efficiency (even if broadly conceived) should be the *only* goal of labour law has also been advanced.[55]

A somewhat similar articulation is that labour law plays (and should play) a role in improving 'the competitiveness of businesses and national economies'.[56] Here as well the idea is to look beyond the simplistic claim that deregulation is always best for competitiveness; it has been argued that cooperation from the workforce (for example) is necessary to be truly competitive. It appears, though, that the concept of competitiveness is best understood as trying to capture some balance between efficiency and other goals.[57]

It has also been argued on a somewhat broader scale that labour law contributes to economic development.[58] Simon Deakin explains that while neo-classical economists view labour law as 'limiting' the market, and new institutionalists—recognizing the prevalence of market imperfections—understand labour law as sometimes 'correcting' the market, there are also systemic approaches which view labour law as an institution necessary for economic growth and development. On this view, labour law has evolved as a component of advanced economies alongside other economic and political institutions, and has a 'market constituting' or 'market creating' role. Rather than being an intervention in the free market, according to this view it is an integral and necessary part of the market.

Human freedom and capabilities

The most fashionable attempt to articulate the goals of labour law is based on the work of Amartya Sen,[59] which has served as inspiration for an increasing number of labour law scholars in recent years.[60] Brian Langille has written extensively

Employment Relation (Kluwer 2000) 3; Simon Deakin and Frank Wilkinson, 'Labour Law and Economic Theory: A Reappraisal' in Collins, Davies, and Rideout ibid 29; Steven L Willborn, 'Individual Employment Rights and the Standard Economic Objection: Theory and Empiricism' (1988) 67 Neb LR 101.

[55] Alan Hyde, 'What is Labour Law?' in Guy Davidov and Brian Langille (eds), *Boundaries and Frontiers of Labour Law: Goals and Means in the Regulation of Work* (Hart 2006), has argued that the goal of labour law is to correct market failures. Referring to the possibility of other goals, he argues that while this is theoretically possible, it is impractical, because of enforcement problems (58–59).

[56] Collins, *Employment Law* (n 36) 23; Hugh Collins, 'Regulating the Employment Relationship for Competitiveness' (2001) 31 ILJ 17.

[57] There are some additional articulations (e.g. partnership, trust) that I am not discussing here because they seem to lead to efficiency or to some combination of efficiency and other goals mentioned throughout this chapter. On partnership as part of the competitiveness agenda see Hugh Collins, 'Is There a Third Way in Labour Law?' in Joanne Conaghan, Richard Michael Fischl, and Karl Klare (eds), *Labour Law in an Era of Globalization: Transformative Practices and Possibilities* (OUP 2002) 449.

[58] Simon Deakin, 'The Contribution of Labour Law to Economic and Human Development' in Davidov and Langille, *The Idea of Labour Law* (n 9) 162.

[59] See especially Amartya Sen, *Development as Freedom* (OUP 1999).

[60] Deakin and Wilkinson, *The Law of the Labour Market: Industrialization, Employment and Legal Evolution* (n 20) 290; Brian Langille, 'Labour Law's Back Pages' in Davidov and Langille, *Boundaries and Frontiers of Labour Law: Goals and Means in the Regulation of Work* (n 55) 13;

about the need to come up with a new theory of justice for labour law.[61] Following Sen, he offers to rely on a rich concept of 'human freedom'. Not freedom in the traditional liberal sense, which can quickly lead to freedom of the employer to impose detrimental work conditions and the 'freedom' of the worker to accept such conditions without interference from the State. Rather, Langille refers to what he calls *substantive* human freedom, meaning 'the real capacity to lead a life we have reason to value'.[62] He argues that one of the components of this freedom is human capital, which, Langille argues, is not only instrumental, 'but also an end in itself (directly contributing to a more fulfilling and freer life)'.[63] He then argues that we should understand (or reframe) labour law as the law which 'structures... human capital creation and deployment'[64] and its goals are 'both the instrumental and intermediate end of productivity and the intrinsic and ultimate end of the maximizing of human freedom'.[65]

The idea of maximizing 'substantive' human freedom is inspiring and probably uncontroversial. This is a strength but also an obvious weakness. When goals are articulated at such a high level of abstraction—in a way which would please everyone—they do not lead to any concrete programmes.[66] Because they can support everything, in practice they support nothing. Otherwise put, Langille's vision for labour law is both too narrow and too broad at the same time. It fails to take into account the conflicts of interest and imbalance of power between employers and employees, so it includes no recipe for addressing such conflicts and imbalance (and in practice, no justification for existing labour laws that are aimed at addressing them). At the same time, it includes too much. Because the goals are articulated in an extremely abstract and general way, Langille's vision appears to include many areas of law which are currently seen as entirely separate from labour law. Indeed, he is unapologetically imperialistic in the way he conceives of this 'new' labour law; although he has not provided much detail yet, he makes clear that education, child care, and unpaid work are all part of 'labour law' under this vision.[67] But these are very diverse areas and it is doubtful that they have enough in common to be seen as one coherent area of law.[68]

Brian Langille, 'Labour Law's Theory of Justice' in Davidov and Langille, *The Idea of Labour Law* (n 9) 111; Fudge (n 21); Judy Fudge, 'Labour as a "Fictive Commodity": Radically Reconceptualizing Labour Law' in Davidov and Langille, *The Idea of Labour Law* ibid 132; Freedland and Kountouris (n 8) 377; Supriya Routh, *Enhancing Capabilities through Labour Law: Informal Workers in India* (Routledge 2014).

[61] Langille, 'Labour Law's Theory of Justice' ibid, and see footnote 30 there for a list of his previous contributions on this subject. See also, most recently, Brian Langille, '"Take These Chains From My Heart and Set Me Free": How Labor Law Theory Drives Segmentation of Workers' Rights' (2015) 36 CLLPJ 257.

[62] Langille, 'Labour Law's Theory of Justice' (n 60) 112. [63] ibid 112.

[64] ibid 112. [65] ibid 114.

[66] For a similar point as well as a more elaborate critique against the use of capabilities as a normative labour law theory, see Alan Bogg, 'Labour Law and the Trade Unions: Autonomy and Betrayal' in Alan Bogg and others (eds), *The Autonomy of Labour Law* (Hart 2015) 73.

[67] Langille, 'Labour Law's Theory of Justice' (n 60) 114.

[68] Finkin (n 1); Weiss (n 39) 49.

The idea of maximizing human freedom can certainly serve as inspiration for these diverse areas of law—and probably some others—but it can hardly be useful for the more concrete reasons that require the articulation of labour law's goals.

A somewhat more concrete direction is taken by Simon Deakin and Frank Wilkinson, who rely on Sen's concept of 'capabilities', which captures the ability of individuals to access 'the processes of socialization, education and training which enable them to exploit their resource endowments'.[69] They use this as justification for social rights (including, but not only, in the labour context).[70] They explain that the right to housing, for example, is necessary as part of the need to provide 'security in the face of risks'—which in turn is a necessary precondition for people to realize their potential, work flexibly, etc.[71] The rules of 'social law' thus have a 'market-creating' function.[72] In another article Deakin has used the same justification to propose a rich concept of 'capacity' in contract law—one that will require conditions for *effective participation* in the market before contracts can have legal force.[73] These are two ways in which Sen's philosophical ideas are translated into legal language and given legal meaning.

At the same time, Deakin and Wilkinson also show how labour laws can be understood to enhance capabilities. A prohibition against dismissals of pregnant women, for example, is necessary in order to make it possible, in practice, for women to enter the labour market (i.e. ensures that their freedom to enter the labour market is not merely formal, but substantive).[74] And a minimum wage law forces employers to invest in new technologies, training, skill development, and health and safety—all strategies enhancing capabilities, which employers have no incentive to pursue when they have the power to lower wages below their market rate.[75] Note, though, that Deakin and Wilkinson do not argue that maximizing capabilities is, or should be, the single all-encompassing idea of labour law.[76]

[69] Deakin and Wilkinson (n 20) 291.

[70] 'Social rights should be understood as institutionalized forms of capabilities which provide individuals with the means to realize the potential of their resource endowments and thereby achieve a higher level of economic functioning' (ibid 347).

[71] Ibid 347–48. Deakin and Wilkinson rely on the Supiot Report (Alain Supiot, *Beyond Employment: Changes in Work and the Future of Labour Law in Europe* (OUP 2001)) for this point.

[72] ibid 348. See also Deakin (n 58).

[73] Simon Deakin, '*Capacitas*: Contract Law, Capabilities and the Legal Foundations of the Market' in Simon Deakin and Alain Supiot (eds), *Capacitas: Contract Law and the Institutional Preconditions of a Market Economy* (Hart 2009). In practice Deakin uses this justification not to suggest reform of contract doctrines, but to justify legislation (such as in labour law) inserting mandatory and default terms into the contract (ibid 28).

[74] Deakin and Wilkinson (n 20) 291–92. [75] ibid 293.

[76] For scepticism about the usefulness of the capabilities approach see Bogg (n 66); Novitz and Fenwick (n 24) 33 (arguing that the concept of capabilities can be used to justify competing claims, and they are not convinced 'that a capabilities approach is the normative basis which should determine any prioritization').

Emancipation/social equality

Adelle Blackett takes a broad view of labour law, challenging us to think beyond familiar borders (particularly, North/South and market/non-market) and to consider the idea of labour law from a global historical perspective.[77] She concludes that '[l]abour law resists the commoditization of the factor of production that is labour; the resistance entails both a protective role for the state but also an enabling role for actors'.[78] Focusing on this enabling role, she argues that the concept of *emancipation* best explains the story of labour law. It captures the ideas of workers' agency, capabilities, empowerment, and ultimately resistance to commoditization. This view emphasizes the transformative and redistributive role of labour law.

A related argument recently made by Samuel Bagenstos stresses the role of employment standards (actual and potential) in advancing social equality in the broad sense—preventing as much as possible social hierarchies.[79] He includes subordination within the workplace—the more 'traditional' argument discussed in the previous chapter—but also subordination and inequality in society more generally, which employment relations contribute to, absent the intervention of labour law. This is obviously related to the ideas of dignity, equality, and social inclusion discussed above; however, the unique focus here is on relations *outside* the workplace and on the breaking of hierarchies between social classes. In this respect as well, there is resemblance to human freedom and capabilities; indeed, Judy Fudge has made this connection when arguing that the normative basis of labour law is 'the achievement of democratic equality through the space of capabilities', referring to equality in society at large.[80] Nonetheless, it seems that the focus of Bagenstos on social equality is distinguishable from that articulated by advocates of the capability theory. He argues that social equality explains and justifies the need for protections in the context of dismissals, privacy, free speech, whistleblowing, maximum hours, and child labour. These ideas were further developed and applied to the minimum wage context by Brishen Rogers.[81]

Part II—A Critical Assessment of Recent Trends

While the goals described in the previous part can all co-exist, there are obviously different views about which goals are more central or important to the labour law enterprise. In recent years we have witnessed a clear trend away from

[77] Adelle Blackett, 'Emancipation in the Idea of Labour Law' in Davidov and Langille, *The Idea of Labour Law* (n 9) 420.

[78] ibid 435.

[79] 'Employment law should be understood as targeting the threat to social equality posed by a boss's ability to leverage her economic power over workers into a more general social hierarchy in and out of the workplace' (Samuel R Bagenstos, 'Employment Law and Social Equality' (2013) 112 Michigan LR 225, 232).

[80] Fudge (n 60) 136. These ideas were further developed by Routh (n 60) ch 5.

[81] Rogers (n 14).

'traditional' goals such as redistribution or the idea of inequality of bargaining power, especially towards efficiency and capabilities. In the current part I offer a possible explanation for this development, then moving to argue that this trend is problematic.

The shift to 'universal' goals—a possible explanation

A review of the 'idea of labour law' literature of recent years reveals that most attention has been given to efficiency and capabilities.[82] The appeal of the new justifications is that they are seen as good for society at large—in contrast to goals protecting the interests of employees, which could be seen as the result of interest-based politics. To the extent that labour law can be justified by goals that are good not only for employees but also for society at large and even for employers, these new articulations of the idea of labour law offer an attractive 'win-win' story. It is not surprising, then, that scholars are drawn to such justifications.

It is perhaps useful to explain this point by borrowing terms from the welfare state literature. In discourse (and literature) concerning the welfare state, universalism and selectivity are key concepts. Universalism generally means that benefits are given to all. Selectivity, on the other hand, is a model that prefers the targeting of benefits to specific groups (or people) that really need them. A child benefit paid by the State for every child, or an old-age benefit paid to every citizen over a certain age, are paradigmatic examples of universal benefits. An income security payment given by the State to people who have no employment and no resources, based on tests aimed to ensure their need, is an example of a selective scheme. Most advanced economies have both universal and selective programmes, but the combination varies. The difference between programmes is often a matter of degree, so it is useful to conceive of the distinction between universalism and selectivity as a continuum rather than a dichotomy. This continuum can also be useful for understanding trends concerning the goals of labour law. I am using the universalism-selectivity spectrum only indirectly, as a heuristic—drawing inspiration from it. I argue that different articulations of goals differ in the degree to which they aim to benefit *everyone* (and in this sense can be seen as *universal* goals) or, alternatively, aim to benefit specific groups (and accordingly can be described as *selective* goals).

Placing the goals of labour law along a spectrum between selectivity and universalism, one can notice the shift from selective to universal justifications for labour law. Instead of inequality of bargaining power and redistribution, the focus is shifting to efficiency and capabilities. Although most labour lawyers have not explicitly backed away from the more traditional (selective) justifications, there

[82] See sources cited in the previous part. I discuss this point at more length in Guy Davidov, 'The (Changing?) Idea of Labour Law' (2007) 146 ILR 311 and Guy Davidov, 'The Goals of Regulating Work: Between Universalism and Selectivity' (2014) 64 UTLJ 1.

appears to be a preference to avoid such justifications, resorting instead to more universal goals.

There is voluminous literature on the pros and cons of universalism vs. selectivity in the welfare state. For the most part it is not relevant for the current context. There is, however, one important advantage associated with universal programmes which should be mentioned here: the political support they enjoy. Programmes targeted at the poor often lack broad political support. In tough economic times, even though such programmes are needed the most, they are likely to suffer cuts—much more than programmes that cost more but benefit a larger share of the population.[83] This was traditionally explained by self-interest: members of the middle class are more likely to support social or welfare programmes which they directly enjoy. Recently another explanation was added: universal programmes fit the psychological tendency for reciprocity.[84] It appears that labour lawyers are drawn towards more universal goals for the same reasons—thinking that it could result in broader societal support.

The risks of 'universal' goals

The attempt to provide new justifications for labour law should certainly be welcomed. It helps in defending labour market regulations against neo-liberal attacks. It can also help improving labour laws, and interpreting them, in a way which is more refined and sophisticated—taking into account the broad range of advantages which labour laws can bring. It is, nevertheless, important to add a word of caution here.[85] There are several difficulties—or risks—with the shift away from 'selective' justifications.

First, and most fundamentally, the new ('universal') articulations are highly unlikely to support the entire body of labour law or even significant parts of it. By ignoring or downplaying the conflict of interests between employer and employees, and the inequality of power which requires redistribution, such views run the risk of losing support for regulations that are in fact—for various other reasons considered in this and the previous chapter—justified and important. For the same reasons, universal justifications would not help us when interpreting—or

[83] William Julius Wilson, *The Truly Disadvantaged: The Inner City, The Underclass, and Public Policy* (U Chicago Press 1987); Theda Skocpol, 'Targeting within Universalism: Politically Viable Policies to Combat Poverty in the United States' in Christopher Jencks and Paul E Peterson (eds), *The Urban Underclass* (Brookings Institution 1991) 437; Amartya Sen, 'The Political Economy of Targeting' in van de Walle and Nead (n 13) 14; Thandika Mkandawire, 'Targeting and Universalism in Poverty Reduction' (Social Policy and Development Programme Paper No 23, UN Research Institute for Social Development 2005).

[84] Gillian Lester, 'Can Joe the Plumber Support Redistribution? Law, Social Preferences, and Sustainable Policy Design' (2011) 64 Tax LR 313.

[85] For other critiques along the same lines see Eric Tucker, 'Renorming Labour Law: Can We Escape Labour Law's Recurring Regulatory Dilemmas?' (2010) 39 ILJ 99; Ruth Dukes, *The Labour Constitution: The Enduring Idea of Labour Law* (OUP 2014) Ch 5.

thinking about improving—specific labour laws that cannot be explained by those (limited) justifications.[86]

Second, it is doubtful that replacing selective justifications with universal ones will actually lead to broader support. As noted above, in the welfare state context universal benefits enjoy broad support because more people enjoy them, compared with targeted (selective) programmes, and also because they are based on ideas of reciprocity. Universal justifications for labour law aim to enlist support from *employers* (and governments who are attuned to their interests), but employers are not likely to become supporters of labour law. They are likely to argue that advancing capabilities should not be done at their expense. And if they are supposed to benefit from these advancements—or otherwise enjoy increased efficiency—they would argue that there is no need for regulations forcing them to do what is good for them. At the end of the day labour laws are bound to limit managerial flexibility, at the very least, and so in all likelihood will continue to attract employers' resistance.

Third, universal articulations of the goals of labour law could further obscure the somewhat neglected issue of intra-worker conflicts. As noted above, this is part of the idea of redistribution through labour law, and is rightly gaining increased attention because conflicts between groups of workers (whether actual or potential) are on the rise. Large numbers of workers are excluded from the scope of labour law, sometimes as a result of excessive protections for the 'insiders'. Others work through subcontractors or temporary employment agencies, with much less benefits compared to their peers. Yet others find themselves in the bottom tier of a two-tier collective agreement. These are just a few examples of current intra-worker distributive problems which labour law faces. Universal justifications for labour law not only ignore or downplay distributive considerations between employers and employees, but also between workers themselves.

It must be admitted that the shift towards universal justifications reflects some real concerns—it responds to a perceived failure of traditional (selective) justifications in some sense. However, given the difficulties just described, a better solution is to improve the 'traditional' articulations—to offer a more sophisticated, accurate, and nuanced account—and also to add the 'universal' justifications *alongside* the selective ones (to supplement them rather than replace them). This is the approach taken in this book.

[86] And see Ron McCallum, 'In Defence of Labour Law' (2007) University of Sydney Legal Studies Research Paper 07/20, 8 <http://ssrn.com/abstract=985006> accessed 15 October 2015 ('I am concerned that if… scholars lose sight of the imbalance of bargaining power between employees and employers… they may blow labour law off its central vocational course'). See also Horacio Spector (n 37) 1125 ('The notion of capabilities is too broad to identify our fundamental concerns in labor law, because it encompasses most economic consequences. What we need is a philosophical approach to labor law capable of showing that, even if a piece of labor legislation is detrimental to welfare or capabilities, it still deserves our allegiance'). See also Collins (n 57) (arguing that an approach focusing on competitiveness neglects distributive issues in the workplace).

5

The Goals of Specific Labour Laws: Some Examples

Inbal Malka worked as a waitress at a restaurant in Eilat, a resort town near the Red Sea. The terms of employment were that her wage consisted only of tips received from the restaurant's clients; in practice this was much more than the Israeli minimum wage. Nonetheless, after the employment ended, Ms Malka filed a suit, arguing before the labour court that she was entitled to a minimum wage from her employer and that tips should not count to this end.[1]

A few thousand miles away, Susan Watts was providing home care services for her disabled daughter, and was paid by the State of Illinois as part of the federal Medicaid programme. According to Illinois legislation from 2003, while the care recipients are considered the 'employers' the caregivers are nonetheless seen as 'public employees' for the purpose of unionization. This allowed the Service Employees International Union (SEIU) to become the exclusive representative of the caregivers and bargain on their behalf; it also allowed the union to charge union dues. Ms Watts and several other caregivers filed a petition to the court, claiming that the duty to pay dues to a union they did not support violated their constitutional rights.[2]

A more procedural issue, but also one that reached the highest court, was raised by Lauren Barratt, who was employed by a small charitable organization in the UK. In 2006 she was summarily dismissed for gross misconduct; the claims against her related to alleged inappropriate behaviour at a private party. Barratt filed a complaint to an employment tribunal, arguing that this was unfair dismissal. According to UK legislation such claims must be submitted within three months from the date the termination takes effect. There was a dispute whether she submitted the claim in time, which required the court to decide whether the effective date was the day in which she was actually able to read the letter of dismissal, or the day it was formally received at her place of residence. While it might appear to be a mere technicality, the result obviously carried with it significant implications for Ms Barratt.[3]

[1] *DGMB Eilat Restaurants Ltd v Malka* 40 PDA 769 (2005) (Israeli National Labour Court).
[2] *Harris v Quinn* 573 US ___ (2014).
[3] *Gisda Cyf v Barratt* [2010] UKSC 41, [2010] IRLR 1073, [2010] 4 All ER 851.

The three cases described are just examples for the numerous cases that require courts to inquire into the goals of specific labour laws, on a daily basis. When the Israeli National Labour Court had to decide whether to consider tips as part of the minimum wage or not, it had to fill a lacuna in the legislation; there was no sensible way to do so without asking what the law is trying to achieve. When the US Supreme Court had to decide whether it was constitutional to impose the payment of union dues on workers, it was necessary to consider the justifications for 'agency shop' regimes which allow this arrangement and are often considered an inseparable part of the collective bargaining system. When the UK Supreme Court had to interpret the term 'effective date of termination', included in s 97(1) of the Employment Rights Act 1996, the justices realized that this must be done in light of the goals of the unfair dismissal arrangements.

In Chapter 8 some examples will be given for purposive interpretation of specific labour law rules; I will discuss these three cases (and several other timely interpretive questions) there.[4] At this stage the three examples were put forward merely to emphasize the importance of uncovering and articulating the goals of specific labour laws. This chapter is dedicated to this task, focusing on three labour laws as examples.[5]

There are obviously differences between the laws of different legal systems. The discussion below is performed at a rather abstract level which is similar to many countries; I ask why (generally speaking) a society would want to set a minimum wage, to allow and encourage collective bargaining, and to prohibit unjust/unfair dismissals. At this level, all the systems that have such regulations share the same basic purpose. When interpreting specific provisions, or thinking about specific reforms, an additional inquiry into the specifics of the national context would also be necessary.

Part I—The Purpose of Minimum Wage Legislation

When the National Minimum Wage Act 1998 was introduced in the UK, the Low Pay Commission was assigned an official consultation role.[6] In its first report the Commission listed a number of goals for the new Act.[7] The broad aim of the Act has been defined by the Commission as to 'make a difference to the low paid while minimising burdens to business'.[8] More specifically, the Commission

[4] Partial spoiler: All three workers won. But the precedents for future cases are complex.

[5] The text below reproduces (and updates) parts from three different articles: Guy Davidov, 'A Purposive Interpretation of the National Minimum Wage Act' (2009) 72 MLR 581; Guy Davidov, 'Collective Bargaining Law: Purpose and Scope' (2004) 20 IJCLLIR 81; and Guy Davidov, 'In Defence of (Efficiently Administered) "Just Cause" Dismissal Laws' (2007) 23 IJCLLIR 117.

[6] National Minimum Wage Act 1998 ss 5–8.

[7] Low Pay Commission, 'The National Minimum Wage: First Report by the Low Pay Commission (1998)' <http://webarchive.nationalarchives.gov.uk/20070603164510/http://www.dti.gov.uk/files/file37987.pdf> accessed 11 October 2015.

[8] ibid 15.

considered the Act as intended to reduce inequalities of income among workers and minimize social exclusion; to create a greater incentive to work by rewarding work more highly (thus complementing the tax and state benefits systems); to remove 'gross exploitation'; to prevent competition that focuses on low wages and creates a 'downward spiral' leading to low morale and low productivity, which is detrimental to both workers and businesses; to prevent the transfer of costs by some employers onto the benefits system, akin to taxpayers subsidizing wage exploitation and unfair competition; and to support a competitive economy, with greater development of workers' skills (as opposed to competition focused on the lowest price of labour).[9]

The Commission was also well aware of the possible implications of the minimum wage in terms of employment levels, and in particular the fact that the consequences might be more burdensome for specific types of employers and sectors, noting that this must be taken into account. It further emphasized the importance of allowing employers to maintain diverse pay systems.[10]

This list of purposes is a good starting point for a purposive analysis of the minimum wage laws. Nonetheless, for the most part, these purposes are not articulated at a level of generalization which could assist the task of legislative interpretation. Just as it would be futile to describe the goal as 'ensuring that each worker earns at least a minimum wage', it is equally useless for interpretation purposes to refer to terms such as 'removing exploitation'. While both descriptions may be correct, the former is too specific, and the latter too broad and vague. The challenge is to articulate the purposes of the Act at the level of *concrete justifications*—the Act could then be interpreted so as to best realize these justifications. Without detracting from the importance of legislative and governmental documents, it would be useful to start by looking for explanations and insights from the academic literature.

A brief historical background—and some possible purposes

The first governments to experiment with modern minimum wage legislation, towards the end of the nineteenth century, were New Zealand and Australia.[11] The experiments proved to be successful. The British Parliament, after a 'careful study of the Australian systems',[12] passed a minimum wage law (though very limited in scope) in 1909.[13] At the end of the First World War, when the ILO was set up following the realization that 'peace can be established only if it is based upon social justice',[14] the provision of an 'adequate living wage' was mentioned as one

[9] ibid 15–19. [10] ibid 18.

[11] See International Labour Office, *Minimum Wage-Fixing Machinery: An International Study of Legislation and Practice* (1927) 9.

[12] ibid.

[13] Trade Boards Act 1909. For an analysis see TJ Hatton, 'Trade Boards and Minimum Wages, 1909–39' (1997) 17 Economic Affairs 22.

[14] Treaty of Peace between the Allied and Associated Powers and Germany, and Protocol (signed 28 June 1919) [1920] ATS 1 (Versailles Treaty) pt XIII s I (creating the International Labour Organization).

of the conditions necessary to prevent social unrest.[15] Over the next few decades minimum wage laws became common around the world, initially limited to specific industries or to workers deemed to be especially vulnerable (e.g. women, children, home-workers), but gradually broadening in scope throughout the twentieth century.[16] The UK enacted national minimum wage legislation in 1998, and Germany has just recently joined.[17]

Minimum wage laws in advanced capitalist economies are usually *general*, i.e. not limited to specific industries or specific groups of workers, and *relatively low*, i.e. they only regulate the wages of a relatively small percentage of the workforce, those at the bottom of the wage ladder. The discussion below is limited to this form of minimum wage legislation. The choice of a general but relatively low minimum wage necessarily relies on a particular understanding of the objective of this measure. It would be useful to start by considering and rejecting a number of possible explanations. Three objectives merit special attention; they are frequently mentioned in the literature, but in my view they cannot explain contemporary minimum wage legislation.

First, minimum wage legislation is not intended to be a major instrument of macro-economic policy (as in some developing countries[18]), i.e. it is not designed to alter the entire structure of wages or to become the applicable wage for a significant number of workers.[19] In advanced capitalist economies the belief is that, for the most part, wages should be set by the market (whether through collective bargaining or not[20]). It is only when the wage is exceptionally meagre that minimum wage laws intervene.

[15] ibid. See also art 427 of the Treaty. And see ILO Convention (No 26) Concerning the Creation of Minimum Wage-Fixing Machinery (adopted 16 June 1928) 39 UNTS 3, and the broader ILO Convention (No 131) Concerning Minimum Wage Fixing (adopted 22 June 1970) 825 UNTS 77.

[16] See Gerald Starr, *Minimum Wage Fixing: An International Review of Practices and Problems* (ILO 1981) ch 1.

[17] Andrea Thomas, 'Germany's Cabinet Adopts Minimum Wage Bill' *Wall Street Journal* (New York, 2 April 2014).

[18] See Starr (n 16) 47–53.

[19] And see Bob Simpson, 'The National Minimum Wage Five Years On: Reflection on Some General Issues' (2004) 33 ILJ 22, 39–41 (rejecting the ability of the National Minimum Wage Act to radically alter wages). Admittedly, when the national minimum wage was introduced in the US, inducing growth by boosting the purchasing power of workers was one of the main goals (see Robert Pollin and Stephanie Luce, *The Living Wage: Building a Fair Economy* (New Press 1998) 27–28). It is still being argued by some that the minimum wage promotes economic growth (see, e.g., Robert E Prasch and Falguni A Sheth, 'The Economics and Ethics of Minimum Wage Legislation' (1999) 57 Review of Social Economy 466; and see Bruce E Kaufman, 'Institutional Economics and the Minimum Wage: Broadening the Theoretical and Policy Debate' (2010) 63 ILRR 427). Still, it would be difficult to accept a claim that inducing growth is a *major* purpose of contemporary minimum wage legislation (and many actually believe that by lowering profits and thus investments minimum wage legislation has the opposite effect). Furthermore, there is a counter-argument—that minimum wages will trigger inflation. However, this has proved to be insignificant; indeed, this argument is rarely advanced by critics anymore.

[20] In this regard it is appropriate to add that contemporary minimum wage laws are not intended to replace collective bargaining or otherwise serve as an instrument for industrial peace, although

Second, it is misleading to describe the minimum wage as directed at reducing overall poverty. Although it may certainly help to reduce poverty among working families,[21] it is only a rather negligible component of broader policies in this regard. The relatively low level of the minimum wage, and its inapplicability to those without employment, make it quite obvious that minimum wage legislation cannot be presumed to substantially reduce poverty. Moreover, if the goal had been to reduce poverty, a minimum wage law would need an additional accompanying justification to explain why the burden of this expense is placed on employers.[22] Critics of the minimum wage that bemoan its record in reducing poverty[23] or suggest a set of other policies that can better achieve this goal[24] are, therefore, misguided. It is simply not the intention of minimum wage laws—at least not their *main* intention—to reduce general poverty.[25]

Third, current minimum wage laws are not limited in their purpose to the advancement of efficiency, or the correction of market failures, as was perhaps the case with some of the early laws at the beginning of the twentieth century.[26] A minimum wage set as a single rate (at most with one or two varying rates for specific groups) is much too crude to capture instances of market failure in numerous different settings. As a consequence, minimum wage legislation does both too much and too little in a significant number of cases. This cannot be presumed to be the idea of minimum wage laws.[27]

this was one of the goals of the very first minimum wage laws in Australia and New Zealand (see the description in AN Holcombe, 'The Legal Minimum Wage in the US' (1912) 2 Am Econ Rev 21). Similarly, Paul Davies and Mark Freedland note that although the wage councils machinery was designed not only to set wages but also to support collective bargaining, 'for the Labour government of 1997 support for collective bargaining was to be provided via the statutory recognition machinery, leaving the wages legislation to concentrate wholly on the substantive level of pay' (Paul Davies and Mark Freedland, *Towards a Flexible Labour Market: Labour Legislation and Regulation Since the 1990s* (OUP 2007) 185).

21 See Low Pay Commission, 'The National Minimum Wage: The Story So Far' (Second report of the Low Pay Commission) (2000) Appendix 3 <http://webarchive.nationalarchives.gov.uk/20130626202215/http://www.lowpay.gov.uk/lowpay/report/pdf/complete.pdf> accessed 11 October 2015; David Card and Alan B Krueger, *Myth and Measurement: The New Economics of the Minimum Wage* (Princeton UP 1995) ch 9.

22 TM Wilkinson, 'The Ethics and Economics of the Minimum Wage' (2004) 20 Econ & Phil 351, 361.

23 See, e.g., Donald O Parsons, *Poverty and the Minimum Wage* (American Enterprise Institute for Public Policy Research 1980) 61–62.

24 See, e.g., George J Stigler, 'The Economics of Minimum Wage Legislation' (1946) 36(3) Am Econ Rev 358.

25 See also Noah Zatz, 'The Minimum Wage as a Civil Rights Protection: An Alternative to Antipoverty Arguments?' (2009) U Chi Legal F 1; Simon Deakin and Frank Wilkinson, 'Minimum Wage Legislation' in Kenneth G Dau-Schmidt, Seth D Harris, and Orly Lobel (eds), *Encyclopedia of Labor and Employment Law and Economics* (Edward Elgar 2009) ch 5; Kaufman (n 19) 430–31.

26 ILO (n 11) 11–13. See also Starr (n 16) 40.

27 There is plenty of evidence in recent years to show that a minimum wage does not cause *inefficiencies* (see below). While such evidence is important to defend the minimum wage, it says little about its goals. In addition, there is a compelling view which supports the minimum wage as a measure to prevent externalities. I discuss this view below, where I argue that the idea of internalizing indirect social costs is best understood in terms of ensuring respect by employers for the human dignity of their employees, rather than correcting market failures to maximize efficiency.

Having rejected these aims as the basis of minimum wage legislation, two further aims seem more suitable. One aim is the redistribution of wealth in favour of low-wage workers. The other is the idea that human labour should not be sold for less than a certain minimum that represents minimal respect for the dignity of the worker as a human being. These two basic goals of minimum wage legislation are discussed in turn below.[28]

Redistribution

Minimum wage laws redistribute resources in favour of low-wage workers. As a positive matter, this has been a major goal of minimum wage laws around the world.[29] As Mark Freedland and his colleagues have argued, one of the goals of the minimum wage law has been to 'make work pay'—to replace (to some extent) welfare benefits and shift some of their costs to employers.[30] This in effect shows that the law has a redistributive goal. The aim of this section is to argue that this is not only the case as a positive matter; redistribution is also a *justified* goal of minimum wage laws.

The basic assumption behind the redistributive goal is that since employers are forced to raise the wages of the lowest-paid, these workers are better off.[31] Empirical evidence supports this assumption and shows that the minimum wage has the effect of compressing the distribution of earnings.[32] The crucial question is who pays for this. One can expect, and presumably so do legislatures, that firms will shift the extra labour costs to consumers by raising prices as much as possible, and perhaps to some extent absorb these extra costs themselves by accepting lower profits. If this is the case, it seems to be a desirable redistribution, whether because employers (who are assumed to be better off) end up paying, or because

[28] In a recent contribution Brishen Rogers argues that minimum wage laws are justified because they advance 'social equality', mitigating work-based class distinctions and enhancing workers' self-respect (Brishen Rogers, 'Justice at Work: Minimum Wage Laws and Social Equality' (2014) 92 Tex LR 1543). Self-respect is part of my conception of dignity. Mitigating class distinctions—or more generally advancing equality/distributive justice—is part of the idea behind redistribution, as discussed below. The elaborated theoretical discussion by Rogers can therefore be used as further support for the arguments below.

[29] See Guy Standing, *Global Labour Flexibility: Seeking Distributive Justice* (Macmillan Press 1999) 295.

[30] Mark Freedland and others, *Public Employment Services and European Law* (OUP 2007) 290–93. See also Davies and Freedland (n 20) 189 ('the NMW represented the transfer to employers…and away from the state…of part of the cost of the welfare to work programme').

[31] As well as those who used to earn less than the minimum wage, others who might benefit are those who used to earn a little more and will now get a raise to maintain differentials, and those who did not bother to work for the lower (market) wage and will now enter the job market.

[32] See the comprehensive review of the evidence in David Metcalf, 'Why Has the British National Minimum Wage Had Little or No Impact on Employment?' (2008) 50 JIR 489. See also Richard Dickens, Stephen Machin, and Alan Manning, 'The Effects of Minimum Wages on Employment: Theory and Evidence from Britain' (1999) 17 J of Labor Econ 1; OECD, *Employment Outlook June 1998* (OECD Publishing 1998) 48; Barry T Hirsch, Bruce E Kaufman, and Tetyana Zelenska, 'Minimum Wage Channels of Adjustment' (2011) IZA Discussion Paper No 6132 <http://www.econstor.eu/bitstream/10419/58927/1/690181728.pdf> accessed 11 October 2015.

consumers and perhaps shareholders or other stakeholders pay a small fraction of the cost so that the few lowest-paid workers will have a meaningful raise.[33] It is interesting to note that according to polls conducted in the United States a large majority supports the minimum wage (although most do not enjoy it themselves) even if it means higher prices.[34]

Many economists believe that minimum wage laws have the direct effect of higher unemployment among those who were the lowest paid to begin with. It is obviously not the intention of legislatures to create unemployment, and, more specifically, to redistribute from the lowest paid workers to those who earn a little more. Indeed, that would be contrary to the Act's goals. So the allegation is serious and must be examined before any suggestions are made regarding the interpretation of minimum wage legislation. Although debates on the minimum wage usually focus on its impact on employment levels, much of the controversy can be understood as revolving around its suitability as a redistributive measure. Critics of minimum wage legislation have long been arguing that it benefits specific groups of workers to the detriment of the lowest-paid. This argument is based on a simple supply and demand analysis which maintains that if employers have to pay more than what the market dictates, they will buy less labour hours at the new price. This means reduction in employment levels, and naturally the people who are disadvantaged are those who add the least value to the firm, i.e. the lowest-paid.[35]

The standard neo-classical model relies on a long list of simplifying assumptions, which often do not hold in real life. In particular, it is assumed that all parties are fully informed; there is full employment; firms operate efficiently; firms can recruit all the workers they want at the going wage; and there are no costs associated with turnover (for the employers) or with switching jobs (for workers). Wages in this model are determined by the market and the employer is simply a 'wage-taker', as opposed to a 'wage-setter'. However, the picture changes if these assumptions are not made.[36] First, if a firm is not efficient, the minimum wage can give it an incentive to make the necessary changes to improve productivity (which presumably it did not care about when paying meagre wages). Workers' marginal productivity can thus be brought up to match the new wage, avoiding the need to reduce employment levels.[37] More importantly,

[33] There is no reason to believe that products of minimum wage workers are bought proportionally more by the poor, especially since minimum wages are often paid in service sectors like restaurants and hotels that are used more by the wealthy (see Richard B Freeman, 'The Minimum Wage as a Redistributive Tool' (1996) 106 The Economic Journal 639, 640).

[34] See ibid 641, and see Jerold Waltman, *The Politics of the Minimum Wage* (U of Illinois Press 2000) ch 3.

[35] See, e.g., Stigler (n 24); Richard A Posner, *Economic Analysis of Law* (5th edn, Aspen Law & Business 1998) 362.

[36] See generally Hugh Collins, 'Justifications and Techniques of Legal Regulation of the Employment Relation' in Hugh Collins, Paul Davies, and Roger Rideout (eds), *Legal Regulation of the Employment Relation* (Kluwer 2000) 3.

[37] In fact, to some extent workers' productivity can also be expected to rise, together with their motivation, as a direct result of earning higher wages. See Adam Smith, *The Wealth of Nations* (Edwin Cannan ed, Methuen 1961) 91 (explaining how high wages encourage industry).

if an employer has some market power and is able to influence the wage rate (a 'monopsonist', in economists' terms), the employer may pay a wage which is lower than the worker's marginal product, and in such a case the legislated minimum can help bring the wage closer to what it should have been in a competitive market. In this scenario, employment is expected to *increase* as a result of the minimum wage, rather than decrease, because more workers will come to work for the higher wage and it is still efficient for the firm to employ them.[38] So the firm may lose some of its profits in favour of low-wage workers, but there is no risk of unemployment.[39]

Traditionally, economists considered monopsony as little more than an intellectual curiosity. Labour economics textbooks commonly equated monopsony with the 'company town', which is rarely found in contemporary labour markets. More recently, 'dynamic monopsony' theories suggest that firms can have market power even when they are not very large employers in a particular labour market.[40] This is explained by the fact that a higher wage helps firms to recruit workers, keep them motivated, and maintain low turnover ('efficiency wage'), and at the same time workers are willing to accept wages below their marginal productivity because of costs associated with job search, lack of information, and moving costs. Firms are thus left with some discretion regarding the wage rate. Such analyses, which can still be seen as within the neo-classical economic model, are in accordance on this point with the long-held views of those who doubt the basic assumptions of the competitive model with regard to labour markets, arguing that wages are determined more by customs and institutions (and often sheer discrimination) than by the actual productivity of any individual worker;[41] and that in real life there is usually inequality of bargaining power between the individual employer and employee.[42]

Whether minimum wage legislation actually has the effect predicted by the competitive model or not is difficult to resolve empirically. There seems to be a consensus that a minimum wage set *too high* will bring down employment

[38] This was recognized already by Stigler (n 24) although he was quick to add that a uniform, national minimum wage was unsuited for this purpose. He assumed it would be too high (above the workers' marginal product) in some cases.

[39] In fact, there is not necessarily a loss of profit either. There may be two equally profitable options for the firm, one based on a low-wage, low-motivation, low-trust, high turnover workforce, another based on higher wages but also higher productivity. A minimum wage may simply force the firm to shift from the first strategy to the second one (from the 'low road' to the 'high road'), which in some cases might be equally profitable. Indeed, it may even be *more* profitable, and has not been chosen because of imperfect information or other market failures. See Simon Deakin and Frank Wilkinson, 'Labour Law and Economic Theory: A Reappraisal' in Gerrit de Geest, Jacques Siegers, and Roger van den Bergh (eds), *Law and Economics and the Labour Market* (Edward Elgar 1999) 27.

[40] See Card and Krueger (n 21) ch 11; Dickens, Machin, and Manning (n 32); Alan Manning, *Monopsony in Motion: Imperfect Competition in Labor Markets* (Princeton UP 2003).

[41] See Simon Deakin and Frank Wilkinson, 'The Law and Economics of the Minimum Wage' (1992) 19 J of Law and Society 379; and see generally Bruce E Kaufman, 'The Evolution of Thought on the Competitive Nature of Labor Markets' in Clark Kerr and Paul D Staudohar (eds), *Labor Economics and Industrial Relations: Markets and Institutions* (HUP 1994) 145.

[42] See Chapter 3.

levels.[43] But there is an ongoing and heated debate among economists about the actual impact of a modest, relatively low minimum wage on employment. Early empirical research, which concentrated on what actually happened *on the ground*, did not substantiate the fears that minimum wage legislation caused significant reduction in employment.[44] Later, in the 1970s, a large body of time-series studies conducted mainly in the United States emerged to confirm the neo-classical predictions—although the effect they have found was very modest and mainly limited to teenagers.[45] The near-consensus among economists regarding the negative impact of minimum wage legislation (however small) was challenged in the 1990s by a new body of case studies, which focused on specific labour markets, and found no negative impact (indeed in some cases the effect was positive) on employment.[46] More generally, there is some evidence that workers commonly accept wages below their marginal productivity;[47] or in other words, 'aside from unreconstructed neoclassical economic ideology, there is little evidence that low-wage workers are being paid according to the value of their marginal product'.[48] There is also evidence to suggest that minimum wages cause a modest reduction in profits and a modest rise in prices[49]—both benign developments from a redistributive point of view, and helping to explain how employers can pay the higher wages without dismissing workers.

[43] On this point the leading critics of the conventional economic model agree that it applies: see Card and Krueger (n 21) 13; Stephen Machin and Alan Manning, 'Employment and the Introduction of a Minimum Wage in Britain' (1996) 106 The Economic Journal 667, 669.

[44] See RH Tawney, *The Establishment of Minimum Wages in the Chain Making Industry under the Trade Board Act of 1909* (Bell 1914); RH Tawney, *The Establishment of Minimum Wages in the Tailoring Industry under the Trade Board Act of 1909* (Bell 1915); Richard A Lester, 'Shortcoming of Marginal Analysis for Wage-Employment Problems' (1946) 36 Am Econ Rev 63.

[45] These studies, which measured overall levels of employment before and after a minimum wage increase, typically found that a 10 per cent increase in the minimum wage reduced teenage employment by 1–3%. An authoritative survey regarded the lower part of this range more plausible; see Charles Brown, Curtis Gilroy, and Andrew Kohen, 'The Effect of the Minimum Wage on Employment and Unemployment' (1982) 20 J of Econ Lit 487, 508. The effect on adult employment, when examined, was found to be even smaller (ibid 512). When the data was extended through 1986, the negative effect on teenage employment was only 0.6%, and no effect was discernible for young adults (ages 20–24); see Alison J Wellington, 'Effects of the Minimum Wage on the Employment Status of Youths: An Update' (1991) 26 J of Human Resources 27.

[46] Most influential was a series of studies by David Card and Alan Krueger, culminating in their 1995 book *Myth and Measurement* (n 20). Similar conclusions were reached at about the same time in the UK by Stephen Machin and Alan Manning, 'The Effects of Minimum Wages on Wage Dispersion and Employment: Evidence from the U.K. Wages Councils' (1994) 47 ILRR 319. Evidence from other European countries was found to be consistent with these new findings; see Stephen Machin and Alan Manning, 'Minimum Wages and Economic Outcomes in Europe' (1997) 41 Euro Econ Rev 733.

[47] See Duncan Watson, 'U.K. Wage Underpayment: Implications for the Minimum Wage' (2000) 32 Applied Economics 429. As explained above, this is characteristic of monopsony power, and means that a forced raise would not necessarily make the employment inefficient.

[48] Sar A Levitan and Richard S Belous, *More Than Subsistence: Minimum Wages for the Working Poor* (Johns Hopkins UP 1979) 161.

[49] See the review in Metcalf (n 32); and see Sara Lemos, 'A Survey of the Effects of the Minimum Wage On Prices' (2008) 22 J of Economic Surveys 187; Mirko Draca, Stephen Machin, and John Van Reenen, 'Minimum Wages And Firm Profitability' (2011) 3 American Economic Journal: Applied Economics 129.

Recent studies of the relatively new UK law have similarly found that it did not have any negative impact on employment, except perhaps for a very modest reduction in the working hours of some low-wage workers.[50] At the same time, other studies continue to maintain the validity of the traditional competitive model and the resulting negative impact of any minimum wage setting.[51] One explanation which was offered for the conflicting conclusions is that employers have some short-term monopsony power, but minimum wages will decrease employment in the long run.[52] From an opposite direction it has been suggested that a statutory wage floor can bring long-term efficiencies, but there may be some 'short-run adjustment costs as some enterprises go out of business and workers retrain'.[53]

The empirical debate continues, but it seems fair to conclude from the evidence that the impact of minimum wages on employment is minimal, if any.[54] Nonetheless, the mere possibility of unemployment resulting from the minimum wage (however minimal) is troubling, especially since the impact might be felt more strongly amongst vulnerable groups such as young people and people from minority groups.[55] If such vulnerable groups are worse off because of the minimum wage, then this would amount to regressive redistribution.[56] A minimum

50 See the review in Metcalf (n 32). And see Mark B Stewart and Joana K Swaffield, 'The Other Margin: Do Minimum Wages Cause Working Hours Adjustments for Low-Wage Workers?' (2008) 75 Economica 148. See also most recently the *Low Pay Commission Report 2015* <https://www.gov.uk/government/uploads/system/uploads/attachment_data/file/413415/The_National_Minimum_Wage_Low_Pay_Commission_Report_2015.pdf> accessed 12 October 2015.

51 For a review see David Neumark and William Wascher, 'Minimum Wages and Employment: A Review of Evidence from the New Minimum Wage Research' (2008) NBER Working Paper No 12663 <http://www.nber.org/papers/w12663.pdf> accessed 11 October 2015. See also David Neumark and William Wascher, 'Reconciling the Evidence on Employment Effects of Minimum Wages—A Review of Our Research Findings' in Marvin H Kosters (ed), *The Effects of the Minimum Wage on Employment* (AEI Press 1996) 55; Richard V Burkhauser, Kennet A Couch, and David C Wittenburg, 'A Reassessment of the New Economics of the Minimum Wage Literature with Monthly Data from the Current Population Survey' (2000) 18 J of Labor Econ 653; Nicolas Williams and Jeffrey A Mills, 'The Minimum Wage and Teenage Employment: Evidence from Time Series' (2001) 33 Applied Economics 285; Stephen Bazen and Nicolas Skourias, 'Is There a Negative Effect of Minimum Wages on Youth Employment in France?' (1997) 41 Euro Econ Rev 723.

52 See Daniel S Hamermesh, 'Myth and Measurement: The New Economics of the Minimum Wage (Book Review)' (1995) 48 ILRR 835; Michael Baker, Dwayne Benjamin, and Shuchita Stanger, 'The Highs and Lows of the Minimum Wage Effect: A Time-Series Cross-Section Study of the Canadian Law' (1999) 17 J of Labor Econ 318.

53 Simon Deakin and Frank Wilkinson, 'Minimum Wage Legislation' in Boudewijn Bouckaert and Gerrit de Geest (eds), *Encyclopedia of Law and Economics*, vol III (Edward Elgar 2000) 566. For an updated version of this chapter, which includes a very useful summary of theoretical and empirical developments in the study of minimum wage laws, see Deakin and Wilkinson (n 25).

54 And see Richard B Freeman, 'Myth and Measurement: The New Economics of the Minimum Wage (Book Review)' (1995) 48 ILRR 830.

55 In the United States, although Brown, Gilroy, and Kohen (n 45) were not convinced by the evidence to this effect, a number of studies who found a negative effect in general also found a stronger impact on such vulnerable groups; see, e.g., Richard V Burkhauser, Kenneth A Couch, and David C Wittenburg, 'Who Minimum Wage Increases Bite: An Analysis Using Monthly Data from the SIPP and the CPS' (2000) 67 Southern Economic Journal 16.

56 Harry Hutchinson, 'Toward a Critical Race Reformist Conception of Minimum Wage Regimes: Exploding the Power of Myth, Fantasy, and Hierarchy' (1997) 34 Harv J on Legis 93, went as far as to argue that the minimum wage 'constitutes a form of institutionalized racism' (ibid 133).

wage can certainly be expected to do more good than harm *overall*, in terms of redistribution, but this would hardly console the few (if there are any) who lose their jobs.

Indeed, the desire to avoid unemployment explains why many legal systems have set a lower minimum wage rate for young workers, trainees, the disabled, and sometimes others who are thought to have the lowest marginal productivity.[57] Such exceptions can be justified when the risk of unemployment seems real given the relative level of the minimum wage (compared with the average wage) and the overall situation of the economy at a given time. When used prudently, these exemptions may help achieve the redistributive goals of the minimum wage by making sure that perversions are avoided. Another 'safety valve' to minimize or prevent any impact on employment levels is, of course, the level of the minimum wage itself; different legal systems have set mechanisms for setting the minimum wage in ways that ensure ample consideration of employment concerns.[58]

Overall, given the most recent evidence as summarized above, and the 'safety valves' just mentioned, it seems fair to describe progressive redistribution as one of the main goals of minimum wage laws.

Respect for human dignity

A second major justification for minimum wage laws relies on the concept of dignity. Respect for the dignity of the worker as a human being dictates that human labour should not be sold for less than a certain minimum. The idea that 'labour should not be regarded merely as a commodity or article of commerce'[59] represents a long-standing understanding that labour power cannot be separated from the self. Since human beings are not things and cannot be bought and sold as such, neither can their labour power.[60] This does not mean that we cannot or should not sell our labour power for a price, but it does mean that some limitations are necessary, and labour and employment regulations accordingly try to protect our health and our rights at work.[61] Some of these regulations are designed

Three decades earlier, Milton Friedman dubbed the minimum wage 'the most anti-Negro law on our statute book' (Milton Friedman, 'Minimum Wage-Rates' in Paul A Samuelson (ed), *Readings in Economics* (6th edn, McGraw-Hill 1970) 247).

[57] See Starr (n 16) 55–59. And see the UK National Minimum Wage Regulations 1999, regs 12, 13.

[58] In the UK, for example, the Low Wage Commission was given an advisory role, and is conducting studies about the impact of the law before making recommendations to the government about the appropriate minimum wage rates (see National Minimum Wage Act 1998 ss 5–8).

[59] Versailles Treaty art 427 (guiding principles for the ILO).

[60] See Karl Polanyi, *The Great Transformation* (first published 1944, Beacon Press 1957) 73.

[61] Ethical justifications were commonly advanced when the idea of minimum wage was first raised around the beginning of the twentieth century. See particularly John A Ryan, *A Living Wage: Its Ethical and Economic Aspects* (Macmillan 1906) (arguing that there is an individual, natural, and absolute *right* to a living wage).

to ensure respect for our *dignity* as human beings.[62] The minimum wage can be seen in a similar light.[63]

Respect for human dignity requires that, as a society, we make sure that each individual's dignity is being respected. Yet to what extent should *the employer* take responsibility? To what extent should the employer be required to pay more than what the 'free market' allows? Arguably there is a minimum of compensation below which employment is not very different from slavery, and is therefore illegitimate.[64] We do not allow slavery not only because the work is not freely chosen (in many contemporary cases the freedom to choose a job is quite illusory), but also because it is not compensated. One should not have to work for the benefit of another person without compensation. Similarly, it is quite obvious that one penny—to take an extreme example—cannot be considered compensation for a full working day. The question is what constitutes sufficient compensation, and for this purpose the fact that the worker sells part of herself is material. By working a full day for the benefit of another, the worker relinquished her freedom to do what she pleases.[65] Our ability to do what we choose with our time is valuable. It is part of our human dignity which everyone else and society at large must honour. Our dignity cannot be sold for money, of course. But *respect* for our dignity, for the value of our time and for the fact that we sell part of our selves, dictates a minimum level of compensation at work.

The argument is strengthened when we consider the importance of one's ability to 'make a living' to all aspects of life. Self-esteem, self-respect, and often the health of family relations largely depend on one's ability to provide for oneself and one's family. It is also, in most cases, a necessary precondition for participation in activities in the community and in the broader political life.[66] Indeed, minimum wage laws 'promote a measure of economic security which is a precondition for anyone to be free'.[67] All this can also be seen as part of our ability to live in dignity.

[62] See the discussion on dignity in Chapter 4.

[63] Indeed, various international covenants recognize a *right* to a minimum wage, including the European Social Charter (Revised) (adopted 3 May 1996, entered into force 1 July 1999) ETS 163 art 4(1); International Covenant on Economic, Social and Cultural Rights (adopted 16 December 1966, entered into force 3 January 1976) 993 UNTS 3 art 7(1)(a); ILO Convention No 26 Concerning the Creation of Minimum Wage-Fixing Machinery (n 15) and ILO Convention No 131 Concerning Minimum Wage Fixing (n 15). And the Charter of Fundamental Rights of the European Union [2000] OJ C364/1 art 31(1) explicitly makes the connection between working conditions and human dignity: 'Every worker has the right to working conditions which respect his or her health, safety and dignity.'

[64] See Arthur M Okun, *Equality and Efficiency: The Big Tradeoff* (Brookings Institution 1975) 20 ('minimum-wage laws…can be viewed most fruitfully as further examples of prohibitions on exchanges born of desperation, extending the logic of the ban on indentured service').

[65] See Frances Raday, 'Individual and Collective Dismissals—A Job Security Dichotomy' (1989) 10 Comp Lab LJ 121, 149.

[66] See Waltman (n 34) 142. And see further the discussion of the social/psychological importance of work in Chapter 3.

[67] David M Beatty, *Putting the Charter to Work: Designing a Constitutional Labour Code* (McGill UP 1987) 81–82.

An additional aspect of the same argument focuses on the fact that work is never toll-free. Whether one works in the office or the factory, at home or on the road, work takes a toll on our health and well-being. The impact can be direct and visible in the short-run, as in workplace accidents, which are covered (to some extent by employers) under specific programmes. However, in many cases the impact is less visible and occurs slowly and over a long period of time. In many cases, the impact is not an observable accident, but a more subtle (yet significant) toll on our well-being, whether our physical, psychological, or social well-being. Although the costs associated with such work-related damages are sometimes difficult to quantify, they are nonetheless real. Respect for human dignity implies that these costs must be taken into account when the worker is compensated. Employers must acknowledge the fact that workers, being humans and not machines, are affected by work in various complicated ways that sometimes have real costs. When compensation is below a certain minimum, one could argue that the employer could not have taken into account the long-term costs associated with the work. In such cases, businesses in fact externalize the indirect costs that flow from their profit-making activities. Workers should not be forced to subsidize such activities by accepting wages that do not cover their long-term costs associated with the work. Nor should society provide such subsidies.[68] Indeed, it has been argued for some time that employers who make their profits by 'sweating' workers are parasitic; a business that can only survive by paying meagre wages is a burden on society rather than an asset.[69] This failure to internalize costs can simply be regarded as a market failure, causing the payment of wages less than what is necessary to ensure the health and continued productivity of workers.[70] But the minimum wage is more appropriately understood as an attempt to ensure respect for human dignity—including taking into account the indirect costs of employment—than a much too crude attempt to correct market failures. There can be different views about what is sufficient in this respect, but one way or another, minimum wage legislation is based on the belief that people, who are not commodities, should not be required to work for wages below a certain minimum that represents respect for their human dignity.

An argument which is often made in favour of minimum wage legislation is that it prevents (or limits) 'unfair' competition among employers[71]—a 'race to the bottom'—which will not only hurt employees but also employers who want to pay higher wages. This argument appears to be based on the same considerations of human dignity. Generally speaking, competition (with regard to commodities, for example) is not considered 'unfair' just because it is especially tough and prices are

[68] See *West Coast Hotel Co v Parrish* 300 US 379, 399 (1937).

[69] Sydney Webb and Beatrice Webb, *Industrial Democracy* (first published 1897, Longmans, Green and Co. 1926) 749–52, 811. See also Holcombe (n 20) 34; ILO (n 11) 12; Waltman (n 34) 15–16.

[70] See Webb and Webb, ibid 589–91, 752–53. For an up-to-date and elaborated resurrection of this argument see Bruce E Kaufman, 'Promoting Labour Market Efficiency and Fairness through a Legal Minimum Wage: The Webbs and the Social Cost of Labour' (2009) 47 BJIR 306. See also Marc Linder, *Migrant Workers and Minimum Wages: Regulating the Exploitation of Agricultural Labor in the US* (Westview 1992) 96.

[71] See, e.g., ILO (n 11) 11, 13; Low Pay Commission First Report (n 7) 17.

very low. It is recognized, however, that competition with regard to wages is different; that human beings are the subject of such competition and their lives are directly affected. When wages get below a certain point they are no longer in accordance with our values regarding respect for human dignity. It is at this point that competition is considered 'unfair' and illegitimate. Implicitly, then, the 'unfair competition' argument is just another face of the human dignity justification explored above.

Conclusion

Minimum wages are controversial among economists; their impact is contested. However, a review of the economic literature shows that the areas of disagreement are in fact quite narrow. Even if there *is* some impact on employment levels, it is surely very low as long as the wage is set at a reasonable level. In the current part I reframed the economic debate and suggested that it should be read as part of the question of whether minimum wage laws have a redistributive goal (and to what extent such laws can achieve progressive redistribution). The conclusion is that, in general (assuming a reasonable level and 'safety valves'), minimum wage laws are an important redistributive tool. At the same time, they are needed to ensure respect for the dignity of low-wage workers. These two justifications seem to offer the best understanding of the idea behind minimum wage laws. Accordingly, they can (and should) serve as a benchmark for any interpretation of minimum wage laws and for assessing reform proposals.

Part II—The Purpose of Collective Bargaining Legislation

The minimum wage law was used as an example (in the previous part) because it is often considered the most basic form of employment protection, and it exists in most advanced economies.[72] The second form of labour regulation that can be seen as fundamental and common throughout the world concerns the ability to bargain collectively. It is therefore appropriate to take it as another example for a purposive analysis. Although in this context there are more significant variations between countries (exclusive/non-exclusive representation, the level of bargaining, the duties on employers, and to what extent they can resist unionization, etc.), there is a basic regulation common to most systems: workers are allowed to bargain collectively (through a union) with their employer. At the very least, the law provides a structure for collective bargaining; in many countries the law also encourages collective bargaining.[73] I will focus on this general level. Obviously, when dealing with concrete questions, it might be necessary to supplement the analysis with a discussion of more specific purposes of specific arrangements and otherwise refer to the national context.

[72] The few exceptions are usually countries with high union density (e.g. Sweden) in which a minimum level of wages is secured for the large majority of workers through collective agreements.

[73] Susan Hayter, 'Introduction' in Susan Hayter (ed), *The Role of Collective Bargaining in the Global Economy* (Edward Elgar 2011) 1.

Regulations that allow, promote, or provide structure for collective bargaining can be justified on several different grounds; most important seem to be workplace democracy, redistribution, and efficiency.[74] All three justifications/purposes are fiercely contested. There are those who believe that labour unions are nothing but monopolies,[75] and that collective bargaining through unions achieves the exact opposite of its intentions: less democracy, regressive redistribution, and inefficiency. It is my view that such criticism is for the most part misguided, and that collective bargaining can be beneficial on all three fronts. Below I consider each of them in turn. Before doing so it must be acknowledged that collective bargaining has been in decline in most countries. Because of the dramatic changes in labour markets, specifically outsourcing and subcontracting (both sham and real) that shifted many jobs into small entities,[76] it is difficult to rely on collective bargaining these days as a vehicle for workers' rights. Nonetheless, it is still a viable (even if less common) option, which the law encourages for the reasons stated below. I do not argue here that it is sufficient, or that it is necessarily still the best method to protect workers; I simply explain the justifications behind this (still existing) legal option.

Workplace democracy

Probably the most important justification for workers' collective action is found in its democratic attributes. We have already seen that the employment relationship is characterized by democratic deficits.[77] By joining forces and acting in concert, workers can rectify this situation, to one extent or another, since the employer can be expected to be much less nonchalant about the prospect of losing the work of *all* its employees (even if only for a limited time), compared with the threat of any individual employee to quit. A union can also provide some financial backing for a prolonged struggle. By bargaining collectively employees are thus able to gain some bargaining power—'countervailing power' to the power of their employer.[78] This does not necessarily mean that both parties to the negotiations possess equal

[74] It has been noted that collective bargaining also plays an important part in the maintenance of social order (see, e.g., Allan D Flanders, *Management and Unions: The Theory and Reform of Industrial Relations* (Faber and Faber 1970) 252; ILO, *World Labour Report 1997/98: Industrial Relations, Democracy and Social Stability* (ILO 1998) 27). However, 'industrial peace' falls today more under considerations of efficiency; labour–capital conflicts are hardly a threat to the social order in current times. Indeed, in more recent reports the ILO has focused much more on the potential efficiency gains of collective bargaining (see ILO, *Your Voice At Work: Global report under the follow-up to the ILO Declaration on fundamental principles and rights at work. Report of the Director-General, 2000* (ILO 2000) part I <http://www.ilo.org/wcmsp5/groups/public/@dgreports/@dcomm/@publ/documents/publication/wcms_publ_9221115046_en.pdf> accessed 12 October 2015; ILO, 'Collective Bargaining and the Decent Work Agenda' (Committee on Employment and Social Policy 300th Session GB.300/ESP/1, November 2007) <http://www.ilo.org/wcmsp5/groups/public/---ed_norm/---relconf/documents/meetingdocument/wcms_084557.pdf> accessed 12 October 2015.

[75] Richard A Posner, 'Some Economics of Labor Law' (1984) 51 U Chi LR 988.

[76] See David Weil, *The Fissured Workplace: Why Work Became So Bad for So Many and What Can Be Done to Improve It* (HUP 2014).

[77] See Chapter 3.

[78] The term 'countervailing power' was coined by John Kenneth Galbraith to describe power that is used to *restrain* private economic power when competition does not perform this function (and in

bargaining power,[79] but the imbalance of power can be expected to be much less dramatic under a regime of collective bargaining.[80] And once the bargaining position of employees is improved, the problem of democratic deficits is also expected to be alleviated.

More specifically, collective bargaining has two separate attributes that can be considered democratic. One is its 'civilizing' impact on employment relationships, or the subjection of the employer to a 'rule of law'.[81] Collective agreements commonly set rules on how workers should be treated, thus limiting the arbitrariness of being subjected to the complete control of the employer. There are rules on who is entitled to a raise and other benefits (usually based on seniority); how to evaluate and promote employees; why and how to discipline and dismiss; and so on. There are also commonly procedures for arbitration by a neutral third party in case of disagreements. This completely changes the situation of the individual employee, who was previously subject to the whims of his managers, lacking both the contractual right and the bargaining power to challenge arbitrary decisions. Under a collective agreement, management decisions must conform to the rules and procedures set out in the agreement, and accordingly are bound to be less arbitrary. And if they are not, the union can challenge such decisions in the name of the employee before a neutral arbitrator. Collective bargaining thus ensures that the employer will not be able to do anything it pleases (like a ruler in a dictatorship), but will rather be subject to a 'rule of law', albeit privately negotiated, at least to some extent and with regard to some decisions. This makes the relationship between the employer and its employees much more democratic.[82]

The second democratic attribute of collective bargaining is found in the ability it gives employees to voice their views, concerns, and demands, and more generally, to participate to some extent in the self-government of the workplace.[83] When organizing collectively, employees can voice their concerns without fear

modern economies, and particularly in labour markets, it rarely does). See John Kenneth Galbraith, *American Capitalism: The Concept of Countervailing Power* (Houghton Mifflin Co. 1956) ch 9.

[79] See Karl E Klare, 'Countervailing Workers' Power as a Regulatory Strategy' in Collins, Davies, and Rideout (n 36) 63, 70.

[80] In a sense, by organizing into a collective association employees merely mirror the parallel association of shareholders into the firm; see John R Commons and John B Andrews, *Principles of Labor Legislation* (rev edn, Harper & Brothers 1927) 99–100, and see the National Labor Relations Act (1935) § 1, 29 USC § 151 (National Labour Relations Act) (referring to the 'inequality of bargaining power between employees who do not possess full freedom of association or actual liberty of contract, and employers who are organized in the corporate or other form of ownership association').

[81] See Archibald Cox, *Law and the National Labor Policy* (first published 1960, Greenwood Press 1983) 12; Flanders (n 74) 41–42; Paul Weiler, *Reconcilable Differences: New Directions in Canadian Labour Law* (Carswell 1980) 30–31.

[82] For an argument that high union density is correlated with a stronger rule of law more generally (outside of the workplace), see Christopher David Ruiz Cameron, 'The Rule of Law Goes to Work: How Collective Bargaining May Promote Access to Justice in the United States, Canada, and the Rest of the World' (2014) 20 UC Davis J of Int Law & Policy 211.

[83] It is often noted with regard to the National Labor Relations Act in the US that the democratic objective of collective bargaining was one of its unstated goals when enacted. This goal was explicitly and clearly stated by Senator Wagner. See, e.g., James B Atleson, *Values and Assumptions in American Labor Law* (U of Massachusetts Press 1983) 41–42.

of losing their jobs.[84] They can change the way their workplace operates, and the way they are being treated, rather than just quit. The collective voice can be concerned with the smallest day-to-day actions, or with the broader view on the future and management of the firm, or even with the yet broader sphere of society at large.[85] Indeed, it is concerned with all of these at the same time.[86] The ability to freely voice concerns is democratically virtuous in itself,[87] but collective action offers more than that. By joining forces and threatening to withhold their services together, employees can force the employer into a framework of (albeit limited) joint government. When the union is strong enough, decisions on some issues are only taken after negotiations, with the final outcome representing a compromise between the interests of shareholders (or managers) and those of the employees. And at least to some extent—often more than in the larger political sphere—employees actively take part in this process, thus participating directly in making decisions on matters that affect their daily lives, and indeed, exercising some democratic self-government.[88] The ability to bargain collectively is thus not merely instrumental; it is rather an important component of, as well as a mean towards, human freedom.[89] This explains why the right to bargain collectively is increasingly being considered a basic human right,[90] with constitutional status.[91]

[84] See also the discussion of democracy in Chapter 4. And see Alan Bogg and Tonia Novitz, 'Investigating Voice at Work' (2011) 33 CLLPJ 323.

[85] See Webb and Webb (n 69) ch IV. See also Gillian Lester, 'Beyond Collective Bargaining: Modern Unions as Agents of Social Solidarity' in Guy Davidov and Brian Langille (eds), *The Idea of Labour Law* (OUP 2011) 329.

[86] Keith Ewing calls this the 'representative' and 'regulatory' functions of unions; the former concerned with representing the workers directly, the latter with participating on their behalf in multi-employer bargaining or influencing legislation. He criticized the UK government for diminishing these functions, which he sees as the central core functions of unions. See KD Ewing, 'The Function of Trade Unions' (2005) 34 ILJ 1.

[87] In a recent contribution, Alan Bogg and Cynthia Estlund argue that freedom of association can be normatively justified by reference to a 'right to contest', which is an important aspect of freedom (following Philip Pettit's idea of freedom as non-domination) and cannot realistically be materialized in the context of employment relations without joining forces with others. See Alan Bogg and Cynthia Estlund, 'Freedom of Association and the Right to Contest: Getting Back to Basics' in Alan Bogg and Tonia Novitz (eds), *Voices at Work: Continuity and Change in the Common Law World* (OUP 2014) 141.

[88] See Flanders (n 74); Weiler (n 81) 32–33.

[89] Brian Langille, 'Freedom of Association and the Effective Recognition of the Right to Collective Bargaining: A Reflection Upon Our Fundamental Commitments' (a paper prepared for the ILO, 1999). See also Weiler (n 81) 33.

[90] The right of collective bargaining is embodied in the ILO Constitution (International Labour Organization Constitution (Adopted by the Peace Conference in April 1919, the ILO Constitution was Part XIII of the Treaty of Versailles)) 15 UNTS 40 annex art III(e), as well as in a number of ILO conventions, most importantly ILO Convention (No 98) concerning the Application of the Principles of the Right to Organize and to Bargain Collectively (adopted 1 July 1949, entered into force 18 July 1951) 96 UNTS 257 art 4. It has also been included with the 'core labour standards' which have been reaffirmed in the Declaration on Fundamental Principles and Rights at Work (adopted 18 June 1998) 37 ILM 1233 art 2(a) and are understood to be accepted by all ILO members (see there). All documents are available at www.ilo.org. On human rights justifications for 'voice' at work, see Virginia Mantouvalou, 'Democratic Theory and Voices at Work' in Bogg and Novitz (n 87).

[91] The Supreme Court of Canada and the European Court of Human Rights have both decided in recent years that the right to bargain collectively is derived from freedom of association

The process of collective bargaining is far from being democratically perfect. Three counter-arguments should be considered in this context. *First*, critics of collective bargaining assert that in practice, unions are often undemocratic, detached from the true interests of local employees, and corrupt. There is probably some truth to such accusations—unions are not immune to the ills of all large bureaucratic organizations—and indeed, different regulatory reforms can and have been suggested to address these concerns. But the prevalence of such problems should not be overstated.[92] And in any case, such problems are not an inherent part of the collective bargaining system; they can, and should, be confronted and minimized.[93]

Second, from a Marxist direction it has been argued that unions (and collective bargaining) help to legitimize management and fail to challenge the capitalistic system which favours the rich and powerful.[94] It is certainly true that collective bargaining is a corrective measure to the capitalistic system but at the same time part of it. Revolutionary challenges are beyond the scope of the current discussion, which is concerned with identifying and understanding the goals of *existing* regulations. While I try to give the legal arrangements the best possible reading,[95] such a fundamental critique is out of the scope of the current analysis.[96]

Third, the process of collective bargaining has been criticized for (undemocratically) giving more weight to those who have more bargaining power because of their wealth or their specific—often accidental—work environment.[97] Indeed, the voices of large employers, and of some specific groups of better-positioned

and therefore constitutionally protected (see, respectively, *Health Services and Support v British Columbia* [2007] 2 SCR 391 and *Demir and Baykara v Turkey* App no 34503/97 (ECtHR, 12 November 2008)). The Canadian Court later gave a somewhat narrow reading for this right (*Fraser v Ontario (Attorney General)* [2011] 2 SCR 3). These cases are the subject of a heated and ongoing debate (see, e.g., Brian Langille, 'The Freedom of Association Mess: How We Got Into It and How We Can Get out of It' (2009) 54 McGill LJ 177; Alan Bogg and Keith Ewing, 'A (Muted) Voice at Work? Collective Bargaining in the Supreme Court of Canada' (2012) 33 CLLPJ 379). This debate has no bearing on the current chapter, which is about the justifications for the basic existing structure, rather than the question of which deviations from this structure are constitutionally allowed.

92 See Richard B Freeman and James L Medoff, *What Do Unions Do?* (Basic Books 1984) ch 14 (concluding, based on empirical evidence, that the American picture of unions as non-democratic institutions run by corrupt labour bosses is a myth); John Godard, 'The Exceptional Decline of the American Labor Movement' (2009–2010) 63 ILRR 82, 94–96.

93 For example, in Israel the National Labour Court has decided to apply duties from administrative law on the Histadrut (Israel's major union). See *Markovic Leon v Health Clinic Labour Organization* (1975) 6 PDA 197, 208; *National Organization of Naval Officers v Tzim* (1994) 26 PDA 3, 28.

94 See, e.g., Richard Hyman, *Marxism and the Sociology of Trade Unionism* (Pluto 1973) 11–25; Harry J Glasbeek, 'Voluntarism, Liberalism, and Grievance Arbitration: Holy Grail, Romance, and Real Life' in Geoffrey England (ed), *Essays in Labour Relations Law* (CCH Canadian Ltd. 1986) 57.

95 See Chapter 2.

96 It is interesting to note, however, that other critical labour law scholars, while arguing that current collective bargaining jurisprudence serves to reinforce hierarchy and domination (see Karl E Klare, 'Labor Law as Ideology: Toward a New Historiography of Collective Bargaining Law' (1981) 4 Ind Rel LJ 450, 452), nonetheless remain committed to the idea of collective bargaining itself (see Klare, 'Countervailing Workers' Power as a Regulatory Strategy' (n 79) 3–4).

97 David M Beatty, 'Ideology, Politics and Unionism' in Kennet P Swan and Katherine E Swinton (eds), *Studies in Labour Law* (Butterworths 1983) 299, 325ff.

employees, are more strongly heard. One could answer that this is not unique to collective bargaining; it is rather a problem of the democratic process as a whole, which gives more weight to the rich and powerful. In a sense, giving power to unions which in some cases will turn out to be excessive is only a balance to the excessive power enjoyed by large corporations in democratic systems (through political donations etc.). This is hardly a satisfactory answer as far as the relations between different groups of workers are concerned, but the redistributive questions (including intra-worker distributional issues) are discussed separately in the next section.

Overall, the democratic benefits of collective bargaining—and certainly the potential democratic benefits—far outweigh the pitfalls.

Redistribution

A second purpose of collective bargaining, one that appears to be straightforward, is to redistribute power (and as a result resources) from employers to employees. This is based on two background assumptions: that employers usually possess superior bargaining power vis-à-vis individual employees; and that this power imbalance, and the resulting terms of engagement, are unfair or unjust. While both assumptions are contested by some,[98] they are obviously accepted by legislatures; both assumptions stand behind any regulation that allows and promotes collective bargaining.[99] Without dwelling on a detailed discussion, I will take this redistributive purpose to be justified (in principle) normatively as well.[100] The question remains, can collective bargaining indeed lead to progressive redistribution?

It is undisputed that through collective bargaining employees can and do achieve better terms and conditions.[101] The question, nevertheless, is who pays for this betterment. To some extent, it is possible that unionization increases productivity (see the next section below), and this increase pays for the higher wages.[102]

[98] See Chapter 3.

[99] In some cases this is stated explicitly; see, e.g., the US National Labor Relations Act s 1 (declaring that the Act is intended to redress the inequality of bargaining power).

[100] For a brief discussion see Chapter 4.

[101] The union/non-union wage differential in North America is approximately 15%; see Peter Kuhn, 'Unions and the Economy: What We Know; What We Should Know' (1998) 31 Can J of Econ 1033; Lawrence Mishel, 'Unions, Inequality, and Faltering Middle-Class Wages' (2012) Economic Policy Institute Issue Brief No. 342. The union wage premium is usually smaller in other parts of the world, but still significant (see Richard B Freeman, 'American Exceptionalism in the Labor Market: Union-Nonunion Differentials in the United States and Other Countries' in Kerr and Staudohar (n 41) 272; David G Blanchflower and Alex Bryson, 'Changes over Time in Union Relative Wage Effects in the UK and the US Revisited' (2002) National Bureau of Economic Research Working Paper 9395 <http://www.nber.org/papers/w9395.pdf> accessed 12 October 2015). See also Erik Bengtsson, 'Do Unions Redistribute Income from Capital to Labour? Union Density and Wage Shares Since 1960' (2014) 45(5) Ind Rel J 389.

[102] Collective bargaining does not have to be a 'zero-sum game'; it can be beneficial for both parties. See Richard E Walton and Robert B McKersie, *A Behavioral Theory of Labor Negotiations* (McGraw-Hill 1965) (distinguishing between 'distributive' and 'integrative' bargaining), and see Richard N Block, 'Rethinking the National Labor Relations Act and Zero-Sum Labor Law: An

But it is highly doubtful that increased productivity can cover the whole additional cost, so one can assume that employers will shift as much as they can of the additional cost to consumers. In other contexts, such as with minimum wage laws, similar cost-shifting could result in desirable redistribution—from many (consumers) to the few employees who are the worst paid. But the situation is radically different with collective bargaining. It is quite possible that the average unionized employee is actually better off than the average consumer, so redistribution from the latter to the former would be unjustified. However, since employers usually have to compete with non-unionized firms, it is doubted whether in practice they can shift much of the additional cost to consumers (if at all).

It has also been argued, as with other employment standards, that the betterment in unionized workers' terms and conditions, which makes employment more costly for the employer, will result in reduced demand for employees in the unionized sector. Thus, it is argued, the most vulnerable (lowest paid) employees will end up paying for their collective bargaining rights with their jobs. According to this theory, workers released from the unionized sector will then look for work in non-unionized firms, creating a larger supply of workers and bringing down wages there.[103]

To a large extent, then, the desirability of collective bargaining in terms of redistribution depends on the empirical verdict as to who exactly pays for the higher union wages. Is it, for the most part, employers (i.e. shareholders), consumers (i.e. the public at large), or rather the lowest-paid and non-unionized workers? The evidence suggests that unionization markedly reduces firms' profits, at least in the United States;[104] to the extent this is the case redistribution from employers to employees occurs. On the other hand, there appears to be no convincing evidence that unionization reduces employment.[105] This can be explained by the fact that collective agreements do much more than set wages; unions also do their best to preserve jobs, whether directly (by insisting on employment levels and layoff policies) or indirectly (various other terms and conditions constrain the firm's employment level).[106] It can also be explained by the fact that unions are just as

Industrial Relations View' (1997) 18 BJELL 30. For more recent reviews of relevant studies see Joseph Slater, 'Homeland Security vs. Workers' Rights? What the Federal Government Should Learn from History and Experience, and Why' (2003–2004) 6 U Pa J Int'l Bus L 295, 338–44; Zafiris Tzannatos and Toke S Aidt, 'Unions and Microeconomic Performance: A Look at What Matters for Economists (and Employers)' (2006) 145 ILR 257.

[103] See, e.g., Milton Friedman and Rose Friedman, *Free to Choose: A Personal Statement* (Harcourt Brace Jovanovich 1980) 233–34; Posner, *Economic Analysis of Law* (n 35) 350–51.

[104] For summaries, see Freeman and Medoff (n 92) ch 12; Freeman (n 101); Kuhn (n 101) 1039; Hristos Doucouliagos and Patrice Laroche, 'Unions and Profits: A Meta-Regression Analysis' (2009) 48 Ind Rel 146.

[105] Freeman and Medoff (n 92) 120; Kuhn (n 101) 1044; John H Pencavel, *Labor Markets under Trade Unionism: Employment, Wages, and Hours* (Blackwell 1991) 44; William M Boal and John Pencavel, 'The Effects of Labor Unions on Employment, Wages and Days of Operation: Coal Mining in West Virginia' (1994) 109 The Quarterly J of Econ 267; Garry Sran and Jim Stanford, 'Further Tests on the Link between Unionization, Unemployment and Employment: Finding from Canadian National and Provincial Data' (2009) 15 Just Labour: A Canadian J of Work and Society 29.

[106] Kuhn (n 101) 1040–44, 1051.

rational as employers, and will usually stop short of demanding raises that will end up hurting their own members.[107] Indeed, there is evidence that unionization does not come with a decrease in the wages of non-union workers (which one would expect if indeed there are job losses in unionized firms); on the contrary, unionization triggers a voluntary increase in wages at non-unionized firms, as part of their efforts to counter the 'threat' of unionization.[108] Overall, then, while one should not belittle the potential impact on consumers and non-unionized workers, for the most part by joining forces workers appear to better their lot at the expense of the employer's profits.[109]

Another important issue that should be examined in this context concerns the impact of collective bargaining on wage inequalities. Within the unionized firm itself, collective bargaining is credited with reducing inequalities by creating pay policies that limit managerial discretion.[110] Thus, by forming determinate policies and taking some subjectivity out of the process of wage determination, collective bargaining decreases pay differences that are often unjustified.[111] It has further been shown that through collective bargaining, unions are able to achieve some standardization of wages—lower wage differentials—across firms within the same industry.[112]

On the other hand, collective bargaining has an opposite impact on wage inequalities between unionized and non-unionized workers. This is obviously the case if collective bargaining causes the involuntary shift of workers from the unionized to the non-unionized sector, which brings down wages in the latter. But even if, as suggested above, unions have a positive effect on wages in non-unionized firms, workers in non-unionized firms will usually enjoy a smaller average increase. And since higher-paid workers are generally better positioned to

107 See in this regard Galbraith (n 78) 115 (arguing that, as a general rule, one finds the strongest unions where markets are served by strong corporations and there are rewards that can be shared).

108 See, e.g., Giacomo Corneo and Claudio Lucifora, 'Wage Formation under Union Threat Effects: Theory and Empirical Evidence' (1997) 4 Labour Economics 265 (finding empirical support for the 'threat effect' theory; the effectiveness of the threat is shown to be correlated to local union density); but see Henry S Farber, 'Non Union Wage Rates and the Threat of Unionization' (2005) 58 Industrial and Labor Relations 335 (finding mixed results).

109 See Dale Belman, 'Unions, The Quality of Labor Relations, and Firm Performance' in Lawrence Mishel and Paula B Voos (eds), *Unions and Economic Competitiveness* (M.E. Sharpe 1992) 41; Kemmet G Dau-Schmidt, 'A Bargaining Analysis of American Labor Law and the Search for Bargaining Equity and Industrial Peace' (1992) 91 Mich LR 419.

110 Freeman and Medoff (n 92) ch 5.

111 While reducing inequalities that are based on irrelevant differences (such as sex or race) and are thus completely unjustified, collective agreements can also be expected to reduce differences in pay between more productive and less productive employees. The justifiability of better pay based on *merit* may be contested, but there is no doubt that more *effort* justifies higher wages. In this sense, the lessening of wage differences by collective bargaining may be both inequitable and inefficient. However, it is doubted that this is a major problem, especially since collective agreements often include variations in pay for productivity-related reasons (e.g. bonuses).

112 Freeman and Medoff (n 92); Thomas Lemieux, 'Unions and Wage Inequality in Canada and the United States' in David Card and Richard B Freeman (eds), *Small Differences That Matter: Labor Markets and Income Maintenance in Canada and the United States* (University of Chicago Press 1993) 69; Bruce Western and Jake Rosenfeld, 'Unions, Norms, and the Rise in U.S. Wage Inequality' (2011) 76 Amer Soc Rev 513.

unionize, wage inequalities can be expected to increase.[113] Furthermore, through collective bargaining, those who are better positioned (because of their wealth or the work environment) are able to get more than others; teachers, for example, have always been able to get more from collective bargaining than retail workers. This can also exacerbate existing inequalities, between different unionized sectors.[114] So collective bargaining can have regressive intra-worker distributive impacts. This is becoming ever more problematic because collective bargaining is not realistically available for a growing number of workers, due to outsourcing, subcontracting, privatization, as well as growing employer resistance to unions.[115]

The final verdict concerning the impact of unions (and collective bargaining) on equality will depend on empirical estimates as to the relative weight of inequality-reducing versus inequality-increasing effects. In their 1984 influential book, Richard Freeman and James Medoff estimated that the reduction in inequality far outweighed the increase.[116] This has been corroborated by more recent studies; it has been shown that the fall in union density in the United States accounts for some of the rise in wage inequalities in recent years.[117] There is also some evidence—although not unequivocal—that unions have the effect of reducing wage inequalities based on race and gender.[118] All this certainly serves to alleviate some of the fears that collective bargaining has the perverse effect of increasing inequalities. Still, concrete adaptations are needed, in many countries, to minimize the problem of increasing gaps between the groups of 'haves' (who have access to collective bargaining) and the 'have-not'.[119]

Overall, the process of collective bargaining appears to be a reasonable (though certainly not perfect) redistributive process. While specific legal arrangements

[113] See Milton Friedman, *Capitalism and Freedom*, (U of Chicago Press 1962) 124; Beatty (n 97).

[114] See Beatty (n 97). Freeman and Medoff found that unionism *reduces* inequalities between white-collar and blue-collar workers, since 'union wage gains accrue primarily to blue-collar workers in the United States' (Freeman and Medoff (n 92) 89). But since the service sector is continuously growing relative to manufacturing, and union membership has dropped especially in manufacturing, the relevance of this estimate for today is doubtful.

[115] See Adelle Blackett and Colleen Sheppard, 'The Links Between Collective Bargaining and Equality' (2002) ILO Working Paper <http://www.ilo.org/wcmsp5/groups/public/---ed_norm/---declaration/documents/publication/wcms_decl_wp_12_en.pdf> accessed 12 October 2015.

[116] Freeman and Medoff (n 92) 90–93 (concluding that, overall, trade unionism in the US reduces wage inequality by around 3%. For the reasons mentioned in note 114, among others, such an estimate is necessarily limited to a specific time and place).

[117] This is especially true for men, since among women unionization rates declined for low-waged workers but increased for higher-waged ones. Significantly, a US comparison between the private sector (where unionization declined) and the public sector (where it rose) showed that unionization substantially slowed the growth in wage inequality in the latter. See David Card, 'The Effect of Unions on Wage Inequality in the U.S. Labor Market' (2001) 54 ILRR 296; Bruce Western and Jake Rosenfeld (n 112); David Card, Thomas Lemieux, and W Craig Riddell, 'Unions and Wage Inequality' (2004) 25 JLR 519.

[118] Re race, see Freeman and Medoff (n 92) 49–50. Re gender, see Abul FM Shamsuddin, 'The Effect of Unionization on the Gender Earnings Gap in Canada: 1971–1981' (1996) 28 Applied Economics 1405; Marta M Elvira and Ishak Saporta, 'How Does Collective Bargaining Affect the Gender Gap?' (2001) 28 Work and Occupations 469.

[119] The terms are borrowed from Marc Galanter, 'Why the "Haves" Come Out Ahead: Speculations on the Limits of Legal Change' (1974) 9 Law & Society Rev 95.

require reform to address the problem of intra-worker gaps,[120] progressive redistribution can definitely be described as one of the general goals of this system.

Efficiency

Perhaps the most complicated question regarding the justifications for collective bargaining concerns its impact on economic efficiency. Generally speaking, laws promoting collective bargaining were designed to limit industrial conflict, which was obviously seen as detrimental to efficiency.[121] But the actual impact of unions (or collective bargaining) in terms of economic efficiency is highly controversial.

In terms of allocative efficiency, standard neo-classical analysis suggests that collective bargaining wage effects cause misallocation of resources, since they bring down the number of workers employed and the quantity of goods produced in the unionized sector from their (efficient) market levels.[122] However, as already noted, in practice unionization does not appear to reduce employment. And in any case, even if such inefficiencies exist, they are estimated to be rather trivial in magnitude.[123]

Much more significant is the impact of collective bargaining on productivity. Here one can expect to see competing forces. On the one hand, the reward for effort (and so presumably, motivation) is reduced; and restrictive work rules may limit management's ability to utilize the workforce in the most efficient way. On the other hand, under a collective agreement regime, turnover rates are lower, since voice is used instead of exit;[124] more information is expected to flow between workers and from workers to management (information which without job security workers may prefer to withhold[125]); morale (and so presumably motivation) is often higher; firm-specific investments are increased, since there is less risk of losing them;[126] and management, induced by the higher costs to reduce prior inefficiencies, is expected to be more rational and professional (the 'shock effect'). To be sure, lower turnover, higher information flows and increased firm-specific investments can result, to some extent, from job security even when voluntarily instituted (i.e. without the presence of unions). But this is rarely offered in recent decades.[127]

[120] Blackett and Sheppard (n 115).

[121] See, e.g., the US National Labor Relations Act s 1 ('the refusal by some employers to accept the procedure of collective bargaining lead[s] to strikes and other forms of industrial strife and unrest, which... impair[] the efficiency... of commerce').

[122] See Barry T Hirsch and John T Addison, *The Economic Analysis of Unions: New Approaches and Evidence* (Allen & Unwin 1986) 181.

[123] See also Robert H DeFina, 'Unions, Relative Wages, and Economic Efficiency' (1983) 1 J of Labor Econ 408.

[124] Freeman and Medoff (n 92) ch 6; Roderick D Iverson and Douglas B Currivan, 'Union Participation, Job Satisfaction, and Employee Turnover' (2003) 42 Ind Rel 101.

[125] For example, it is speculated that without some job security, senior workers may not willingly train juniors if their jobs are threatened, and workers in general will not provide information to management about labour-saving innovations.

[126] See Oliver E Williamson, *The Economic Institutions of Capitalism* (Free Press 1985) 255.

[127] Richard Posner has argued that if job security is not offered, it must be inefficient, and more generally, if unions enhance productivity they should be growing, and so the decline of the unionized sector tells us that they are not (n 35 at 357). This argument, however, is circular; it assumes

The empirical evidence suggests that the positive effects of unionization on productivity are stronger, at least potentially.[128] Unsurprisingly, the potential for increased productivity does not materialize when the parties adopt a particularly adversarial stance.[129] Indeed, it is 'the state of labor relations, rather than unionization and collective bargaining per se, [that] determines productivity.'[130] The impact is also smaller, or even negative, when there are no competitive pressures to improve productivity (as in the public sector).[131] Arguably, such negative effects result from job security that is too strong (inability in practice to dismiss incompetent employees), but this is not an inherent consequence of collective agreements.

No less important is the impact of collective bargaining on productivity growth, which is considered to ultimately determine the increase in a society's standard of living. Since collective bargaining results in lower profits, this can be expected to lower investment in unionized firms, including investment in research and development, which in turn can lower productivity growth. Lower productivity growth can also be expected if unions oppose technological change. On the other hand, higher union wages may induce management to look for new (labour-saving) technologies. The empirical evidence on these conflicting hypotheses is far from conclusive. It appears that unions do not generally hinder technological change.[132] There is evidence that unionization reduces investment

that the market currently works perfectly (efficiently) to prove that current market structures/choices are efficient. But several market failures can explain the objection to unions, most obviously the reluctance of managers to relinquish some of their unilateral powers, even when such a step is efficient. Moreover, Posner appears to equate profitability with efficiency, but in fact, firms might fail to introduce job security for distributive reasons, even when this is efficient.

[128] For summaries of the evidence, see Freeman and Medoff (n 92) ch 11; Kuhn (n 101) 1045–50; Tzannatos and Aidt (n 102). For a concrete example see Kim B Clark, 'The Impact of Unionization on Productivity: A Case Study' (1980) 33 ILRR 451 (finding productivity gains of 6–8% in the cement industry in the US as a result of unionization). For a slightly different view see Barry T Hirsch, 'What Do Unions Do for Economic Performance?' (2004) 25 JLR 415, 430 (concluding that 'the average union effect [on productivity] is very close to zero, and as likely to be somewhat negative as somewhat positive').

[129] Freeman and Medoff (n 92) ch11; Kuhn (n 101) 1048.

[130] Freeman (n 101) 291 (summarizing the research in different countries). See also Paul Davies, 'Efficiency Arguments for the Collective Representation of Workers: A Sketch' in Alan Bogg and others (eds), *The Autonomy of Labour Law* (Hart 2015) 367 (arguing that the efficiency of collective representation depends on supporting mechanisms within and outside the company). For additional evidence from Australia, Japan, and Canada (respectively) see Stephen J Deery and Roderick D Iverson, 'Labor-Management Cooperation: Antecedents and Impact on Organizational Performance' (2005) 58 ILRR 588; Masayuki Morikawa, 'Labor Unions and Productivity: An Empirical Analysis using Japanese Firm-Level Data' (2010) 17 Lab Econ 1030; Dionne Pohler and Andrew Luchak, 'Are Unions Good or Bad for Organizations? The Moderating Role of Management's Response' (2015) 53 BJIR 423.

[131] On the importance of competition for increased productivity see Freeman and Medoff (n 92) 179. On the public sector, see Hirsch and Addison (n 122); Caroline Minter Hoxby, 'How Teachers' Unions Affect Education Production' (1996) 111 The Quarterly J of Econ 671; Tzannatos and Aidt (n 102) 262–63.

[132] See Jeffrey H Keefe, 'Do Unions Hinder Technological Change?' in Mishel and Voos (n 109) 109. But see Barry T Hirsch and Albert N Link, 'Labor Union Effects on Innovative Activity' (1987) 8 JLR 323; Tzannatos and Aidt (n 102) 265.

in research and development (in the specific firm), at least in some countries.[133] Richard Freeman concluded a number of years ago that productivity growth is slower in unionized settings, but only 'to a modestly and statistically insignificant degree'.[134] This seems to be a reasonable summary even after taking into account the more recent studies.[135]

A related concern is whether firms invest the optimal amount of resources in workers' training. The importance of such training transcends the particular firm's productivity considerations; it is directly related to the competitiveness, adaptability and growth of the economy as a whole, especially in the modern economy which puts more emphasis on knowledge and skills. Absent unionization, firms may under-invest in training because they fear losing their investment as a result of quits. By reducing quits, collective bargaining can bring the investment in training closer to what is socially optimal.[136]

There are other efficiency attributes that should be considered. The process of collective bargaining can reduce transaction costs (the costs of bargaining).[137] It can also improve the administration and enforcement of workers' rights, since unions are often much more capable of enforcing such rights—even legislated rights—than labour inspectors or the courts.[138] No less important, collective bargaining can correct a number of market failures that impinge on overall efficiency, even when this is not (at least not necessarily) captured by workers' productivity. First, many aspects of the work setting are 'public goods', which will be under-produced because of collective action (or 'free-riding') problems. Whether it is safety conditions, lighting, heating, grievance procedures, pension plans, or other policies, once the 'good' is in place everyone can enjoy it, but no individual employee will be willing to 'pay' for it, or even invest the time in fighting for it, by herself. By acting together they can choose what is in fact rational for all of them.[139] Second, by bargaining collectively workers can share information, which should help them overcome barriers to informed bargaining.[140] Indeed, to this

[133] See Barry T Hirsch, 'Firm Investment Behavior and Collective Bargaining Strategy' (1992) 31 Ind Rel 95; Julian R Betts, Cameron W Odgers, and Michael K Wilson, 'The Effects of Unions on Research and Development: An Empirical Analysis Using Multi-Year Data' (2001) 34 Canadian J of Econ 785; Tzannatos and Aidt (n 102) 267–68. But see Naercio Menezes-Filho, David Ulph, and John Van Reenen, 'R&D and Unionism: Comparative Evidence from British Companies and Establishments' (1998) 52 ILRR 45. See also Tzannatos and Aidt (n 102) 266–67.

[134] Freeman (n 101) 292.

[135] See also Hirsch (n 128) 431.

[136] See Alison L Booth and Monojit Chatterji, 'Unions and Efficient Training' (1998) 108 The Economic 328; Alison L Booth, Marco Francesconi, and Gylfi Zoega, 'Unions, Work Related Training and Wages: Evidence from British Men' (2003–2004) 57 ILRR 68. The simplistic assumption that unions equal rigidity which equals competitive disadvantage has been exposed as baseless. See, e.g., the different contributions in Mishel and Voos (n 109).

[137] Williamson (n 126) 255.

[138] For a summary of the studies see David Weil, 'Individual Rights and Collective Agents: The Role of Old and New Workplace Institutions in the Regulation of Labor Markets' in Richard B Freeman, Joni Hersch, and Lawrence Mishel (eds), *Emerging Labor Market Institutions for the Twenty-First Century* (U of Chicago Press 2004) 13. For further discussion see Chapter 9.

[139] See Cass R Sunstein, *After the Rights Revolution: Reconceiving the Regulatory State* (HUP 1990) 49–51.

[140] Cass R Sunstein, 'Human Behavior and the Law of Work' (2001) 87 Va LR 205, 210.

end, 'unions can both serve as a source of information regarding employee needs and preferences (with respect, for example, to fringe benefits) and assist employees in evaluating complex wage and benefits offers'.[141] Third, union representation can limit occurrences of workers' short-sightedness (as a result of 'bounded rationality') that might produce outcomes that are not in the workers' long-term interest.[142] Fourth, management will be restricted by the collective agreement from some inefficient actions, whether it is discrimination between workers, 'arbitrary and capricious behavior by foremen',[143] or opportunistic decisions such as firing senior workers just before they become eligible for pension rights. Indeed, 'economic theorists of all persuasions have increasingly recognized that unions' ability to enforce labor agreements, particularly those with deferred claims, creates the possibility for improved labour contracts and arrangements and higher economic efficiency'.[144] To some extent collective bargaining can also correct externalities, that is, minimize the problem of wage setting policies (and other management decisions) that ignore their effect on others.[145] Finally, unions make sure that the preferences of all workers are considered, including older workers who are more tied to the firm. Without the existence of a union firms' signals and incentives are based only on the preferences of the 'marginal' worker, 'the one who might leave because of (or be attracted by) small changes in the conditions of employment'.[146]

There is thus ample theory and evidence to suggest that the process of collective bargaining has some efficiency-enhancing attributed. At the very least, the discussion so far seems enough to refute the once-common claim that unions (and collective bargaining) significantly impair efficiency.

Conclusion

We have seen that collective bargaining is most strongly justified in terms of democracy, but can also serve to achieve (even if not without some complications) progressive redistribution and economic efficiency. Because the details of the law differ from one legal system to another, these goals are obviously achieved to very different degrees. Moreover, various improvements and adaptations might be required to minimize the disadvantages attached to collective bargaining, as described in this part. Still, the analysis shows that the gains outweigh the costs, and explains why all advanced economies have chosen to allow and support collective bargaining (to different degrees)—and why this is justified.

141 Williamson (n 126) 254. This was recognized already by John Stuart Mill, *Principles of Political Economy with some of their applications to social philosophy* (William J Ashley ed, first published 1848, AM Kelley 1961) 937.

142 Sunstein (n 140) 210.

143 Williamson (n 126) 256.

144 Freeman and Medoff (n 92) 11. And see Williamson (n 126) 255.

145 See Joseph Stiglitz, 'Democratic Development as the Fruits of Labor' (Keynote Address, Industrial Relations Research Association, Boston, January 2000) <http://www0.gsb.columbia.edu/faculty/jstiglitz/download/2000_Democratic_Development_KEYNOTE.pdf> accessed 12 October 2015.

146 Freeman and Medoff (n 92) 9–10.

Part III—The Purpose of Unjust Dismissal Laws

The third example I chose for performing a purposive analysis of a specific labour regulation is more controversial than the previous two. 'Unjust dismissal' laws are not universally available. In some jurisdictions—notably the United States—the controlling legal rule is 'employment at will' (EAW), which gives an employer the freedom to terminate the contract 'for good cause, for no cause or even for cause morally wrong'.[147] Sometimes the law prohibits specific impermissible reasons for dismissals, like pregnancy, trade union membership, or racial discrimination; and there are proposals to expand the list of 'bad' causes.[148] Sometimes there are procedural limitations such as a duty to perform a hearing or to give advance notice prior to dismissals.[149] Some legal systems also have regulations that create disincentives to dismissals or 'cushion' their economic impact, such as mandatory severance payments.[150] But such regulations leave the basic rule—the right of employers to terminate the employment for any reason they see fit—intact. In contrast, 'unfair dismissal' (or 'just cause') laws give employees a degree of entitlement to the job, or more correctly to the continuance of the employment relationship, subject only to dismissal for a permissible reason. These legal protections are enjoyed by employees in the UK,[151] in most continental European countries,[152] in some Canadian jurisdictions,[153] and elsewhere.[154] The focus of this part is on such regulations.

[147] *Payne v Western & Atlantic Railroad Co* 81 Tenn. 507 (Tenn 1884) para 6. There are some exceptions in the case law (see Katherine VW Stone, 'Revisiting the At-Will Doctrine: Imposed Terms, Implied Terms, and the Normative World of the Workplace' (2007) 36 ILJ 84; and see American Law Institute, *Restatement of the Law (Third): Employment Law* (2015) ch 2) and also in one state legislation (Montana's Wrongful Discharge from Employment Act of 1987, Mont Code Ann § 39-2-901 (1987)). And of course, employers can agree to a 'just cause' regime in a collective agreement. But the default rule is dominant.

[148] Nicole Porter, 'The Perfect Compromise: Bridging the Gap Between At-Will Employment and Just Cause' (2008) 87 Neb LR 62.

[149] For a useful comparative review see Samuel Estreicher and Jeffrey M Hirsch, 'Comparative Wrongful Dismissal Law: Reassessing American Exceptionalism' (2014) 92 North Car LR 343, 370–76. For proposals to adopt advanced notice in the US see Daniel J Libenson, 'Leasing Human Capital: Toward a New Foundation for Employment Termination Law' (2006) 27 BJELL 111; Rachel Arnow-Richman, 'From Just Cause to Just Notice in Reforming Employment Termination Law' in Cynthia L Estlund and Michael L Wachter (eds), *Research Handbook on the Economics of Labor and Employment Law* (Edward Elgar 2012) 296.

[150] See, e.g., the Israeli Severance Pay Law, 1963; Ontario Employment Standards Act, 2000, SO 2000, C 41, s 64. Other legal systems offer specific remedies for situations of plant closure or otherwise mass dismissals (see, e.g., Worker Adjustment and Retraining Notification Act 1988, 29 USC § 2101 (60-day pre-notification)).

[151] Employment Rights Act 1996 ss 94ff.

[152] For a survey of employment protection laws in some of the European countries see Klaus Schomann, Ralf Rogowski, and Thomas Kruppe, *Labour Market Efficiency in the European Union: Employment Protection and Fixed-Term Contracts* (Routledge 1998) ch 3; European Labour Law Network, 'Thematic Report 2011: Dismissal—Particularly for Business Reasons—and Employment Protection' (2011) <www.labourlawnetwork.eu/frontend/file.php?id=218&dl=1> accessed 12 October 2015.

[153] Canada Labour Code, RS 1985, c L-2, s 240; Nova Scotia Labour Standards Code, RS, c 246, s 71; Quebec's Act Respecting Labour Standards, CQLR, c N-1.1, s 124ff.

[154] For useful comparative reviews see Malcolm Crotty and others (eds), *Termination of Employment Digest* (International Labour Office 2000); OECD, *Employment Outlook 2004* (OECD

Unjust dismissal laws usually allow dismissals due to *incapability* (personal reasons), *misconduct* (disciplinary reasons), and *redundancy* (economic/operational reasons).[155] The protection is usually limited to employees who have been employed for more than a specified minimum term (e.g. twelve months in the Canadian federal jurisdiction).[156] The regulations are also sometimes limited to employers with more than a specified number of employees (e.g. ten employees in Germany).[157] In some countries there have been changes of detail as part of the trend towards deregulation of labour markets, but for the most part the basic structure remained intact.[158]

Unjust dismissals laws are constantly under attack. They are cited as a major cause for European unemployment and inefficiency (due to 'rigidity'). They are often considered anachronistic. Nonetheless, they have strong justifications; as explained in this part, they are based on the need to provide risk-averse and vulnerable workers with *security*, both economic and social/psychological. Below I explore the nature of this security and its place within the employment contract, and consider the effect it might have on employment levels and on the unemployed. I then examine the impact of a 'just cause' regime on economic efficiency and on the autonomy of the employer.

Providing security

The basic idea behind 'just cause' regulations is straightforward: to provide security against arbitrary, opportunistic, or otherwise 'unfair' dismissals.[159] Such security can be seen as *implied* in long-term relationships like employment. Some commentators support the adoption of a *default* 'just cause' rule—an implied

Publishing 2004) ch 2; *OECD Employment Outlook 2013*, ch 2 <http://www.oecd-ilibrary.org/employment/oecd-employment-outlook-2013_empl_outlook-2013-en> accessed 12 October 2015; Estreicher and Hirsch (n 149).

155 These three grounds for dismissals are found in the international instruments instituting protection against unjust dismissals; see ILO Termination of Employment Recommendation 1963 No 119 art 2(1) and the ILO Termination of Employment Convention 1982 (No 158) art 4; and see the Charter of Fundamental Rights of the European Union art 30.

156 Canada Labour Code, RS 1985, c L-2, s 240(1)(a).

157 Protection against Dismissals Act, s 23 (Germany).

158 Deregulation during the 1990s and onwards usually took the form of relaxing limitations on temporary employment, which is exempted in one way or another from employment protection laws, without changing these laws themselves. See OECD, *Employment Outlook 2004* (n 154) 73. This approach, which strengthens the polarization into dual labour markets, is obviously problematic.

159 By providing security, the law will also redistribute power from employers to employees, since 'it is the fear of being discharged which above all else renders the great majority of employees vulnerable to employer coercion' (Lawrence E Blades, 'Employment at Will vs. Individual Freedom: On Limiting the Abusive Exercise of Employer Power' (1967) 67 Colum LR 1404, 1406). But a 'just cause' rule will not make much difference in this regard, since (a) employers will still have a broad ability to discharge employees, and (b) employees tend to believe anyway that they have more job security than they actually do (see below). It seems to me, therefore, that any redistribution of power would be quite minimal, and should be seen merely as a side effect. Providing security to employees is valuable for other reasons, as explored below.

term of the employment contract which can be refuted.[160] But the regulations discussed here go much further—a 'just cause' regime is explicitly imposed on the parties. The assumption behind such regulations is that the vast majority of employees are interested in the security they provide, but in most cases employers have both the interest and the bargaining power to contract out of such restrictions, should this remain an option. They have the *interest* because a 'just cause' regime imposes some costs on them (although, as we shall see, not as much as is often believed), not all of which they can shift to others,[161] and especially because employers, and particularly managers, prefer to maintain full powers and flexibility to dismiss employees for whatever reason they see fit. And in most cases employers have superior bargaining power that allows them to impose such conditions.[162] Indeed, experience shows that where this was possible, most employers have been quick to contract out of any restrictions on their ability to dismiss employees.[163]

Admittedly, a default 'just cause' rule can be useful in overcoming information asymmetries, particularly since employees tend to believe that the law provides more job security for them than it actually does.[164] It could thus be useful, in terms of the availability of information, to require the employer to state explicitly any contradictory arrangement.[165] But for most employees, the problem is more acute. The information will not change the fact that they have to accept the contract 'as is', or risk unemployment.

So if society wants all employees to enjoy some security, the law must make it a mandatory part of the contract.[166] It remains to be explained *why* employees

[160] See, e.g., Arthur S Leonard, 'A New Common Law of Employment Termination' (1988) 66 North Car LR 631; Michael J Phillips, 'Toward a Middle Way in the Polarized Debate Over Employment at Will' (1992) 30 Am Bus LJ 441. This is also the approach adopted by the American Uniform Law Commissioners in their Model Employment Termination Act (1991); see Theodore J St Antoine, 'The Model Employment Termination Act: A Fair Compromise' (1994) 536 Annals Am Acad Pol & Soc Sci 93.

[161] See Jeffrey L Harrison, 'The "New" Terminable-at-Will Employment Contract: An Interest and Cost Incidence Analysis' (1984) 69 Iowa LR 327.

[162] On the inequality of bargaining power see Chapter 3. There are also a number of market failures that prevent the voluntary making of 'just cause' arrangements in non-unionized settings, some of which will not be solved by changing the default rule. See Paul C Weiler, *Governing the Workplace: The Future of Labour and Employment Law* (HUP 1990) 74–78; Guy Mundlak, 'Information-Forcing and Cooperation-Inducing Rules: Rethinking the Building Blocks of Labour Law' in de Geest, Siegers and van den Bergh (n 39); Note, 'Protecting at Will Employees Against Wrongful Discharge: The Duty to Terminate Only in Good Faith' (1980) 93 Harv LR 1816. For a different view see Mayer G Freed and Daniel D Polsby, 'Just Cause for Termination Rules and Economic Efficiency' (1989) 38 Emory LJ 1097.

[163] J Hoult Verkerke, 'An Empirical Perspective on Indefinite Term Employment Contracts: Resolving the Just Cause Debate' (1995) 1995 Wis LR 837, 867–68.

[164] Pauline T Kim, 'Bargaining with Imperfect Information: A Study of Worker Perceptions of Legal Protection in an At-Will World' (1997) 83 Cornell LR 105 (89% of the respondents erroneously believed that American law forbids an employer from discharging employees out of personal dislike).

[165] Although admittedly it is not easy to ensure that workers will actually receive the information, as opposed to simply signing standard contracts without reading them. See JH Verkerke, 'Legal Ignorance and Information-Forcing Rules' (2015) 56 William & Mary LR 899.

[166] This does not exclude creative alternatives such as 'a constrained-penalty-default rule that allows derogation of the just-cause statutory standard, contingent on developing an internal dispute

should be granted such security, from a societal point of view. In other words, we need to explain why the regular laws of contract—which allow each party to terminate an indefinite contract at any time (subject only to reasonable notice)—should not apply. My answer is comprised of two separate parts. The first focuses on the importance of the job for the life of the employee, both in economic and in social/psychological terms; the second on the nature of the exchange (subordination for security).

The unique characteristics of employment relationships

It hardly needs to be stated that for most of us, work is crucial in *economic* terms. But as we have seen in Chapter 3, work is also important for the individual in *social and psychological* terms. It is an important part of our identity, and it plays a crucial part in our quest for self-realization and in the shaping of our self-esteem. It is also an important source for social relationships.[167] Such are the characteristics of *work*; they are not limited to employees. Employment relations are characterized, as I have argued in Chapter 3, by the one-sided *dependency* of the employee on the relationship with the specific employer, both economically and for the fulfilment of those social and psychological needs. While some workers—those properly called 'independent contractors'—are able to spread their economic risks as well as their social and psychological ties among many separate relationships, employees are tied to a specific employer and this puts them in a vulnerable position.

Admittedly, a discharged employee will usually be able to find a new job instead of the old one.[168] But this is not always the case; the most vulnerable employees—the old, the less healthy, and more generally women and minorities—often face significant difficulties in finding new jobs; even more so after they have been discharged from their previous employment.[169] And the implications of losing a job in terms of personal well-being are dramatic; empirical research connects job insecurity with stress, depression, alcohol dependency, and other health-detrimental factors.[170] Furthermore, even if a new job is secured, and even if it

resolution mechanism modelled on the premises of European works councils legislation' (Mundlak (n 162) 84). For our purposes here, the important point is that such arrangements would still make sure that some security is provided to *all* employees.

[167] These social/psychological aspects of employment were given much attention, in the context of wrongful dismissals, by the Supreme Court of Canada. See *Machtinger v HOJ Industries Ltd.* [1992] 1 SCR 986, 1002; *Wallace v United Grain Growers Ltd.* [1997] 3 SCR 701; *McKinley v BC Tel* (2001), 200 DLR (4th) 385.

[168] See Richard A Epstein, 'Agency Costs, Employment Contracts, and Labor Unions' in John W Pratt and Richard J Zeckhauser (eds), *Principles and Agents: The Structure of Business* (Harvard Business School Press 1985) 140.

[169] 'It is far easier for a wrongfully discharged employee to obtain comparable other employment in the fertile imagination of Professor Epstein than it is in reality' (Martin H Malin, 'The Distributive and Corrective Justice Concerns in the Debate over Employment at Will: Some Preliminary Thoughts' (1992) 68 Chi-Kent LR 117, 143).

[170] See World Health Organization, *Closing the Gap in a Generation: Health Equity Through Action on the Social Determinants of Health* (CSDH 2008) <http://whqlibdoc.who.int/publications/2008/9789241563703_eng.pdf> accessed 12 October 2015; Marianna Virtanen and others,

appears to be comparable to the old one, in most cases there are significant costs to the employee, who loses firm-specific investments, various seniority-related benefits (formal and informal), as well as existing social ties.

Some commentators have justified a 'just cause' regime on the basis of an implicit contract of deferred payment. The argument is that career employees invest in the firm, and accept given terms at the beginning, in the expectation—implicitly encouraged by the firms—of improving those terms along with seniority. They accept less than their marginal product at the beginning under the implicit understanding that they will get *more* than their marginal product as they get older—an arrangement preferred by the firms since it promotes a longer (and more efficient) service. Career employees therefore have a legitimate expectation for tenure.[171] Employees who have a more casual relationship, on the other hand, do not have such an expectation, so if one follows this justification they should be excluded from any 'just cause' legislation.[172] My own focus is not on what the parties have implicitly agreed upon, or what they should be conceived as if they agreed, but rather on the protection that employees need in light of their one-sided dependency on the relationship.[173] This dependency is perhaps more obvious in the case of career employees, but exists in precarious work relations as well, and it is often not less significant given the workers' lack of alternative opportunities.

This does not mean that a 'just cause' regime is justified in any relation of economic dependency. Such vulnerability also appears in relations between cooperating firms. In such cases it may be justified to provide some protection against termination of long-term contracts,[174] but not in the form discussed here. The economic interests of firms can be protected by means of monetary compensation. There is no reason, in such cases, to give the dependent firm a right to the continuance of the relationship, such as the right usually given by 'just cause' laws to employees. Employees have the right to be reinstated if unjustly dismissed, because their dependency is not only economic but social/psychological as well.[175]

'Temporary Employment and Health: A Review' (2005) 34 Int J of Epidemiology 610. See also Theodore J St Antoine, 'A Seed Germinates: Unjust Discharge Reform Heads Toward Full Flower' (1988) 67 Neb LR 56, 67; David M Beatty, 'Labour is Not a Commodity' in Barry J Reiter and John Swan (eds), *Studies in Contract Law* (Butterworths 1980) 313.

171 See Weiler (n 162) ch 2. For an argument that American courts already provide more security when employer opportunism is more likely (especially after long terms of employment), see Stewart J Schwab, 'Life-Cycle Justice: Accommodating Just Cause and Employment at Will' (1993) 92 Mich LR 8.

172 See Weiler (n 162) 68.

173 I am thus generally concerned with considerations of distributive, rather than corrective, justice; see Malin (n 169).

174 Indeed, franchisees and exclusive distributors, for example, are often entitled to reasonable notice before termination of an indefinite contract, and rightly so.

175 It does not matter, for our purposes, if in practice employees prefer reinstatement or not, or if reinstatement is successful (often it is not absent the support of a union; see Samuel Estreicher, 'Unjust Dismissal Laws: Some Cautionary Notes' (1985) 33 Am J Comp L 310, and see Genevieve Eden, 'Reinstatement in the Nonunion Sector: An Empirical Analysis' (1994) 49 Ind Rel 87). The right itself still provides an important protection for employees.

This last point may explain why commentators who focus only or mainly on *economic* dependency end up supporting legislation which gives employees no right to reinstatement in cases of unjust dismissals. Paul Weiler, for example, directed most of his attention to the economic aspects of long-term employment relationships.[176] The protection he ended up proposing against arbitrary dismissals is significantly weaker than what is common in Europe. Importantly, his model offers no right to the continuance of the relationship. When attention is shifted to the social and psychological aspects of employment, one reaches very different conclusions.

Hugh Collins rightly focused on these aspects in articulating a rationale for job security laws, and this led him to conclude that employers should be required to show respect for the *dignity* of their employees, and that work relations should be structured in a way conducive to workers' *autonomy*.[177] Arbitrary dismissals naturally do not stand up to these standards. But this does not explain why the same standards should not apply in other relationships, like the relationship between the firm and an independent contractor. The difference, I believe, lies in the *dependency* of the employee on the specific relationship for those social/psychological needs. The importance of the work as well as the work environment for the individual are crucial, but the independent contractor can significantly mitigate the blow of any termination by concurrently maintaining other similar relationships. Those who require protection in this context are the workers who depend upon a specific relationship.

This unique attribute of employment relationships plays a crucial role in explaining the purpose of 'just cause' laws. Employees depend on the relationship with the employer for important aspects of their personal well-being. Society therefore has a strong interest in the continuance of these relationships and so would be justified in demanding that they shall not be severed without a good reason. Another way of putting this is by pointing attention to the significant *power* that employers hold over employees who depend on them. Power should be used responsibly. To avoid dismissals that cannot be justified, neither on incapability, nor misconduct, nor on operational reasons, seems like a rather modest requirement in this regard.

The nature of the employer–employee exchange

A second justification for 'just cause' regulations, also based on the need for security, is concerned with making the exchange between the parties a fair one. A prominent characteristic of employment relationships is the existence of

[176] Weiler (n 162) ch 2. And see *Wygant v Jackson Board of Education* 476 US 267, 283 (1986): 'the rights and expectations surrounding seniority make up what is probably the most valuable asset that the worker "owns," worth even more than the current equity in his home' (quoting Richard H Fallon Jr and Paul C Weiler, 'Firefighters v. Stotts: Conflicting Models of Racial Justice' (1984) 1984 Sup Ct Rev 1, 58).

[177] Hugh Collins, 'The Meaning of Job Security' (1991) 20 ILJ 227; Hugh Collins, *Justice in Dismissal: The Law of Termination of Employment* (Clarendon 1992) ch 1.

democratic deficits, or as it is often put (somewhat more narrowly) the subordination of the employee to the employer.[178] Economists explain the agreement of employees to submit themselves to the control of others in the *security* they get in return from frequent fluctuations in the demand for their labour. This can be seen as *insurance* that employees buy from their employers; employees agree to submit themselves to the control of the firm in return for the security of getting more or less the same compensation every month (as long as they are employed), regardless of the actual demand for the products or services of the firm in a given month.[179]

It may be an exaggeration to see this as an 'agreement', since many employees just have to take what they are offered. But it is certainly true that more often than not this is the basic structure of the contract of employment: subordination in exchange for security. It is the *level* of security that changes according to the employee's bargaining power. Weakly positioned employees often have to endure more risks (and less security) in irregular and otherwise contingent relationships. In recent years the bargaining power of many employees has diminished because of new economic pressures, and as a result the exchange with the employer is sometimes more akin to a discrete market transaction, with no security at all.[180] On the other hand, when they are unionized, employees are usually able to gain *more* security through some kind of a job security agreement.

Because the laws of contracts, in themselves, do not always ensure that exchanges meet certain standards of fairness, society often finds it necessary to insert some terms into contracts that were created in conditions of unequal bargaining power. In some cases, such terms simply set out the minimum standards that society finds acceptable, like the maximum hours of work per day. But in other cases, such as the 'just cause' requirement, the regulations can be seen as inserting some fairness into the existing conditions of the exchange. There is nothing particularly 'fair' about setting a maximum of, say, nine hours of work per day. If the employee is well paid to work ten hours that can be just as fair. For various other reasons, which will not be explored here, society still finds this unacceptable. But the case of security is different at least once it is acknowledged that contracts of employment involve an exchange of security (at whatever level) for subordination. When entering into an employment relationship, employees sacrifice some of their *freedom*. They submit themselves to the control of others; to a regime that is democratically deficient. This freedom does not have a monetary value. It should not be sold for money. Indeed, employees normally get more than an hourly compensation from their employers; they get a measure of security. They get some

[178] See Chapter 3.

[179] See Frank H Knight, *Risk, Uncertainty and Profit* (Houghton Mifflin Co. 1921) 269–70; Costas Azariadis and Joseph E Stiglitz, 'Implicit Contracts and Fixed Price Equilibria' (1983) 98 (Supp) The Quarterly J of Econ 1.

[180] See Peter Cappelli and others, *Change at Work* (Oxford University Press 1997); Katherine VW Stone, *From Widgets to Digits: Employment Regulation for the Changing Workplace* (Cambridge UP 2004); Leah Vosko, *Managing the Margins: Gender, Citizenship, and the International Regulation of Precarious Employment* (OUP 2010); Guy Standing, *The Precariat: The New Dangerous Class* (Bloomsbury Academic 2011).

assurance that, at least as long as they are employed, they will get compensated regardless of the conditions of the market. In a sense, in return for some of their freedom, they get some freedom from the daily worries on whether they will have money to put food on the table tomorrow; they get some peace of mind.

The question is whether, absent 'just cause' regulations, the non-unionized employees are getting enough; whether the minimal security commonly offered as part of the EAW arrangement is reasonably fair. It seems to me that it is not. Respect for the human dignity of employees and for the value of their freedom dictates a higher level of security. If employers want to control others—to maintain a workplace with democratic deficits—at the very least they must avoid arbitrary and opportunistic dismissals. This minimal standard of fairness is instituted by 'just cause' regulations. Employers retain the freedom to dismiss employees for any reasonably justified cause. Employees do not get absolute security; far from it. But they know that as long as they perform and behave adequately, and assuming that their job is still needed, this job will remain available for them. Such a level of security seems more appropriate and fair once the nature of the employer–employee exchange is taken into consideration.

Free-market enthusiasts argue that the State should not impose on the parties 'just cause' requirements, but rather assume that both parties prefer the specific combination of wages, benefits, and insurance they agreed upon. A 'just cause' requirement is seen as a higher level of insurance, and by making such additional insurance mandatory, it is argued, legislatures leave employees with lower wages and/or lower levels of other benefits, a new combination which they did not want and is less efficient. It is plausible, however, that employees actually prefer 'just cause' arrangements, but in practice they are prevented by market failures. There is no reason to believe that non-unionized employees have different preferences than unionized ones, who commonly opt for 'just cause' protections.[181] No less important, it is misleading to equate 'just cause' rules with insurance. A 'just cause' rule is, for the most part, a requirement for due process. A due process requirement should not be seen as 'insurance' against arbitrary actions. By setting a standard of acceptable conduct we do not 'buy insurance' against unacceptable conduct, even if there are some indirect costs (discussed below) as a result of this standard-setting. It is plausible to describe as insurance the basic agreement to pay a fixed salary in return for the employee's work, and plausible as well to argue that employees pay for such insurance, at least in part, by submitting themselves to the control of others (to a regime with democratic deficits). But legislation that puts limits on the exercise of employers' power—that minimizes to some extent the democratic deficits by setting acceptable standards—should not be seen as mandating additional insurance. Society simply demands that employers adhere to minimal standards of justice, fairness, and democratic rule. This is properly imposed as a non-negotiable part of the employment relationship.

[181] See Weiler (n 162) 73.

The impact on 'outsiders'

We have seen that 'just cause' regulations are designed to provide workers with some security, and two separate justifications have been advanced to support this goal. However, security does not come without a price. It has been argued that the most vulnerable are the ones paying for employees' security—in this case, the unemployed as well as workers in precarious arrangements who for various reasons remain out of the scope of 'just cause' regulations. Proponents of deregulation have focused much attention on European dismissal laws, chastising them as a major factor contributing to the persistently high rate of unemployment in many European countries. According to this line of thought, by making employment more costly, 'just cause' regulations reduce the demand for labour and hence the level of employment.[182] Alternatively, but usually at the same time, firms try to avoid these additional costs by preferring non-standard work relationships that are not covered by the regulations.[183] In such cases, the workers lose not only security but various other rights and benefits as well. Finally, those who hold the jobs in the first place (the 'insiders') gain unfair advantage since the cost of labour turnover is increased, thus making it practically impossible for the unemployed and contingent workers (the 'outsiders') to compete for those jobs.[184]

This line of argument is hopefully not intended to suggest that arbitrary and opportunistic dismissals are an acceptable method of distributing jobs among workers. If the critics wish to suggest a revolutionary system of job sharing, according to which the unemployed will somehow replace current employees every once in a while, surely this cannot be done through arbitrary dismissals. The argument is equally weak if it is based on the idea that 'just cause' regulations interfere with the ability of the unemployed to underbid current employees in competition for jobs. Such underbidding, while expected in neo-classical economic theory, does not exist in real life.[185]

[182] See, e.g., Richard A Posner, 'Hegel and Employment at Will: A Comment' (1989) 10 Cardozo LR 1625, 1634.

[183] See David H Autor, 'Outsourcing at Will: The Contribution of Unjust Dismissal Doctrine to the Growth of Employment Outsourcing' (2003) 21 J of Labor Econ 1; *OECD Employment Outlook 2014*, ch 4 <http://www.oecd-ilibrary.org/employment/oecd-employment-outlook-2014_empl_outlook-2014-en;jsessionid=fo13dthqolf0p.x-oecd-live-03> accessed 13 October 2015.

[184] See generally Assar Lindbeck and Dennis J Snower, *The Insider-Outsider Theory of Employment and Unemployment* (MIT Press 1988). It has also been shown that given the high cost of firing, employers prefer the safer bet of hiring from among those already employed, thus further disadvantaging the unemployed (Adrianna D Kugler and Gilles Saint-Paul, 'How do Firing Costs Affect Worker Flows in a World with Adverse Selection?' (2004) 22 J of Labor Econ 553). For an up-to-date theoretical and empirical discussion see *OECD Employment Outlook 2013* (n 154).

[185] Many explanations have been offered for this discrepancy between theory and reality. For example, efficiency wage and insider-outsider theories both explain why employers will not accept offers from the unemployed for lower wages. According to the former, employers get enhanced productivity by paying more. According to the latter, employers fear a disruption of the balance they have reached with current employees. A third explanation, which focuses on the fact that the unemployed do not appear to even attempt underbidding, is that workers act according to a social norm, which is strategically beneficial for them in the long run since they can be on the other side (i.e. employed) in a latter episode of this 'repeated game'. For a useful review of the first

It is true that when replacing an employee becomes more costly, an employer can be expected to be more hesitant before doing so. This is good news for the employee and bad news for the unemployed vying for scarce jobs. It is similarly true that a rise in the total cost of employment might sometimes discourage employers from taking new employees. But these claims can hardly be used as a serious argument against 'just cause' laws, because—as it will be argued below—the additional costs that such laws impose on the replacement of employees are rather minimal.

Different employment protection regulations are usually considered together in this regard, and this has caused some confusion. Laws setting notice periods and severance payments indeed translate into relatively significant costs attached to the replacement of employees.[186] The justification for such laws is beyond the scope of this chapter. Laws setting a 'just cause' regime, on the other hand, should be analyzed separately. The question is what are the costs when the firm has—or at least believes it has—a just cause for replacing the employee. This is analyzed in the next section, as part of the discussion on efficiency. I shall argue that these costs are quite insignificant for medium and large firms, although they may be high for small firms. Leaving aside the small firms, who are often excluded from the scope of 'just cause' laws, it appears that such regulations do not significantly raise the costs of replacing employees. The impact on 'outsiders', therefore, is bound to be (if at all) rather small.

An equity-efficiency trade-off?

The impact of job security regulations on economic efficiency has been at the forefront of discussions on labour market (de)regulation. Proponents of deregulation, who as we have seen criticized European dismissal laws as a cause of unemployment, further rebuked them as the paradigmatic example of labour market 'rigidities', that hamper the efficient management of enterprises and impair the 'flexibility' so necessary for maintaining competitiveness in the New Economy.

It appears that there is indeed some adverse impact on efficiency, but it will be argued here that this impact is rather trivial in magnitude. This chapter is

two explanations and a defence of the third see Robert M Solow, *The Labour Market as a Social Institution* (Blackwell 1990) 31–44. See also Deakin and Wilkinson (n 39).

186 Even this does not necessarily mean higher (overall) unemployment; while costs related to firing may deter employers from hiring in the first place, they also lessen the incidence of firing for those already employed. Empirical studies on the question of the overall impact on employment are inconclusive. See OECD, *Employment Outlook June 1999* (OECD 1999) ch 2; OECD, *Employment Outlook 2004* (n 154). Some studies have found that as a result of employment protection laws the employment rate among prime-age men is increased, while employment among young workers and women is decreased (see OECD, *Employment Outlook 2004* ibid). If this is the case, such laws are obviously problematic in terms of distributive justice, although this can probably be corrected with other policies (see Friedrich Buttler and Ulrich Walwei, 'Employment Security and Efficiency: Assumptions in the Current Debate and Empirical Evidence for West Germany' in Christoph F Buechtemann (ed), *Employment Security and Labor Market Behavior: Interdisciplinary Approaches and International Evidence* (ILR 1993) 264–65).

concerned only with regulations that are mandatory, in the sense that employers cannot contract out of them. Such a broad application of the 'just cause' rule implies that there are bound to be specific cases in which the opposite (EAW) regime would have been more efficient. Thus, for example, some young high-tech workers may feel secure enough in their ability to find good alternative jobs that they would rather 'sell' their 'just cause' rights in return for higher compensation, and such an arrangement might sometimes be altogether more efficient. But this seems like a relatively rare possibility. Much more important is whether a 'just cause' rule prevents efficient discharges. As we have noted, the laws under consideration here allow dismissals if an employer can substantiate incapability, misconduct, or redundancy. This covers almost any efficiency-related reason for dismissals.[187]

The inefficiency, where it exists, arises from the costs associated with having to *prove* the 'just cause': litigation costs (including related costs such as gathering the evidence), possible errors by adjudicators (which mean that a just cause was mistakenly not recognized),[188] and time lost until the need for redundancy dismissals is proven and, where necessary, the resulting dismissals negotiated. Such costs could be very significant for small employers.[189] Even litigation in one single case can prove to be highly costly for a very small business; and even just one incapable employee (reinstated in error) is a big problem for a business with, say, five employees overall. Moreover, the imposition of a personal employment relationship on a small employer may have a demoralizing effect which can further impair the efficiency of the small business. This explains the exclusion of small businesses from the scope of 'just cause' regulations in many countries.

The situation is completely different, however, with medium and large enterprises. Since employees have much less ability to endure costly litigation than their employers, the number of cases, and the accompanying costs, are bound

[187] See Christoph F Buechtemann, 'Introduction: Employment Security and Labor Markets' in Buechtemann (ed) ibid 61–62. Much of the discussion in Richard A Epstein, 'In Defense of the Contract at Will' (1984) 51 U Chi LR 947 and Epstein (n 168) shows why the ability to dismiss a worker is efficient, not why it is efficient to allow such dismissals even without a just cause. For example, Epstein puts much emphasis on the advantages of the at-will rule for monitoring performance, but seems to ignore the fact that a 'just cause' regime still allows dismissals for incapability or misconduct.

[188] If the laws are applied too rigidly, providing in effect *too much* job security, this is bound to cause inefficiencies. See, e.g., Andrea Ichino and Regina T Riphahn, 'The Effect of Employment Protection on Worker Effort: A Comparison of Absenteeism During and After Probation' (2004) IZA Discussion Paper No 385 <http://www.econstor.eu/bitstream/10419/21245/1/dp385.pdf> accessed 12 October 2015) (showing that 'just cause' regulations increase worker absenteeism).

[189] Although interestingly the empirical results are mixed; see Lothar Funk, 'Survey finds that Statutory Protection against Dismissal Hurts Small Firms' 2003 EIROnline 6 <http://www.eurofound.europa.eu/observatories/eurwork/articles/survey-finds-that-statutory-protection-against-dismissal-hurts-small-firms> accessed 12 October 2015; Benoit Freyens and Paul Oslington, 'Dismissal Costs and Their Impact on Employment: Evidence from Australian Small and Medium Enterprises' (2007) 83 The Economic Record 1; Dorothea Alewell, Eileen Schot, and Franziska Wiegand, 'The Impact of Dismissal Protection on Employers' Cost of Terminating Employment Relations in Germany: An Overview of Empirical Research and Its White Spots' (2008–2009) 30 CLLPJ 667.

to remain rather small when seen in light of larger firms' revenues.[190] Since the overall costs would remain rather small for the larger firms, a 'chilling effect' (i.e. hesitance by management to take the 'risk' of discharging employees even when there *is* a just cause) is not very likely. Similarly, since an incapable employee (reinstated in error) is only one of many for the larger employer, the resulting inefficiency is rather insignificant when seen in light of its overall operations.[191] The time lost before redundancy dismissals can be materialized could indeed be significant when too much 'red tape' is involved, but it certainly does not have to be so. At least in some countries there is evidence that the proceedings are prompt and efficient.[192]

'Just cause' regimes instituted in collective agreements often include procedural guarantees—a process for settling disputes about what constitutes 'just cause'. Sometimes these guarantees create cumbersome and lengthy proceedings, or even give the union *de facto* power to veto dismissals. When this is the case, obviously the risk of inefficiency is much higher.[193] This chapter is not concerned with justifying such arrangements, but only the substantive right not to be dismissed without cause.

There are two additional scenarios that should be considered in terms of potential inefficiencies. One is the possibility of replacing a senior employee with a younger (and just as good) employee who is cheaper to employ. The long-term efficiency of such a move is highly questionable given the adverse impact on the firm's reputation. Not to mention that in many cases such a move would amount to a breach of an implicit contract. One can always save some money in the short run by running away from commitments after enjoying the gains, but this is hardly efficient for society at large, nor even to oneself in the longer run. The second scenario is the replacement of an employee who is 'capable' but not extremely productive with someone who is more productive. This is presumably banned by 'just cause' regulations, yet efficient. But the standard of 'incapability' should allow employers to discharge employees who are less productive than what is reasonably expected. So the only margin left for an efficient yet banned management

[190] In this regard one must not look at the situation concerning wrongful discharge suits in the US, where litigation is particularly long and costly and damages awarded by juries are exceptionally high. In other countries, where a 'just cause' regime has been legislated, cases are referred to either an administrative tribunal or binding arbitration, where the proceedings are significantly faster and cheaper, and awards are much more modest. And see Walter Kamiat, 'Labor and Lemons: Efficient Norms in the Internal Labor Market and the Possible Failures of Individual Contracting' (1996) 144 U Pa LR 1953, 1964–65 (arguing that the problem of high costs in the context of wrongful discharge litigation in the US can be solved by the creation of low cost alternative dispute resolution systems for the enforcement of the right).

[191] For another assessment that the costs of unjust dismissal laws are modest, see Jeffrey M Hirsch, 'The Law of Termination: Doing More with Less' (2008) 68 Maryland LR 89, 152–57.

[192] See Schomann, Rogowski, and Kruppe (n 152). And see Thomas J Carter and Paul R De Lancey, 'Just, Unjust, and Just-Cause Dismissals' (1997) 19 J of Macroeconomics 619 (arguing that a law that requires employers to have greater evidence of shirking before firing a worker will have no effect on output or profits).

[193] See Guy Davidov and Edo Eshet, 'Intermediate Approaches to Unfair Dismissal Protection' (2015) 44 ILJ 167.

decision concerns the replacement of an employee who performs reasonably well with an *exceptionally* productive employee. There is no reason to believe that such occurrences are common.

The relatively modest inefficiencies are further counteracted by the efficiency-*enhancing* attributes of 'just cause' regulations. By preventing opportunistic and arbitrary dismissals, a 'just cause' regime diminishes irrational (and thus inefficient) decisions. It can also raise motivation and effort.[194] Perhaps most importantly, a 'just cause' rule may force firms to internalize some of the costs of dismissals and thus minimize externalities, which can be significant given the economic and social/psychological importance of the employment relationship to the employee. It can also promote the making of efficient firm-specific investments, and generally promote long-term and cooperative relationships, which are often efficient but do not fully materialize because of various market failures.[195] In addition, by making dismissals a bit more difficult, a 'just cause' regime can focus firms on their long-term interests, and prevent dismissals (which may turn out to be inefficient) in response to small fluctuations in demand.

The employer's autonomy

An additional argument against 'just cause' regulations concerns their impact on the employer's autonomy—her liberty to conduct the business as she sees fit and to employ whomever she wants. This argument is often couched in property terms. The business is seen as the property of the employer (or the shareholders), and this in turn is considered to imply a right to control every aspect of the business and its organization. Notwithstanding, as the legal realists taught us, there is nothing sacred or natural about the concept of 'property' and no rights are necessarily inherent in it. 'Property' is just a tool, which we can fill with content as we see fit. The business can just as well be seen as the property of the workers; and the rights of the employer to run the business can be qualified to ensure that societal values are respected. If one wishes to invoke the concept of property in the sense of control over resources, this must be based on the *justifications* for such control in a given context. The two main justifications that have been advanced in this regard revolve around efficiency and autonomy. Generally speaking, a right to control one's 'private property' can be justified on efficiency grounds and because of its importance to the realization of individual autonomy. In our own context, the question is whether 'just cause' laws are unjustified either because they are inefficient or because they infringe upon individual autonomy. The question of

[194] See Thomas Eger, 'Opportunistic Termination of Employment Contracts and Legal Protection against Dismissal in Germany and the USA' (2004) 23 Int Rev of Law and Econ 381. The contradictory argument, according to which effort will decline with job security since employees are certain of keeping their jobs, is untenable in the context of 'just cause' regulations that list incapability as a legitimate cause for dismissals.

[195] See Eger (n 194) 57.

efficiency has been discussed in the previous section. The employer's autonomy is considered below.

In the case of very small businesses, where the owner works alongside the employees, imposing the continuation of the relationship would be highly intrusive. Just as we would never impose the continuation of the employment relationship on an employee (that would be slavery) we should not impose such a personal relationship on the small employer. This would be inefficient, as noted in the previous section, but more importantly, it would seriously impinge upon the employer's personal liberty and autonomy. This does not mean that the small employer should not be required to give reasonable notice, pay severance payments, and so on (where these are deemed appropriate by society). It also does not mean that society should not invalidate dismissals due to specific impermissible reasons, such as pregnancy, even in small businesses. But small employers should be able to dismiss an employee whom they do not like, even if there are no objectively justified reasons for that. These considerations provide a further explanation for the exclusion of small employers from 'just cause' regulations.[196] In some legal systems the threshold may be in need of change. Perhaps it should be based more on the personal involvement of the owner than on the exact number of employees. But for our own purposes it is sufficient to note that the significant intrusions into the owner's autonomy in small businesses can and have been dealt with through their exclusion from the scope of the regulations.

The situation is completely different with medium and large enterprises, where the owners have no direct relationship with the employees. Considerations of liberty and autonomy and imposed personal relationships lose their weight. Aside from the case of small employers, then, arguments based on the employer's autonomy cannot justify termination without just cause.

Conclusion

We have seen that a 'just cause' law, which provides employees with some security, is justified on two main grounds: preventing unnecessary injuries to the social/psychological well-being of workers who depend on a particular relationship for such purposes; and ensuring a fair 'price' in terms of security in return for workers' submission to a democratically deficient regime. A number of considerations to the contrary have been discussed: the distributive impact of 'just cause' legislation (in terms of the impact on workers who are 'outsiders'), the potential inefficiencies and the infringement on the employers' autonomy.

[196] The issue is not merely the availability of reinstatement as a remedy. This can be solved simply by awarding damages instead of reinstatement when the latter is inappropriate or impractical due to the personal nature of the relationship (see Clyde W Summers, 'Individual Protection against Unjust Dismissal: Time for a Statute' (1976) 62 Va LR 481, 525). The issue is more generally the right of an employer not to work side by side with a worker she dislikes. If such a right is recognized, damages cannot be justified either.

The overall impact of the law changes from one legal system to another and from time to time. In some countries, the 'just cause' requirement is probably being applied too rigidly, with undesired results such as avoidance by employers of hiring 'risky' (e.g. young and inexperienced) employees.[197] In other countries, courts may be leaving too much room for managerial discretion.[198] This chapter cannot replace the need for a country-specific analysis. It does, however, provide a basis for such analyses.

[197] On this fear see Posner (n 182) 1635.

[198] See, e.g., Linda Dickens, 'Comparative Systems of Unjust Dismissal: The British Case' (1994) 536 Annals Am Acad Pol Soc Sci 43. An attempt by the British Employment Appeal Tribunal to change this interpretation of the law and institute a more 'interventionist' approach was overruled by the Court of Appeal soon afterwards. See *Haddon v Van der Bergh Foods Ltd* [1999] IRLR 672 (EAT) and *Foley v Post Office* [2000] ICR 1283 (CA), respectively. For additional critiques of the UK regime (which is seen as weak and ineffective), see Simon Deakin and Gillian S Morris, *Labour Law*, 6th edn (Hart 2012) 595–7; Joanna Howe, 'Poles Apart? The Contestation between the Ideas of No Fault Dismissal and Unfair Dismissal for Protecting Job Security' (2013) 42 ILJ 122, 149–50; David Cabrelli, *Employment Law in Context: Text and Materials* (OUP 2014) 585, 687–89.

II

MEANS

6

The Building Blocks of Labour Law: Employee and Employer

The questions of 'who is an employee' and 'who is an employer' have always been central problems in labour law, and they can be expected to remain so, due to the following structure which is common throughout the world. First, the coverage of labour legislation is usually defined by reference to 'employer' and 'employee' (or similar terms), so being in these groups carries with it significant implications in terms of rights or obligations. Second, labour legislation rarely includes any guidance regarding the meaning of these terms, so courts were given in practice broad discretion to interpret them and decide the scope (coverage) of labour laws.

In recent years a broad agreement has emerged among academics, as well as courts, that the terms 'employee' and 'employer' should be interpreted purposively.[1] Such proclamations—although important—have not yet led to an in-depth discussion of goals/purposes, and even more uncommon is any attempt to draw direct conclusions from such a discussion for setting the scope of the law. Rather, the reference to a purposive approach has usually meant sensitivity to economic realities, with a focus on the real arrangements between the parties instead of a formalistic reliance on the written terms of the contract. The adoption of a purposive approach in principle and the attempt to decipher the reality of the relationship are welcome and highly important developments. But they are not sufficient. The next (and crucial) step is to understand the purpose of these legislative terms and offer an interpretation based on such an analysis. This is the goal of the current chapter. I will supplement this interpretive discussion with some suggestions, along the way, for specific legislative corrections that can assist in advancing the goals of labour law.

Part I is devoted to the age-old distinction between 'employee' and 'independent contractor', which over the years has attracted most of the interest in the

[1] See, e.g., Marc Linder, 'Dependent and Independent Contractors in Recent U.S. Labor Law: An Ambiguous Dichotomy Rooted in Simulated Statutory Purposelessness' (1999) 21 CLLPJ 187; Brian Langille and Guy Davidov, 'Beyond Employees and Independent Contractors: A View from Canada' (1999) 21 CLLPJ 6; Mark Freedland and Nicola Kountouris, *The Legal Construction of Personal Work Relations* (OUP 2011). And see *Autoclenz Ltd v Belcher* [2011] UKSC 41 (UK Supreme Court); *Pointe-Claire (City) v Quebec* (1997) 1 SCR 1015 (Supreme Court of Canada); HCJ 4601/95 *Sarusi v National Labor Court* (1998) 52(4) PD 817 (Supreme Court of Israel); *Konrad v Victoria Police* (1999) 165 ALR 23 (Federal Court of Australia).

case-law and literature. Part II will address the issue of intermediate categories, such as 'dependent contractors', 'employee-likes', or 'workers'. Finally, Part III examines the 'employer' concept, first in the context of temporary employment agencies and then in the context of subcontracting.

Part I—Employee vs Independent Contractor

Paul Huntington worked as a car cleaner for 17 years. He was engaged by a company named Autoclenz. Together with nineteen other 'valeters', Huntington sued because they were paid less than the minimum wage (as set by the UK National Minimum Wage Act) and were not given paid leave (as required by the UK Working Time Regulations). The company claimed that they were not entitled to such rights, because they were self-employed sub-contractors; so said, very explicitly, the contract. Eventually, the UK Supreme Court decided to look beyond the written terms drafted by the employer's lawyers, and to consider the *real* agreement between the parties—as reflected by their actual expectations from each other. This has led quite easily to the conclusion that the car cleaners were, in fact, employees.[2]

The Court maintained that the general laws of contract apply, and require an examination of unwritten and implied terms alongside the written explicit ones. Importantly, it added that employment relations are different from other commercial relations, and 'the relative bargaining power of the parties must be taken into account'.[3] This was described by Lord Clarke, writing for the Court, as a 'purposive approach'.[4]

Towards a rich purposive approach

The insistence of the Court in *Autoclenz* on examining the reality of the relationship can genuinely be described as purposive, in the sense that the National Minimum Wage Act and the Working Time Regulations were obviously enacted to protect workers who need such protection, rather than be limited to those designated by their employers as entitled to protection. A formalistic approach to the interpretation of 'employee' which relies mostly on the terms of the contract is quite obviously anti-purposive. It gives significant weight to provisions drafted by the employer (or its lawyers), often with the explicit intention of avoiding responsibility towards the worker. There is little doubt that labour laws were not enacted with the purpose of allowing employers an easy route to exclude their workers from the scope of protection.

Preventing sham arrangements—in which the facts 'on the ground' make it very clear that the work is performed through an employment relationship—is thus a crucial starting point.[5] But a purposive approach offers much more. Alan

[2] *Autoclenz Ltd* (n 1). [3] ibid para 35. [4] ibid.

[5] And see ACL Davies, 'Sensible Thinking about Sham Transactions: Protectacoat Firthglow Ltd v Szilagy' (2009) 38 ILJ 318. See also ILO R198: Employment Relationship Recommendation (95th ILC Session Geneva 15 June 2006) art 9.

Bogg and Julie McClelland have both called on the Court to take the purposive approach further. For Bogg, this could mean resolving any interpretive doubts in favour of the putative worker, perhaps even creating a presumption of employee status.[6] For McClelland, a truly purposive approach would lead the courts to insert a degree of fairness into contracts based on unequal bargaining power.[7] My own proposal is less far-reaching in terms of the role of courts and their legitimacy, yet arguably could have even more impact. By using purposive interpretation we can (and should) rethink the tests and indicia used to distinguish between employees and independent contractors in 'grey areas'—when the real characteristics of the relationship do not point clearly in one direction. These tests and indicia were developed by courts, so there is no doubt that courts can also change them. Also it is difficult to justify tests and indicia that have been developed to decide who should be covered by labour laws, but are detached from the purpose of such laws.[8]

The term 'employee' appears in various pieces of labour legislation. Should it have the exact same meaning in all of them? General principles of statutory interpretation suggest that this should be the starting point, although it is possible to deviate from this rule. When the legislature refers to the same term in different laws that deal with the same subject-matter—laws *in pari materia*—there is a presumption that the term has the same meaning.[9] This makes perfect sense when thinking about labour legislation. The assumption behind the various pieces of labour legislation is that people can sell their labour power either as 'employees' or as independent contractors. Performing work for the benefit of others is not always subject to labour laws. When people have their own independent business—when they work as independent contractors—the general contract laws apply, and labour regulations do not. While this cannot be a clear-cut dichotomy,[10] the basic distinction is still valid. In some general sense, then, the reasons for enacting a minimum wage law are similar to the reasons behind working time regulations, and any other labour legislation: there is something about some work relations (which we usually call employment) that separates them from other work relations (which we classify as contractor–client relations) and justifies the subjection of the

6 Alan L Bogg, 'Sham Self-Employment in the Supreme Court' (2012) 41 ILJ 328, 343.

7 Julie McClelland, 'A Purposive Approach to Employment Protection or a Missed Opportunity?' (2012) 75 MLR 427, 433.

8 In his highly important and influential contribution, Hugh Collins expressed scepticism about a purposive approach (Hugh Collins, 'Independent Contractors and the Challenge of Vertical Disintegration to Employment Protection Laws' (1990) 10 OJLS 353, 377). But apparently this was only directed against a case-by-case subjective analysis which tries to reach a solution in line with the purpose, as opposed to the method supported here which is to devise the tests purposively. In fact, Collins himself throughout his article made it clear that he was looking for a solution that will ensure a connection between the group of 'employees' and the goals of addressing subordination and dependency.

9 See Francis J McCaffrey, 'The Rule in Pari Materia as an Aid to Statutory Construction' (1949) 3 Law & L Notes 11; William N Eskridge Jr, 'Public Values in Statutory Interpretation' (1989) 137 U Pa LR 1007, 1039–40.

10 See Douglas Brodie, 'Fair Dealing and the World of Work' (2014) 43 ILJ 29; Guy Davidov, 'Setting Labour Law's Coverage: Between Universalism and Selectivity' (2014) 34 OJLS 543.

former to heavy regulatory intervention (which we call labour law). Different laws will surely have some additional, more specific goals—which could lead to some adjustments in the interpretation of basic terms.[11] But the general goals are the same and should inform our interpretation of the legislative terms setting labour laws' scope.

So a purposive approach means that the term 'employee' should be interpreted in light of the purposes (goals) of labour law. It is used in labour legislation as the term setting the scope of the law (its coverage). It is not defined, at least not in detail, so courts were intentionally given the power to give this term meaning and set its boundaries. They should do so with the goals of labour law in mind—to ensure that the purpose behind these laws is advanced rather than being frustrated. This brings to the forefront the question: what is the goal (or what are the goals) of labour law that should be the basis of our interpretation?

Choosing the goals that can guide interpretation

In Chapters 3 and 4 various different goals and articulations were considered. For current purposes we will have to choose a level of abstraction/generalization that can help us make the differentiation between the different groups. The 'universal' goals seem less helpful for this task. If we think about labour laws as designed to maximize capabilities or human freedom, for example, it would be difficult to explain why some people performing work (employees) need such regulations and others (independent contractors) do not.[12] Current labour laws clearly were not intended to cover independent contractors, and we need to interpret them accordingly. Similarly, if we see capabilities as our main goal, we will have to provide an additional explanation of why some labourers need legislative intervention to maximize their capabilities, while others can presumably achieve a sufficient level of capabilities' materialization when operating in the 'free market' with the general law of contracts. The distinction between these two groups is, after all, the whole point of purposive interpretation in this context, and by pointing to capabilities we do not address this problem at all. The same is true with regard to advancing democracy or human rights—or any other goal of the more 'universal' kind (or otherwise abstract values).

What about countering inequality of bargaining power? This will probably be the intuitive response of most labour lawyers, when asked to identify the basis for the distinction between employees and independent contractors. However, as explained in Chapter 3, inequality of bargaining power is too vague to offer such guidance. Notwithstanding the rhetorical power of this phrase, we know that in fact there is never equality between the parties to a contract, nor do we expect or

[11] Brian Langille and Pnina Alon-Shenker, 'Law Firm Partners and the Scope of Labour Laws' (2015) 4 Can J Hum Rts 211.

[12] This could, indeed, lead some to conclude that labour laws should be extended to independent contractors as well. I discuss such claims separately in the next section.

require such equality. I have argued that inequality of bargaining power is best understood as a shorthand for market failures and subordination, but added that it would be better to refer directly to these characteristics.

It seems, then, that the most useful level of abstraction is the one focusing on the unique characteristics of employment relations: on the vulnerability of employees in terms of (a) democratic deficits (or subordination, broadly conceived) and (b) dependency on the specific relationship for economic as well as social/psychological needs (in the sense of inability to spread risks). When these vulnerabilities exist, the person performing the work for another appears to be in need of protection—the kind of protection provided by labour laws. Some laws address only one of these vulnerabilities (for example, dependency, even without the existence of subordination). Others have additional goals that may require, as noted above, adjustments. But a general look at the body of labour laws as a whole suggests that they are designed to counteract these two vulnerabilities.[13]

This means that any tests or indicia used to identify 'employees' should be based—at least as a starting point (before the goals of the specific regulation are considered)—on democratic deficits and dependency. This will ensure that people who work for others and suffer from these vulnerabilities will be covered by labour laws, while those who are not vulnerable in these ways will be excluded. If one agrees that the goal of labour law—or at least one important goal of labour law—is to counteract these vulnerabilities, or solve problems resulting from them, then designing tests and indicia based on these vulnerabilities is what the purposive approach requires.

Can subordination (democratic deficits) and dependency serve as the actual tests? In other words, is it possible to examine, in every specific case, whether these vulnerabilities exist, and decide the status of the person performing work accordingly? Given the need for a reasonable degree of determinacy and a reasonable ability of workers and employers to know their rights and duties, this does not seem realistic. There is no choice but to develop some more concrete indicia that will help the courts, and especially the parties themselves, understand the legal situation. It is nonetheless possible, and advisable in my view, to consider the two vulnerabilities as ultimate tests that can assist in difficult cases. Otherwise put, when applying the more concrete indicia, one must always remember what their ultimate goal is: to identify situations of subordination and dependency.

Pausing to reconsider the distinction

Although the main goal of this chapter is interpretive—in the context of the current part, to give meaning to the term 'employee' that appears in labour legislation—it would be pertinent to pause, at this stage, and ask whether the entire employee–independent contractor distinction makes sense. Some scholars

[13] This approach was recently adopted by the Supreme Court of Canada; see *McCormick v Fasken Martineau DuMoulin* [2014] 2 SCR 108.

have argued that independent contractors have become so similar to employees, that there is no discernible difference that can justify the distinction any longer.[14] If this is correct, then the purpose of the distinction is no longer being served; or to put this otherwise, the distinction no longer advances the goals of labour law. Nevertheless, if we think about the genuine independent contractor—i.e. a plumber, or a consultant, or otherwise the owner of a very small business operating the business by herself—there are obvious differences from the paradigmatic employee. Such a small business can certainly suffer economic vulnerability, and perhaps have little bargaining power when contracting with bigger enterprises. But the unique vulnerabilities described in Chapter 3 as characterizing employment are not there. Neither the subordination to someone else; nor the inability to spread risks, resulting in dependency on the specific relationship, for economic as well as social/psychological needs. So in principle, the difference *does* exist. The genuine independent contractor does not require protection of laws designed to counter these specific vulnerabilities.

Let us pinpoint the possible arguments against the distinction, then. One argument could be that the 'genuine independent contractor' just described simply does not exist any longer. This would be untenable on its face; we see small businesses of independent contractors (who do not appear to be in a situation of subordination and dependency) around us, in any developed economy. The less extreme version of the argument is this: The number of genuine independent contractors is relatively small,[15] and in contrast, the costs of administering the distinction are high, especially in terms of employees close to the 'grey area' who end up being excluded. Given these costs, the 'price' of maintaining the distinction is higher than the benefit—we should simply extend labour law's protection to all people that perform work for others. A third argument is that the distinction is overused, in the sense that some protections that are given only to employees are not in fact directed against the two vulnerabilities of employees, and so should be extended to independent contractors as well. This is not an argument against the distinction in principle, only against the way it is being used by the legislature. A fourth and final argument is this: the clear-cut distinction between 'employees' who are subject to subordination and dependency and independent contractors who are subject to none fails to represent the complexities of real life. In practice,

[14] See Adrian Brooks, 'Myth and Muddle–An Examination of Contracts for the Performance of Work' (1988) 11 U of New South Wales LJ 48; Linder (n 1); Richard R Carlson, 'Why the Law Still Can't Tell an Employee When It Sees One and How It Ought to Stop Trying' (2001) 22 BJELL 295; Eric Tucker, Judy Fudge, and Leah Vosko, 'Employee or Independent Contractor? Charting the Legal Significance of the Distinction in Canada' (2002) 10 CLELJ 193.

[15] Fudge brings data to show that many of those currently considered independent contractors in fact have some of the characteristics of employees (Judy Fudge, 'Fragmenting Work and Fragmenting Organizations: The Contract of Employment and the Scope of Labour Regulation' (2006) 44 Osgoode Hall LJ 609). However, this should be read together with the fact that the percentage of self-employment in the labour market has been on the rise (see Leah F Vosko, *Managing the Margins: Gender, Citizenship, and the International Regulation of Precarious Employment* (OUP 2010) ch 6). Arguably this rise is mostly the result of growing misclassification, and the number of genuine independent contractors has not changed much.

there are many people who fall in-between, especially those who have a small business but are dependent on one or two major clients.[16]

The last three arguments are valid and important; they should lead to major changes in the way the employee–independent contractor distinction is being used and applied. They do not, though, justify the abolition of the distinction altogether. If one accepts the basic premise that there are genuine independent contractors in the market alongside people who have the characteristics of employees, then it is important to limit the protection directed at counteracting subordination and dependency to those who really need it. Otherwise, if we extend such protection too broadly, it will necessarily lead to lowering the level of protection. Imagine that when you invite a plumber to fix your sink, or consult with a self-employed lawyer, you will have the duties of an employer—and they will have the rights of employees—in terms of vacations, maximum hours, etc. How much can we demand from clients of independent contractors? Not a lot. Certainly less than what we currently demand from employers whose employees are subordinated to them and dependent on them. So the standards can be expected to quickly deteriorate.[17]

Still, the problems with the employee–independent contractor distinction can (and should) be addressed, in several ways. First, the distinction should be applied in a way that ensures that people who are formally considered independent contractors but in fact are not genuine contractors—those who actually have the characteristics of employees—will be legally considered 'employees'. This is the goal of the current part: to offer tests that can achieve the goals of the distinction and better prevent misclassification. Second, some laws that are included in labour law and apply only to employees should be extended to others as well—if they are not limited (given their purpose) to addressing the vulnerabilities of employment. In some cases protection should be extended to all residents (e.g. health care), in other cases to all those working for others, including independent contractors (e.g. health and safety, anti-discrimination).[18] But there is still a significant body of regulations designed to address the vulnerabilities of subordination and dependency. Third, an intermediate category should exist to ensure protection for those who are dependent but not subordinate—the small businesses that have characteristics of an independent business in terms of making their own decisions (i.e. no subordination) but are still dependent on one major client. This intermediate category of 'dependent contractors'—which exists in a growing number of legal systems—is a necessary correction to the rigidity of the original distinction. This is discussed in Part II below.

[16] I discuss some of these arguments in more detail in Guy Davidov, 'The Reports of My Death are Greatly Exaggerated: "Employee" as a Viable (Though Overly-used) Legal Concept' in Guy Davidov and Brian Langille (eds), *Boundaries and Frontiers of Labour Law* (Hart 2006) 133.

[17] See also Jessica A Clarke, 'Beyond Equality? Against the Universal Turn in Workplace Protections' (2011) 86 Indiana LJ 1219, 1225.

[18] See Alain Supiot, *Beyond Employment: Changes in Work and the Future of Labour Law in Europe* (OUP 2001).

The structure of the test

So we need to distinguish between employees and independent contractors. We need to identify the group of workers that should enjoy the protection of labour laws. Is it possible to create a clear-cut definition in legislation? The advantage would be clear: indeterminacy is extremely costly, leading to never-ending litigation; but even more troublesome, it plays to the hands of the stronger party. The more 'grey areas' there are, the more employers can legitimately claim ignorance or good faith when misclassifying employees as independent contractors. Indeterminacy means that a large number of workers in 'grey areas' will not be able to enjoy labour laws unless they go to court to enforce their rights—an unlikely prospect for most of them. Nonetheless, as tempting as it is, a clear-cut definition is likely to fail, which explains why such attempts have been very rare and were not considered successful.[19] It is not possible to capture the entire complexity of work relations. If we define employment relations based on concrete characteristics A, B, and C, employers are likely to alter the relationship to some extent (for example, using D instead of C) to evade the costs and responsibility attached to employment. It is not possible to list all the characteristics that justify protection, unless we use more abstract tests, at a higher level of generalization—making the distinction more indeterminate.

There are some useful methods to gain more determinacy, without opening the door for employers to 'work around' a detailed definition. This is possible by creating *presumptions* alongside the general tests. The legislature can say, for example, that a worker earning less than X Euros per month, or who has only one or two 'clients', is an 'employee'—unless proven otherwise; without detracting from the possibility that a worker earning more or having more clients is also an employee—if the tests lead to that conclusion. In recent years presumptions have been adopted in many legal systems.[20] An additional method to gain more determinacy is by determining in regulations that workers in a specific sector doing a specific kind of work will be *deemed* to be employees automatically, without leaving room for employers to contest this status.[21]

Another structural question is whether we need one single test—a unified meaning of the term 'employee' for all labour law purposes—or rather allow room for variations and nuances. Otherwise put: should the coverage of labour law be

[19] See Guy Davidov, Mark Freedland, and Nicola Kountouris, 'The Subjects of Labor Law: "Employees" and Other Workers' in Matthew Finkin and Guy Mundlak (eds), *Research Handbook in Comparative Labor Law* (Edward Elgar 2015) 115.

[20] ibid. See also ILO 2006 (n 5), art 11(b); and see International Labour Conference (91st Session) Report V: The Scope of the Employment Relationship (Geneva 2003); ILO, 'The Employment Relationship: an Annotated Guide to ILO Recommendation No. 198' (2007) 27<http://www.ilo.org/wcmsp5/groups/public/@ed_dialogue/@dialogue/documents/genericdocument/wcms_172417.pdf> accessed 13 October 2015 (ILO 2007); ILO, 'Regulating the Employment Relationship in Europe: a Guide to Recommendation No. 198' (2013) 28 <www.ilo.org/wcmsp5/groups/public/---ed_dialogue/---dialogue/documents/publication/wcms_209280.pdf> accessed 13 October 2015 (ILO 2013).

[21] See ILO 2006 (n 5), art 11(c); ILO 2007, ibid 29; ILO 2013, ibid 30.

universal, or should we also leave room for *selective* schemes that apply only for specific groups? Obviously there is some selectivity within labour laws, which sometimes include exceptions/exemptions. The question is whether more nuances in the scope of labour law should be achieved through purposive interpretation of the term 'employee'.

Universalism has several important advantages, which can be learned from the welfare state literature.[22] First, universal labour laws are likely to enjoy broader support and more durability and stability, compared with laws that protect only a small specific group. Second, they are more likely to reach a larger segment of the population that needs them: the fact that the same laws apply to all workers makes it easier for them to know their rights and enforce them (and more difficult for employers to evade). This is highly important in the labour law context: it means more determinacy and higher levels of compliance with the law. Third, universal labour laws are better in fostering solidarity and promoting social cohesion.

In contrast, selective labour laws have their own advantages. They are more efficient and arguably more just in targeting benefits to those who really need them. There is an advantage in providing special protection for those with special needs/vulnerabilities—regulations that are better tailored to the actual needs of different workers. Universal laws are likely to be designed based on the lowest common denominator, or at best the needs of the mean worker—not the most vulnerable. In a similar vein, selective programmes can be used to provide partial protection for those who need only the protection of some laws (and not the entire bundle of rights)—for example dependent contractors. Under a universal scheme such workers are usually excluded altogether because they do not fall into the 'regular' group of employees; but if we assume that they share some of the characteristics (and vulnerabilities) of employees, they can and should enjoy selective application of relevant laws.

We need, therefore, a balance between universalism and selectivity. In the current context, the optimal balance can be achieved by having a universal system but allowing some exceptions. The default rule should be universal: if one is an 'employee' then the entire bundle of labour laws applies. Room for exceptions can be achieved in two ways: first, the category of dependent contractors (or a similar intermediate category)—if one exists in legislation; second, extensions or exceptions based on the purpose of the specific legislation—when this is justified. The first 'selective' solution is discussed in Part II below. The second is not considered here; but would be based on an analysis of specific goals as performed in Chapter 5.[23]

[22] I discuss this at more length in Davidov (n 10); Guy Davidov, 'Special Protection for Cleaners: A Case of Justified Selectivity?' (2015) 36 CLLPJ 217. For further discussion of these issues see Einat Albin, 'From Domestic Servant to Domestic Worker' in Judy Fudge, Shae McCrystal, and Kamala Sankaran (eds), *Challenging the Legal Boundaries of Work Regulation* (Hart 2012) 231; Einat Albin, *Sectoral Disadvantage: The Case of Workers in the British Hospitality Sector* (Unpublished PhD dissertation, University of Oxford, 2010).

[23] For an example of interpreting the term 'employee' based on the goals of a *specific* regulation see Langille and Alon-Shenker (n 11) (arguing that the concept of 'employee' should receive broad interpretation for the purpose of age discrimination claims).

The test that has been developed by courts in different countries usually includes one or more indicators that are considered necessary—one cannot be considered an 'employee' without them—and then a long list of indicia that are not necessary, nor sufficient, but are rather considered together to create one whole picture. This seems like a logical structure. Accordingly, I start below by asking which indicators (if at all) are necessary, and should form a preliminary test.

The preliminary (threshold) requirements

Are there threshold requirements that must be met, as a preliminary matter, in order for one to be considered an employee rather than an independent contractor? Courts and legislatures in many legal systems require the work to be performed personally.[24] If the agreement is for certain work to be performed but the person providing the service can send whoever he wants to actually perform the work, this is seen as a clear sign of an independent business, negating the possibility of access to employment rights.[25] Is this justified, from a purposive point of view? Mark Freedland and Nicola Kountouris insist that it is.[26] Because they see the goals of labour law as maximizing dignity, capabilities, and stability, they envision a focus on the person and personhood.[27] In contrast, Douglas Brodie has recently argued that there is a trend towards convergence in the standards that apply on contracts for the provision of work, whether as part of employment or not.[28] He sees this as justified because contracts for services are often characterized by inequality of bargaining power very similar to the one characterizing employment relations.[29] Brodie's analysis is limited to general standards of good faith and fair dealing (as opposed to the application of employment legislation), and he does not refute the relevance of personal relations to the need of protection altogether;[30] notwithstanding, his analysis does raise doubts about the insistence on a personal commitment to perform the work as a necessary precondition for entering into labour law's scope.

As far as economic dependency is concerned, there is indeed much resemblance between the employee dependent on one employer and a very small business dependent on one client. This could justify the application of some labour laws on this group: for example laws setting minimum wages, permitting collective bargaining, requiring advance notice before termination, and ensuring that wages

[24] See, e.g., *Ron Shmuel v Representatives of the Condominium* (1970) 1 PDA 42 (Israeli National Labour Court); Employment Rights Act 1996 (UK) s 230. In some countries this is not a threshold requirement but rather considered together with the other indicia. This is also the way it appears in ILO 2006 (n 5), art 13. However, it seems that in practice it is usually applied as a threshold requirement even when this is not explicit.

[25] Usually a rare instance of asking someone for help or to replace you is not seen as preventing employee status. See, e.g., *Ready-Mixed Concrete (South East) Ltd v Minister of Pensions* [1968] 2 QB 497 (QB).

[26] Mark Freedland and Nicola Kountouris, *The Legal Construction of Personal Work Relations* (OUP 2011) 33.

[27] ibid 369ff. [28] Brodie (n 10). [29] ibid 46. [30] ibid 46–47.

are paid in time and in cash (wage protection laws)—all regulations that address, at least for the most part, economic dependency. Indeed, I will argue below (in the next part) that these regulations should be extended to all dependent contractors as well. However, there are several reasons to retain the requirement of personal relations as far as employment relations are concerned. First, the degree of dependency will usually be different, because even a very small business has at least *some* ability to spread risks through the different contracts with employees, suppliers, etc. Moreover, even with dependency on one major client, a small business will usually have additional clients as well, adding some more ability to spread risks. I assume, of course, that the small business has some characteristics of a 'real' business and is not part of a sham arrangement designed to avoid employment rights (in which case, the relationship could actually be personal). If the business is real, then even if it is very small and has only one major client, economic dependency is likely to be lower than that experienced by employees in a personal relationship.

Second, while some labour laws confront economic dependency, other labour laws directly address problems of individuals working in person, for example laws setting maximum hours, rights to annual vacation or sick days, time off for maternity/parental leave, and protection against unfair dismissals. Such regulations address the other vulnerabilities mentioned above: democratic deficits and dependency for social and psychological needs. Or they can be seen, at another level of abstraction, as designed to protect dignity, health, etc.—all *human* needs not relevant for non-personal relations. Obviously at the end of the line there is work performed by people, but the point is that only the people personally can be seen as employees entitled to such rights, and not the company/small business employing them. It could be that the 'client' should in fact be considered their 'real' employer, or a joint employer, in some cases—this will be discussed separately in Part III below.

The third justification for the 'personal relations' threshold is the limits of statutory interpretation. We can decide to extend specific regulations to non-personal relations as well, but this will have to be done through legislative amendments, because the term 'employee' or 'worker' probably cannot bear a non-personal meaning. Sometimes this is made explicitly clear in the legislation; the UK Employment Rights Act, for example, defines 'employee' as working under a 'contract of employment', which in turn is defined as a contract 'of service'—a term contrasted with a contract 'for services', the former being inherently of a personal nature.[31] The definition of the broader 'worker' category in the same legislation further clarifies this point: a 'worker' includes those working under a contract of employment, as well as other contracts 'whereby the individual undertakes to do or perform *personally* any work…' not through a business undertaking.[32] In other countries, even when there is no definition explicitly excluding non-personal

[31] Employment Rights Act 1996 (UK) ss 230(1) and 230(2).
[32] ibid s 230(3) (my emphasis).

relations, arguably this is implied by the linguistic meaning of the term—placing an outer boundary on the breadth of possible interpretations.[33]

So while it seems justified to extend some specific regulations (perhaps many) to non-personal work relations as well, this is not true for all labour laws; it is not clear that it is justified to apply such regulations in the exact same way (given differences in the degree of economic dependency); and it is not possible to do by way of interpretation. It seems best, therefore, to retain the personal relations requirement as a general rule, and consider extensions by way of legislative amendments for specific regulations.[34]

Another threshold requirement, which has been applied specifically by UK courts, is 'mutuality of obligations'.[35] Although it is increasingly being questioned if the employment relationship must be considered contractual,[36] this is relevant mostly for special situations such as the rights of elected officials or prison labour. Even if one accepts the proposition that an employment relationship is possible without a contract, it will not change the fact that in most cases—the paradigmatic cases—employment is based on a contract. As in any contractual relationship, there is mutuality of obligations in the sense of reciprocal promises—and in common law, consideration is necessary for the creation of a binding contract. Yet, the threshold developed in the UK for the purpose of identifying 'employee' status is quite different:[37] It is a requirement of an 'umbrella' or 'global' contract for continuous employment, as opposed to a series of short-term engagements. Although UK courts have recognized the possibility of 'intermittent' employment contracts—i.e. a series of one-time separate engagements, without an 'umbrella' contract—such cases lead to very minimal protection, because many labour rights and benefits depend on the existence of some tenure.[38] The mutuality of obligations doctrine attracted stringent critiques, and rightly so.[39] It provides employers with an easy route to evade responsibilities towards those working for them,[40]

[33] The recently adopted restatement of US employment law–which attempts to offer a clear and simplified description of US law–defines 'employee' by reference to 'an individual' (American Law Institute, *Restatement of the Law: Employment Law* (2015) s 1.01).

[34] Thus, for example, FedEx drivers who hire others to help or replace them on a regular basis should be classified as 'dependent contractors' and not employees. See the next part for this intermediate category. However, if in practice the drivers almost always perform the work themselves, they should be treated as employees notwithstanding the theoretical right to hire replacements. For conflicting decisions about the status of FedEx drivers in the US, see *Slayman v FedEx Ground Package Sys*, 765 F 3d 1033 (9th Cir 2014); *FedEx Home Delivery v NLRB*, 563 F 3d 492 (DC Cir 2009).

[35] On the British exceptionalism in this context see Nicola Countouris, 'Uses and Misuses of "Mutuality of Obligations" and the Autonomy of Labour Law' in A Bogg and others (eds), *The Autonomy of Labour Law* (Hart 2015) 169.

[36] See, e.g., Freedland and Kountouris (n 26) 47; HCJ 1163/98 *Ofer Sadot v Israel Prison Service* 55 PD 814 (2001) (Supreme Court of Israel).

[37] Simon Deakin and Gillian S Morris, *Labour Law* (6th edn, Hart 2012) 164.

[38] See, e.g., Employment Rights Act 1996 s 108(1). And see Deakin and Morris (n 37) 200; ACL Davies, 'The Contract for Intermittent Employment' (2007) 36 ILJ 102.

[39] See, e.g., Deakin and Morris (n 37) 165–69; Hugh Collins, 'Employment Rights of Casual Workers' (2000) 29 ILJ 73; ACL Davies, 'Casual Workers and Continuity of Employment' (2006) 35 ILJ 196; Countouris (n 35).

[40] Prime examples are *O'Kelly v Trusthouse Forte plc* [1983] ICR 728 (CA); *Carmichael v National Power plc* [2000] IRLR 43 (HL).

by adding clauses defining the relationship as casual (on a daily basis) with no obligation on either side to work or employ the next day—even when in practice the work is regular and continuous. This route is perhaps partially closed now as a result of the *Autoclenz* decision in which the Supreme Court showed greater willingness to reject sham arrangements. But the basic requirement has not been withdrawn; so in cases of relations that are truly with 'no obligation'—for example when a restaurant owner has a pool of waiters, telephoning several of them each evening and offering them work, without engaging anyone on a regular basis—the workers will be excluded from the scope of most labour laws.

From a purposive point of view this cannot be justified. Quite obviously, in the sham 'no obligation' contracts that actually attach to regular ongoing employment, there are subordination and dependency and a need for labour laws' protection. The truly casual workers are not less in need of protection—in fact they are even more vulnerable. Even if there is no 'umbrella contract' for continuous and regular employment, this does not point to the existence of an independent business. Moreover, arguably there is still an 'umbrella contract' by which the employer and the worker agree that the latter will be on the former's 'on-call' list, and they agree on the wage that shall apply when the worker is called and agrees to come to work. It is highly likely that subordination and dependency still exist in such cases, exacerbated by lack of stability and security. It is the purpose of labour laws to protect workers whether they have an 'umbrella contract' for continuous and regular employment or not.

To conclude, the only preliminary (necessary) requirement that can be justified is that the work has to be performed personally (subject to insignificant exceptions of occasional help). This will exclude from the scope of 'employee' businesses that have to provide a service and can send their own (different) employees to do so.

The possible indicia determining employment status

Once a relationship has passed the preliminary requirement, we are still left with the task of separating employees from independent contractors who perform the work personally. The purposive approach makes it clear that our goal is to distinguish between workers who need the protection of labour laws and those who do not. As noted above, ultimately the difference seems to be based on the existence of two vulnerabilities: subordination and dependency. The various indicia used by courts to determine 'employee' status should be understood in this light: as aides to identify these vulnerabilities. It must be stressed that the meaning of 'subordination' and 'dependency' should be based on an understanding of the vulnerabilities characterizing employment and explaining the need of labour laws—as explained in detail in Chapter 3—as opposed to the more technical meaning often adopted by courts for these terms.

The first question we are faced with is whether both of the vulnerabilities are required for one to be considered an 'employee'. Given the use of the same term in various labour laws, our starting point (as noted above) is that we need a general understating of who is an employee, which we can later deviate from if and when there are specific justifications to do so. The general understating has to be based on the typical case, of an 'employee' subject to the full 'package' of labour laws. It has already been noted that some labour laws could be justified for anyone in a position of economic dependency, but others provide protection specifically for people in a position of subordination. This leads to the conclusion that the term 'employee' should be based on the existence of both vulnerabilities.[41]

The list below includes various indicia that are used in different legal systems. I consider the suitability of each indicator, in turn, to identify subordination or dependency. The first eleven indicia are taken from the ILO's Employment Relationship Recommendation,[42] which itself is based on indicia common in many different countries.[43]

(1) The worker (W) is performing the work under the control/instructions of the employer (E). This indeed indicates the existence of subordination, in the sense of democratic deficits. Courts usually look for the *right* to control rather than actual control, to avoid the exclusion of workers who because of the nature of their occupation/tasks are not subject to daily instructions.[44] This may seem confusing, because as noted we are not interested in the written terms, but in the reality of the relationship. However, it is indeed important to note that direct day-to-day control is not necessary for the creation of subordination. This has led many legal systems to adopt the next indicator.

(2) W is integrated into E's organization. This includes being subject to organizational rules and discipline,[45] which can be termed 'administrative'

[41] The degree can vary, as I explain in the next section; i.e. a minimal degree of subordination can suffice if there is strong dependency, and vice versa. Still, one might wonder, if many labour laws should apply based on dependency alone, why not use the term 'employee' based on this characteristic and extend the additional protections to some 'employee plus' category which includes subordination as well? The reason is a practical one: the large majority of workers are still in a position of both dependency and subordination. It is therefore useful to treat them as the default category, and deviate from this category as needed, rather than the other way around.

[42] ILO 2006 (n 5), art 13. For explanations see also ILO 2007 (n 20) 42.

[43] For comparative reviews of the tests used to distinguish between 'employees' and independent contractors, see Guy Davidov, 'The Three Axes of Employment Relationship: A Characterization of Workers in Need of Protection' (2002) 52 UTLJ 357, 365–71; Nicola Countouris, *The Changing Law of the Employment Relationship: Comparative Analyses in the European Context* (Ashgate 2013); Giuseppe Casale (ed), *The Employment Relationship: A Comparative Overview* (Hart 2011); Davidov, Freedland, and Kountouris (n 19). In the US, a different test is used for different laws; the 'common law' test which is most common focuses on control, but for purposes of the Fair Labor Standards Act courts give more weight to economic dependency, and recently the Department of Labor has advocated focusing *exclusively* on dependency (see US Department of Labor Wage and Hour Division, Administrator's Interpretation No. 2015-1 (July 2015) <http://www.dol.gov/whd/workers/misclassification/AI-2015_1.htm> accessed 17 October 2015.

[44] In the US this has long been the prevailing formulation. See, e.g., *Smith v Dutra Trucking Co* 410 F Supp 513 (ND Cal 1976), affd 580 F 2d 1054 (9th Cir 1978) (US Court of Appeals); *Cobb v Sun Papers Inc* 673 F 2d 337 (11th Cir 1982) (US Court of Appeals); *Slayman v FedEx Ground Package System, Inc* 765 F 3d 1033 (9th Cir 2014) (US Court of Appeals); *O'Connor v Uber Techs*, 2015 US Dist LEXIS 116482, 80 Cal Comp. Cases 852 (ND Cal 2015). For the use of this test elsewhere see *Stevens & Brodribb Sawmilling Co Pty Ltd* (1986) 160 CLR 16 (High Court of Australia); Chris Engels, 'Belgium' (Special Issue: Employed or Self-Employed) (1992) 24 Bull Com Lab Rel 29, 34–35.

[45] The last point was made more explicitly in the draft ILO Recommendation concerning contract labour, which later led to the Employment Relationship Recommendation. See International

or 'bureaucratic' control. It can also include, for example, an obligation to attend regular staff meetings.[46] Being a part of the organization and subject to a degree of control in this way is indeed a clear indicator of democratic deficits.[47]

Another common formulation is to ask whether 'the work performed is integrated into the normal activities' of E.[48] But this can result in the exclusion of workers performing work that is marginal to the business of the organization, which cannot be justified by a purposive analysis. A business can hire someone to do something which is not part of its 'normal activities' and the worker could still be in need of protection. If the *worker* is integrated into the organization—subject to bureaucratic control—this is highly relevant. Whether the work itself (the task/job) is integrated or not is immaterial.

(3) W is working solely or mainly for E's benefit (a single employer). Another way this is sometimes put is by reference to remuneration from E being W's sole or principal source of income. This is obviously an indicator of dependency.

(4) The work has to be carried out within specific working hours and/or a specified workplace.[49] Working in regular hours and at the employers' premises is obviously a common characteristic of employees, but it is not an indicator that can be justified purposively: one can work on irregular hours at home and still be in need of labour law's protection. However, if W is not free to choose when and where to do the work—if E controls these important aspects of W's work life—this indicates democratic deficits.

(5) The engagement is continuous. This indicator appears to be losing some ground,[50] but it was still included in the ILO Recommendation. A continuous relationship can exist between a client and an independent contractor just as it exists in employment relationships; consider for example a lawyer or a consultant engaged on a retainer basis. The question, however, is whether the lack of continuity can be used to point *against* employee status. Otherwise put, can one be an 'employee' if hired on a one-time basis? Or

Labour Conference (86th Session) Report V (2B) Addendum: Committee on Contract Labour (Geneva June 1998) (ILO 1998), para (c).

[46] IRS instructions, form SS-8 (Rev. 8-2011) pt II, s 8 (United States).

[47] See also Matthew T Bodie, 'Participation as a Theory of Employment' (2013) 89 Notre Dame LR 661, 666: 'Because employees participate in the common economic enterprise as organized into a firm, the firm in turn must take care of its employees within that common enterprise.' This seems to be similar to integration. However, Bodie moves away from a connection that can be justified purposively, when he explains that '[i]t is not that employees are controlled by the firm that makes them employees. It is rather that they are part of a process of joint production, acting together within one unit' (ibid 705).

[48] See ILO 1998 (n 45), para (h). See also *Municipality of Netanya v Birger* 3 PDA 238 (1972) (Israeli National Labour Court).

[49] Sometimes 'the location of the work' is listed as the relevant indicator; see *Nationwide Mutual Insurance Co v Darden* 503 US 318 (1992).

[50] See ILO 2007 (n 20) 40.

occasionally? I do not refer here to 'zero hours' contracts or other forms of atypical employment used to evade responsibility when the relationship is in fact continuous. If E hires W today on a one-time basis, and then does so again tomorrow and the next day, this should be seen as continuous.

In cases of a one-time engagement, or very sporadic and rare engagements, there is no dependency. And while there could be subordination during the time of the work, a one-time short engagement does not require a structure of governance, which is a precondition for the creation of democratic deficits in the sense considered here. In contrast, repeated engagements, even if they are irregular, certainly create subordination and dependency. Overall, then, lack of a continuous relationship is an indication against employee status—but only if the engagement is one-time (e.g. daily) or rare.

(6) W is required to be available for work at specified times. This is sometime formulated as W is not free to refuse work. Again these are indicators of subordination—being subject to the control of an employer.

(7) Tools, materials, and machinery are provided by E. More generally, E makes the financial investments needed;[51] W in contrast does not have to incur expenses.[52] These are relevant indicia in the sense that financial investments by the worker are signs of economic independence. However, this is the case only if there is a real ability to spread risks. If, for example, W is buying the tools with a loan from E, and has no real control over the price or an ability to use the tools for other engagements, this is hardly a sign of independence.

(8) Remuneration is paid on a periodic basis, rather than through invoices or at the end of the contract period. This does not seem to be a justified indicator. It points to what is common for employees, but the form of payment says nothing about the existence or lack of subordination and/or dependency.

(9) Part of the remuneration is paid in kind, for example for food or lodging. This is seen in some legal systems as an indication of employment. Once again, however, such an indicator is difficult to justify from a purposive analysis. The method of payment is immaterial for the need of protection.

(10) W has a right for entitlements/benefits such as weekly rest, annual leave, and reimbursement for travel expenses. It is quite obvious that the *lack* of such entitlements should not be seen as an indication of being an independent contractor. If E is interested in misclassifying W as an independent contractor, such benefits will not be given—and this should not be used as a relevant consideration because it will simply validate the employer's evasion attempt. What if these entitlements are given, but W is not considered by E as an 'employee'? This seems unlikely. But if there is such a case, it will be justified to use these entitlements as an indication of employment, because

[51] See ILO 1998 (n 45), para (d).
[52] IRS instructions, form SS-8 (Rev. 8-2011) pt III, ss 3–4.

they point to control by E over W's time. An independent contractor does not need to agree with clients on a weekly rest or annual leave, because she retains residual control over her own working time.

(11) W assumes no financial risk. Another and perhaps broader way to put this is by asking whether W has a chance to make profits and runs a risk of losses in the performance of the work.[53] This is a good indicator of economic dependency: if W is assuming risks and at the same time is enjoying the potential for higher profit as a result of business decisions, this suggests an ability to spread risks, less dependency on E, and no vulnerability justifying protection. This does not mean that by basing a large part of the salary on bonuses, E can evade the employment relationship. The reference is to risk of loss and chance of profit connected to decisions within E's control (and not merely to the decision to work more, or to E's level of success in performing the work).

(12) W does not exercise 'entrepreneurial control' over important business decisions, 'including whether to hire and where to assign assistants, whether to purchase and where to deploy equipment, and whether and when to provide service to other customers'.[54] These are indeed good indicators of independence, in the sense of ability to spread risks.

Having control over the level of payment required for the service/product is also sometimes seen as an indication of independence.[55] This cannot be justified; the price of a service/product can be set by employees of the organization on behalf of their employer—it does not make them independent.

(13) E provides job-specific training to W.[56] This training can be seen as an indicator of employment from W's viewpoint: job-specific investments, as well as any other job-specific ties, heighten the level of dependency on the specific employer.

(14) E has the right to assign additional projects to W.[57] This appears to suggest control over W's time. However, clients can 'assign' additional projects to their contractors as well. The vulnerability justifying protection here is the fact that (within certain limits) W cannot refuse the work assignments—she has to be available for work during specific times. This was already mentioned in point (6) above.

(15) W lacks special skills—according to US jurisprudence, lack of skills suggests that an independent business is unlikely.[58] At the same time, high skills do not negate the possibility of an employment relationship.[59]

[53] See ILO 1998 (n 45), para (e). This is known in the UK as an 'economic reality' test; see Deakin and Morris (n 37) 162.

[54] Restatement (n 33) s 1.01(b).

[55] IRS instructions, form SS-8 (Rev. 8-2011) pt II, s 10.

[56] See ILO 1998 (n 45), para (i).

[57] *Darden* (n 49).

[58] See, e.g., *United States v Silk* 331 US 704 (1947); *Darden* (n 49).

[59] Restatement (n 33) s 1.01 comments d and f.

It is difficult to see a connection between the level of skills and the vulnerability justifying protection. While it is certainly true that unskilled workers are much more likely to be employees rather than independent contractors, this is not necessarily so, and the lack of skills in itself does not seem relevant from a purposive analysis.[60]

(16) The work performed is typical for an employee according to 'common view'.[61] Once again, this is not an indicator that can be justified.

(17) E (the hiring party) is 'in business'.[62] This is probably meant to distinguish between businesses that usually employ staff, and individuals who do not usually have their own employees, but are more likely to contract with others as clients. However, this again seems to be based on what is common, rather than any justification for separate treatment. Individuals who are not 'in business' nonetheless sometimes hire others as employees (e.g. to take care of their children or to clean their house). In terms of the workers' need of protection, the question of whether the hiring party is 'in business' or not is entirely irrelevant.

(18) W is not treated as an independent contractor for tax purposes.[63] The presentation of W as an independent contractor before the tax authority or other third parties is seen as an indication that she is, in fact, such a contractor. This seems odd: as noted, the whole idea is to prevent evasion by employers. If they decide to misclassify an employee as an independent contractor, it is very easy for them to create such an impression for the tax authorities as well. This in itself should not be an indication concerning the real status of W.

From an opposite direction, it could be suggested that when W is presented as an employee to customers, this suggests that she is, in fact, an employee.[64] For similar reasons this does not seem justified. E may have various reasons to present W in certain ways to customers, but this does not have any impact on the actual level of vulnerability justifying protection.

(19) W has agreed to a non-competition clause.[65] This is unlikely to be part of an agreement in which W appears to be an independent contractor. However, if such a case exists, should it be an indication of employee status? A limitation on the ability of W to pursue other work opportunities suggests being under the control of E and is therefore relevant.

(20) W has no ownership stake. In the UK, recent legislation exempts employees from unfair dismissal protection if they are given shares in the employing

[60] Admittedly, lack of skills will usually lead to lower bargaining power, which in turn can be understood as proxy to economic dependency (see Noah Zatz, 'Beyond Misclassification: Tackling the Independent Contractor Problem Without Redefining Employment' (2011) 26 ABA J Lab & Emp L 279, para accompanying fn 39). But the connection is too indirect, in my view, to justify using the level of skill as an indicator of employment.

[61] The German Social Security Code (SGB) IV sec 7 para 4.

[62] *Darden* (n 49).

[63] ibid.

[64] IRS Instructions, form SS-8 (Rev. 8-2011) pt IV, s 9.

[65] ibid pt IV, s 4.

company valued at £2,000 or more.[66] This was rightly criticized as offering employers an easy way out of employer liabilities.[67] In the US, according to the recent Restatement the law includes a less extreme variation of the same idea: 'An individual is not an employee of an enterprise if the individual through an ownership interest controls all or a part of the enterprise.'[68] If W really controls the enterprise (wholly or partly) this is obviously relevant—see point (12) above—but there is no justification for the additional rule. The formal ownership should not matter. Indeed, in a recent case, the Supreme Court of Canada refused to accept the view that an equity partner can never be an employee of the partnership, stating that 'the key is the degree of control and dependency'.[69]

A summary of the relevant indicia

The above analysis suggests twelve relevant indicia, which can be divided into three groups. The first group contains indicia that, if they exist, point to an employment relationship, but their non-existence does not point to the opposite: direct day-to-day control; right to weekly rest, annual leave, etc.; a non-competition clause. In the second group, the lack of the characteristic points *against* an employment relationship, but its existence does not point to the opposite. Here I would include continuous engagement (in the rather minimal sense explained above). The third group includes indicia that when they exist suggest employee status, and their non-existence suggests the opposite. Most of those discussed in the previous part fall under this heading: bureaucratic control; single/main employer; inability to choose when/where to work; obligation to be available/not to refuse work; tools and materials provided by the employer; no chance of profit/risk of loss; no entrepreneurial control; job-specific investments.

The structure of assessing a large number of indicia and deciding whether one is an 'employee' or not based on the overall picture emerging is not ideal. It is inherently indeterminate. Nonetheless, as we have seen, there is no better alternative. Moreover, when applying this long list of indicia, one must remember that the ultimate question is whether the relationship is characterized by subordination and dependency. The many different indicia are just aids that can assist in answering

[66] Employment Rights Act 1996 s 205a, added by the Growth and Infrastructure Act 2013. The 'employee shareholders' still have some minimal protection, especially in cases of discrimination; see s 205(a)(9).

[67] Jeremias Prassl, 'Employee Shareholder Status: Dismantling the Contract of Employment' (2013) 42 ILJ 307.

[68] Restatement (n 33) s 1.03.

[69] *McCormick v Fasken* (n 13) at 119. The Court relied (at 122–3) on Davidov (n 43), among others. At issue was a claim by a partner at a large law firm against its policy of mandatory retirement at the age of 65. The plaintiff claimed age discrimination, which is prohibited for 'employees'. The Court concluded based on the facts that there were no control and dependency. This conclusion was not based on the formality of having an equity stake, but on the actual characteristics of the relationship. But see Langille and Alon-Shenker (n 11) 215 (criticizing the Court for focusing on the *general* purposes of labour law and not the *specific* goals of anti-discrimination laws).

this question. Focusing our attention on the two main characteristics can assist in applying these indicia and help prevent employer evasion.

The final decision cannot be based on counting the number of indicia pulling to each direction. The analysis must be qualitative rather than quantitative. A useful aid can be a three-axes graph in which subordination, economic dependency, and social/psychological dependency are all featured together. The stronger the presence of one vulnerability the lower the level required at the other axes for employment relations to be created.[70] The idea is that we are looking for a combination of those three axes—put simply, a combination of subordination and dependency. One can be stronger than the other; there are different combinations of vulnerabilities in different employment relations. As long as both vulnerabilities exist (to some non-negligible degree) this is a relationship that requires the intervention of labour laws. Overall, we are looking for vulnerability in the relationship that justifies getting out of the 'free market' zone and into the heavily regulated labour law zone. The cumulative degree of vulnerability is thus relevant, as long as there is at least *some* showing of both subordination and dependency.

The proposed purposive interpretation for the term 'employee'—when it needs to be distinguished from an independent contractor—can be summarized based on the following steps:

1. Is there a personal relationship, in which the worker has to perform work personally? If the answer is negative—there is no employment relationship. Otherwise proceed to step 2.
2. Is the relationship characterized by subordination (in the sense of democratic deficits) and dependency (in the sense of inability to spread risks)? If there is some degree of both, this is an employment relationship. The following indicia can be used to assist in this examination (in parenthesis, it is noted whether they are relevant for s-subordination or d-dependency):
    a. Indicia that suggest the existence of an employment relationship, and the lack thereof suggest otherwise: Bureaucratic control (s); inability to choose when/where to work (s); obligation to be available/not to refuse work (s); single/main employer (d); tools and materials provided by the employer (d); no chance of profit/risk of loss (d); no entrepreneurial control (d); job-specific investments (d).
    b. If the engagement is not continuous, i.e. it is a one-time or rare engagement, this will point against an employment relationship.
    c. Indicia that suggest the existence of an employment relationship, but lack thereof does *not* suggest otherwise: direct day-to-day control (s); right to weekly rest, annual leave, etc. (s); a non-competition clause (s).

[70] See Davidov (n 43). A similar structure was previously proposed by Collins (n 8). Collins suggested two axes, one denoting the level of risks imposed on the workers, the other the level of bureaucratic controls. My own focus is on the vulnerabilities justifying protection.

3. Consider if exceptions or extensions to the meaning of 'employee' are need in light of the goals of the specific regulation under consideration.

Part II—Dependent Contractors

So far the discussion assumed a binary divide between 'employees' and independent contractors. Legal systems that refer only to the term 'employee' when setting the scope of labour law are generally limited to this solution, because one can either be an 'employee' (and enjoy the protection of labour law) or can not. Although purposive interpretation of the term 'employee' leaves room for some variation—a somewhat different meaning in different contexts—this room is relatively limited.

Nonetheless, a growing number of countries now have a third, intermediate category. The addition of a third category in-between employees and independent contractors offers a better balance between universalism and selectivity. It opens more possibilities for a nuanced, targeted application of labour laws. Furthermore, adding a third (intermediate) category can be useful for advancing the goals of labour law. The rigidity of the binary divide often leads to the unjustified exclusion of some workers, who fall in between the categories, thus frustrating some of labour law's purposes. This can be prevented, or at least minimized, by the additional category, thanks to the (partial) inclusion of workers who share only *some* of the characteristics of employees and require some of the protections. At the same time, this solution takes into account the advantages of universalism as well, avoiding the creation of numerous different categories (or even no categories at all) which could make it impossible for people to know their status and rights.[71]

The proliferation of intermediate categories

A category of 'dependent contractor' has existed in Sweden and Canada for decades; a very similar category has been part of the law in Germany ('employee-like') and in Italy (*parasubordinati*) for many years.[72] Other legal systems in Europe have followed suit in more recent years, sometimes under the names 'economically dependent worker' or 'dependent self-employed'.[73] These intermediate categories

[71] Freedland and Kountouris (n 26 at 276ff) prefer a 'family of contracts' with multiple variations, which seems to downplay the importance of determinacy (and the advantages of universalism). I discuss this more fully in Guy Davidov, 'The (Incomplete) Purposive Revolution: A Review of Freedland & Kountouris' (2013) 7 Jerusalem Rev of Leg Stud 87. On the need to balance between universalism and selectivity see further Davidov (n 10).

[72] For brief reviews see Langille and Davidov (n 1); Nicola Countouris, 'The Employment Relationship: A Comparative Analysis of National Judicial Approached' in Giuseppe Casale (ed), *The Employment Relationship: A Comparative Overview* (Hart 2011) 35.

[73] For useful comparative information see Roberto Pedersini and Diego Coletto, *Self-Employed Workers: Industrial Relations and Working Conditions* (European Foundation for the Improvement of Living and Working Conditions 2010) ch 4. See also Jaime Cabeza Pereiro, 'The Status of

aim to capture people who have *some* characteristics of independent businesses, but at the same time some of the vulnerabilities of employees, especially in the sense of depending entirely or mostly on a single employer/client.[74] In these cases, legislatures have chosen to apply *some* labour laws (e.g. in Canada, the right to bargain collectively) but not others. Technically, this can be achieved by stating in specific laws that they apply not only to 'employees' but also to 'dependent contractors', or alternatively, stating that for the purpose of the specific law, the term 'employee' also includes dependent contractors.[75]

The proliferation of intermediate categories in recent years is not always problem-free. The backdrop is usually vast evasion of the law through misclassification of employees as independent contractors, which courts are unable or unwilling to stop. Legislatures in the UK, Austria, and Spain have introduced a third category in the last two decades in order to provide at least *some* protection for such workers. But these protections are often quite minimal (usually the focus is on social security rather than direct employer obligations),[76] and the worrying side-effect is the legitimizing of the existing order in which workers who often have *all* the characteristics of employees are excluded from full protection. The failure of courts to prevent such misclassification is surely no excuse

Self-Employed Workers in Spain' (2008) 147 ILR 91; Esther Sánchez Torres, 'The Spanish Law on Dependent Self-Employed Workers: A New Evolution in Labor Law' (2010) 31 CLLPJ 231; Juan Pablo Landa Zapirain, 'Regulation of Dependent Self-Employed Workers in Spain: A Regulatory Framework for Informal Work?' in Fudge, McCrystal, and Sankaran (n 22) 155; Judy Fudge, 'A Canadian Perspective on the Scope of Employment Standards, Labor Rights, and Social Protection: The Good, the Bad, and the Ugly' (2010) 31 CLLPJ 253; Orsola Razzolini, 'The Need to Go Beyond the Contract: "Economic" and "Bureaucratic" Dependence in Personal Work Relations' (2010) 31 CLLPJ 267; ILO 2007 (n 20) 22; Davidov, Freedland, and Kountouris (n 19).

[74] For an empirical study showing that a significant group of dependent self-employed exists in the UK, see René Böheim and Ulrike Mühlberger, 'Dependent Self-employment: Workers between Employment and Self-employment in the UK' (2009) 42 J Labour Market Res 185.

[75] A similar result can also be achieved using a slightly different structure, when a legislature introduces a new concept which is broader than the regular 'employee'. Thus, for example, in the UK some labour laws apply to all 'workers', a concept defined in legislation in much broader terms than those developed by the courts to identify employees. As a result, there is the group of 'employees' who enjoy all labour laws, and those who are 'workers' but not 'employees' who enjoy only *some* labour laws. The technique is slightly different, but the result is the same. On the UK intermediate category see Guy Davidov, 'Who is a Worker?' (2005) 34 ILJ 57. Another technique could be to provide some independent contractors with the possibility of exemption from competition laws that generally prevent collective bargaining. This technique exists in Australia, although it appears to be difficult to employ; see Shae McCrystal, 'Organising Independent Contractors: The Impact of Competition Law', in Fudge, McCrystal, and Sankaran (n 22) 139. See also the Canadian Status of the Artist Act 1992, which extends the right to bargain collectively to self-employed writers, performers, and other artists. Yet another technique developed in Australia—again not without practical weaknesses—creates a special regulatory regime for franchisees, a group that has some of the characteristics of employees but not others; see Joellen Riley, 'A Blurred Boundary between Entrepreneurship and Servitude: Regulating Business Format Franchising in Australia' in Fudge, McCrystal, and Sankaran (n 22) 101. For a comparative discussion examining the different techniques to include some self-employed workers in collective bargaining regimes, see Shae McCrystal, 'Collective Bargaining Beyond the Boundaries of Employment: A Comparative Analysis' (2014) 37 Melbourne U LR 662.

[76] They are less minimal in Spain and in the UK. See the sources cited in n 73 above.

for legislatures, who only went half-way (or even less) to protect workers in need of protection—and despite the good intentions have helped to perpetuate their unjustified exclusion.

But let us leave this difficulty aside. Even if courts would function perfectly and interpret the term 'employee' in the best possible way, there is still room, as we have seen, for an intermediate category. The next section offers an optimal definition for this category, before moving to examine how it corresponds with the actual definitions in some legal systems.[77]

Defining 'dependent contractors'—in theory

Consider the following example: John is a copyeditor of books. He has his own company, issues invoices, and so on. But he has no employees, he works alone. In practice, he only has one client—he does all the editorial work for one single publisher. The publisher considers him to be a 'freelancer' and works with several other such 'freelancers'. To a large extent John has control over his own time. He is not committed to take all the work that the publisher sends him; if he wants to take a vacation or a day off, he will simply tell the publisher to send any urgent materials to other editors. He chooses when to work, where to work, and how many hours per day to work. He is also not subject to any organizational rules of the publisher.

What is John's legal status? We should probably not consider him an 'employee'. Although he has just one client, he does not appear to suffer from all the same vulnerabilities as internal employees of the publisher. Specifically, his relationship with the publisher is not characterized by subordination. On the other hand, it is obviously characterized by dependency. He has no real ability to spread risks. He relies entirely on work provided by the specific publisher. So it would be fair to argue that he should be entitled to *some* labour law protection. For example, he should be allowed to bargain collectively with other 'freelance' editors, so as to improve their bargaining position vis-à-vis the publisher. People like John should also enjoy the protection of minimum wage laws and other laws setting minimum monetary terms. On the other hand, there is obviously no justification to apply working time laws or workplace privacy laws, for example, in this case.

In such cases, when the relationship is characterized by dependency but no subordination, it is useful to call the worker a 'dependent contractor' and apply at least some labour laws. In other words, dependency alone should be sufficient to justify a floor of basic labour-related rights, with additional rights (which are tied to subordination) granted only to 'employees'. A purposive approach, therefore, leads to identifying the category of 'dependent contractors' with a common vulnerability (dependency) and the category of 'employees' with the intersection

[77] The following section is based partly on Guy Davidov, 'Freelancers: An Intermediate Group in Labour Law?' in Fudge, McCrystal, and Sankaran (n 22) 171.

of two common vulnerabilities (dependency and subordination). At the legislative level, my proposal is therefore simple: define the intermediate category based on the existence of dependency only.

In specific cases it will still be difficult to decide where to put the line. Should we consider John an 'employee' (as opposed to a 'dependent contractor') if he receives ongoing instructions from the publisher, for example, about how to perform the work, or has agreed to coordinate his vacations with the publisher in advance? From the other direction, should we consider John an independent contractor—with no entitlement to labour-related rights whatsoever—if he works with two or three publishers rather than one, or if he is assisted by one or two employees of his own? These are difficult questions with no clear-cut answers. But it seems that the basic questions remain the same: what is the degree of subordination and what is the degree of dependency in the relationship between the two parties. It is sometimes a judgment call to decide where to put the line, and some degree of indeterminacy is inherent in this process. Yet it is wise to leave some latitude of discretion to courts, to avoid the pitfall of specific clear-cut rules that create an illusion of determinacy but bring about exacerbated levels of evasion. At the same time, there is benefit in introducing presumptions about what it means to be dependent (e.g. 75 per cent of total income), to ensure a degree of determinacy and guidance to the courts.[78]

When discussing the meaning of 'employee', we have seen that an obligation to perform the work *in person* is a necessary requirement. Should it be required to be considered a 'dependent contractor' as well? To answer this question, we have to consider the list of rights and benefits that will be given to dependent contractors. The answer should be based on the vulnerability that these rights and benefits are designed to confront—whether it is mainly *economic* dependency or rather social/psychological dependency. If it is the former, there is no reason to limit the protection to individuals performing the work in person; the vulnerability of economic dependency affects small businesses in much the same way. In contrast, social/psychological vulnerabilities are obviously personal in nature, and thus protection against them should be limited to individuals who are subject to these vulnerabilities *in person*. Putting aside regulations that should cover only 'employees'—because they address subordination (e.g. concerning working time, vacations, privacy)—most other labour laws seem to address especially economic dependency. Thus the right to bargain collectively, for example, and rights to minimum wage, severance pay, or wage protection. A notable exception is regulation limiting dismissals to just cause (where it exists), which seems to protect also—perhaps especially—from social/psychological dependency. So adaptations might be needed for specific regulations. But in the interest of maintaining some clear categories, it would be useful to rely on the purpose of the majority of dependent

[78] On the use of presumptions in this context as well, see ILO 2013 (n 20) 28. In Spain a 75% requirement is included as a strict rule rather than a mere presumption (see Sánchez Torres (n 73) 236), which means higher determinacy but also a higher risk of evasion by employers working around the rule.

contractor protections, and extend them to non-personal relations as well (i.e. to small businesses who are dependent on one client, even if the owner of the business is not obligated to perform all the work herself).

A final issue that should be considered is whether a 'dependent contractor' category can be created by courts in legal systems that lack an intermediate category in legislation. While courts would overstep the limits of legitimacy by creating a new category, setting its boundaries and deciding on the rights to be accorded to this category, in practice a partial solution can be reached by way of purposive interpretation of the term 'employee'. If the legislature fails to differentiate between employees and dependent contractors, but leaves the interpretation of the term 'employee' to courts, it would be perfectly justified to interpret the term in a way that includes dependent contractors for the purpose of *some* protections.

Interpreting intermediate categories—in practice

Is it possible to interpret existing laws setting intermediate categories in light of the proposed distinction between subordination and dependency? And extend protection to non-personal relations as well? Below I examine several examples.

In Canada, different definitions of 'dependent contractor' appear in different provincial laws. The Ontario Labour Relations Act, for example, offers the following definition:

> a person, whether or not employed under a contract of employment, and whether or not furnishing tools, vehicles, equipment, machinery, material, or any other thing owned by the dependent contractor, who performs work or services for another person for compensation or reward on such terms and conditions that the dependent contractor is in a position of economic dependence upon, and under an obligation to perform duties for, that person more closely resembling the relationship of an employee than that of an independent contractor.[79]

This definition obviously puts most emphasis on dependency, and rightly so. However, there is also a requirement of 'an obligation to perform duties' for the employer/client. This suggests that some level of subordination is also necessary, which is unfortunate; but purposive interpretation should lead to requiring a very minimal level of subordination (given the need to maintain a distinction from the concept of 'employee'). As for the question of whether the relations must be

[79] Ontario Labour Relations Act 1995 s 1. Definitions in other provinces are very similar. The Federal legislation includes a similar definition, but also adds that truck owner-operators and fishers who are part of joint fishing ventures shall be considered 'dependent contractors' under certain conditions, that do not include any reference to subordination. See Canada Labour Code 1985 s 3. A report prepared by Harry Arthurs for the Federal government proposed extending some employment standards to 'autonomous workers' on top of the right to bargain collectively which is currently extended to 'dependent contractors'. See Harry Arthurs, *Fairness at Work: Federal Labour Standards for the 21st Century* (Human Resources and Skill Development Canada 2006) ch 4. The proposed category of 'autonomous workers' appears to be very similar to dependent contractors, the main difference being that the Minister should have the power, according to the proposal, to decide who is part of that group and for which purposes.

'personal', it seems that the Ontario legislation does not include such a requirement. Although the definition refers to a 'person' this can also include a 'legal person' (a corporation).

In Spain, the category of 'dependent self-employed workers' introduced in 2007 is based entirely on indicia of economic dependency: most notably, 75 per cent of the worker's income is derived from the same 'client'. There is no requirement of subordination; on the contrary, it is explicitly made clear in the legislation that dependent contractors 'must carry out their activity using their own organizational criteria without prejudice to the technical indications they may receive from their client',[80] which seems to suggest that the existence of subordination should lead to the conclusion that the worker is an 'employee' rather than a 'dependent self-employed worker'. This definition allows the adoption of the purposive interpretation proposed above. In contrast, the Spanish legislation is explicitly limited to workers that perform all their work in person[81]—a significant limitation difficult to explain from a purposive perspective.

In the UK, the category of 'worker' has been defined to include any individual who has entered into or works under any other contract 'whereby the individual undertakes to do or perform personally any work or services for another party to the contract whose status is not by virtue of the contract that of a client or customer of any profession or business undertaking carried on by the individual'.[82] Although hopelessly cumbersome and circular, the definition does make a couple of intentions clear. The first intention is to include all employees and then some others. The second is to maintain a number of requirements associated with the term 'employee', in particular the contractual relationship, the personal nature of the engagement, and the lack of an independent business undertaking. It does seem to leave sufficient room for judicial interpretation that will put all emphasis on economic dependency, without any requirement of subordination.[83]

The proposed interpretation for the intermediate group is thus quite similar to the one that already exists in some countries, but with a number of differences. First, the focus of the examination should be the ability or inability to spread risks. The more specific indicia can be useful as aids, but they can also more easily be manipulated. Second, social/psychological dependency should be examined as well, rather than just economic dependency. Third, we should not demand any level of subordination for this group. Finally, the intermediate group of workers should enjoy much broader protection than what is common in most of the countries that have so far recognized such a group.

[80] Sánchez Torres (n 73) 236. [81] ibid.

[82] Employment Rights Act 1996 ss 13 and 230(3); National Minimum Wage Act 1998 s 54(3); Working Time Regulations 1998 reg 2; Employment Relations Act 1999 ss 10–13; Part-Time Workers (Prevention of Less Favourable Treatment) Regulations 2000 reg 1.

[83] I have advocated this approach in Davidov (n 75). It has not been adopted by the courts; see the judgments discussed there. For further discussion of this proposal in the UK context see Douglas Brodie, 'Employees, Workers and the Self-Employed' (2005) 34 ILJ 253; Patricia Leighton and Michael Wynn, 'Classifying Employment Relationships: More Sliding Doors or a Better Regulatory Framework?' (2011) 40 ILJ 5, 38–39.

Part III—Identifying the Employer

Assuming a worker is an 'employee', or a 'dependent contractor', based on the tests discussed in the previous parts various labour laws apply. But one still has to identify the legal employer in order to know where the duties resulting from these laws lie. In most cases this is obvious: the employer is the one commissioning the work, enjoying it, paying for it. But in an increasing number of cases there is now more than one body involved, and it often becomes difficult to decide which entity should shoulder the burden of responsibility towards the employee. It is useful to distinguish between sham arrangements, designed entirely to evade responsibilities, and truly triangular relations. The former should be ignored and the legal responsibility of an employer should be placed with the 'real' employer. The latter of the case types, in which the characteristics of an employer are divided between two or more bodies, are much more complex. The main contemporary examples are employment through a Temporary Employment Agency (TEA) for a limited period, and employment through subcontractors. I discuss these different situations in turn.[84] I then briefly consider whether an entity with no characteristics of an employer can still be required to bear at least *some* employer responsibility—most notably in the case of supply/production chains. I conclude with a summary of the legal questions raised and the possible solutions.

Sham triangular relations

Assume a triangular work relationship that includes a worker, entity A using her work, and entity B that is presented as the legal employer. B can be a TEA or a subcontractor. Now assume (and this is unfortunately common in real life) that all the characteristics of an employer lie with A. In other words, presenting B as the employer is a sham. If it is accepted that employers should not be able to 'contract out' of their legal responsibilities, it should be obvious, from a purposive point of view, that this sham arrangement should be ignored. Just as we do not allow employers to evade their duties simply by having the worker sign a contract saying that she is an independent contractor, so we cannot give force to a contract saying that some other body is the employer, if the facts suggest otherwise. An organization is allowed to outsource some of its tasks—to 'buy' a product or service from another entity rather than 'make' it in-house—but not to outsource only the 'employer' legal status. If the service is *really* outsourced, the characteristics of the employer (or at least some of them) will be found with B. Otherwise it is not outsourcing but a sham.[85]

[84] Some parts of the discussion are reproduced (with updates) from Guy Davidov, 'Joint Employers Status in Triangular Employment Relationships' (2004) 42 BJIR 727.

[85] The meaning of 'sham' adopted here is thus much broader than what courts in the UK have accepted. See Michael Wynn and Patricia Leighton, 'Agency Workers, Employment Rights and the Ebb and Flow of Freedom of Contract' (2009) 72 MLR 91.

What are the 'characteristics of an employer' just mentioned? The discussion in Part I suggested—based on the discussion in Chapter 3—that employer–employee relations are characterized by subordination and dependency. Because these are the vulnerabilities that justify protection and explain the need for labour law, I have argued that these should be the ultimate tests to decide if someone is an 'employee' (i.e. should be subject to labour law) or not. In a very similar way, we should identify the 'employer' by looking at the other side of these vulnerabilities. If the worker is subordinate to A, and dependent on A, then A is the entity that should be under the obligations of labour law vis-à-vis that worker.[86]

The situation does not change when B has some minor role to play as the long arm of A. For example, if B is providing 'payrolling' services, taking money from A and using it to pay wages to the workers, deduct taxes, and otherwise deal with the formalities of employment—it does not in itself change the reality of the relationship in terms of subordination and dependency on A.[87] Even if B assumes some other 'human resources' tasks—such as recruitment[88] or perhaps communicating dismissal decisions—this should not make a difference for determining who is the employer. The firm can outsource some of the bureaucracy attached to employment relationships to another firm, but this hardly makes a real difference for the employees, their relationship with the user firm, or their need of protection.

Employers sometimes explain the resort to triangular relations by citing 'screening' purposes: they want to be able to dismiss the worker swiftly during a 'trial' period, and plan to hire her directly afterwards.[89] Yet laws that limit the ability to dismiss employees to a provable 'just cause', and laws that establish rights to notice before dismissals or to severance pay, all become applicable only after some minimal period of work for the same employer.[90] The law thus already recognizes the need for a 'trial period' and sets the appropriate maximum for it in the context of each regulation. In such cases as well, then, the use of TEAs or subcontractors is only designed to circumvent the law and lengthen the permissible trial period.

A useful legal technique for limiting sham arrangements is by creating a maximum period of employment through TEAs with the same user. In the context of employment through TEAs, engagement that is not temporary in nature is

[86] Jeremias Prassl lists five functions of the employer: Inception and termination of the contract of employment; receiving labour and its fruits; providing work and pay; managing the enterprise internally; managing the enterprise externally (Jeremias Prassl, 'The Notion of the Employer' (2013) 129 LQR 380). However, he does not explain why these functions are relevant for the workers' need of protection.

[87] See also Frances Raday, 'The Insider-Outsider Politics of Labor-Only Contracting' (1999) 20 CLLPJ 413, 424.

[88] Leah F Vosko, *Temporary Work: The Gendered Rise of a Precarious Employment Relationship* (U of Toronto Press 2000) 140–48.

[89] ibid 152; S Smith-Vidal, 'France' (1999) 36 Bull Com Lab Rel 245, 245, 247; Susan N Houseman, 'Why Employers Use Flexible Staffing Arrangements: Evidence from an Establishment Survey' (2000) Upjohn Institute Staff Working Paper <http://research.upjohn.org/cgi/viewcontent.cgi?article=1084&context=up_workingpapers> accessed 14 October 2015.

[90] For example, in the UK, Employment Rights Act 1996 s 108.

necessarily a sham; there is no justifiable reason to employ someone indirectly through a TEA for a long period (or indefinitely). The only explanation for such a structure is a desire to evade employer obligations. So legislatures can set a maximum period (e.g. nine months) of employment through B, after which a worker will automatically become an employee of A. Indeed, some legal systems have such provisions.[91] This method entails a risk that workers will be dismissed just before the maximum period ends, so some complementary protections are needed to prevent this scenario.[92] Moreover, it has two additional limitations. First, it will not prevent sham arrangements during the period which is considered legitimate for temporary engagement by the legislation—even though it is entirely possible that arrangements will be fictive during this period as well. Second, and more fundamentally, it does not provide any solution for subcontracting arrangements, which could be a sham or not, unrelated to the length of the engagement. A worker employed through a TEA is by definition providing labour power to the user. B is just an intermediary, facilitating the work of the worker for A. In contrast, subcontracting arrangements are based on the premise that B is selling a product or service to A—the contract between them is for the delivery of some 'end result', which is delivered by using the workers. This could also turn out to be a sham; but the length of the engagement does not make it a sham, because A could certainly contract with B for a long or even indefinite period while maintaining a real separation between A and the workers employed by B.

So legislation prohibiting employment through TEAs for more than a maximum period is useful, perhaps even necessary, but not sufficient. It must be supplemented with judicial assessment of the characteristics of employment—and the invalidation of sham arrangements which present B as the employer when in fact subordination and dependency are all vis-à-vis A.

Some examples of sham arrangements

Sometimes it is patently obvious that an arrangement is fictive, but apparently it is not always clear to the courts that this is illegitimate. Maintaining a clear view of the purpose of labour laws is essential to prevent such arrangements. A set of four Israeli cases, all of them dealing with indirect employment by the Government, is highly illustrative of this point. In the first of these cases, a secretary who worked at the Israeli Ministry of Labour—Ilana Levinger—was employed for eleven years (from 1980 through to 1991) as an 'independent contractor'.[93] Officials at

[91] See, e.g., Belgium (OECD data as of 2013, <http://www.oecd.org/els/emp/Belgium.pdf> accessed 14 October 2015); Israel (Employment of Employees by Manpower Contractors Act 1996 s 12A).

[92] The Israeli National Labour Court has unfortunately failed to appreciate this point. When an employer dismissed a worker just before the end of nine months, for no other reason but the desire to avoid direct employment, the Court refused to see this as an infringement of the 'good faith' duty. See *Zohar Golan v ORS*, judgment of Sep 12, 2010 (Israeli National Labour Court).

[93] *Ilana Levinger v The State of Israel*, judgment of Oct 2, 2000 (Israeli National Labour Court).

the Ministry then realized that according to the tests developed by the courts Levinger is surely, in fact, an 'employee'. Instead of hiring her directly, their solution was to employ her through a TEA. For nine more years she continued to do the same job as before, and indeed the same job as other secretaries employed directly by the Ministry. During those nine years, the TEAs formally employing Levinger had changed almost on a yearly basis (the Ministry issued tenders every year and chose the cheapest supplier each time). Every time a new TEA was engaged by the Ministry, the workers were formally transferred to a new legal employer. Levinger had no contact with these employers; she only noticed that the employer's name on her wage slips had changed from time to time. Her supervisors were from the Ministry and had not changed. After a period of twenty years at the Ministry she was dismissed, for the sole reason that Ministry officials became worried that after such a lengthy period she could be considered a Ministry employee. She petitioned to the court and won; the National Labour Court had harsh words to say about the Ministry's actions. It was ruled that Levinger was an 'employee' of the Ministry for the entire period and should enjoy the protections attached to State employees. In such an extreme case it was apparently obvious to the judges that the employer has acted to circumvent the law by evading employer responsibilities and this should not be allowed.

The second case seemed to be about a patently clear sham as well, but ended differently. This time it involved the Ministry of Agriculture, which has a unit for market research. Apparently *all* of the workers in this unit (except for the unit head) were employed through intermediaries—first a company that appeared to be a contractor, providing the service of market research for the Ministry, and later (during another period) through a number of changing TEAs. In practice the workers were indistinguishable from Ministry employees in terms of subordination and dependency. When one of those workers—Dovrat Schwab—was dismissed, she asked the Court to recognize her rights as a State employee. Two of the judges (out of five) at the National Labour Court thought that this was a sham arrangement and accepted her petition. However, the Majority (headed by President Steve Adler) decided that employers (including the State) should be able to enjoy the flexibility of employing through intermediaries rather than directly.[94] The Court realized that workers are paying the price of this 'flexibility', and so decided to require the Ministry, as the user of the work (A), to guarantee compliance with labour legislation by the employing intermediary (B). So if the workers do not get the minimum wage or other basic rights from B, they can sue A for the same amount. Such residual responsibility is better than none at all, but a far cry from full employer responsibility.[95] As a Ministry employee, Schwab was supposed to enjoy various benefits included in collective agreements, as well as various other rights and benefits granted to State employees. There is no justification for excluding workers from the full scope of protection only in the name

[94] *Dovrat Schwab v The State of Israel*, judgment of Nov 2, 2006 (Israeli National Labour Court).

[95] The difference can also be described as between 'primary' and 'secondary' liability (see Jeremias Prassl, *The Concept of the Employer* (OUP 2015) 186).

of flexibility. The desired level of employer flexibility chosen by a given society is already represented in the contents of its labour laws; allowing employers to decide unilaterally to exclude some workers from part of these laws is entirely contradictory to their purpose.

The third and fourth cases both dealt with outsourcing by the Ministry of Education. The case of Moshe Hagabee concerned security of school trips. The people providing the actual security at school trips are employed by security companies, and this was not challenged in this case. The Ministry not only outsourced the security tasks themselves, but also wanted to outsource the tasks of managing all the security issues, including supervision, training, and so on—to a different company. Altogether sixteen workers were employed by a company contracted to handle the security at school trips.[96] The case of Hanna Aloni concerned another relatively peripheral task of the Ministry: road safety instruction. Altogether nineteen workers were employed as road safety instructors for schoolchildren, and once again they were employed indirectly through a contractor.[97] In practice, in both cases the facts suggested that the workers were not different, substantively, from 'regular' employees of the Ministry, but they were excluded from many rights and benefits as a result of their indirect employment. In both cases, the workers were employed in this indirect structure for many years.

The approach of the National Labour Court differed between the two cases. In *Hagabee*, most emphasis was placed on the terms of the contract between the Ministry and the contractor. Not surprisingly, those terms—drafted by the Ministry lawyers with the explicit intention of preventing direct liability towards the employees—painted a picture of separation between the workers and the Ministry. The facts suggested that in reality such separation did not exist; on the contrary, the workers were actually subordinated to the Ministry and dependent on the Ministry. But the Court was more minded (in line with its decision in *Schwab*) to the employer's flexibility needs. In contrast, in the more recent case of *Aloni*, the Court referred to the reality of the relationship, rather than the contractual stipulations. In addition, the judges explicitly resorted to a purposive analysis, explaining that triangular relations should be examined in light of the purpose of labour laws, to ensure that sham arrangements designed to evade these laws are prevented. For current purposes it is not necessary to speculate on the reasons for the different results in those two cases; to some extent this is simply related to timing and the identity of the judges deciding the case. The pertinent point is that all four cases illustrate sham outsourcing arrangements which courts do not consistently prevent.

It is sometimes argued by those sceptical of a purposive approach that it would always lead to the same decision—in favour of the employees. This is certainly not the case. To illustrate, consider one more case of the Israeli National Labour

[96] *Ministry of Education v Moshe Hagabee*, judgment of Feb 2, 2006 (Israeli National Labour Court).
[97] *Ministry of Education v Hanna Aloni*, judgment of Jan 24, 2012 (Israeli National Labour Court).

Court, this time dealing with outsourcing of computing services by the Jerusalem Municipality.[98] The plaintiff, Itzhak Hassidim, provided information technology (IT) services for the Municipality for twenty-six years. He was employed through ATG, a company dedicated to providing IT services to municipalities, partially owned by an association of Israeli municipalities. Hassidim did not work for any other client, so his indirect employment certainly appeared suspicious; and after his engagement ended, he petitioned the court to be recognized as a Municipality employee. However, the facts showed that the outsourcing was real and not fictive. ATG was not just the long arm of the Municipality, a funnel for wages to employees. Rather, the company was truly providing IT services to the Municipality, and the Municipality bought the service (rather than just the labour power). Obviously to provide the service ATG needed employees, and Hassidim was employed for this specific ongoing project for a long time. It also meant that he had close connections with the Municipality; but this in itself did not make him a Municipality employee. The Court explicitly resorted to a purposive approach in this case as well, making clear that the goal is to prevent sham arrangements and to place employer responsibilities based on the purposes of labour law. Although the judgment does not rely on subordination and dependency specifically, the analysis is based on other (more specific) factors leading to the same conclusion: that the vulnerabilities of the employee were vis-à-vis ATG and not the Municipality.

Truly triangular employment through TEAs

The analysis is much more difficult when we consider relations that are *truly triangular*, i.e. when A and B both have some substantive (rather than fictive) relationship with the worker—and with regard to the same work. Let us consider first employment through TEA that is not a sham (where the TEA is used to employ someone long-term) but truly temporary. If A is the entity using the work and B is the TEA, during the period of the engagement there is clearly subordination to A—this is the organization that determines what the worker should do and supervises her. At the same time, there is some subordination in the relationship with B, which controls when and where the worker will be placed. The latter becomes more pronounced when the worker is moved from one job to another more frequently. As for economic dependency, the worker depends mostly on B, not because it is the one that delivers the remuneration, but rather because it is B that determines whether the worker will have additional work whenever a particular assignment is completed. Social and psychological ties are rather minimal in temporary employment relationships, assuming the placements are for short periods of time; but to some extent workers rely on B for the continued supply of work as a precondition for the fulfilment of social/psychological needs.

[98] *Itzhak Hassidim v Jerusalem Municipality*, judgment of Jan 13, 2011 (Israeli National Labour Court).

The tangled web of relationships faced by the worker explains why the law has difficulties in tackling such cases. If the relationship with B is characterized by subordination and dependency, but at the same time the relationship with A is characterized by subordination, there are two possible solutions: dividing the responsibilities between them or placing all responsibilities on both of them jointly and severally as 'joint employers'.[99]

The model adopted by the EU Directive on Temporary Agency Work of 2008[100] can be seen as a division of responsibilities. Formally only the agency (B) is considered the employer;[101] but some specific duties have been placed on the user (A). In terms of access to new (permanent) positions, access to collective facilities (such as child care facilities or transportation), and potentially also training, the workers have rights *as if* they were A's employees.[102] Moreover, the main protection offered by the Directive—the principle of equal treatment—places an obligation on the legal employer (B) to offer the workers pay and working conditions equal to those they would have received as employees of A.[103] This rule has many exceptions which significantly limit its applicability.[104] But overall the Directive can be seen as attempting to divide the employer responsibilities: For the most part employer duties are placed with B, but some minimal duties are placed with A, and also B has some extra duties to ensure equality with A's employees.

The Directive fails to give sufficient weight to the fact that during the time of placement with A, which could be significant, workers are subordinated to A. This vulnerability is ignored; even though it is A that controls the workers on a day-to-day basis, A has no obligation in terms of maximum hours or protecting their privacy (for example). Such obligations are legally imposed on B even though B has no impact and no control over these matters.

A proposal to divide employer responsibilities more in line with a purposive approach was put forward by Simon Deakin, who argued that employers in bilateral relationships are characterized by two functions, coordination ('managerial control') and risk ('a mechanism for absorbing and spreading certain economic and social risks').[105] Once a TEA gets into the picture, these functions are split: coordination vests with the user firm, while the risk function is left with the agency or with the worker. Accordingly, Deakin suggested that the user firm should assume obligations that attach to coordination, like the maintenance of health and safety, while the agency should be under an obligation to provide continuing

[99] The concept of 'joint employers' is already used in several legal systems. See Davidov (n 84); Luisa Corazza and Orsola Razzolini, 'Who is an Employer?' in Matthew W Finkin and Guy Mundlak, *Comparative Labor Law* (Edward Elgar 2015) 132. Note however that the proposal advanced here is for a much broader understanding of this concept. The recent US Restatement (n 33) exemplifies the extremely narrow approach, defining 'joint employer' only as situations in which both employers control the employee (s 1.04(b)).

[100] Council Directive 2008/104/EC of 19 November 2008 On Temporary Agency Work [2008] OJ L327/9.

[101] ibid, art 2. [102] ibid, art 6. [103] ibid, art 5.

[104] See Vosko (n 15) ch 5.

[105] Simon Deakin, 'The Changing Concept of the "Employer" in British Labour Law' (2001) 30 ILJ 72.

employment to the worker and to provide access to pension and occupational employment benefits, as is the case in some European systems.

While there are obvious similarities between Deakin's analysis and my own, I believe that subordination and dependency better capture the characteristics of employment relationships in light of the general goals of protective labour and employment laws. And given the existence of subordination vis-à-vis both the user firm and the TEA, a division of responsibilities is bound to be more complicated and might fail to ensure that workers are protected. In some specific contexts—such as tax or unemployment insurance payments—legislatures must explicitly assign the role of the employer to one specific entity (as many of them have done) to avoid confusion. But in the context of employment standards and collective bargaining laws, the best solution seems to be placing responsibility jointly and severally on both entities, i.e. allowing the employee to sue either one or both.[106] This seems justified in light of the unique vulnerability of TEA workers and the need to ensure that the most vulnerable employees are protected. To examine whether (and how) this solution can work in practice, let us consider several regulations as examples: minimum wage, working hours, and collective bargaining regulations.

Take the minimum wage first. Once they are considered joint employers, A and B will have to coordinate in order to ensure compliance with minimum wage laws. B is the one that actually pays the wage. But A, which uses the worker, must be held responsible for that as well. It will therefore have to take steps to ensure that B pays the minimum wage (e.g. stipulate this duty in its contract with B, and refuse to accept offers from TEAs that are 'too good to be true' leading to non-compliance with legal requirements). And if B becomes insolvent, or for any other reason does not pay the worker a minimum wage, A should be required to do so for the particular work that it enjoyed. The right of the worker to be paid a minimum wage for a particular assignment would be vis-à-vis both the TEA and the user firm. There would therefore be some risk for A involved in using B. But it is indeed A, not the temporary worker, that should assume this risk, both because A profits from the temporary nature of the employment, and because A is in a better position to evaluate the financial stability of B and its attitude towards compliance with legal requirements, and to take collaterals as needed.

[106] To clarify further: in theory, it makes perfect sense to divide responsibilities between two or more employers (see also Prassl (n 95)); however in practice it is likely to be counter-productive. Many workers already face a situation of inability to enforce their rights. Forcing them to seek redress from more than one employer, depending on the law in question, will only exacerbate the situation. The solution of joint liability, in contrast, allows them to demand compliance from (and sue) either one of the employers or both at the same time. Note that this is not like the proposal of abolishing the distinction between employees and independent contractors altogether, discussed in Part I. Admittedly, in both cases the idea is to sacrifice a 'pure' purposive solution in favour of better ability of workers to enforce their rights. But in the context of the 'employee' concept, this would significantly broaden the relationships falling within labour law, leading to diluting of standards; while in the current context, there is no broadening of the scope of labour law, only a question of how to allocate existing liabilities.

In respect of working hours, as long as the worker stays with A, then A should bear the primary responsibility for compliance with such laws. If the worker is asked to work overtime on a given day, it will usually be by the immediate supervisor. B cannot be expected to be directly involved. At the same time, when there are limits on the hours to be worked over a week, or a month, and the worker moves from one user firm to another during that time, B must be the one responsible for compliance. So A should be the employer while it uses the employee, and B should have overall responsibility as the employer throughout and in between her different assignments. It can be seen that even with regard to such specific regulations there is no sensible way of dividing the responsibility. The best solution is to place joint responsibility on both A and B during the period of work for A.

The issue of collective bargaining is more complicated. Since we are working under the assumption that the work for A is temporary—otherwise engaging the worker through B is a sham—the natural site for collective bargaining is vis-à-vis B. Those who are truly 'temps' have some concerns that differ from the concerns of permanent employees of A, in particular their rights between assignments. These matters can be discussed only with B. At the same time, it is A that ultimately bears the burden of their remuneration for any given assignment, so their best chance of improving their wages is by bargaining vis-à-vis A. Similarly, it is A that controls working conditions in the workplace, so any attempt to bargain with B with regard to such conditions is likely to be fruitless. Moreover, both the 'temps' and the permanent workers of A have an interest in bargaining together vis-à-vis A. For the 'temps', this is a chance to achieve parity of terms and conditions (to the extent this is not dictated by law). For the permanent employees, this is a way to make sure that their interests are not undermined by competition from the 'temps'. And since one of the goals of collective bargaining is to prevent competition between workers, such joint bargaining can certainly be justified.[107]

Nonetheless, as a matter of practice, if the workers work for A only for a brief period it would be unrealistic to consider them part of the collective that bargains with that firm. The true 'temps' can only bargain, as a matter of fact, vis-à-vis B, which presumably has a longer relationship with them. This should be allowed and encouraged. Importantly, this does not preclude the possibility of applying collective agreements that cover employees of A, by legislation, to comparable agency workers as well (mutatis mutandis), as required by the European Directive. Still, as far as the true 'temps' are concerned, for the purpose of actual collective bargaining it appears that B alone should be considered the employer. Indeed, collective bargaining with TEAs is a common practice in many European countries.[108]

Having said that, it must be acknowledged that the line between the true 'temps' and those workers that should be considered employees of A for all purposes is

[107] In Chapter 5 this goal is not mentioned explicitly, but it is implicit in the discussion.
[108] Donald Storrie, *Temporary Agency Work in the European Union* (European Foundation for the Improvement of Living and Working Conditions 2002).

often far from clear. A worker can start working on a short-term assignment, then stay with the same user firm for an additional assignment, eventually working long-term for the same firm. At first it appears that only B should be the employer for purposes of collective bargaining, but as time goes by this is less and less clear. The worker may be party to a collective agreement with B (if she and her peers were able to overcome the barriers to unionization), but after a year or two with the same user firm it becomes for the most part irrelevant. At this stage the worker will be less interested in her theoretical rights between assignments, and more interested in parity with her colleagues at A and the conditions of work there. From the point of view of A's employees, as well, this worker should be part of their bargaining unit at this stage. So a 'community of interest' may build over time. Workers through agencies have their own interests as long as they frequently switch assignments, but the longer they stay with the same user firm the more their interests converge with those of the permanent employees.

If they stay with A for what is, in practice, an indefinite period, workers should be considered employees of that firm. But often it is not clear when exactly that point has been reached. A useful solution could be to allow the workers to choose where they want to exercise their collective bargaining rights at any given time. In other words, workers should be able to move from one bargaining unit to another as their situation changes. Once again, then, according to this suggestion, both A and B would be considered 'employers'. In this context, there is not much room for coordination between them, and they should not be considered as one employer, but rather both should be considered (separately) employers for purposes of allowing the worker to be part of collective bargaining with them.

Truly triangular employment through subcontractors

The same 'joint employer' solution is applicable, and justified, in the context of subcontracting as well—when it is truly triangular. Consider, for example, the situation of cleaners employed at a university (A) through a cleaning contractor (B). There are different ways in which A can buy the cleaning services. Imagine at one extreme that A contracts with B to provide cleaning services, but in practice A controls the number of cleaners, the identity of the cleaners, and the number of hours they work; A also supervises their work and makes the decision about dismissals; the payment is based on the cost of wages per hour of work as determined by A, plus a small commission for B ('cost plus'). Such characteristics suggest that the workers are subordinated to A and dependent on A; their employment through B is merely a sham designed to evade labour laws. In such a case, a purposive interpretation of the term 'employer' should lead to a conclusion that A is in fact the legal employer.

At the other extreme, it is also possible for A to contract with B to deliver a clean campus. B gets a lump sum and retains complete discretion on how many cleaners to employ, their identity, where and how they will work, including supervision. In this scenario, although the workers work on the premises of A, they have no real contact with A in terms of subordination and dependency. They should be considered employees of B. It may seem unfair that they do not enjoy the rights and benefits of university employees, even though they clean the university and work alongside university employees, but the geographical location of the work is not indicative of an employment relationship. Arguably, the fact such cleaners are part of the same community should lead to *some* liability on the university, but as a guarantor and not an employer—I discuss this separately in Chapter 9.

The most difficult cases are, of course, those in between the two extremes. If work relations are (truly) triangular, both A and B have some characteristics of employers. Consider the following (realistic) scenario: A wants a specific number of cleaners in each building/area, and it pays B by hours of work, on a 'cost plus' basis. A also has its own employees that check if the work is done properly (i.e. supervise the work). Furthermore, if A is not satisfied with the work in a specific area, it will ask B to replace the employee there, which will usually lead to dismissals. However, B can generally decide who to hire, and B also has its own supervisors—so direct supervision is performed by B, while A only checks the overall performance from time to time. Direct orders are given to the workers by B's supervisors, who are also the ones who deal with requests for vacations, time-off, changing shifts, and so on.

In subcontracting as well, then, the truly triangular relations are characterized by a mixture of vulnerabilities. There is (some) subordination, and also dependency, vis-à-vis A. There is also (some) subordination, and also dependency, vis-à-vis B. In this situation, once again a division of responsibilities would be difficult and is likely to fail in terms of preventing evasion. The solution of placing responsibility on both A and B as 'joint employers'—jointly and severally—is thus suitable here as well.

There is also an additional argument in favour of joint responsibility if we take into account the problems of enforcement—and assume (realistically) that non-compliance is prevalent. A is better positioned, compared with the workers, to *prevent* violations of labour laws by B, by choosing only reliable contractors and by insisting on collaterals.[109] Moreover, economic analysis suggests that in principal–agent relations, it is generally recommended to place liability on the principal, to ensure that she behaves socially optimally in controlling her agents to reduce harm.[110] The same logic applies with regard to client–contractor relations when these are characterized—as in the cleaning sector—by the client's ability to

[109] Compare David Weil, 'Crafting a Progressive Workplace Regulatory Policy: Why Enforcement Matters' (2007) 28 CLLPJ 125, 140–42; and see Lora Jo Foo, 'The Vulnerable and Exploitable Immigrant Workforce and the Need for Strengthening Worker Protective Legislation' (1994) 103 Yale LJ 2179.

[110] A Mitchell Polinsky and Steven Shavell, 'The Theory of Public Enforcement of Law' in A Mitchell Polinsky and Steven Shavell (eds), *Handbook of Law and Economics: Vol 1* (Elsevier 2007) 403. And see also Michael C. Harper, 'Defining the Economic Relationship Appropriate for Collective Bargaining' (1998) 39 Boston College LR 329 (arguing that the direct capital provider should be considered a joint employer for collective bargaining purposes, based on the goals of the US National Labor Relations Act); David Weil, *The Fissured Workplace: Why Work Became So Bad for So Many and What Can Be Done to Improve It* (HUP 2014) 260 (discussing the possibility of a collective agreement with both the direct employer and the lead company).

minimize the harm, both at the contracting stage and during implementation.[111] In such cases, supervision is possible because of the physical placement of the workers on the client's premises.[112] By making A legally responsible, we can create a 'community of fate' between A and B,[113] thus encouraging A to take steps to ensure compliance by B with labour standards.[114]

In practice the 'joint employer' solution can work in much the same way as in the TEA context discussed in the previous section. The one additional issue that we need to consider, which was not relevant in the context of *temporary* relations, is long-term rights and benefits included in A's collective agreements. This is particularly crucial when 'just cause' protections are not available in legislation, but can be available in collective agreements. Workers through subcontractors can work for the same client for many years. Should the cleaners employed indirectly at a university, for example, be entitled to the same job security ('just cause') rights secured by university administrative staff in their collective agreement? It seems that such non-pecuniary rights should apply as well, *mutatis mutandis*, otherwise there will be an incentive for indirect employment in order to evade these specific collective agreement obligations. From a purposive point of view, there is no justification for allowing an employer who has signed a collective agreement, in accordance with labour law, to evade some of the obligations included in the agreement by unilaterally excluding some workers from its scope (assuming, of course, that the agreement itself does not explicitly exclude these workers—which raises other issues that are out of the scope of this chapter).

So far I have argued that in relations of subcontracting, to examine an argument that A should be directly responsible as an 'employer' for employees of B, we must check where subordination and dependency lie. If they are entirely towards A, this is a sham arrangement; A is the employer. If they are entirely towards B, then B alone is the employer. If these two vulnerabilities are found in both of the relationships—towards A as well as B—then both of them should be liable together and separately, as 'joint employers'.

From a purposive perspective this seems to be the most appropriate solution in principle; still, it may not always be optimal in terms of the balance between universalism and selectivity. Specifically, such a case-by-case examination is likely to

[111] Compare Fiona Haines, *Corporate Regulation: Beyond 'Punish or Persuade'* (Clarendon 1997) 235.

[112] See also Bruce Goldstein and others, 'Enforcing Fair Labor Standards in the Modern American Sweatshop: Rediscovering the Statutory Definition of Employment' (1999) 46 UCLA LR 983. Compare also with the heightened willingness of courts to place responsibility on clients for health and safety violations occurring on their premises. See, e.g., in the United States, *Heiman v Worker's Compensation Appeals Board* (2007) 149 Cal App 4th 724 (California Court of Appeals).

[113] John Braithwaite, *Regulatory Capitalism: How it Works, Ideas for Making it Work Better* (Edward Elgar 2008) 95.

[114] In Chapter 9 I discuss similar proposals to place liability on the 'lead company' towards employees of a contractor, but show more reluctance to rely on the argument that the lead company has the power to prevent the harm. Note, however, that the discussion there is limited to situations in which there are no direct relations between the lead company and the workers, while in the current context our assumption has been that the relations are truly triangular, meaning that A shares some of the characteristics of an employer alongside B.

fail in sectors that suffer from severe enforcement problems. In these sectors, the lack of a clear-cut solution might give employers too much leeway to evade labour laws, arguing that dependency and subordination exist only vis-à-vis B. Even if after a case-by-case factual examination this proves to be incorrect, this conclusion will often not be obvious on its face but rather costly and lengthy to reach. As a result, employees who face significant barriers to self enforcement are unlikely to challenge their status and sue A. This can be solved by making a clear-cut decision that in specific sectors—for example cleaning and security—all workers employed by B to do work at A are in fact jointly employed by both of them, regardless of the specific facts of the case. This entails some costs in terms of placing liability on A in some cases which do not justify it. But in sectors that experience vast enforcement problems, and also when most cases are likely to be classified as either sham arrangements or joint employment, the cost will be low indeed—and the contribution to advancing the goals of labour law will be significant.

Supply chain employment

The final issue that must be considered here—if we are to address the main problems confronted by contemporary employment structures—is the identification of the 'employer' in supply chain contexts. Consider, for example, the facts of *Lian v J Crew*, a case considered by a court in Ontario, Canada.[115] The plaintiff, Fan Jin Lian, is a Chinese immigrant, who worked from her own home in Toronto sewing and assembling garments. Among the clothes she made were shorts later sold under the label of J Crew, a large American retailer. The J Crew Group (hereinafter A) contracted with a company named Yee Tung Garment Co (B), of Hong Kong, to manufacture the shorts. Yee Tung in turn contracted with E Knitted Garment Inc (C), a Canadian corporation, to do the same. E Knitted then contracted with several subcontractors, among them Eliz World Inc (D). The last subcontractor hired Lian on an hourly basis.

Alongside J Crew shorts, Lian also produced in her home 'Northern Elements' clothing as well as 'Costa Blanca' garments. In these cases as well, Eliz World (Lian's direct employer) was a subcontractor at the end of a supply/production chain. So Eliz World received orders from several sources, and hired workers in Toronto—among them Lian—to do the actual work. Lian claimed that her wages were below the legislated minimum wage, and that she was not paid overtime payments as well as vacation pay—and she sued (in a class action) not only the direct employer, but the entire three chains. The legal argument was that J Crew and the other companies up the chain(s) were 'associated or related employers' together with Eliz World; according to applicable Ontario legislation, if two or more entities are associated or related and the intent or effect of the combination was to defeat the

115 *Lian v J Crew Group Inc* (2001) 54 OR (3d) 239 (Ontario Superior Court of Justice). For a similar case see *Doe v Wal-Mart Stores Inc* 572 F 3d 677 (9th Cir 2009) (US Court of Appeals).

purpose of the law, they shall be considered 'joint employers'.[116] Unsurprisingly, this argument was rejected by the court; with so many degrees of separation, it was difficult to see J Crew as 'associated' with Eliz World. There was also no evidence to suggest that the subcontracting arrangement was intended to evade the law (and thus defeat its purpose). The question of 'effect' is more complicated, but in any case cannot come instead of the 'associated' requirement.

It is still pertinent to ask: is it justified to place responsibility on A for employees of D? The 'joint employer' solution does not seem applicable here, because it leads to seeing the employees of the subcontractor as employees of the client as well *for all intents and purposes*. Seeing Lian as an employee of J Crew for all intents and purposes would be unreasonable on its face. A large corporation works with thousands of suppliers, as well as other entities who do work for it (such as consultants). It usually has no knowledge of the workers who perform the work on behalf of these suppliers—not about their number, or their identity, or their work conditions. There is certainly no subordination of these employees vis-à-vis the ultimate client. Dependency is very indirect, if at all. To require a large corporation to treat all of the workers employed by its numerous subcontractors as its own employees would be against the entire structure of the market and cannot be justified.

The more modest alternative is to hold A responsible for D's employees in some specific limited sense: for example, to place 'residual responsibility' on A, as a guarantor for D's debts to employees. Under such a rule, A will only have to pay if D does not pay some of the mandatory payments to its employees. This means that A will have an incentive to make sure that all its subcontractors comply with labour laws, which can be done by limiting the number of links in the chain; by ensuring that all the subcontractors are recognized, law-abiding corporations; by insisting on collaterals; and perhaps even by operating an inspection/monitoring apparatus.[117] All of these steps have costs and they will limit the flexibility of businesses. Is it still justified to impose residual responsibility? This is not obvious on its face and requires a normative discussion. I address this issue in Chapter 9, as part of the inquiry into possible methods to improve compliance with labour law (in this case, indirect pressure through the clients to improve compliance by their subcontractors).

Conclusion

This part attempted to offer solutions for a number of common legal problems concerning the identity of the employer. By way of conclusion it would be useful to set out the stages of the required analysis and the possible solutions. Assume once again a triangular work relationship that includes a worker, entity A enjoying

[116] The Court in *Lian* (n 115) considered s 12 of the Ontario Employment Standards Act 1990. A similar section now appears as s 4 of the Ontario Employment Standards Act 2000. For analyses of this case see Benjamin Kates, 'The Supply Chain Gang: Enforcing the Employment Rights of Subcontracted Labour in Ontario' (2012) 16 CLELJ 449; Brian Langille, '"Take These Chains from My Heart and Set Me Free": How Labor Law Theory Drives Segmentation of Workers' Rights' (2015) 36 CLLPJ 257.

[117] See also Brishen Rogers, 'Toward Third-Party Liability for Wage Theft' (2010) 31 BJELL 1.

her work, and entity B that is presented as the legal employer. B could be a TEA or a subcontractor.[118] Assume also a supply/production chain that includes a worker, A as the lead company/brand, B as a subcontractor that contracts with C that in turn contracts with D that is the direct employer.

When considering legal responsibility, we should start by asking: who has the characteristics of an employer? That is, which entity has, vis-à-vis the worker, the characteristics that justify the application of labour laws? I have argued, relying on the analysis in previous chapters, that the relevant characteristics are democratic deficits (subordination, broadly conceived) and dependency. There are three possible answers when asking who has the employer characteristics:

First, if the answer is A—i.e. if all (or almost all) the characteristics of an employer lie with A, even though another entity is presented as a legal employer—then this is a sham arrangement. In such cases we should ignore the sham and place full employer responsibility on A. Ignoring (looking beyond) sham arrangements is indeed the law in many countries, although in practice this rule is often not applied, at least not consistently.

Second, if the characteristics of an employer are shared by two or more entities, in theory there are four options in terms of ascribing responsibility. We can either:

(a) Decide that one of them is the only legal employer, e.g., always the user, or always the TEA/subcontractor; or
(b) Divide the responsibilities of an employer between them, e.g., for purposes of the minimum wage law A would be the employer, for purposes of a working hours law B would have to assume responsibility; or
(c) Place joint responsibility on both/all of them, i.e. both/all will be jointly and severally liable as if they are the employer for all purposes (and the worker will have all the rights enjoyed by employees of A as well); or
(d) Place full responsibility on the direct employer and residual responsibility (sometime called subsidiary or secondary responsibility) on the other(s), i.e. A will have to guarantee the payments by B (or D) to the worker, if these were not paid, but the worker will not enjoy the same rights as A's employees.

It is possible to find examples in the laws of different legal systems to all four solutions, although probably the most common result is simply to leave the responsibility with the entity that was designated as the employer by the formal contractual arrangements. This is unfortunate, because it legitimizes a system by which A evades responsibility, and the rights of the workers are harmed. I have argued above that the best solution is (c), i.e. placing full responsibility on both A and B (or D) as 'joint employers'.

[118] I have not discussed in this chapter situations of franchising—and the potential responsibility of the franchisor towards the workers employed by the franchisee. I discuss this to some extent in Guy Davidov, 'Indirect Employment: Should Lead Companies Be Liable?' (2015) 37 CLLPJ 5. For an extensive discussion of franchising see Weil (n 110).

The third option regarding the initial question is that the direct employer (B or D) has all the characteristics of an employer. In such cases it would not be justified to hold A legally responsible as a full employer. There is still a question of whether A should be liable residually, as a guarantor. I discuss this separately in Chapter 9.

7

Using Open-Ended Standards to Advance Labour Law's Goals

At the beginning of this book (Chapter 1) I briefly referred to two main aspects of the 'crisis of labour law'. First, the widespread enforcement problems—specifically, the fact that many workers are unable to enjoy labour laws due to employer evasion and other instances of non-compliance; and second, the inadequate response to changing realities, i.e. the fact that labour laws are not being sufficiently adapted to new circumstances and challenges. Both of these problems have been exacerbated by the decline in union density and union power. Unions play an important role in ensuring compliance with labour and employment laws, and collective agreements are one of the main methods of adapting the law to changing and unique circumstances. But in most countries, this route is now relevant for a rather small and decreasing number of workers.[1] In both respects, the results are highly troublesome for workers, especially those in precarious arrangements. When labour laws are becoming irrelevant—whether they are unenforceable or outdated—the result is the reign of 'free market' private law rules, giving unfettered control to employers. The goal of this chapter is to show that among the many possible solutions to this crisis, one potential component is to rely more heavily on open-ended standards. Addressing the two problems will also serve to advance labour law's goals, in line with the purposive approach. Another goal of the chapter is to examine which standards are most suitable for labour law; I offer a combination of three standards that seem to optimally cover the needs of this legal field.

Examples of open-ended standards are good faith, proportionality, reasonableness, fairness, mutual trust and confidence, and the managerial prerogative. Unlike concrete rules, which are obviously very common in labour law, such standards give broad discretion to courts and as a result have the potential to alleviate, to some extent, both of the above-mentioned problems. First, they are more

[1] On the decline in union density around the world, see Claus Schnabel, 'Union Membership and Density: Some (Not So) Stylized Facts and Challenges' (2012) Diskussionspapiere No. 81, Universität Erlangen-Nürnberg, Lehrstuhl für Arbeitsmarkt- und Regionalpolitik, <http://www.econstor.eu/bitstream/10419/66786/1/730117782.pdf> accessed 15 October 2015. For up-to-date data see also <http://stats.oecd.org/Index.aspx?DataSetCode=UN_DEN> accessed 15 October 2015.

difficult to evade, because it is more difficult to work around a standard than a rule. A rule would state that in concrete circumstances X an employer must pay the workers a sum Y.[2] The employer can then try to avoid circumstances X by structuring the relationship a little differently (say, X-1).[3] In contrast, a standard is designed to capture a more general idea: if the demand from the employer is to act 'fairly' or 'reasonably' (for example), this could easily capture a broad range of circumstances (including both X and X-1). Second, standards have an inherent capacity for ongoing adaptation to change. If changes in the labour market necessitate (justify) it, a court can change what 'reasonableness' or 'fairness' requires. The content of these open legal requirements can develop from case to case, adapting relatively easily and quickly. Thus, for example, a court can decide that circumstances not previously foreseen (say, X + 1) should also trigger the imposition of a certain duty. Open-ended standards are thus a legal technique that can be used to address the crisis and advance the goals of labour law (although, obviously, they are no panacea; most notably, they can only help those who can overcome the barriers to reaching the courts).

None of this is intended to suggest that standards should generally replace rules in labour law; my argument is rather that standards should be used *on top of* rules to supplement and address their shortcomings. For the purpose of ensuring the payment of Y in circumstances X, it may well be more useful to clearly state this duty as a rule.[4] And if the legislature or the government are quick enough to respond, and enact a new rule placing the duty in circumstances X + 1 as well, this should be welcomed. Nonetheless, there will always be cases that seem to justify the same legal treatment, but are not covered by the rule (X-1, X + 2, and so on).

It appears that in many countries, the resort to standards in labour law has increased in recent years.[5] This chapter offers a possible justification for this development, as well as a call for further development along the same lines. Part I provides a summary of the pros and cons of rules versus standards, giving special attention to the point of view of advancing labour law's goals. It concludes with some possible solutions that attempt to maximize the advantages of both techniques. I then move to examine which standards are best suited for labour law purposes, and briefly justify them (Part II) before moving to examine in detail the three chosen standards: good faith (Part III), the managerial prerogative

[2] Isaac Ehrlich and Richard A Posner, 'An Economic Analysis of Legal Rulemaking' (1974) 3 JLS 257, 258.

[3] As one employer was quoted as saying: 'Give us the rules and we'll play the game' (John Braithwaite, 'Rules and Principles: A Theory of Legal Certainty' (2002) 27 Aust J of Legal Phil 47, 64). See also Cass R Sunstein, 'Problems with Rules' (1995) 83 Cal LR 953, 995: 'Because rules have clear edges, they allow people to "evade" them by engaging in conduct that is technically exempted but that creates the same or analogous harms.'

[4] Certainly the criminal aspects of labour law must be defined in a clear and precise way—as rules. The discussion below refers to civil obligations only.

[5] See, e.g., the special issue on 'Good Faith and Fair Dealing in the Individual Employment Relationship' (2010–2011) 32 CLLPJ; Joellen Riley, *Employee Protection at Common Law* (Federation Press 2005) ch 3; ACL Davies, 'Judicial Self-Restraint in Labour Law' (2009) 38 ILJ 278; Aline Van Bever, 'Open Norms and Employment Law's Foundations: A Legal Examination of Hidden Patterns in Employment Relationships' (2012) 2 ELLJ 173.

(Part IV), and proportionality (Part V). In each of these cases, I will attempt to show that the standards can indeed prove useful for preventing evasion and for adapting the law. Part VI concludes and also addresses some possible critiques.

Part I—Rules vs Standards

When a legislature wishes to advance a goal, it has to choose a legal technique to do so. It is common and useful to distinguish between legal regulations based on their level of specificity.[6] On a spectrum between the most specific and most general, the more specific commands are termed 'rules'; for example: within city borders (which let us assume are clearly defined in the legislation) driving at a speed of over 50km/h is prohibited. In contrast, commands that are more open-ended are termed 'standards'; for example: driving in a pedestrian-heavy area at a dangerous speed is prohibited. Or consider an example from the labour law field: a legislature can command an employer to pay every employee £6.50 per hour of work, or alternatively it could say that an employee must be paid 'fair' wages, or perhaps the minimal amount required to cover reasonable living expenses. If this last example seems unrealistic, then consider a law that requires the employer to act in good faith, or respect employees' privacy unless there is a reasonable business reason justifying an infringement. To be sure, even the specified minimum wage requirement leaves some room for judicial discretion (who is an 'employee'? who is an 'employer'? what is an 'hour of work'?) but on the specificity spectrum it is much closer to the rule pole, while a fairness/good faith/reasonableness requirement is much more open-ended and thus appropriately classified as a standard.

Each of these methods has its own advantages. A seminal article by Isaac Ehrlich and Richard Posner is a useful starting point for the discussion. The authors conducted an economic analysis of the problem, which at first sight could be seen as offering only a narrow and partial point of view, but in fact their cost-benefit analysis is highly useful for our current purposes, as they (rightly) considered 'discouraging socially undesirable activities and encouraging socially desirable ones' as a benefit.[7] And because the decision of what is socially desirable is based on the legislation itself, their model can be understood as designed to advance the goals of the legislation (among other things).

On the face of it, a rule appears to offer better chances of maximizing the achievement of the legislative goal. If the undesirable activity is defined in a precise manner (as a rule) there are better chances of catching it and preventing it.[8] A rule is also associated with more clarity, predictability, and certainty;[9] consistency in its application is also understood to assure fairness and equal treatment.[10]

[6] Ehrlich and Posner (n 2) 258. [7] ibid 262. [8] ibid.

[9] Duncan Kennedy, 'Form and Substance in Private Law Adjudication' (1976) 89 Harv LR 1685, 1688.

[10] Kathleen M Sullivan, 'Foreword: The Justice of Rules and Standards' (1992) 106 Harv LR 22, 62; Sunstein (n 3) 974.

Importantly for current purposes, rules are also easier for enforcement agencies and courts to enforce and litigation costs are smaller.[11] Once we enter the city, we know exactly what the speed limit is; and it is equally clear to the police and the courts whether driving at a certain speed has violated the law or not. However, these advantages depend on whether (or to what extent) it is possible to define the undesirable activity in a precise manner. Certainly, if we think it is dangerous to drive at a speed of over 50km/h within city limits, we should say so explicitly. But it has to be acknowledged that such a rule is likely to be both over-inclusive and under-inclusive, if the actual goal is to prevent dangerous driving. There are circumstances in which 50km/h would be too speedy, i.e. the rule will fail to prevent dangerous driving, and other circumstances in which the limitation will be too strict, i.e. will slow drivers down unnecessarily. A legislature can respond to this problem by making the rule more detailed, with exceptions and separate rules for some circumstances. Nevertheless, it is impossible to anticipate every contingency in advance,[12] especially so in an area such as labour law, dealing with long-term complex relations. Moreover, the more detailed the rule is, the higher the costs (and disadvantages). If instead of one simple rule for the maximum driving speed in cities we will end up with twenty different rules for various unique circumstances, this is costly to create and to enforce, and perhaps most importantly, we lose a lot of clarity and predictability.[13]

A standard ('driving at a dangerous speed is prohibited') can have a 'chilling effect', preventing desirable activity alongside the undesirable activity, because of its imprecision. This could be especially problematic because those who are prone to violating the law are likely to be less risk-averse than those who have a tendency to obey.[14] Therefore, a standard can over-deter the 'good' employers, while under-deterring the 'bad' ones. Nonetheless, it has been shown empirically that regulations creating self-interest incentives can undermine ethical motives and reduce

[11] Ehrlich and Posner (n 2) 264–65. On the high litigation costs incurred as part of the process of giving content to standards, see also Louis Kaplow, 'Rules versus Standards: An Economic Analysis' (1992) 42 Duke LJ 577, 622.

[12] 'The inherent ambiguity of language and the limitations of human foresight and knowledge limit the practical ability of the rulemaker to catalog accurately and exhaustively the circumstances that should activate the general standard. Hence the reduction of a standard to a set of rules must in practice create both overinclusion and underinclusion' (Ehrlich and Posner (n 2) 268). See also Sunstein (n 3) 992.

[13] As argued by Braithwaite, with some empirical support, 'with complex actions in changing environments where large economic interests are at stake principles are more likely to enable legal certainty than rules' (Braithwaite (n 3) 53). One of the main reasons for this counter-intuitive uncertainty of rules is that in complex settings there are so many of them, making it impossible, certainly for lay persons, to understand what the rules require them to do (ibid 57). Complexity also means that those in charge of enforcing the rules have more discretion to choose which rule to apply. For an overview of additional studies supporting these points see Doron Teichman and Eyal Zamir, 'Judicial Decisionmaking: A Behavioral Perspective', in Eyal Zamir and Doron Teichman (eds), *The Oxford Handbook of Behavioral Economics and the Law* (OUP 2014) pt 10.

[14] Ehrlich and Posner (n 2) 262–63.

intrinsic motivation;[15] so in this respect, specific detailed rules are arguably more problematic, while standards can be less destructive for the 'good' employers.[16]

Furthermore, standards have several other important advantages. *First*, they can cover unforeseen situations. If the regulated behaviour is relatively homogenous, a rule is appropriate; but when the conduct regulated tends to be heterogeneous, it would be especially costly and cumbersome to come up with detailed and precise rules.[17] It also means that problems of over-inclusion and under-inclusion are likely exacerbated.[18] Labour relations, which are complex and ever-changing in nature, seem to be a prime example for heterogeneous conduct. *Second*, and relatedly, standards are much better suited to accommodate change. The desirable solution to a problem is likely to change over time, together with economic, technological, social and other factors shaping the problem.[19] If we choose rules, we have to take into account the cost of updating and adapting them to change, including the cost (which is social and not only economic) of having outdated laws for significant periods of time. Standards, in contrast, because they are articulated at a much higher level of abstraction without reference to specific circumstances, are much less vulnerable to obsolescence.[20] *Third*, it has been argued by Duncan Kennedy that rules are associated with individualism, while standards are associated with altruism.[21] If this is correct, standards are more suited to achieve distributive goals—which are among the main goals of labour law.[22] Admittedly, there does not seem to be any necessary connection between open-ended standards and a progressive development of the law.[23] But the structure of standards does seem to open more possibilities for developing the law in a way that will achieve the redistributive goal—if judges are willing to use their power in such direction. *Fourth*, standards offer a solution to problems of opportunism—they can be seen as creating a 'safety valve' that prevents the stronger party from taking unfair advantage of imperfections in the law (or incompleteness in the contract).[24]

[15] Samuel Bowles, 'Policies Designed for Self-Interested Citizens May Undermine "The Moral Sentiments": Evidence from Economic Experiments' (2008) 320 Science 1605.

[16] Yuval Feldman and Henry E Smith, 'Behavioral Equity' (2014) 170 J of Institutional and Theoretical Econ 137 offer a sophisticated analysis of this point, showing how the law can send different messages to different people at the same time. For 'good faith' people, the goal would be not to interfere with their intrinsic motivation to do the right thing (they cite empirical studies showing that specific detailed rules sometimes have this detrimental effect). For 'bad faith' people, the goal is to prevent evasion. Standards could potentially achieve both goals simultaneously.

[17] Ehrlich and Posner (n 2) 266–67. A similar point is made by Kaplow (n 11) who puts the emphasis on 'the frequency with which a law will govern conduct' (ibid 621). If the conduct is frequent, it is more efficient to invest in creating a rule, however detailed. Nonetheless, if the law governs heterogeneous behaviour, 'in which each relevant type of act may be rare' (ibid 564), a standard could be appropriate. In other words, the regulated activity itself could be frequent—such as work that repeats every day—but if new problems arise frequently, the heterogeneity could make a standard more fitting.

[18] Ehrlich and Posner (n 2) 270.

[19] ibid 277.

[20] ibid; Sullivan (n 10) 66; Sunstein (n 3) 994.

[21] Kennedy (n 9) 1741–51.

[22] See Chapter 4.

[23] See Sullivan (n 10) 96 (arguing that standards are not necessarily progressive, but can be used to advance conservative goals as well).

[24] See Kenneth Ayotte, Ezra Friedman, and Henry E Smith, 'A Safety Valve Model of Equity as Anti-Opportunism' (2013) Northwestern Law & Econ Research Paper no 13-15 <http://ssrn.com/abstract=2245098> accessed 15 October 2015.

This is especially relevant for the context of employment relations, where one of the parties is consistently stronger, and the relationship is structured in a way that keeps one party subordinated and the other with powers to make decisions,[25] thus creating a high risk of opportunism and abuse of power.

There is also an option of combining a rule with a standard—which would be helpful for tackling the problem of under-inclusion (e.g. within city limits, it is prohibited to drive at a speed of over 50 km/h, or at a lower speed which a reasonable person would consider dangerous in the circumstances). Ehrlich and Posner note that this would diminish to some extent the advantages of the rule,[26] but it has been argued in contrast by Braithwaite that a prudent mix of rules and standards can achieve the highest level of certainty.[27] Moreover, labour laws are not symmetrical. They aim to prevent abuse by the stronger party. From the point of view of protecting the weaker employees, the advantages of the rule are still achieved, and the standard is helpful for closing loopholes and allowing for adaptations. As noted by Kathleen Sullivan, 'bright-line rules create incentives for exploitation in situations in which knowledge or access to information is distributed unequally';[28] and this is certainly true in the labour market. Standards can potentially remedy this problem. In addition, a standard can be reduced over time, through a case-by-case development, to a set of rules when appropriate.[29]

Another option for combining the two methods is to use standards and leave room for private actors to create more specific rules, thus addressing the demand for more specificity.[30] The same mechanism can be used to open some room for adaptations.[31] Collective agreements are a prime example of such private rule-making. In this respect, with the declining coverage of collective agreements arguably more rules are needed to replace those previously created by the collective partners. At the same time the decline in collective bargaining diminishes opportunities that previously existed for adapting the law to specific circumstances, which suggests the need for *more* standards that can have such capacities.[32]

[25] On the inherent inequality of power in employment relations see Chapter 3.

[26] Ehrlich and Posner (n 2) 268.

[27] Braithwaite (n 3) 65, 79–80.

[28] Sullivan (n 10) 66.

[29] Ehrlich and Posner (n 2) 266. Ehrlich and Posner also argue that rules could be more fitting when a problem is 'older', because at first a problem seems complex, but over time commonality is expected to emerge (ibid 273). So rules can be derived from standards over time, whether by courts or by the legislature, and they can also be codified. But in an ever-changing world this cannot be expected to reduce the need for standards. For a recent attempt to find another middle ground between rules and standards, see Gideon Parchomovsky and Alex Stein, 'Catalogs' (2015) 115 Colum LR 165 (arguing that it is often preferable to use a third option that includes several examples and a residual category, e.g., by using 'such as' or 'and the like').

[30] Ehrlich and Posner (n 2) 261.

[31] Cass Sunstein has made several proposals that aim to achieve an optimal balance between rules and standards. One of them is a presumption in favour of 'privately adaptable rules' (Sunstein (n 3) 958–59).

[32] In discussing 'good faith', one important labour law standard, Alan Bogg has argued that 'many of the functions of contractual good faith were performed instead by an effective system of collective bargaining' (Alan Bogg, 'Good Faith in the Contract of Employment: A Case of the English Reserve?' (2011) 32 CLLPJ 729, 746). In this sense as well, the decline in union power explains the increased need for an explicit good faith requirement. Indeed, as described by Bogg, UK judges have explicitly referred to the declining fortunes of collective bargaining as necessitating

To summarise this part: standards can potentially offer a solution (obviously, only a partial solution) to some of the main problems that labour law is facing. Rules are necessary, but a combination with open-ended standards on top of them can prove useful to confront pervasive problems of employer evasion and obsoleteness. Standards can thus contribute to the advancement of labour law's goals. However, this depends to a large extent on the actual ability and willingness of courts to use standards in a way that materializes the potential. For example, the idea of 'good faith' can be taken to suggest mainly a duty on the employee to adhere to the economic interests of the business, perversely giving more power to the stronger party to the relationship—which usually can use market power to protect itself and does not need additional protection from the law. Or it can be used to prevent abuse of power and unfair actions mostly by the employer (and by the employee when power is held and abused at the other end).[33] From the other side there is potentially a risk that 'good faith' will become an untamed tool, leading to excessive and unpredicted limitations on employers (and thus on economic activities). So what can experience teach us about the actual application of standards in labour law? Have they succeeded in advancing labour law's goals? Parts III through to V below examine the actual application of three main standards in labour law. But first, the next part asks which standards are most appropriate and justified to employ.

Part II—Which Standards?

David Cabrelli has shown that UK labour laws impose many different standards in different contexts, and argued in favour of some simplification and convergence.[34] Indeed, it is sometimes difficult to explain why employers are subjected to proportionality in one context but only required not to act irrationally in other contexts; and why courts assess the actions of employers against an objective standard in some cases, but a subjective standard in others. It is certainly possible from a purposive point of view to have different levels of expectations, depending on the context; as Cabrelli explains, the more important the protected rights/interests, the higher the standard demanded from an employer to justify an infringement.[35] However, the question is whether we need a variety of different standards to achieve this result, or rather can have the flexibility within a small

creative regulatory responses, including the development of a good faith duty (ibid 749). See also Aditi Bagchi, 'Unions and the Duty of Good Faith in Employment Contracts' (2003) 112 Yale LJ 1881 (arguing that the duty of good faith is not self-enforcing in individual employment relations, and not easily enforced by courts—and unions provide a solution because they create an institutional framework for self-enforcing good faith).

33 See Bogg (n 32) 734–36.

34 David Cabrelli, 'The Hierarchy of Differing Behavioural Standards of Review in Labour Law' (2011) 40 ILJ 146.

35 ibid 172–73.

number of standards to place changing demands on employers depending on the context.

I will argue that three standards offer together a comprehensive and coherent solution for labour law: good faith, the managerial prerogative, and proportionality. While acknowledging the possibility that a legislature could find it justified, when striving to achieve a specific purpose, to adopt some other standard, for the most part these three seem to be sufficient.

A duty to act in good faith has a dual purpose. First, it can be used to prevent actions and decisions taken in 'bad faith', i.e. when one of the parties (usually the employer) treats the other in a way that in the specific circumstances is considered unacceptable (to a degree that society finds it justified to intervene).[36] This includes malicious intentions—bad faith in the sense of wanting to harm the other party—but goes much beyond such occurrences, which are likely to be rare. If an employer is oblivious to the implications of its actions for the employee, there is no intention to harm but it can certainly be considered bad faith. Second, a good faith standard can be used to derive norms that can guide employers and employees, explaining in a more general and forward-looking way what kinds of behaviour will be considered unacceptable. With this structure in mind, there is little difference between good faith, fairness, or 'mutual trust and confidence'.[37] I prefer the former term, especially because it also captures the situations of bad intentions, but as noted they are only a small part of the story. As far as creating an objective standard the title is hardly important. The point is to have a standard that supplements labour law rules (which tell us that *specific* conducts are unacceptable) with (a) a *general* prohibition to act in a way that is unacceptable—to a degree that can justify judicial intervention, and (b) a legal tool that allows judges to adopt rules that they find necessary in light of cases they are exposed to, derived from the general standard. There is of course a difficult question of how far this can be taken in terms of legitimacy—an issue which I discuss briefly in the concluding part of the chapter—but such questions are not affected by the title of the standard.[38]

In some sense the good faith duty can be seen as a limitation on the managerial prerogative: the employer generally has the right to make managerial decisions

[36] See Robert S Summers, '"Good Faith" in General Contract Law and the Sales Provisions of the Uniform Commercial Code' (1968) 54 Va LR 195.

[37] Joellen Riley has argued that 'mutual trust' is unique to employment and therefore imposes a somewhat higher standard compared with 'good faith' which applies to some other contracts as well (Joellen Riley, 'Siblings But Not Twins: Making Sense of "Mutual Trust" and "Good Faith" in Employment Contracts' (2012) 36 Melbourne U LR 521). Such distinctions are certainly possible, but it is equally possible to use the same standard (good faith) and apply it contextually, taking into account the unique features of employment relations. See also n 41 below and accompanying text.

[38] Hanoch Dagan argues that while 'standards that refine the regulative principle...are generally unobjectionable...open-ended references to justice, fairness, good faith, or reasonableness...cannot provide proper predictability and should be criticized as an invitation to discretionary ad hoc adjudication' (Hanoch Dagan, 'Lawmaking for Legal Realists' (2013) 1 Theory and Practice of Legislation 187). This is true if standards are used as methods for unconstrained case-by-case decision-making. In fact, as will be shown below, good faith has been used in practice mostly to develop new rules.

unilaterally (including by variation of working arrangements), but these are subject to the limitations of good faith. However, quite apart from these limitations there is also a question of how broad the managerial prerogative is. Even if we only examine decisions that were taken in good faith, we still have to ask whether they can be taken unilaterally or rather require an agreement between the parties. This is the role of the managerial prerogative standard. Here as well, it is not possible to use concrete rules for setting the boundaries of the managerial prerogative, without being exposed to a significant degree of the disadvantages of rules. Just to give a few examples: should the employer be allowed to transfer an employee from one job to another? To move the place of business from one city to another? To transfer the employee from day shifts to night shifts? In some legal systems there is perhaps a clear-cut rule for these questions (which is likely to be 'yes'); but it is not clear at all that the employer should enjoy the power to do all of these things entirely unilaterally. As I show in Part IV, in some legal systems the managerial prerogative to take such decisions has limits—and rightly so—and these limits are best captured by way of an open-ended standard.

Finally, and perhaps most importantly, there is the principle of proportionality, which (like good faith) also has a dual purpose. First, it provides a structure to examine whether infringements of rights are justified. Assume for example that an employee's privacy has been infringed by covert video recording, and that privacy in the employment context is protected by law. The employer argues that this was justified in the circumstances for legitimate business reasons. The three proportionality tests—described in Part V below—create a structure to examine whether the means chosen to achieve the legitimate goal are 'proportionate' and thus justified. The same structure is useful to examine managerial decisions that affect other rights. Decisions taken by labour unions can similarly be subject to this standard. The second role of proportionality, at least potentially, is to create a general system that places limits on managerial decision-making. In this respect, the good faith standard might seem broad enough—indeed it may even seem *too* broad potentially—but its actual breadth is much more limited. Leaving aside occurrences of bad faith in specific circumstances, the rules derived from the good faith standard can be either quite specific (e.g. do not make unsubstantiated allegations) or procedural (e.g. give notice before dismissal or changes). Such rules are highly important, but they do not offer any system to limit decision-making by employers more generally. It is here that the principle of proportionality can come into play, by subjecting decisions of an employer to the proportionality tests not only when they infringe rights, but also when they negatively impact other employee interests. The same is true for decisions by labour unions, which can be limited by the proportionality tests when harming employers' interests. Otherwise put, proportionality is a tool that helps to decide conflicts of rights and/or interests between employers and employees. This is very common, and the three proportionality tests provide a legal structure to balance such conflicting rights/interests.

Hopefully it now becomes clear how the three standards complement each other. The starting point is that employers have a lot of power in the employment relationship. They control the business and accordingly the workplace. Labour law acknowledges that this default position is necessary and justified. Nevertheless, employment relations are still contractual, and there is a question of which changes are within the employer's unilateral power, and which require agreement. This is captured by the concept of managerial prerogative, which has a changing content (setting its boundaries) and thus can be considered a standard. Decisions that do not require agreement are still subject to many limitations, designed to ensure that the power of the employer is not abused, and also that all the important goals of labour law (discussed in Chapters 3 through to 5) are advanced. In most cases such limitations are set in concrete rules (in legislation), but a good faith standard adds an important protection, allowing courts to decide that certain actions/decisions are unacceptable, even if they were not foreseen (and thus not prevented) in advance by legislation. Finally, the principle of proportionality adds three structured tests that aim to ensure the rationality and necessity of decisions that harm employees, and also to prevent occurrences of gross disproportion between costs and benefits.

Let us turn, then, to examine how the three standards have worked—and can work—in practice. There are several ways in which one can try to support an argument about the actual usefulness of standards in labour law. One is to examine the overall impact of the standard in different countries. Another is to follow more closely the historical development of a standard in one specific country. A third option is to ask how the standard has been used (and can be used) in specific circumstances (cases). Below I use all of these approaches, to show that the virtues of standards can be seen through different kinds of analysis. When discussing good faith, I will take a broad comparative approach; when considering the managerial prerogative, I will focus mainly on one legal system (Israel) and consider development over time; when analysing proportionality, I will examine how it can be helpful in a number of specific cases. I believe that each of these methodologies can be successfully used for the other two standards as well. I do not follow all three methods here for each standard, not only to avoid excessive length, but also because it is not crucial for my argument. I have no pretentions of presenting an empirical proof for the usefulness of standards here. I do, however, believe that the three parts below provide much support for this argument, showing that standards are helpful and important for advancing labour law's goals not only in theory (as argued above) but also in practice.

Part III—Good Faith

In some legal systems, notably Germany, good faith is a fundamental overarching principle, embracing all kinds of contracts and other relationships.[39] If two commercial entities dealing at arm's length with each other must do so in good

[39] Bernd Waas, 'Good Faith in the Law of the Employment Relationship: Germany' (2011) 32 CLLPJ 603.

faith it is obviously all the more required when the relationship is characterized by one-sided subordination (opening the possibility of abuse of power). Other characteristics of the employment contract—the fact that it is long term (usually indefinite), incomplete, requires changes from time to time, and highly important for the worker to make a living, and also for the fulfilment of social and psychological needs—similarly suggest the need for more protection and intervention, compared with commercial contracts.[40] So systems that cherish the idea of good faith in general, are likely to demand an even higher standard ('heightened' good faith) in employment relations.[41] Other legal systems, notably the UK, are more suspicious about a general requirement of good faith, but have nonetheless seen the need to create a similar demand ('mutual trust and confidence') for contracts of employment.[42] Overall, then, there is significant experience with a 'good faith' standard (whether by this or some other name) in various jurisdictions and the noticeable trend has been in the direction of further extending the role accorded to this standard.[43]

Experience with the 'good faith' standard has been positive, at least from the point of view of labour law scholars (which is a good indication in terms of the advancement of labour law's goals). In Germany, Bernd Waas explains that the principle of good faith—which appears explicitly in legislation—has permitted the courts to ensure that the law is sufficiently dynamic and capable of responding to change. It is used to fill lacunas and to adapt legislative demands to new situations.[44] Specifically, as a result of the good faith standard, employers are prevented from abusing their rights, for example by transferring part of the business

[40] On these characteristics see Chapter 3.

[41] When discussing the situation in Germany Waas (n 39) talks about 'a particular need to protect trust' in the context of employment and an increased willingness of courts to apply the principle of good faith (628–29). In Israel, the National Labour Court explicitly maintains that the duties of good faith are 'heightened' (*Avraham Tzur v Calibre 87 Ltd* 23 PDA 115, 120 (1991); *Osnat Nitay v Beit Hatfutsot* 37 PDA 311, 319 (2002); *Amos Sofer v ORT Israel network*, judgment of 29 December 2005). The US appears to be an exception; an implied covenant of good faith is broadly recognized in contract law generally, but not in the employment context (James J Brudney, 'Reluctance and Remorse: The Covenant of Good Faith and Fair Dealing in American Employment Law' (2011) 32 CLLPJ 773). This is explained mostly by the perceived inconsistency of a good faith duty with the employment at-will doctrine. Nonetheless, US courts do recognize other causes of action that are in some respects similar (ibid 788) and the National Labor Relations Act places a duty to bargain in good faith at the collective level (s 8(d)).

[42] On the similarity between good faith and mutual trust and confidence, see Bogg (n 32); Riley (n 37); Katherine M Apps, 'Good Faith Performance in Employment Contracts: A "Comparative Conversation" Between the U.S. and England' (2006) 8 U Penn J Lab & Emp L 883.

[43] In the UK, see Bogg (n 32), and see David Campbell, 'Good Faith and the Ubiquity of the Relational Contract' (2014) 77 MLR 460 (describing a recent resort to 'good faith' by courts in the context of relational (non-employment) contracts). Mark Freedland and Nicola Kountouris, *The Legal Construction of Personal Work Relations* (OUP 2011) 194–99 explain that in the early and central decades of the twentieth century, good faith was used in many European countries to impose strong duties of fidelity and obedience to the employer. As a result it was treated with suspicion during the years following. Notwithstanding, in later years it has resurrected as a very different concept, imposing standards of fair dealing, mostly in a worker-protective sense. They note that this has been the development in continental European countries as well as the UK.

[44] Waas (n 39) 604–06.

to a separate legal entity to evade labour laws; the parties are prevented from 'contradictory behaviour', for example by trying to renege a reference letter; the employee has a right to actually work (and not only to receive wages); both parties are obligated to disclose relevant information; and employers are sometimes bound by custom (e.g. to pay a Christmas bonus).[45] Moreover, as a result of recent amendments to legislation, employment contracts are subject to standard form contract rules, and coupled by the requirement of good faith, this has led to the invalidation of some unfair terms (e.g. provisions that allow an employer to revoke certain promises unilaterally).[46]

Finally, there are limitations on dismissals above and beyond those included in legislation: most notably, the good faith principle was used to extend protection to small businesses (with less than ten employees) and during a 'probationary period' (the first six months of employment). Even though the German legislature explicitly excluded these situations from the scope of the (legislated) protection against dismissals, the courts decided that at least in some instances the duty to act in good faith creates similar limitations on small businesses and during probationary periods as well.[47] Specifically, a dismissal is considered in violation of the good faith duty if it 'lacks any sense of social thoughtfulness'; if it is made in a surprising fashion (after contradicting statements); or 'declared in an unreasonable manner' (e.g. in a humiliating way, or immediately after the death of a spouse). It appears, though, that these protections are based on the existence of a degree of subjective 'bad faith': Waas notes that in other cases German courts allowed dismissals on Christmas Eve, or right after the employee suffered a miscarriage, because there was no indication that the employer had any intention to harm.[48]

In Israel, a duty to act in good faith appears in the Contracts Act,[49] and has similarly been elevated by the courts to an overarching principle. This is nowhere more evident than in the employment context. In the last two decades, especially, the National Labour Court has often relied on the good faith standard when filling gaps and adapting the law to new realities. This was crucial, because union density (and with it union power) have plummeted drastically,[50] employer evasion attempts and resistance to unions proliferated and became ever more sophisticated, and the legislature has largely failed to respond. New questions and problems were presented to the Court, and it responded with various new rules derived from the good faith standard, most notably: (a) a right to a hearing before dismissals or other significant changes (although the Court did not go so far as to require 'just cause', absent such a right in legislation or in a collective agreement); and (b) duties of information and consultation, in some circumstances, and a duty

[45] ibid 609–15. [46] ibid 615–17. [47] ibid 621–28. [48] ibid 627–28.

[49] Contracts Act (General Part) 1973, ss 12, 39.

[50] Membership declined from 80–85% in the 1980s to 40–45% in 2000 to 25% in 2012. See Yinon Cohen and others, 'Unpacking Union Density: Union Membership and Coverage in the Transformation of the Israeli Industrial Relations System' (2003) 42 Industrial Relations 692; Israeli Central Bureau of Statistics, 'Selected Data from the 2012 Social Survey on the Organization of Workers' (Press Release of June 9, 2013) <http://147.237.248.50/reader/newhodaot/hodaa_template_eng.html?hodaa=201319151> accessed 16 October 2015.

to bargain with a new union.[51] Admittedly, these rights are procedural in nature and not substantive,[52] but they have proved to be highly important and meaningful for employees.

In another set of Israeli cases, good faith was used to reject employee claims that the courts considered opportunistic and unfair—for example, some extreme situations of workers earning high income as independent contractors and then arguing that they are employees, or employees enjoying some beneficial legal arrangement (e.g. in terms of working hours) and then arguing that it is illegal because the employer failed to register the agreement it was based upon.[53] The Court has also relied on good faith to create an implied covenant not to compete, when senior employees have used their position within the employer's business to elicit clients to move with them to a competing business. It is considered to be against the good faith duty if such actions are taken while the employee is still being employed by the first employer.[54]

In the UK, a comprehensive review by Alan Bogg describes the introduction of good-faith-like norms in the last few decades as revolutionary.[55] The concept of 'mutual trust and confidence' has been used to create an impressive array of rights and duties: (a) it prevents the 'infliction of a dignitarian injury' by the employer, through coercion, intimidation, insults, humiliation, making unsubstantiated allegations, and so on;[56] (b) there is a limitation on the exercise of contractual rights, which must be 'rational', based on legitimate reasons (e.g. when using the power of disciplinary suspensions, or making decisions regarding 'discretionary bonus');[57] (c) employers are required to give notice before some decisions, to treat different employees consistently, to protect their legitimate expectations, and to provide information in some contexts—all described by Bogg as 'rule of law' duties;[58] (d) employees are prevented from engaging in industrial action that is seen as unfair or not conductive to goodwill and confidence between the parties (such as 'work to rule').[59]

The impact of this standard has been somewhat limited by the choice of technique: the duty of mutual trust is seen as an 'implied term', meaning that it can be overridden by explicit terms, and also requiring an existing contract (thus it is not applicable to the pre- and post-employment stages).[60] Further, it appears that

[51] Sharon Rabin Margalioth, 'Regulating Individual Employment Contracts Through Good Faith Duties' (2011) 32 CLLPJ 663 explains that the decline in collective agreements has created a 'procedural gap' in Israeli labour law—lack of rules governing the procedural aspects of the employment relationship—which the Court attempted to fill. The good faith duty was 'a natural vehicle for advancing these objectives' (ibid 664).

[52] ibid.

[53] *Issac v Tahal Ltd* 36 PDA 817 (2002) (National Labour Court); *Shmueli v The State of Israel—Israel Broadcasting Authority* 36 PDA 577 (2001) (National Labour Court).

[54] *Euroca International Ltd v Kori*, judgment of 3 March 2001 (National Labour Court).

[55] Bogg (n 32) 747. [56] ibid 754–56. [57] ibid 756–57. [58] ibid 759–63.

[59] ibid 766–67. For other useful reviews and discussions, see Simon Deakin and Gillian S Morris, *Labour Law* (6th edn, Hart 2012) 363; Freedland and Kountouris (n 43) 194–99.

[60] Bogg (n 32) 751ff. See also Hugh Collins, 'Implied Terms: The Foundation in Good Faith and Fair Dealing' (2014) 67 CLP 297. But see Douglas Brodie, 'Beyond Exchange: The New Contract of

British judges have shown a high degree of self-restraint in applying this standard as far as employers' obligations are concerned,[61] and in contrast have been less shy when using it against industrial action.[62] Overall, though, it seems fair to conclude based on the local observers that the good faith/mutual trust standard has done more good than bad, especially in more recent years: it served as a useful measure to close gaps in legislation and otherwise respond to new problems, and it was used as a replacement for protections previously provided by unions.[63] There is further potential for its usefulness if judges will soften their deferential stance.[64] Recently there are some signs of increased willingness to do so, for example by extending the reach of the doctrine to the pre-employment stage.[65]

In Canada, good faith (or 'fair dealing') developed as an implied duty as well, especially since the late 1990s.[66] Kevin Banks notes that this development followed mounting calls from labour law scholars, who argued in favour of a good faith obligation for two main reasons: first, as a reciprocal duty on employers alongside the duty of fidelity, which was long imposed on employees; second, to offset the inherent vulnerability of employees in the relationship. Interestingly, despite the common roots, Canadian jurisprudence developed quite differently from the British one—at least until recently, a good faith duty applied only in dismissal decisions.[67] However, Banks shows that doctrines from contract and tort law have led in practice to similar results in a number of contexts during the life of employment as well. Overall, the impact of the good faith standard in Canada has been significant. It prevents '(1) abuse of power or dishonesty affecting personal integrity interests such as the employee's health, dignity, or reputation; (2) opportunistic deprivation of contractual or statutory rights; (3) lack of candor directly inducing reasonable reliance to the employee's economic detriment; or, (4) failure to meet basic standards of care and respect for employee health, personal dignity, and reputation interests.'[68]

Until very recently Canadian courts refused to require good faith from employers in the context of 'employment policies or how an enterprise carries

Employment' (1998) 27 ILJ 79 (arguing that contracting out of the mutual trust obligation should be considered illegitimate).

61 Bogg (n 32) 770–71.

62 ibid 767–68. On the deferential stance of the judiciary towards employers see generally Davies (n 5).

63 See Bogg (n 32); Freedland and Kountouris (n 43) 194–99; Douglas Brodie, 'The Heart of the Matter: Mutual Trust and Confidence' (1996) 25 ILJ 121; Lizzie Barmes, 'Common Law Implied Terms and Behavioural Standards at Work' (2007) 36 ILJ 35.

64 Douglas Brodie in particular has strongly advocated the use and expansion of good faith norms, especially through the 'mutual trust' doctrine, in a series of articles. See especially Brodie, 'The Heart of the Terms' (n 63); Brodie, 'Beyond Exchange' (n 60); Douglas Brodie, 'Mutual Trust and the Values of the Employment Contract' (2001) 30 ILJ 84.

65 *Tullett Prebon Plc v BGC Brokers LP* [2011] IRLR 420, para 42. Thanks to Douglas Brodie for referring me to this case.

66 *Wallace v United Grain Growers* [1997] 3 SCR 701, [95].

67 Kevin Banks, 'Progress and Paradox: The Remarkable Yet Limited Advance of Employer Good Faith Duties in Canadian Common Law' (2011) 32 CLLPJ 547, 553–54.

68 ibid 585.

on business'.[69] But commentators have been pushing in the direction of further expanding good faith obligations.[70] In a recent case, the Supreme Court proclaimed good faith as a 'central organizing principle' of contract law,[71] and soon afterwards this has been applied to invalidate a decision to suspend an employee, i.e. a decision during the life of the employment contract.[72]

In New Zealand (NZ), Gordon Anderson explains that a good faith duty was inherent in the arbitral system that existed between 1894 and 1991. In the 1990s this was changed by neo-liberal legislation as well as judgments of the Court of Appeal that reversed 'several decades of progressive developments' by specialist labour courts.[73] However, since 2000 there is a legislated duty of good faith in employment relations.[74] The legislation explicitly stipulates that it is wider in scope than trust and confidence (which was narrowly constructed by the Court of Appeal), and requires the parties to be 'active and constructive' towards maintaining a 'responsive and communicative' relationship. This means, in particular (according to the legislation itself) a hearing before any decision that can lead to dismissals, with access to relevant information beforehand.[75] The main impact of the good faith standard to date has been in personal grievance cases, specifically concerning disciplinary proceedings. It appears that the NZ courts have so far limited the use of good faith to procedural guarantees (notifying an employee of allegations, being responsive in the hearing, consultation before restructuring),[76] but the previous 'trust and confidence' cases are also likely to be re-evaluated, in a way that will limit managerial prerogative and require 'good management' practices.[77] Anderson concludes with some optimism about the possibility of the good faith standard to change employer behaviour, although he adds, based on the NZ experience, that specialized labour law courts are a crucial factor.[78]

A duty of good faith does not change the basic structure of the contract of employment or purports to offer a full remedy for the inequality of power or the

[69] ibid 554.

[70] Geoffrey England, 'Recent Developments in the Law of the Employment Contract: Continuing Tension between the Rights Paradigm and the Efficiency Paradigm' (1995) 20 Queen's LJ 557, 589; David Doorey, 'Employer "Bullying": Implied Duties of Fair Dealing in Canadian Employment Contracts' (2005) 30 Queen's LJ 500; Banks (n 67) 588–91.

[71] *Bhasin v Hrynew* [2014] 3 SCR 494.

[72] *Potter v Legal Aid Services Commission* [2015] 1 SCR 500. And see the analysis in Claire Mummé, '*Bhasin v. Hrynew*: A New Era for Good Faith in Canadian Employment Law, or Just Tinkering at the Margins?' (2016) 32 IJCLLIR 117.

[73] Gordon Anderson, 'Good Faith in the Individual Employment Relationship in New Zealand' (2011) 32 CLLPJ 685, 687.

[74] Employment Relations Act 2000.

[75] ibid s 4(1A).

[76] Anderson (n 73) 714–15, 717–19.

[77] ibid 715–17.

[78] In Australia there was some debate about the extent to which a duty of good faith is part of the law. Compare Riley (n 5) with Andrew Stewart, 'Good Faith: A Necessary Element in Australian Employment Law Good Faith and Fair Dealing in the Individual Employment Relationship' (2011) 32 CLLPJ 521. Joellen Riley in particular has strongly advocated the adoption of such standards in a series of publications. See also Riley (n 37); Joellen Riley, '"Mutual Trust and Confidence" On Trial: At Last' (2014) 36 Sydney LR 151. Recently the High Court of Australia decided that implying a term of mutual trust and confidence is 'beyond the legitimate law-making function of the courts' and therefore a step that should not be taken (*Commonwealth Bank of Australia v Barker* [2014] HCA 32 at [1]).

inherent vulnerability of employees.[79] It does offer a useful tool in response to ever-changing challenges in the labour market—as a supplement to concrete labour law rules. Perhaps most importantly, the good faith standard can be used to derive rules that help to address the constant need to adapt labour laws to changing circumstances. At the same time, an open-ended standard is helpful in fighting the crucial problem of employer evasion, by creating a periphery of protection around the concrete rules that are more easily evaded.

Part IV—The Managerial Prerogative

Otto Kahn-Freund famously stated that '[t]here can be no employment relationship without a power to command and a duty to obey'.[80] This assertion is embodied in labour law; the 'power to command' is legally framed as a 'managerial prerogative'—the right of an employer to make unilateral decisions with regard to the business/workplace, including decisions that affect its employees. Otherwise put, the managerial prerogative is the legal recognition of the subordination characterizing the employment relationship (as discussed in Chapter 3). As stated by Mia Rönmmar, '[t]he employer's right to direct and allocate work constitutes a general principle of law'.[81] In this part I use the term 'managerial prerogative' to refer to this right, following the common usage in some (although not all) legal systems. The current part will discuss the regulation of this 'prerogative', focusing mostly on innovative developments introduced in Israel by the National Labour Court, as an example of the potential for adaptation within this doctrine. Because the concept of the managerial prerogative is a judicial creation, and it is open for judges to give it meaning from a broad range of options, I believe it is justified to treat it as an open-ended standard.

Of course, in some respects it is very different from good faith. Modern labour laws are generally designed to protect employees because of their vulnerabilities. They are added on top of private law rules—contract, tort, corporate law, and so on—which create the so-called 'free market'. The interests of employers are generally protected through these private laws, and labour laws usually provide the counterbalance to those rules. However, in some respects labour laws also include within them an additional balance with the rights and legitimate interests of employers. It is easy to see how a duty of good faith fits into this structure: it is generally used to place limits on employers' actions; at the same time it is also used in some contexts to place limits on the actions of employees and unions. The structure of the managerial prerogative is different: unlike other labour law

[79] The critique of Frank Carrigan, 'The Implications of Implied Terms in Law in the Common Law Contract of Employment' (2009) 9 Oxford U Commonwealth LJ 73, is thus based on unrealistic expectations in my view.

[80] Paul Davies and Mark Freedland, *Kahn-Freund's Labour and the Law* (Stevens 1983) 18.

[81] Mia Rönmmar, 'The Managerial Prerogative and the Employee's Obligation to Work: Comparative Perspectives on Functional Flexibility' (2006) 35 ILJ 56, 61.

rules, which for the most part are designed to protect employees, the managerial prerogative is a doctrine used first and foremost to facilitate unilateral decision-making by employers. It embodies and even extends the private law rules that give power to the employer. To a large extent, such a rule, together with the duty of fidelity imposed on employees, are relics of pre-modern labour laws, which for the most part were not protective but were rather designed to strengthen the control over employees.[82] It remains part of labour law, but over the years the main question became what are the *limits* of the managerial prerogative. An analysis of the regulation of the managerial prerogative from an historical perspective can shed light on the way it can be used to respond to new challenges. I will focus on the law in Israel as it developed over the last few decades, as an example.[83] The discussion is limited to the context of individual employment relations, although the concept of the managerial prerogative has been invoked in collective labour law as well.

The wide latitude approach

It is quite obvious that employment relationships are characterized by ongoing change. There is, nevertheless, nothing in Israeli legislation to set the rights and duties of the parties when they wish to make changes to the status quo of their relationship. The legislature chose to ignore the unique feature of the employment contract—the fact that changes to the status quo are unavoidable during the life of the contract—and left it for regulation by the courts (in Israel as in many other legal systems). General contract laws are unsatisfactory, because employment contracts are characterized by the existence of an open-ended (usually implied) 'subordination' clause. While the employer is bound by concrete contractual obligations, such as the obligation to pay a specific sum as the wage, the employee has to submit herself to the command and control of the employer, without knowing in advance what this duty will entail. We have seen in Chapter 3 that this arrangement is a necessary part of employment relationships. Courts have accordingly recognized the employer's 'prerogative'—in fact a right—to make managerial decisions, including changes in the workplace that affect the employees.

The term 'prerogative' first appeared in Israel in the context of the employment relationship in the National Labour Court's jurisprudence of the mid-1970s.[84] The cases usually referred to dismissals or to disciplinary steps which resulted in demotion of some sort—the legal questions being whether the dismissal was legally justified, or whether the disciplinary steps taken by the employer amounted

[82] Simon Deakin and Frank Wilkinson, *The Law of the Labour Market: Industrialization, Employment, and Legal Evolution* (OUP 2005) 61.

[83] The following sections are based on Guy Davidov, 'Unbound: Some Comments on Israel's Judicially-Developed Labor Law' (2009) 30 CLLPJ 283. Parts of this article are reproduced here, and updated.

[84] See *Mekorot Water Co Ltd v Tsvi Markovits* 6 PDA 125 (1974); *Ramat-Gan Municipality v Leibo Merchel* 6 PDA 337 (1975); *Zim v Ze'ev Ne'eman* 10 PDA 225 (1979).

to constructive dismissals, justifying in turn a claim by the employee for severance payments. Underscoring the power of an employer to manage the business as she sees fit—including by making changes that affect the employees—the Court has not deviated from earlier precedents. But the explicit framing of this power as a legal right (the 'prerogative') has probably helped to fortify it.[85]

The Court made it clear that the managerial prerogative is subject to limitations as set out by legislation, by collective agreements, or by an individual employment contract. From this point of view, the prerogative has shrunk significantly over the years from the inception of the Israeli state in 1948 through to the mid-1970s. The extent of protective laws and collective agreements has grown significantly over this period. However, it is perhaps more useful to describe the managerial prerogative as the sphere allotted to employers to make unilateral decisions on matters *not resolved by legislation, collective agreements or an individual employment contract.* The doctrine does not come into play—and legal questions are not raised—when the issue is already settled by one of these sources. The Court refers to the prerogative—and considers its boundaries and limits—when neither of these sources determines whether a particular change to the status quo is allowed.

From this perspective, the early cases in which we find reference to the concept of 'prerogative' reveal wide latitude given to employers to make changes as they see fit. This approach is exemplified in the case of Uri Ganani, who was employed as the secretary and treasurer of a cooperative village (*Moshav*).[86] He was engaged under certain conditions, most of which—as is often the case in employment relationships—had not been agreed explicitly, but were rather based on the shared understandings of the parties. Either way, it was not disputed that there were certain work conditions that the employer wanted to change, following some changes in the composition of the *Moshav* administration. In the past, Ganani had flexible working hours—later they wanted him in the office from 8am to 4pm. In the past, he was allowed to use the car that he got from the employer for personal purposes (after work) as well—later they prohibited it. Moreover, Ganani was required by the new *Moshav* administration to coordinate its tourism activities, a significant task which was not within his responsibilities before; and he was further asked to report daily on his schedule and prepare written reports on his activities, which he did not have to do previously. The National Labour Court ruled that *all* of these changes—including changes that can be characterized as affecting work conditions—are within the employer's prerogative and could be introduced unilaterally.

This approach, which gives wide latitude to employers, is in line with the approach adopted in the UK.[87] It rests (usually implicitly) on three grounds: first,

[85] In *Itzhak Guy v Tel-Aviv-Yaffo Municipality* 15 PDA 409 (1984), the Court noted that the term 'power' is more suitable than 'prerogative', as the latter could be identified with arbitrariness. But soon afterwards the Court went back to using the same term (see *Binymain Gur-Arie v The State of Israel* 17 PDA 61 (1985)), and continues to do so today.

[86] *Uri Ganani v Amirim* 19 PDA 419 (1988).

[87] Freedland and Kountouris (n 43) 212; David Cabrelli, *Employment Law in Context: Text and Materials* (OUP 2014) 219.

the view that efficiency-wise it is imperative to give the managers/employers wide latitude to make managerial decisions, and this is beneficial for the economy as a whole; second, the view that the business/workplace is the property of the employer, which in turn gives the employing entity the right to 'control' it and make unilateral decisions; and finally, a view of the employment contract as being 'open-ended' and 'loose'—as the Court sometimes put it, a contract which could be likened to a tree, with new branches growing and old ones falling down from time to time.[88]

The contractual approach

The Israeli National Labour Court never explicitly said that an employer could change the contract of employment unilaterally. The Court's approach regarding the contract remained rather vague. But it appeared from the earlier case-law (up until the late 1980s) that work conditions could often be changed by the employer, without the employee's consent, whatever the contractual explanation for this phenomenon may be.

This approach did not resonate well with Justice Aharon Barak of the Supreme Court, when the issue came before him in 1987. While in principle there is no appeal on judgments of the National Labour Court in Israel, the Supreme Court sitting as the High Court of Justice is sometimes willing to hear petitions against the Labour Court and intervene when it believes the issue to be of general importance and considers the Labour Court's decision to be grossly mistaken. The case of Yeoshua Milfelder and his colleagues, a group of firemen, was one of those rare cases in which the Supreme Court overturned the Labour Court's judgment.[89] The firemen had an implicit agreement with their employer, according to which when they worked over the weekend (a shift starting on Friday evening and going on until Sunday morning) they were entitled to a 36-hour rest during the next week. The employer then decided, unilaterally, to shorten the rest period to 25 hours. The National Labour Court concluded that the 36-hour rest, although it was not put in writing, became over time part of the (implicit) contract between the employer and each of the firemen. Nonetheless, it added that this does not mean that the employer was prevented from introducing changes—the issue was open for renegotiation. With this last part the Supreme Court vehemently disagreed.

Justice Barak, who wrote the judgment for a unanimous Court, expressed the view that a contract of employment should be analysed like any other contract—a party is not allowed to 'tear out' parts of the contract or otherwise change it unilaterally. Although a contract of employment is usually for an indefinite term, and so can be terminated by each party at any time (subject only to reasonable notice, and to other legal limitations), it does not follow from the right to bring the contract to an end that there is also a right to bring *parts of it* to an end during the

[88] *Miriam Zohar Gelblum v Habima* 6 PDA 309 (1975).
[89] *Yeoshua Milfelder v The National Labour Court* 41(2) PD 210 (1987) (Supreme Court of Israel).

term of the contract. So while the employer could certainly approach the firemen and ask to renegotiate the terms of the contract, and perhaps could also threaten to end the contract if they disagree (subject to limitations flowing from their collective agreement), until any changes are agreed upon by both parties the contract is binding and the employer must continue to give the same rest period. This way, the Court reasoned, the best balance is achieved between the managerial prerogative and employees' rights.

Justice Barak added that there are various ways in which the parties could agree on changes to the contract, including, for example, an explicit or implicit stipulation that allows one party to make changes. Although the Court did not refer to the managerial prerogative in this context, its approach provides an excellent way to understand the prerogative. Alongside the concrete terms of the contract (X wages, Y hours of work, etc.) there is a more open-ended term—an agreement (usually implicit) of the employee to follow the directions of the employer and its managerial decisions. As long as a decision falls within the managerial prerogative, the employer can take it unilaterally and impose it on the employee, without violating the contract. The difficult legal question then becomes: what are the boundaries of the prerogative? What changes can an employer implement unilaterally and what decisions can he take without seeking the agreement of its employees? Obviously business decisions that do not affect the employees do not require their approval. It is similarly clear, on the other hand, that terms such as those setting the level of wages are *not* part of the prerogative and cannot be changed unilaterally by the employer.[90] But there is also a wide range of decisions in between which is not so easy to classify—particularly decisions that are based on a legitimate (good-faith) business reason but have an *indirect* negative impact on the conditions of employment. Who should bear the (indirect) cost of these changes?

The *Milfelder* judgment did not answer these questions. In the following years, two separate and somewhat contradictory lines of thought have developed side by side. On the one hand, there were cases in which some change in the workplace was examined through a contractual lens, and following *Milfelder* was not allowed unilaterally. On the other hand, there were cases in which decisions of the employer were examined through the managerial prerogative lens, with the background (default) understanding being that changes are allowed even if they affect the employee. Strangely, when the Court resorted to one of these doctrines, there was usually no mention of the other and so they lived side by side, as if they were unrelated—while in fact these two doctrines represent two sides of the same coin. The question is always whether the change amounts to a violation of the contract, and in order to answer this question, the Court has to decide whether the work conditions that were changed fall within the conditions that are part of the contract, or whether they fall within the conditions that an employer can change

[90] Deakin and Morris (n 59), para 4.3.

as part of the prerogative. Otherwise put, the question is what are the boundaries (or limits) of the managerial prerogative.

Because of the unique, long-term and complex nature of the contract of employment, these legal questions often arise with regard to changes that have not been foreseen in advance. Although the Court could have framed its decision as an attempt to gauge the intent of the parties, the National Labour Court judges usually refrain from this somewhat fictitious move. Instead, they seem to draw the boundaries of the managerial prerogative based on what reasonable employment relationships ought to look like—i.e. based on public policy considerations. In contrast, in the UK a few cases dealing with similar issues have focused more on contract interpretation. This was mainly due to the fact that employers have inserted *explicit* provisions giving them the power to change work rules and conditions unilaterally, leading the Employment Appeal Tribunal to construct the intentions of the parties regarding the breadth of such provisions.[91] It has recently been suggested that in light of more recent cases of the Supreme Court giving weight to the imbalance of power in the contract of employment, only minor (insignificant) variations to working practices should be allowed.[92]

The internalization approach

During the 1990s, the two doctrines continued to live side by side in Israeli jurisprudence. In some cases, labour courts continued to apply the (older) approach which can be termed the 'wide latitude' approach. On other cases they preferred to follow the *Milfelder* precedent and apply the (somewhat newer) approach which can be termed the 'contractual' approach. As a result, when employees challenged some change in work conditions before the courts, the end-result was always 'all or nothing'—the change was either allowed (if it falls within the prerogative) or prohibited (if the contract prohibits it).

This binary divide has changed following the National Labour Court decision in the case of *Nahari* in 2000.[93] Moshe Nahari worked in a State institution caring for people with intellectual disabilities. When he started to work he was required by the employer to work only night shifts, and although he objected at first, over time he got used to this arrangement. After nine years the employer decided to change the arrangement and wanted everyone (including Nahari) to work day shifts as well. This meant some disruption for the work–life balance that Nahari developed for himself, and, perhaps more significantly, the loss of the night shift allowance which constituted an important part of his salary. Accordingly he objected to the change. The question before the Court was whether this change in the shifts schedule was allowed.

[91] *Bateman v Asda Stores Ltd* [2010] IRLR 370 (EAT); *Malone v British Airways* [2010] EWHC 302 (QB), [2010] IRLR 431.

[92] Frederic Reynold and John Hendy, 'Reserving the Right to Change Terms and Conditions: How Far Can the Employer Go?' (2012) 41 ILJ 79.

[93] *The State of Israel v Moshe Nahari* 35 PDA 318 (2000).

Based on the contractual approach, an employer cannot unilaterally reduce an employee's salary. On the other hand, based on the wide latitude approach, the shifts' arrangement falls within the boundaries of the managerial prerogative—it is up to the employer to make decisions and changes on such matters. In the past, such a case would probably have been decided based on the latter approach. Night shift allowance is paid only to those who actually work at night. It is not considered part of the regular salary. Assuming the employer acted in good faith, i.e. did not change the shifts arrangement just to harm Mr Nahari, but rather had some business reason for this decision, it is safe to assume that in the past Israeli courts would have considered the change to be within the prerogative. The reduction in the employee's total income would have been considered, in the past, an indirect and unavoidable result of a legitimate change. The 'cost' of the change falls, according to this approach, on the employee alone.

But the judgment of the National Labour Court in *Nahari*, written by President Steve Adler, surprisingly separated the change itself and its consequences. The Court reiterated its previous precedents and noted that an employer has the prerogative to change the shifts arrangements without the consent of its employees. Nevertheless, the Court added, after nine years in which Nahari received the night shift allowance it became part of his salary, indeed part of his contract; and as the employer is not allowed to change the contract unilaterally, he may change the shifts arrangement as he wishes but must continue to pay the night shift allowance to Nahari. Otherwise put, the Court required the employer to *internalize* the costs of the change.

In a later judgment dealing with similar facts,[94] the Court acknowledged that it would be unreasonable to require the employer to pay the night shift allowance for an unlimited time, because in practice this will prevent the change and place a dramatic limit on the ability of the employer to take managerial decisions. If they have to pay Nahari the night shift allowance *indefinitely*, there is no way they will move him to day shift and pay the night shift allowance to someone else (who will be moved to night shift) as well. Accordingly, the new approach—which can be termed the internalization approach—was refined to require only *limited* compensation for the 'damages' incurred as a result of the change introduced by the employer. In the context of workers who have lost their night shift allowance after years of getting it regularly (and growing to rely on it), the Court required the employer to pay a sum equivalent to the monthly night shift allowance for a period of twelve months. Otherwise put, the Court in effect required the employer to give a significant notice period before making the change—a period in which the affected employee can (hopefully) make the necessary arrangements to adjust himself to the new setting (and salary).

The new approach is, at least potentially, revolutionary. While in principle employers (or managers) are still considered the sole decision-makers on 'managerial' issues, they are now required to internalize the costs of their decisions—to

[94] *The State of Israel v Avraham Grinshpan*, judgment of 24 April 2006.

bear at least part of the costs inflicted by such decisions on their employees. This will obviously also impact the decision-making process itself—some workplace changes will not be beneficial for the employer anymore once these costs are taken into account. This is hardly revolutionary from an economic analysis point of view; by making employers internalize some of the costs of their actions, the new rule can be seen as correcting a market failure and enhancing efficiency. But it is certainly a major transformation compared with the previous state of the law.

It is perhaps the breadth of this transformation that has so far muted the impact of the *Nahari* precedent. The Israeli labour courts have been slow to acknowledge and understand this change and have so far only rarely applied it. But the new rule can have dramatic consequences for a variety of situations in which employers decide to introduce changes that affect their employees, including, for example, transferring an employee from one department to another, moving offices to a new location (which requires an employee to spend more time commuting), or reducing the overtime hours that an employee is accustomed to working. All of these situations have so far been considered within the employer's prerogative. Today this is still formally the case, but at the same time the employer could be required to pay the employee some compensation when introducing such changes.

Conclusion

The managerial prerogative has not been treated as a 'standard' in the case-law and literature so far, at least not explicitly. But obviously the power accorded to the employer to make decisions regarding the workplace is not unlimited; and quite apart from the various specific limitations explicitly recognized by law, there is also a limitation on the power to introduce changes/variations that affect the employees. Legally it is usually framed as a question of whether the change is an attempt to unilaterally modify the contract (which is prohibited) or rather a decision falling within the managerial prerogative (which is allowed). However, there are no rules leading to clear-cut answers; the managerial prerogative is in fact structured as an open-ended standard.

I have sketched the development of the Israeli law concerning the managerial prerogative in individual employment relations by reference to three different approaches. While there was certainly development over time, each new approach has not replaced the former, but was rather added on top of it. Thus, the wide latitude approach still has a lot of influence, and one often finds in the case-law reference to its main precedents and the use of rhetoric emphasizing the sole decision-making power of the employer. At the same time, though, in other cases the contractual approach is invoked, and changes that affect employment conditions are considered to be in violation of the contract of employment. Yet other times—rarely so far, but we can expect to see more of that in the future—we find an interesting combination (the internalization approach) in which employers are free to make unilateral decisions introducing changes in the workplace, but they must bear some of the consequences and compensate the employee at least partially for losses incurred as a result of this decision.

The development of the law in Israel is a good example of the potential for adaptation and change within the managerial prerogative standard. Limiting the prerogative was much less important when most employees had the protection of a union against changes to work rules and conditions. With the decline of union protection the issue became central. The Court then clarified that unilateral changes to the contract will not be accepted—i.e. that the prerogative has its limits—and later added a duty on the employer to compensate the employee in case of changes. We can see, then, that the standard allows judicial development of the law in response to changing realities. It also gives the courts the power to decide which changes are allowed on a case-by-case basis, taking into account current practices and circumstances. Creating a set of rules determining if and when an employer is allowed to do X unilaterally (whether transferring an employee from one job to another, or from day shifts to night shifts, or moving the place of business from one city to another, and so on) is not possible given the complexity of work relations—unless the employer is given wholesale powers. If we want to place limits on the managerial prerogative, the only realistic way of doing so is by way of a standard.

Part V—Proportionality

The principle precluding the use of power excessively (or gratuitously) is a basic principle of law.[95] It forms an important part of public law in many countries; we expect our representatives to use their powers proportionately, and avoid any unnecessary infringement of our rights. It is accepted as a principle of international law; we expect each country to avoid, for example, over-reactions against threats from other countries. It is used in criminal law; we expect our judges to apply a punishment that is proportional to the crime. And so on. Proportionality appears to be an age-old ethical principle,[96] but as a binding *legal* principle it has its origins in nineteenth-century Germany.[97] It was first used there as a legal tool to limit the use of police powers.[98] It later became a prominent principle of administrative and constitutional law in many European countries. It is also found in a number of constitutions and international treaties.[99] In Israel the principle was adopted by

[95] This part is based on Guy Davidov, 'The Principle of Proportionality in Labor Law and Its Impact on Precarious Workers' (2012) 34 CLLPJ 63. Some paragraphs from this article are reproduced here, and updated. I have also relied on some paragraphs from Pnina Alon-Shenker and Guy Davidov, 'Applying the Principle of Proportionality in Employment and Labour Law Contexts' (2013) 59 McGill LJ 375.

[96] Jeffrey Wattles, *The Golden Rule* (OUP 1996).

[97] Jürgen Schwarze, *European Administrative Law* (Sweet & Maxwell 1992) 685ff; Nicholas Emiliou, *The Principle of Proportionality in European Law* (Kluwer 1996) 23.

[98] Emiliou (n 97) ch 2. See also David P Currie, *The Constitution of the Federal Republic of Germany* (U of Chicago 1994) 309.

[99] See, e.g., Canadian Charter of Rights and Freedom art 1; Constitution of the Republic of South Africa art 36; Basic Law: Human Dignity and Liberty art 8 (Israel); Convention for the Protection of Human Rights and Fundamental Freedoms (European Convention on Human

the Supreme Court in the early 1990s, and has quickly achieved a leading role in administrative law and constitutional law.

The principle of proportionality is usually understood to include three separate requirements (tests), all concerning the means chosen to achieve the State's goals.[100] First, there must be a *rational relation* between the means and the goals, in the sense that the means applied can indeed advance the ends they are supposed to advance. Second, the State must choose the least drastic means necessary to achieve its goals, i.e. any infringement of rights is justified only to the extent necessary (*minimal impairment*). The third requirement, which is somewhat more controversial, goes beyond a mere review of the means chosen. It demands the harm caused by the use of force (in terms of the infringement of rights) to be proportional to the benefit that stems from that action (*proportionality in the strict/narrow sense*). This obviously requires judges to make value judgments about the importance of certain goals, which makes the last test prone to indeterminacy. But it is still considered necessary in public law, in many legal systems, to prevent extreme violations of rights for trivial goals.[101]

In recent years the same tests are increasingly invoked to put limits on the use of power by employers, including employers in the private sector.[102] They are similarly used to put limits on the use of power by unions. As in public law, the principle of proportionality proves invaluable as a legal tool to prevent abuse of power and balance conflicting rights (and other legitimate interests). It is much more structured compared to other standards such as reasonableness, so the ability to maintain some determinacy and predictability is higher. Moreover, the level of intervention in managerial discretion (or unions' discretion) is relatively small when courts follow the three tests. For the most part, the party using power (usually the employer) is free to choose its own goals; but the means chosen have to be rational and avoid gratuitous infringements of rights (and sometimes other interests). Those who hold the power are expected to be considerate to others when using it, if they can achieve the same goals with less intrusive means. The only intervention that might limit the ability of employers to achieve their goals is through the third test, which examines if the benefits to the employer are not outweighed by greater harms to the employees. In practice it seems that judges are especially careful when using this test, and often prefer to avoid it, as the cases

Rights, as amended) (ECHR) arts 8–11; FEU Treaty (Treaty of Rome, as amended) art 5; Charter of Fundamental Rights of the European Union art 52, 2010.

100 See, e.g., *R v Oakes* [1986] 1 SCR 103 (Supreme Court of Canada); *Ben-Atyia v Minister of Education* 49(5) PD 1 (1995) (Supreme Court of Israel). And see David Beatty, *The Ultimate Rule of Law* (OUP 2004).

101 In the UK, originally the formulation of the proportionality test in public law did not include the last test; see *de Freitas v Permanent Secretary of Ministry of Agriculture, Fisheries, Lands and Housing* [1999] 1 AC 69, 80. However, it was later added, see *Huang v Secretary of State for the Home Department* [2007] UKHL 11, [2007] 2 AC 167 (HL).

102 See generally Davidov (n 95); Alon-Shenker and Davidov (n 95); Victoria Lambropoulos, *Rethinking the Employer's Summary Dismissal Power in the Employment Contract* (PhD thesis, Deakin University, Australia, June 2015).

described below show. I do believe that the third test as well is necessary, to ensure that employers (and unions) are not using their powers excessively, in ways that cause great harms to others only to achieve small gains (even if the gains are legitimate). Nevertheless, it is certainly possible to limit the resort to this test if it appears too intrusive. One option is to use the third (balancing) test only when constitutional/human rights are at stake—for example to examine infringements of the right to equality or the right to privacy. Another option is to use it to protect other interests as well, but only with a 'relaxed' version of the test, which will prevent only cases of *gross disproportion* between costs and benefits.

In some labour law contexts courts in different legal systems mention proportionality explicitly, but perhaps even more widespread is the resort to the proportionality tests implicitly, in additional contexts. Although the use of proportionality tests implicitly has not been entirely consistent, and even when it is mentioned explicitly courts sometimes neglect to go through all three tests, overall proportionality has become a leading legal tool in labour law. The following is a brief review of several examples.

Workplace discrimination

Ephraim Rekanat was a flight attendant employed by El-Al Israel Airlines. Based on the collective agreement between the employer and the *Histadrut* (the representative union), he was required to retire at the age of 60, even though other El-Al employees could work until the age of 65. He claimed that this was age discrimination and asked the court to intervene. The case reached the Supreme Court of Israel.[103] When examining whether the differences between different employees could justify the disparate treatment, Chief Justice Barak invoked the principle of proportionality. He did not explicitly apply the three separate tests, but it can be seen that in fact the first two tests have been applied. El-Al had two excuses for the different treatment: that they want the flight attendants to have a young appearance, because this is what the customers want; and that the job requires physical fitness. Barak maintained that a young appearance is irrelevant for the job (thus, in effect, it does not pass the rational relation test); and that the company can ensure physical fitness by individual tests (i.e. the policy which automatically presumed lack of fitness at a fixed age impaired the right to equality more than the minimum necessary). The provision of the collective agreement allowing the practice of retiring flight attendants at the age of 60 was therefore struck down.

Interestingly, individual fitness tests can be discriminatory as well. Tawney Meiorin was hired as a forest firefighter by the Province of British Columbia, but lost her job three years later because of new tests adopted by the Government. There were four aerobic tests; she passed three of them but failed to run 2.5 km in less than 11 minutes (it took her 49 seconds longer). She argued against the fact that the standard was the same for men and women, and had been created

[103] *Rekanat v National Labour Court* 54(5) PD 330 (2000) (Supreme Court of Israel).

based on male physical capabilities. According to applicable legislation, in case of *prima facie* discrimination the employer must present a 'bona fide occupational requirement' to justify it. The Supreme Court of Canada interpreted this provision as including three tests.[104] The employer must show that (1) the standard was adopted for a purpose rationally connected to the performance of the job (i.e. a legitimate work-related purpose); (2) the particular standard was adopted in an honest and good faith belief that it was necessary for the fulfilment of that purpose; and (3) the standard is reasonably necessary to the accomplishment of that purpose, which means specifically that it is impossible to accommodate individual employees without imposing undue hardship on the employer. Although the judges have not made explicit reference to the three-stage proportionality test, the similarities are obvious: all three tests can be found within this articulation. In practice, even if not explicitly, the Canadian Court is using the proportionality tests to decide workplace discrimination cases. There is some variation resulting from the introduction of good faith and reasonableness into the same analysis, in a way that lowers the standard (good faith belief that you did the right thing is sufficient, and instead of a 'necessary' connection between end and means the Court settles for 'reasonably necessary'). But the basic structure is very similar, which led the Canadian Court to conclude that Meiorin should get her job back, and the Government should devise a new aerobic standard that takes into account gender differences (the claim of 'undue hardship' was not proved).

In the UK, the principle of proportionality is now an established, explicit part of discrimination law.[105] According to the Equality Act 2010, indirect *prima facie* discrimination can be justified if it is 'a proportionate means of achieving a legitimate aim'.[106] Proportionality was used by the courts before the new Act as well, following the European conventions and directives.[107] Consider, for example, the case of Lisa Lax, who was employed by the company of Hardys & Hansons as a 'retail recruitment manager'.[108] When she became pregnant with her second child, she asked the employer to be allowed to work part-time after her return from maternity leave, possibly in a 'job share' arrangement. Her request was rejected, but the Employment Tribunal concluded that the difficulties presented by the employer as preventing such an arrangement were overstated. The refusal of the employer to accommodate Lax thus amounted to sex discrimination. When affirming the judgment, the Court of Appeal applied the principle of proportionality, explaining that this means particularly that the employer has to show that a decision with discriminatory effect (here the insistence on a full-time arrangement) is 'reasonably necessary'.[109] The judges made it clear that they are

[104] *British Columbia (Public Service Employee Relations Commission) v BCGSEU* [1999] 3 SCR 3, 32.

[105] Deakin and Morris (n 59), para 6.30; Davies (n 5) 288.

[106] s 19(2)(d).

[107] Aaron Baker, 'Proportionality and Employment Discrimination in the UK' (2008) 37 ILJ 305.

[108] *Hardys and Hansons Plc v Lax* [2005] EWCA Civ 846, [2005] IRLR 726.

[109] ibid [32].

not applying a test allowing the employer to choose between a 'reasonable range of responses' and the employer does not get a 'margin of appreciation'. So it appears that the first two proportionality tests were applied quite strictly; although the third one is not mentioned.[110]

Commentators have criticized the UK courts for adopting deferential versions of proportionality[111] and for applying the tests in a deferential manner towards employers.[112] Recently there is perhaps more willingness on the part of the courts to engage in stricter scrutiny.[113] But it seems that much can be gained from a more structured application of the three proportionality tests separately.

The three anecdotal examples were brought to show how proportionality is used, in different countries, to help in deciding workplace discrimination cases. It is not enough to say that discrimination is prohibited. In cases of indirect discrimination there are sometimes adverse effects based on gender, age, race, etc. that were not intentional, and the question is whether the practice causing them can be justified. The law does not say that such practices are never justified, but rather requires an examination of possible justifications. It is not possible to come up with clear-cut rules that can resolve such disputes. The proportionality tests offer a structure to make this examination. Without relying on such an open-ended standard it would hardly be possible to prevent the many different cases of indirect discrimination, while at the same time not prohibiting too much economic activity (when adverse effects can be justified).

Privacy at work

Canadian Pacific (CP), a railway company, installed six surveillance cameras in its maintenance yard in Scarborough, Ontario. One of the workers on the site, Erwin Eastmond, complained that this was a violation of his and his colleagues' privacy.[114] According to the Personal Information and Protection of Electronic Documents Act 2000 (a Canadian federal legislation), '[a]n organization may collect, use or disclose personal information only for purposes that a reasonable person would consider are appropriate in the circumstances'.[115] A fourfold test was adopted by the Privacy Commissioner, and upheld by the Federal Court. It includes the following questions: 'Is the measure demonstrably necessary to meet a specific need? Is it likely to be effective in meeting that need? Is the loss of privacy proportional

[110] In public law cases UK courts have recognized, even if somewhat belatedly, the third test as well (see *Huang* (n 101)). There are also workplace discrimination cases in which balancing in the form of the third proportionality test was applied (see especially *Allonby v Accrington & Rossendale College* [2001] EWCA Civ 529, [2001] IRLR 364) but this seems to be more rare.

[111] Baker (n 107). [112] Davies (n 5).

[113] Deakin and Morris (n 59) analyse the judgment in *R(E) v Governing Body of JFS* [2009] UKSC 15, [2010] IRLR 136, dealing with discrimination in a non-employment context, and conclude that it shows 'that a strict approach to the test of proportionality can result in a high level of external scrutiny of decisions which result in group disadvantage' (ibid 644).

[114] *Eastmond v Canadian Pacific Railway* [2004] FCJ No 1043, 2004 FC 852.

[115] s 5(3).

to the benefit gained? Is there a less privacy-invasive way of achieving the same end?'.[116] It is quite obvious that these are just (slightly) different articulations of the same three proportionality tests. Applying these tests in the circumstances, the Court concluded that the employer acted legally. There was a legitimate need (given past incidents of theft, vandalism, etc.) to use cameras. Warning signs were displayed. The recorded images are kept under lock and key and only accessed if an incident is reported; otherwise they are later destroyed. Other alternatives (such as using fences and security guards) were examined but would be very expensive. The infringement of privacy, in contrast, is quite minimal.

The proportionality tests were also used by the National Labour Court of Israel when employees of Tel-Aviv University complained that they were required to go through psychological tests—which impinge on their privacy—before applying for any new position within the University. The Court allowed this practice with two important conditions.[117] First, that the specific tests are relevant to the position sought (in effect the rational relation test); and second, that the tests have been proven to conform to scientific standards of validity and reliability and the results are kept confidential (in effect the minimal impairment test).

More recently, in a case setting limits on the right of employers to look into e-mail correspondence of their employees, the Israeli National Labour Court explicitly referred to proportionality, and specifically to the minimal impairment test, as well as the need to balance the gains with the infringement of privacy rights.[118] At issue was an employee named Tali Issakov who worked for an information technology (IT) company named Panaya. After she was dismissed she argued that the dismissal was illegal because she was pregnant at the time. The company argued in contrast that she was in fact dismissed *before* she became pregnant, so the date of the dismissal became central to the dispute. To support its claim in this regard, the employer wanted to submit e-mail communications of Issakov during the disputed period, showing that she was busy looking for new work—most of her e-mails were to job placement companies, with her CV attached. The question before the Court was whether to allow the submission of these communications; the employee argued that they were achieved in violation of her privacy, while the company claimed that because the e-mail address belonged to it there was no such infringement. Israeli legislation prohibits violations of privacy, but does not include any rules that resolve such scenarios. The Court based its decision mostly on the proportionality tests: the company did not have any clear policy prohibiting the use of e-mail for private purposes, nor did it publish any policy to let employees know in advance that their e-mails could be inspected. The company also failed to examine alternative means to achieve its goal. Although the Court did not follow the three separate proportionality tests in its analysis, the principle

[116] *Eastmond* (n 114) at [13] and [126].
[117] *Tel-Aviv University v The Histadrut* 30 PDA 385 (1998).
[118] *Issakov v The State of Israel*, judgment of 8 February 2011.

was explicitly mentioned, and more importantly, the tests themselves (especially minimal impairment) were clearly used.

In the UK, proportionality is brought into the analysis through the European Convention on Human Rights. Section 8 of the Convention enshrines the right to privacy, allowing interference with this right only when it is 'necessary in a democratic society'. The long-established jurisprudence of the European Court of Human Rights maintains that this requires a proportionality analysis (which includes the three tests).[119] According to the Human Rights Act 1998, only public authorities in the UK are *directly* bound by the Convention (s 6), but because all legislation has to be interpreted in a way which is compatible with Convention rights (s 3), in practice private employers have to respect these rights as well.[120] An interesting example concerns dismissals because of activities of an employee outside of the workplace and outside working hours. In the case of *X v Y*[121] an employee had a sexual encounter with another man in a public toilet at a transport café—an incident for which he was arrested. Although he was not charged, he was cautioned, and by signing the caution acknowledged that he committed a criminal offence. The employee was dismissed soon after his employer had learned about this incident. In examining whether this amounted to unjust dismissal, the Court of Appeal made it clear that in principle, the right of privacy applied even though it was a private employer, and once the right of privacy is infringed, the employer must justify it by conforming with the proportionality standard. In the specific circumstances the Court decided that this was not required, because the activity leading to dismissal did not take place in a private sphere, but in a public space. This conclusion was rightly criticized for not treating the life choices and actions of the employee outside of the workplace as private.[122] Virginia Mantouvalou has argued that applying the proportionality test in such contexts should mean that dismissals can be justified only when the off-duty behaviour has a direct impact—or at least a high likelihood of direct impact—on the employee's performance or the business reputation. This was not the case here, although the basic fact that proportionality should be examined when privacy is infringed seems widely accepted.

Questions of workplace privacy are thus another example for the usefulness of proportionality in resolving disputes and determining the boundaries of acceptable behaviour in employment relations. It is necessary to limit the power of employers when they infringe employee privacy. At the same time it is necessary to allow employers to control the business using their own judgment. It is not

[119] See, e.g., *Dudgeon v UK* (1981) 4 EHRR 149, para 53; *MS v Sweden* (1997) 28 EHRR 313, para 41. The ECHR does not explicitly divide the test into the three parts (it was recently suggested that it should; see Janneke Gerards, 'How to Improve the Necessity Test of the European Court of Human Rights' (2013) 11 I-CON 466), but in practice it follows the same basic requirements (see Beatty (n 100)).

[120] *X v Y* [2004] EWCA Civ 662, [2004] IRLR 625 (CA).

[121] ibid.

[122] Virginia Mantouvalou, 'Human Rights and Unfair Dismissal: Private Acts in Public Spaces' (2008) 71 MLR 912.

possible to foresee every contingency in which these rights will conflict. The proportionality tests offer a structure to resolve such conflicts.

Restrictive (non-competition) covenants

Restrictive covenants—in which employees agree not to compete with their employer after the end of the relationship—are another example of a conflict between rights (and/or other legitimate interests) that is difficult to resolve without using an open-ended standard. The structure in many countries is similar: non-competition clauses are viewed as a restraint of trade and are presumed unenforceable (or: against public policy and void), unless the employer can show that the restrictive covenant is 'reasonable' in the circumstances.[123] The Israeli Supreme Court considers a restriction 'reasonable' only to the extent that it is necessary to protect the employer's legitimate interests.[124] This, in effect, means that courts apply the first two proportionality tests (without explicitly mentioning them). The judges are looking for a legitimate business purpose (other than the mere interest in preventing competition), which the restrictive covenant can advance—the rational relation test. Then they aim to ensure that the restriction is limited to the extent necessary to achieve this goal (in terms of length, geographical scope, and substantive scope)—the minimal impairment test. Sometimes judges also add an assessment of the relevant rights and interests and their relative weight—in effect adding a balance of costs vs benefits reminiscent of the third proportionality test.[125]

Over the years the views of Israeli judges regarding which restriction could be considered 'necessary' have changed: in the 1990s, they often allowed restrictions for two years covering the area in which the employee worked; but in the next decade, restrictions were only rarely allowed, and if so usually for much shorter periods.[126] Recently there are signs that labour courts are more willing to accept restrictive covenants, although much narrower in scope than those approved in the 1990s.[127] These developments reflect the standard's ability to adapt to changing market conditions and changing societal views. The high point in this

[123] See Deakin and Morris (n 59), para 4.115; John Dwight Ingram, 'Covenants Not to Compete' (2002) 36 Akron LR 49.

[124] *AES Systems Inc v Sa'ar* 54(3) PD 850 (2005) (Supreme Court of Israel). See also *Frumer v Red Guard Ltd* 34 PDA 294 (1999) (National Labour Court).

[125] *Tony Tuama v Techo Rubber Lisitzki Ltd* 25 PDA 227, 238–241 (1992) (National Labour Court).

[126] Compare *Tony Tuama* (n 125); *Modcon Ltd v David Bash* 31 PDA 613 (1996); *Itzhak Ofri v Electronics Line (AL) Ltd*, judgment of 26 June 1997 with *Frumer* (n 124); *Adi Amihay v Yossi Goldhammer Co Ltd* 35 PD 204 (2000); *Har-Zahav Food Services Ltd v Foodline Ltd* 35 PDA 72 (2002).

[127] See, e.g., *Gamatronic Industries v Goma Kalman*, judgment of 19 September 2006 (Jerusalem Regional Labour Court); *Berman Yehuda Ltd v Mordechai Goldman*, judgment of 14 June 2009 (Tel-Aviv Regional Labour Court); *Dip Tech Ltd v Avi Fineschmidt*, judgment of 4 January 2009 (Tel-Aviv Regional Labour Court); *Kav Manche Ltd v Moshe Yehezkel*, judgment of 5 December 2010 (Tel-Aviv Regional Labour Court).

transformation was the case of *Dan Frumer v Red Guard*.[128] Frumer was the Chief Technology Officer at Red Guard, an IT security company. His contract of employment included a covenant prohibiting him from joining any competitor for a period of twenty-two months after the end of his employment. Frumer left the company after some disagreement with the Chief Executive Officer, who wanted to move him to another position. After resigning, he started to look for a new job, and a few months later he started working for Check Point, another IT security company. There was no doubt that the two companies were direct competitors in the area of Frumer's expertise. Nevertheless, President Adler of the National Labour Court decided to reject Red Guard's petition, refusing to enforce the restrictive covenant. The decision puts much more emphasis on the preliminary inquiry of whether there are legitimate reasons for *any* restriction of competition. Several reasons are listed (protecting trade secrets, protecting an exceptional investment in the employee, protecting ties with customers) but they are all given a narrow reading in the judgment. In effect, the judgment shifted more attention to the rational relation stage. But covenants that pass this test—when the employer can show that there was a legitimate reason for restricting competition—are still limited to the minimal scope necessary (i.e. minimal impairment).

Canadian courts are using very similar tests: to be enforceable, a restrictive clause must be necessary to protect the employer's legitimate proprietary or business interests; it must cover a reasonable length of time and geographic area; and the employer must show that a non-solicitation clause would not suffice to protect the employer's legitimate interests in the circumstances.[129] Although the courts in Canada make no mention of proportionality in this context, it can easily be observed that the three requirements mirror the first two proportionality tests. An explicit resort to proportionality, and a separate application of each of the three tests, can provide better structure and predictability (compared with the vague 'reasonableness' standard) while still offering the advantages of an open-ended standard.

Strikes and picketing

Having considered several examples of the use of proportionality as a check on employers' power, I now move to show that the same tests are helpful to limit the use of power by unions. In this context as well, we have conflicting rights and interests that should be balanced. The starting point is that workers have a right to strike, derived from freedom of association.[130] But a strike could have grave implications for employers and for society at large, both in terms of the economic damages it causes (implicating right to property) and other possible harms (consider, e.g., a strike at an airport limiting the right to movement, or a strike at a

[128] *Frumer* (n 124).

[129] For references and further discussion see Alon-Shenker and Davidov (n 95) 395–96.

[130] The right to strike has recently been recognized as constitutional by the Supreme Court of Canada (*Saskatchewan Federation of Labour v Saskatchewan* [2015] 1 SCR 245).

hospital limiting the right to health). So there has to be a system to place limits on strikes—to ensure that the power is used responsibly—and once again it is not possible to solve this with clear-cut rules.

Germany is the leading example of an explicit use of proportionality in this area. Manfred Weiss and Marlene Schmidt report that proportionality has been 'the governing principle of strike law' since 1971.[131] They summarize the law developed by the Federal Labour Court as follows: a strike must respect a 'peace obligation' agreed upon in a collective agreement; it must be fair, in the sense that it is not intended to destroy the employer's enterprises; it must be preceded by a secret ballot of union members; and, most importantly, it can only be carried out as a 'last resort'.[132]

In Israel, the origins of proportionality in the context of strikes are found in two judgments of the Supreme Court from the mid-1980s, where the Court placed limits on strikes by using—in practice although not explicitly—two of the proportionality tests. In one of those cases, a group of exporters had sued a union representing dockers for damages caused by their strike.[133] The Court decided that the union could be held responsible for such damages, if the strike exceeded its legitimate scope. Among the factors mentioned to decide whether this had happened, the Court included an assessment of the harm expected to be inflicted on third parties due to the strike, balanced against the benefit expected to the strikers as a result of their actions. This cost-benefit analysis in fact closely resembles the third proportionality test, as mentioned above. In a second case from the same period, the Supreme Court considered an appeal on a disciplinary ruling against the chair of the Israeli Broadcasting Authority workers' union.[134] This union official shut down a TV broadcast—at a time when this was the only TV channel available in Israel—because he suspected that management violated a collective agreement. While affirming his disciplinary conviction, the Court emphasized the fact that the union chair's actions were overly aggressive, and that he failed to exhaust all other (less aggressive) options. This, indeed, is exactly the second proportionality test (minimal impairment).

In more recent judgments of the National Labour Court the principle of proportionality is mentioned explicitly.[135] However, this has not been consistent; there are cases in which, for some reason, the Court refrains from any mention of this principle. Further, even when it *is* mentioned, the National Labour Court does not go far enough to clearly embrace and apply the three different proportionality tests. Often when the Court is asked to put limits on strikes, the requirement that unions' actions must be 'proportional' is mentioned, and separately, the

[131] Manfred Weiss and Marlene Schmidt, *Labour Law and Industrial Relations in Germany* (4th revised edn, Kluwer 2008) 203.

[132] ibid 203–04.

[133] *Mif'aley Rechev Ashdod Ltd v Tsizik* 41(3) PD 169 (1987) (Supreme Court of Israel).

[134] *Koka v IBA Chairman* 40(2) PD 406 (1986) (Supreme Court of Israel).

[135] See, e.g., *Mekorot Water Company Ltd v The Histadrut* 36 PDA 560 (2001); *Lishkat Hamischar Tel-Aviv v The Histadrut*, judgment of 14 December 2003; *Sherutey Briut Clalit v The Histadrut*, judgment of 16 May 2005.

Court sometimes examines whether there were less drastic means available, and what is the magnitude of the damage caused by the strike vis-à-vis its importance to the workers' legitimate interests. Thus, for example, when considering an application for an injunction against a strike by Israel's Water Authority workers, the Court explained that 'because the parties were close to an agreement, the strike went on for a long time, disruptions of water supply could risk lives and public safety, and it was possible to limit the strike partially without totally negating the union's bargaining power, we have reached a conclusion that an injunction is warranted…to prohibit any disruptions in water supply'.[136] In another case, at issue was a strike by the workers of a major bank, which involved a refusal to submit reports to the Israeli Securities Authority, at a time when such reports were necessary to allow the bank's sale. The Court issued an injunction, and reasoned that allowing such a move would amount to giving the workers a right to veto the sale.[137] The Court went on to explain that a strike necessarily involves some (legitimate) harm to the employer, but in the specific case the harm was extreme, and the workers had other ways available to further their legitimate aims vis-à-vis their employer. So the principle itself is sometimes mentioned, and one or more of the three proportionality tests can be found between the lines.

The resort to proportionality tests is sometimes more apparent when freedom of speech enters into the analysis: in the case of picketing. Consider, for example, the Canadian case of *Ogden Entertainment*,[138] dealing with workers at the Corel Centre (as it was then known) in the City of Kanata, where NHL (professional ice hockey) games are played. During a strike, workers had set up large picket lines on nights of ice hockey games, impeding the access of vehicles into the Centre's area. Traffic jams resulted, causing traffic on the highway to back up for many miles. The picketers did not distribute leaflets or try to communicate with the occupants of any vehicles. The Ontario Court of Justice held that the picketing amounted to a criminal offence and nuisance, and stressed that the only thing the picketers achieved was the obstruction of vehicles.[139] It also stated that there might be a need for special rules to apply in cases which involve large numbers of people who are not party to the labour dispute.[140] The Court issued an injunction restraining the picketers from interfering, blocking, or delaying any person or vehicle from entering or exiting the Centre.[141]

This is a good example of how courts resort de facto to a proportionality analysis, but a more structured analysis following the three separate tests could have been beneficial. The Court maintained that the picketers did not convey information to the public and achieved nothing other than the obstruction of vehicles.

[136] *Mekorot Water Company* (n 135).

[137] *Israel Discount Bank v The Histadrut* 40 PDA 337 (2004).

[138] *Ogden Entertainment Services v USWA, Local 440* [1998] OJ No 1769, (1998) 159 DLR (4th) 340 (Gen Div).

[139] ibid at [9], [18]–[19].

[140] ibid [25].

[141] ibid [31]. The order was upheld by the Court of Appeal ((1998) 38 OR (3d) 448, [1998] OJ No 1824).

This appears to mean that they failed the first proportionality test: no rational connection to a legitimate goal. However, a better articulation of the union's goal—which recognizes the need to exert economic pressure on the employer—could have led to a different conclusion. Furthermore, the analysis would have benefited from a discussion of the second stage: did the union have other alternatives—less harmful to the employer—to achieve its legitimate goals? The Court held that the picketers committed the tort of nuisance which is clearly harmful to the employer, but it did not consider whether other, less harmful ways to achieve its legitimate goals were actually available to the union. Finally, as part of the 'balance of convenience' examination which courts employ to consider petitions for injunctions, the Court weighed the employees' interest in obstructing traffic against the employer's right to enjoy free access to its premises.[142] Not surprisingly, it concluded in favour of the employer.[143] An explicit resort to the third proportionality test could have led to a better articulation of the rights and interests involved. Employees obviously do not have a right to obstruct traffic per se; but they have a right or at least a legitimate interest to exert pressure on the employer as a way to secure better work conditions. The Court should have considered not only the damage to the employer and the public, but also the importance of the actions for the picketers themselves.

Conclusion

The three proportionality tests, developed in public law, create a useful structure for discretionary decision-making, which aims to ensure that decisions are rational and considerate. Proportionality can help in making decisions more structured and principled and less indeterminate, and substantively, prevent abuse of power. As I have shown above, this structure also fits the intuitions of judges—who in practice have been applying these tests (to one extent or another) in a number of labour law contexts. The examples considered above are not exclusive; proportionality has been used in different countries (usually implicitly) in other contexts as well, such as disciplinary proceedings, dismissals, unfair labour practices, and the managerial prerogative.[144] In France there is even a legislated requirement that every limitation of employees' rights must be subject to the principle of proportionality.[145] The result is that employers, and unions, are legally required to stand up to the standard of proportionality, even in the private sector.

The long-term, complex relations of employment frequently require a delicate balance of rights and interests. It is not possible to anticipate and solve every conflict of rights and interests in advance by way of clear-cut rules. Proportionality is the most general standard, used to place limits on the use of power when rights are infringed (and sometimes other interests). Because it covers such a broad range

[142] *Ogden Entertainment* (n 138) [30]. [143] ibid [28].
[144] For additional examples see Davidov (n 95); Alon-Shenker and Davidov (n 95).
[145] Code du Travail art L1121-1.

of instances—in contrast to rules that cover only a small number of foreseen conflicts—proportionality helps to prevent evasion, i.e. to prevent occurrences of employers avoiding the result expected and justified from a purposive point of view. It also leaves plenty of room for the law to evolve and adapt, thus further contributing to advancing the goals of labour law. Moreover, the analysis invited by the proportionality tests opens the room for contextual considerations, including distinctions between small and large employers, public and private sector, or special characteristics of a sector.[146] Such sensitivity to context is crucial in the quest to advance the goals of labour law and adapt it to new challenges.

Part VI—Conclusions and Possible Critiques

We have seen that good faith, the managerial prerogative, and proportionality have all been used by courts—at least in some countries—to advance the goals of labour law. Such standards provide an important supplement to concrete legislated rules.

There are three possible critiques that require attention. First, the issue of legitimacy: is it justified to give so much discretion to courts, and in some cases for courts to take so much power for themselves? Second, the problem of indeterminacy: is it possible to maintain a sufficient level of determinacy when using open-ended standards, to ensure that employers and workers know their rights and obligations in advance? Finally, the concern of efficiency: are we setting the bar too high, in terms of the standard of behaviour expected from employers—causing significant costs that are likely to create inefficiencies and perhaps even lead to job losses?

In terms of legitimacy, I do not see any difficulty with giving broad discretion to courts, including by allowing them to set rules (derived from open-ended standards) and change them from time to time. Although such rules are not formally published in the same way as legislation, they become known to employers through legal advisors and other channels and are not different from other instances of judicial interpretation which it is important for actors to know about, but which are not formally published as part of the legislation. Issues of legitimacy are more prominent when courts adopt the standard themselves without any basis in legislation; unless, of course, it is part of their role in a common-law system.

In Israel, for example, a duty of good faith is set in legislation (applicable for all contracts); the managerial prerogative is a judicial invention (and so can also be changed/limited by courts without problems of legitimacy); and proportionality is used to protect recognized rights, when the legislature has not set up a clear process to examine infringements of those rights (i.e. the decision on the appropriate process was in practice left for the courts). The legislature is of course also

[146] For a sector-sensitive approach see Einat Albin, *Sectoral Disadvantage: The Case of Workers in the British Hospitality Sector* (Unpublished PhD dissertation, University of Oxford, 2010).

sovereign to change any rules or standards adopted by the judiciary, further minimizing any legitimacy concerns.

Admittedly, there are contexts in which a new rule would have dramatic implications and then it seems illegitimate to judicially institute the change. In Israel, for example, in the context of dismissals, demanding that employers stand up to the proportionality tests would amount to nothing less than replacing the at-will rule with a 'just cause' rule. Such a major change with numerous indirect and significant implications should probably be left for the legislature. Indeed Israeli courts, although using proportionality in other contexts, have refrained from adopting such a requirement in the context of dismissals.

To clarify, I am not arguing that courts are necessarily better than legislatures in addressing labour market problems and advancing the goals of labour law. Quite often (depending on time and place) they are not. The idea as explained in the chapter is not to use standards *instead* of rules, but rather *on top* of them. If a legal system is characterized by hostility of judges towards workers and unions, and a strong belief in freedom of contract and the right of property even in the employment context, then giving more weight to standards as suggested here will not help. However, it will not cause harm either. In other legal systems, where judges have a deeper understanding of the unique characteristics of labour relations, standards can be a useful element in the quest to advance the goals of labour law.

A related concern could be that a system based to some extent on standards will reduce the motivation of the legislature to address new problems. This is plausible in theory, but unlikely in practice in my view. If a legislature is noticing a new problem, and is interested in principle in addressing it, the possibility that courts will also address it at some point can hardly be expected to deter legislative action. Legislators would want the credit for the solution; they would want to see a solution during their time in office; and they would want to control the details of the new regulation. There are many other reasons that can explain the inaction of legislatures, in some countries, in the face of new labour market problems; most notably, pressure from business owners. The existence of standards is unlikely to make much difference in this respect, if at all.

As for indeterminacy, the discussion in Part I has shown that standards are not necessarily indeterminate: a combination of rules and standards can prove more determinate than a system based only on (necessarily numerous) rules. Further, it is important to bear in mind that standards are already pervasive in labour law; courts often examine if specific terms are 'reasonable', are not against 'public policy', and so on—usually based on a specific requirement set in legislation.[147] Consequently the three standards proposed here will not add more indeterminacy; on the contrary, they can be expected to minimize the resort to many different standards, adding more clarity (especially the proportionality tests which are proposed as a general method of examining infringements/harms to rights/interests).

[147] See, e.g., Employment Rights Act 1996 s 98(4) (UK); Health and Safety at Work Act 1974 s 2 (UK); Workplace Relations Act 1996 ss 226(1), 226(4) (Australia).

Still, one might argue, standards are more difficult to enforce. For a low-wage employee, facing multiple barriers to bringing a suit before a labour court/tribunal, suing the employer for infringing a duty of good faith or proportionality is highly unlikely. At most such a worker will sue for the infringement of clear and basic rules (such as a payment below the minimum wage). There are two answers to this critique. First, I am not suggesting that we forgo rules; just that we supplement them. So the worker will still be able to sue for violation of the minimum wage law (or other rules). Second, as explained above, standards are expected to lead to the development of new rules, derived from those standards. Even if such a process is likely to take place as a result of suits brought by high-wage employees, we can expect the low-wage employees—at least many of them, even if not all—to benefit from these derived rules as well.

The concern of efficiency is the most serious one. Admittedly, there are *always* claims that labour laws are inefficient, and as we have seen in Chapters 3 through 5, such claims are often exaggerated. Still, the legislature is usually the one to decide the level of protection for employees, after taking into consideration possible impacts on efficiency and employment levels. New limitations imposed by courts on employers entail more costs, and courts lack the institutional capacity to weigh the negative implications. There are four possible answers to this critique. First, when the legislature enacted a standard, the costs have already been considered. For example, if a duty of good faith appears in legislation, and the courts decide to derive a right to a hearing from this duty, the specific costs of this right have not been anticipated by the legislature, but the existence of *some* costs flowing from the general duty must have been expected. Second, the legislature can always correct judicial mistakes if such mistakes have been made. We have seen why it is useful and important to allow courts the possibility of developing, supplementing, and adapting (to some extent) the law. But if judicially-created rules impose excessive costs, the legislature can quickly intervene. Third, experience from different legal systems (as discussed in the previous parts) shows that judges tend to be quite deferential towards managerial judgment and careful about imposing new duties/limitations. So the fear of judges imposing excessive costs does not seem realistic. Fourth, I would argue that in practice, the three standards discussed in this chapter do not lead to significant inefficiencies. I now turn to explain this final argument.

The good faith standard, as we have seen, has two aspects: it is used to prevent unacceptable conduct in concrete circumstances, and to derive rules explaining *ex ante* that certain kinds of conduct will be considered unacceptable. This standard can be seen as correcting a market failure: the risk of opportunistic behaviour and the fear that the other party will act opportunistically. Without a good faith standard, the parties are likely to be suspicious towards each other, and in long-term personal relations such as employment, this is inefficient.[148] The good faith standard supports trust and cooperation by ensuring the parties that

[148] Simon Deakin and Frank Wilkinson, 'Labour Law and Economic Theory: A Reappraisal' in Hugh Collins, Paul Davies, and Roger Rideout (eds), *Legal Regulation of the Employment Relation* (Kluwer 2000) 29, 56–59.

such a positive attitude will not work against them. Such cooperation is obviously efficient. Moreover, with regard to the rules derived from the good faith standard, we have seen that they are for the most part procedural, with relatively low costs.

The managerial prerogative is first and foremost a legal tool designed to support the employer and give a legal explanation for its unilateral powers. In this sense, it is obviously promoting efficiency. Nonetheless, as we have seen, this standard allows courts to place limits on the prerogative. Usually these limits are based on the understanding of the prerogative's boundaries. If a court decides that a certain decision is not within the managerial prerogative but rather violates the contract with the employee (i.e. requires negotiations and agreement between the parties), this should be seen as supporting the freedom of contract—which is considered an important element of an efficient market economy. The more extreme form of intervention, as found in recent precedents in Israel which require the employer to internalize some of the costs of changes in the workplace, is obviously costly for employers. However, from the point of view of society as a whole, a duty to internalize costs improves efficiency by helping to ensure that decisions are rational and the costs do not outweigh the benefits.

The proportionality tests are in many contexts just a new and improved (and more structured) way to analyse conflicts of rights and interests in the workplace. Thus, for example, when considering violations of privacy, or disciplinary decisions, or discrimination, courts perform judicial review sometimes without a clear structure, or by relying on vague concepts such as reasonableness and public policy. Employees have fundamental rights vis-à-vis their employers (e.g. a right to privacy) emanating from specific legislation or from interpretation of the open-ended employment contract. In such cases, courts are often required to balance competing rights and interests, and the proportionality tests are a useful and principled aid in doing so. To the extent that the three proportionality tests replace other and more 'fluid' forms of doing judicial review, they add clarity and predictability and thus contribute to efficiency.

In other contexts, the proportionality standard could add some *new* limitations on employers that have not previously existed. Where this is the case, it would be useful to separate the first two proportionality tests from the third one when examining the impact on efficiency. The requirements of a rational relation between the goal and the means, and a choice of means that minimally impairs the rights (or interests) of employees, do not present any significant danger to efficiency. There is no limitation on the choice of goals—any legitimate business goal is acceptable. Employers are only asked to act rationally, and consider the interests of the employees as well, as long as they do not compromise their ability to fully achieve their goals. There is nothing inefficient or overly intrusive here. The difficulty for employers, in this regard, is caused only by the submission of their decisions to judicial review. While the first two proportionality tests should not be used to annul any managerial decision that is rational and necessary to achieve the goals that the employer itself has set, there are still costs associated with litigation and with the possibility of judicial mistakes. How significant are these costs? While there is no empirical data on this question, it seems reasonable to believe—given the inherent barriers faced by workers to bring cases to court, and given the deferential attitude of courts towards managerial decisions—that the costs of litigation and judicial mistakes would be small.

The third test—proportionality in the narrow sense—is more problematic. When applied, it requires the employer to balance its own interests against those of the employees before making a decision. This test could therefore prevent otherwise legitimate business decisions only because the benefit they create to the employer is outweighed by the harm they cause to the employees. Such a standard seems acceptable in public law, but is it too demanding when dealing with two 'private' parties? Perhaps it would be useful to distinguish here between harm to employees that involves constitutional or otherwise fundamental rights (such as equality or privacy) and harm that involves other interests. When constitutional/fundamental/human rights are at stake, it seems justified to apply this strict standard. Employers are told, in effect, that society lets them set up a limited liability corporation, own private property that society protects, employ other people, and so on—in the condition that employees are treated fairly, which includes, when the right to privacy, for example, is infringed, a requirement from the employer to show that the gain is greater than the harm. On the other hand, when other interests (which are not considered constitutional or fundamental rights) are involved, it seems that such a burden would be too high. At most, in such cases a relaxed balancing test might be appropriate—in which the burden is on the employee to show *gross* (or *extreme*) disproportion between the harm to her and the benefit to the employer.

8

Purposive Interpretation of Concrete Rules: Some Examples

In Chapter 6 we have seen how the purposive approach can be used to interpret basic terms such as 'employer' and 'employee', setting the scope of labour law. There are also numerous other interpretive questions being raised before labour courts (or other courts, boards, and arbitrators) on a daily basis. The goal of this chapter is to give some examples of purposive interpretation in concrete contexts. I have chosen several timely legal questions to illustrate how the purposive approach can be implemented. The first part considers several interpretive questions related to minimum wage laws: whether tips should be seen as part of the minimum wage; which deductions can be made from the wage for accommodation and related expenses; what are the minimum wage rights of apprentices, trainees, interns, and volunteers; what are the rights for time spent being 'on call'; and whether the minimum wage obligations apply for activities done before and after the actual 'work'. The second part discusses rights related to dismissals. It starts by focusing on the rights of a specific group of vulnerable workers (cleaners) to severance pay. This is a good example to show the importance of a *contextual* analysis—sensitivity to the particular context, here of the specific sector—as part of purposive interpretation. The next example is brought from the area of procedural rules, specifically, what is considered the effective date of dismissals, for purpose of the time limit to file a claim against it. The third and final part is concerned with the interpretation of freedom of association. I discuss the question of what additional rights should be derived from it, which is a good example to show that purposive interpretation is needed at the constitutional level as well. I then move to consider the issue of compulsory union agency fees, which raise the question of the scope of a *negative* freedom of association. The concrete examples throughout the chapter are drawn from Israel, the UK, Canada, and the US.

Part I—Rights Related to Wages

Tips and the minimum wage

Minimum wage laws are designed to ensure a minimal income for every worker. However, there are often difficult questions as to how the income should be calculated. In the case of *Inbal Malka*, for example, the Israeli National Labour Court was faced with the question of whether tips paid by customers directly to a waitress should be considered part of the wage.[1] There is no mention in the Israeli Minimum Wage Act of tips; it is only stipulated that the determinative wage for purposes of the Act is that 'paid by the employer to the employee'.[2] A literal reading of this section can lead one to conclude that sums paid by customers—and not directly by the employer—cannot be part of the wage. Nevertheless, we must avoid such quick and simplistic conclusions. Surely the wording of the legislation permits the opposite conclusion as well; it does not explicitly exclude sums that were paid *indirectly* by the employer, so the question remains whether we should consider the tips as sums paid on behalf of the employer. Most importantly, it is obvious that the Israeli legislature did not consider this specific legal problem and did not attempt to regulate it. There is thus a lacuna that needs to be filled, and to do that, we need to look at the purpose of the legislation, and adopt the solution that best advances this purpose.

The judgment does not tell us how much exactly Inbal Malka has earned for her work as a waitress. This information is difficult to gather, given that the tips have gone directly to her pocket and were never registered in any way. We do know, though, that the employer in this specific case has paid nothing directly—there was no wage except for the tips—and that the hourly tips could amount to sums significantly higher than the minimum wage, sometimes several times higher.

It is quite obvious that informal employment of this kind is not legitimate and contradicts the goals of the Act (and other labour laws). An employer must issue a pay slip and make the necessary deductions for income tax, social security, and so on. This is necessary also to make sure that the employee is getting at least the minimum wage, and that other employment laws are obeyed (e.g. with regard to maximum hours). Employing someone not through the formal payroll—without recording the number of hours worked and the payments made—is a recipe for labour law violations.[3] However, let us assume that records are kept, the exact sums of tips are registered, and the employee gets a formal wage slip. Would it be acceptable, in these circumstances, to count the tips as part of the wage for minimum wage purposes? The Israeli Labour Court answered positively (subject to the condition that the tips are registered and go through the employer's payroll). If the goals of the minimum wage are to protect the dignity of low-wage employees and to redistribute resources in their favour, as argued in Chapter 5, this judgment is justified. Assume that a waiter is earning twice the minimum wage from tips. This is not a situation of low wage that should be seen as an assault to dignity or a need to redistribute in his favour. From a purposive point of view, it does not matter whether the income is paid directly by the employer or by customers as part of the work for this employer. It would be a mistake to decide the issue based

[1] *DGMB Eilat Restaurants Ltd v Malka* 40 PDA 769 (2005) (Israeli National Labour Court).

[2] Minimum Wage Act 1987 s 3.

[3] On the precariousness resulting from reliance on tips see Einat Albin, 'A Worker–Employer–Customer Triangle: The Case of Tips' (2011) 40 ILJ 181.

on an attempt to conclude who has property rights in the tips;[4] they are obviously paid as compensation for the same work that the waiter was hired by the employer to do. The goals of the minimum wage law do not justify the application of this law on people whose income is much higher than the minimum wage.[5]

The legislature can certainly decide otherwise; in the UK, for example, an amendment to the regulations from 2009 clarified that tips cannot be counted towards the minimum wage.[6] This is obviously legitimate and the parties can be expected to adjust accordingly. My point is that absent such a determination in legislation, it is not required by purposive interpretation, quite the contrary.

Deductions from the minimum wage

A related issue concerns which deductions are allowed from the minimum wage.[7] A prominent example is payments in respect of living accommodation. In the UK, for example, when accommodation is provided to the worker by the employer, a deduction is allowed up to a maximum sum determined by the National Minimum Wage Regulations.[8] In *Leisure Employment Services Ltd v HM Revenue & Customs*,[9] at issue was whether an employer can deduct an additional sum for heat and light, on top of the maximum accommodation offset. This may sound like an attempt to evade the minimum wage requirement, but it certainly was not the case in the particular circumstances. Leisure Employment Services Ltd operates holiday resorts, and allows its seasonal staff the choice of being accommodated on site. For those who chose this option—41 per cent of the workforce—the employer deducted the accommodation offset, plus £3.00 per week for heat and light, which are bought by the company for the entire site with no individual meters. It was not in dispute that the sum of £3.00 was less than the market rate for the utility services, and it was not argued that the employer over-charged the workers for those services.

Assuming the workers truly have a choice whether to use the employer's accommodation or not, it seems perfectly justified to require that they pay for utilities out of their wages—just as those living off-site must do. It is therefore

[4] Which was the approach of the UK Employment Appeal Tribunal in *Revenue and Customs v Annabels (Berkeley Square) Ltd* [2008] UKEAT 0562_07_1306, [2008] ICR 1076. The property argument was rightly rejected by the European Court of Human Rights in the case of *Nerva v UK* [2002] IRLR 815, (2003) 36 EHRR 4.

[5] The Israeli Supreme Court created some confusion in a subsequent case, which considered the status of tips as part of the salary not for minimum wage purposes, but for payments owed from the National Insurance Institute as a result of accidental death at work. In a judgment that ignores the reality of the relationship as well as any purposive analysis, the Court decided to view tips as a separate payment, given voluntarily by customers, unrelated to the wage; presumably for the worker this income represents a separate and independent income. See *National Insurance Institute v Esther Cohen*, judgment of 14 April 2013.

[6] National Minimum Wage Regulations 2015, reg 10(m).

[7] This section as well as the parts of the following two sections are based on Guy Davidov, 'A Purposive Interpretation of the National Minimum Wage Act' (2009) 72 MLR 581.

[8] National Minimum Wage Regulations 2015, regs 14–16.

[9] [2007] IRLR 450, [2007] ICR 1056, [2007] EWCA Civ 92.

understandable that at the Court of Appeal, Smith and Wilson LJJ expressed their sympathy with the employer, noting that a ruling preventing the deduction of heat and light provided at 'bargain rates' will deter such arrangements, even when those are beneficial to the workers themselves. Nonetheless, as all the justices agreed, a clear rule preventing such deductions—and requiring wages to be paid in cash without contractual obligations for any purchases by the workers from their employer—is justified. Such a rule is necessary in order to prevent abuse by employers, or even genuine disagreements on whether an arrangement is really beneficial to the workers (disagreements which are bound to be detrimental to low-wage workers who often find it impossible to bring such disputes to court).[10]

This is a good example to show how second-order considerations must enter the analysis as well. It also helps to clarify that a purposive approach does *not* mean a case-by-case determination in light of the circumstances of specific plaintiffs. In the specific case, considerations of dignity and redistribution do not appear to justify accepting the employees' claims; but a rule allowing additional deductions, which are not explicitly authorized in the regulations, could be problematic from the point of view of these goals. The decision of the Court of Appeal to prohibit the additional deduction is therefore in line with the main goals of the Act. It takes into account the understanding that low-wage workers are in a position of vulnerability, and might accept offers from the employer even when those are not always beneficial to them.

Apprentices, trainees, interns, and volunteers

In the UK, the National Minimum Wage Act makes it clear that the right to a minimum wage applies to apprentices, who are considered to be 'employees' for the purposes of the Act.[11] Although some specific apprentices and trainees in publicly funded programmes are excluded,[12] and other apprentices under the age of 19 or in the first year of their apprenticeship are only entitled to a reduced rate,[13] as a general rule the legislature included apprentices and trainees within the group of people entitled to a minimum wage.

In *Edmonds v Lawson*,[14] the Court of Appeal had to decide whether a pupil barrister who received no pay was an 'apprentice' (and hence entitled to a minimum wage) under the Act. The pupil sued the head of her chambers as well as two members of the chambers to whom she was assigned as a pupil during her 12-months pupillage. The Court concluded that there was a binding contract between the pupil and the defendants—but *not* a contract of employment, mainly

[10] See also Low Pay Commission, 'National Minimum Wage: Low Pay Commission Report 2006', ch 4 <https://www.gov.uk/government/uploads/system/uploads/attachment_data/file/273274/6759.pdf> accessed 16 October 2015.

[11] National Minimum Wage Act 1998 ss 54(1) and 54(2).

[12] National Minimum Wage Regulations 2015, regs 51–52, 54–56.

[13] National Minimum Wage Regulations 2015, reg 5.

[14] [2000] 2 WLR 1091, [2000] IRLR 391, [2000] QB 501, [2000] EWCA Civ 69, [2000] ICR 567.

on the grounds that the relationship with pupil barristers is characterized by 'the lack of expectation that they will render services of value'.[15] It is difficult to accept this conclusion, given the Court's own acknowledgement that a pupil works on his 'master's papers (making factual summaries, or drafting chronologies, or writing advices or preparing pleadings)'.[16] Although the pupil will use this experience to acquire professional skills, 'the pupil master will [also] often benefit from the pupil's work and from discussion with him',[17] as the Court itself added. There is therefore obviously *some* value for the so-called 'master' stemming from the pupil's service.

A similar issue came before the Employment Appeal Tribunal in the case of *HM Revenue & Customs v Rinaldi-Tranter*.[18] At issue was whether a trainee hairdresser in the second year of a National Traineeship was entitled to a minimum wage. The trainee worked 35 hours per week at a salon, where she 'was given simple tasks to do such as sweeping, washing hair, passing rollers and making coffee'.[19] She also observed the staff and was able to ask questions and gain some experience. In accordance with the requirements of the governmental Traineeship programme, she was paid £50 per week by the salon's owner, i.e. less than the minimum wage. There was no doubt that during the first year the trainee came within the scope of the exceptions listed in the Regulations, but the question was whether she was a 'worker' during her second year on the programme. The lower Employment Tribunal came to the conclusion that she was not, relying on evidence suggesting that 'had she not been there to learn she would not have been there at all. The qualified hairdressers would have done their own sweeping up etc.... We are satisfied that she made little or no financial contribution to the business and that almost all of the benefit was to herself.'[20]

However, as the Appeal Tribunal rightly observed, the Act does not require (or permit) a calculation of the extent to which an engagement is profitable for the employer. It is difficult to deny the fact that the trainee has undertaken to 'perform personally... work'[21] for the salon. Accordingly she was a worker, entitled to a minimum wage. The idea of having exclusions or reductions in specific circumstances, when the 'work' is assumed to be minimal—merely a by-product of studying—makes perfect sense, but such exceptions should be limited and explicitly stipulated in the legislation. Once a year has passed the suggestion that a trainee hairdresser still does not produce any value to the salon is untenable.

If the goals of the Act are (as I have suggested) redistribution and assuring respect for human dignity, apprentices and trainees must generally be included within the scope of the Act. Such workers are in a position of vulnerability vis-à-vis the employer, to an even greater extent than regular employees. If the idea of redistribution is to transfer resources from a group that is likely to be better-off to a group that is likely to be worse-off, apprentices and trainees are certainly just as

[15] ibid para 34. [16] ibid para 24. [17] ibid.
[18] [2007] UKEAT 0486_06_1309. [19] ibid para 2(16). [20] ibid para 9(52).
[21] National Minimum Wage Act 1998 s 54(3)(b) (definition of 'worker').

likely to fall within the latter group as other employees. Also given the assumption that they perform work that benefits the employer, a situation in which they are not paid for this work—or paid less than the minimum wage—would hardly be in accord with respect for their dignity. This appears to support the logic of the Employment Appeal Tribunal in *Rinaldi-Tranter* rather than the Court of Appeal's reasoning in *Edmonds v Lawson*. Ultimately the question is whether any 'work' has been performed; whether profitable or not is immaterial. Once a person performs such work, even as a trainee or an apprentice, the right to a minimum wage should apply (provided that the specific exceptions listed in the Regulations are not applicable).

One could argue that public policy justifies giving incentives to professionals to supervise apprentices and trainees. Nevertheless, this is no different from arguing that we should allow other employers to pay less than the minimum wage, as an incentive for taking more employees. This is hardly a sound employment policy. Once the basic idea of a minimum wage is accepted, those who enjoy the work of others should be bound to pay at least the minimum wage, with incentives—if they are necessary—provided separately. Moreover, it is just as likely that the requirement of paying minimum wages would *increase* the investment in training (assuming an imperfect labour market)—as a result of employers' desire to quickly make trainees more beneficial to them. Indeed, there is evidence suggesting that the introduction of the National Minimum Wage Act was not detrimental to work-related training,[22] and may have even increased it.[23]

In recent years it has become common, in several countries, to engage people as 'interns' and avoid paying them a minimum wage and other employment benefits.[24] People are often willing to work for free because the internship is seen as a route towards employment (whether at the same place of work or in other places that consider the experience gained an asset). To decide if this should be allowed we have to consider the appropriate legal boundaries of volunteering. Clearly, some room has to be left for people to perform 'work' on a volunteer basis, without being considered 'employees'. This is a social activity that should not be prevented; on the contrary, it should be encouraged. At the same time, it is also clear that this legal construct can be used to evade labour law responsibilities and this must be prevented. The question thus becomes how to set the line and separate between the two scenarios.

Consider first an easy case: Suheir Sarugi worked for the Israeli National Insurance Institute (a governmental agency) for six years as a secretary. When she started, there was no open position available and she agreed to work as a

[22] Andy Dickerson, 'Longer-Term Implications of the NMW: A Re-Examination Of Employer-Provided Training', Report presented to the Low Pay Commission, March 2007 <http://webarchive.nationalarchives.gov.uk/20130626202215/http://www.lowpay.gov.uk/lowpay/research/pdf/t0JK67V2.pdf> accessed 16 October 2015.

[23] Wiji Arulampalam, Alison L Booth, and Mark L Bryan, 'Training and the New Minimum Wage' (2004) 114 Economic Journal 87.

[24] See, e.g., Mitchell H Rubinstein, 'Our Nation's Forgotten Workers: The Unprotected Volunteers' (2006) 9 U Penn J of Lab & Emp Law 1.

'volunteer', which she did for ten months, until she was hired for a short period as a replacement for another worker. She then went back to being a 'volunteer' for another six weeks, before she received a regular paid position. During the entire period, she worked on a full-time basis doing the exact same job. When she was dismissed after six years at the Institute, she sued, asking for a minimum wage for the time she was not paid at the beginning of the relationship (approximately one year).[25] It was clear to the National Labour Court, and rightly so, that this arrangement was beyond any legitimate scope of volunteering. Sarugi worked for the Institute doing the exact same job performed by employees (indeed performed also by herself as an employee in other periods). Because she was desperate for a job she was willing to work for free to put a 'foot in the door' and land a paid position once one became available. The employer used this vulnerability to enjoy her work without pay; this should not be allowed.

It is true that in some sense it was a rational decision—a free choice of Sarugi to invest this time in the hope of securing good employment. It could also be the case that the Institute would not have taken her (or anyone else) if they knew that they had to pay. But this should not change the conclusion. In another Israeli case, a small law office used the services of a recent law graduate doing articling without paying him any wages.[26] The employer had argued that he did the worker a favour when he agreed to supervise him during the articling period, to allow him to get his licence (for which an articling period is mandatory). The employer explained that the plaintiff could not find any paid articling position, and it was beneficial for him in these circumstances to do the articling on a volunteer basis. It was made clear to him that this was the arrangement and he decided to take it. The Court, though, was not impressed with this argument. Just as the right to a minimum wage cannot be waived, even by 'free will', the status of an 'employee' cannot be waived for the same reasons (otherwise it will create a simple route to avoid the minimum wage and other obligations). In practice, a person performed work for the benefit of another, work of the kind that is usually paid; therefore the Court concluded that he *should* be paid.

Is it indeed relevant—perhaps even determinative—that in other cases (or even usually) the same work is provided for pay, from a purposive point of view? On the face of it, this fact does not tell us whether the worker needs the protection of the law; or (otherwise put) whether the goal of the law was to apply to such cases. A starting point could be that people who work for others have to be paid, and we want to ensure that the compensation is above a certain minimum, for both dignity and redistributive purposes. It is not possible to count indirect or potential (future) benefits as part of this compensation without significantly harming these goals. Just as we do not allow an employer to consider uncounted and unregistered tips as part of the minimum wage, without being able to know what these

[25] *Suheir Sarugi v National Insurance Institute*, judgment of 3 May 2004 (Israeli National Labour Court).

[26] *Haim Kazis v Taufic Ariet* 38 PDA 394 (2003). See also *Asher Tweeli v Izchak Dahari* 37 PDA 746 (2002).

sums are and ensure that they are sufficient, we cannot rely on unknown future benefits of an intern as a replacement for the minimum wage. Further, a worker spending his scarce time at work requires compensation now, and not a promise (or potential) of compensation in the future, in order to subsist in dignity. Finally, such a system is also detrimental to other workers, who have to face impossible competition from people who will do the same work for free.

Volunteer status can be justified—for purposes of the minimum wage—only if the work is performed for non-economic reasons (whether present or future economic reasons) and without competing with paid employees. Only then, the goals of protecting dignity and redistributing in favour of low-wage workers become irrelevant. But how can we be sure that this is *truly* the case? Here, the fact that the same kind of work is usually performed for pay can be an indicator that it is economic in nature. It also means that unfair competition with paid employees is likely. Additional indicators may have to be developed over time, in light of new cases.

Being 'on call' and the minimum wage

Minimum wage laws set a minimum hourly rate, but sometimes it is difficult to ascertain the number of hours that count as *working time* entitled to wages, especially when the worker is inactive or free to do as he chooses during time spent at the workplace. Further complications arise when the boundaries between the workplace and the worker's home become blurred. In the UK there is an elaborate attempt to address such cases in the National Minimum Wage Regulations, but much has been left for judicial interpretation.

The Regulations draw a distinction between 'time work' (when payment is made by reference to the time actually worked, usually by the hour); 'salaried hours work' (when a worker is paid on a weekly or monthly basis, regardless of the hours actually worked in a particular week or month); 'output work' (when payment is based on the number of pieces made or some other measure of output); and 'unmeasured work' (any work that does not fall into the previous groups, 'including, in particular, work in respect of which there are no specified hours and the worker is required to work when needed or when work is available').[27] There are also specific regulations dealing with special circumstances, such as being 'on call' or travelling, in each of those circumstances.[28]

In *British Nursing Association v Inland Revenue*[29] the Court of Appeal considered the status of workers operating a twenty-four-hour booking service. During day-time this service was provided from the premises of the employer, but at night

[27] National Minimum Wage Regulations 1999 regs 3–6. For a useful introduction to these complex regulations see Bob Simpson, 'Implementing the National Minimum Wage—the 1999 Regulations' (1999) 28 ILJ 171; S Deakin and GS Morris, *Labour Law* (4th edn, Hart 2005) 288–90. Similar arrangements are now included in the National Minimum Wage Regulations 2015.

[28] National Minimum Wage Regulations 1999 regs 15–19.

[29] [2002] IRLR 480, [2002] EWCA Civ 494, [2003] ICR 19, [2002] Emp LR 668.

calls were diverted to the homes of employees. The legal question was whether the entire night shift should be seen as 'working time', or just the times in which calls actually came in. Affirming the judgment of the Employment Appeal Tribunal, the Court concluded that the workers were entitled to a minimum wage for the entire shift. As Buxton LJ noted, 'the alternative... that the employees are only working when they are actually dealing with phone calls with all the periods spent waiting for calls excluded, would, in my view effectively make a mockery of the whole system of the minimum wage'.[30]

The idea that any idle time at work should be excluded from the definition of 'working time' indeed seems preposterous. If, for example, there are two calls on average each hour, each taking only one minute, the actual working time during a 13-hour night shift (8:00 p.m. to 9:00 a.m.) would amount to merely 26 minutes. But obviously having to answer calls every 30 minutes during the night makes one committed to work during the entire period. Although the overall workload may be smaller than in other settings, having to wait awake for calls throughout the night is certainly 'work' that requires remuneration.

British Nursing Association was decided on the basis of the original Minimum Wage Regulations of 1999, but already in 2000 the regulations were amended in a way that arguably might change the law in similar cases. Regulation 15 starts from the proposition that a period of time during which one is required to be available for work is generally considered working time, but there are now two important exceptions. First, if the worker is required to be available for work (usually known as being 'on call') but his home is at or near the place of work and he is entitled to spend the time at home, it is *not* considered 'working time' for the purposes of the Minimum Wage Act.[31] Second, workers who are required to sleep at or near the place of work will *not* be considered as 'working' except when they are 'awake for the purpose of working'.[32]

It is understandable that the amended regulations consider being 'on call' but asleep as different from regular work. Yet to maintain that these are not working hours at all—with no remuneration required by law—is problematic, given the justifications for minimum wage laws. Any time in which a worker is not free to do as he chooses, and has to be available for work in one form or another, requires at least *some* remuneration.

The issue has hardly been settled by the amended regulations. The situation considered in *British Nursing Association*, for example, arguably does not fall within regulation 15 at all. For people who work from home during the night, the entire night shift is 'working time', even if there is some idle time between tasks (just as there is sometimes idle time for those working on the employer's premises during the day). So the interpretive question that remains is what counts as a worker being 'required to be available for... work'[33] and what constitutes actual

[30] ibid para 19.
[31] National Minimum Wage Regulations 1999, as amended, reg 15(1).
[32] National Minimum Wage Regulations 1999, added in 2000, reg 15(1A).
[33] ibid, reg 15(1).

'work'. Moreover, the arrangement of regulation 15 applies only to 'time work' (or 'salaried hours work'[34]), as opposed to 'unmeasured work'. An additional crucial interpretive question, therefore, is whether the worker is engaged in time work (or salaried hours work). In the case of 'unmeasured work', a daily average of actual work requiring compensation could be agreed upon.[35]

Interestingly, British courts and tribunals have usually refrained from applying regulation 15 in cases that involve sleeping at work. In several cases—one involving a night watchman at a construction site,[36] another concerning a resident manager at senior residences who had to be on site four days a week, twenty-four hours a day,[37] and a third involving a guest care manager at a hotel who had to 'sleep over' several nights each week[38]—the judgments have given the workers a right to a minimum wage *for their entire time at the workplace*, even though they were all allowed to sleep and were only rarely interrupted during the nights. This approach is in line with that of the European Court of Justice.[39] In two additional cases—one concerning a carer who stayed with an epilepsy patient for three days each week, twenty-four hours a day,[40] the other dealing with wardens at a sheltered housing service who had to be on site Mondays through Fridays[41]—the regulations concerning 'unmeasured work' were invoked, and the time spent sleeping or otherwise not actually attending to clients has been ruled *not* to require compensation.[42]

The first line of judgments mentioned above embodies an extremely narrow reading (if not outright contradiction) of regulation 15. Despite the explicit language of the regulation, which excludes time in which workers can sleep at work from the right to a minimum wage, judges have sought to ensure compensation for such time. This is understandable when considering the purposes of the National Minimum Wage Act as a whole—the goals of redistribution and protecting human dignity require a minimum level of remuneration when

[34] There is an arrangement similar to reg 15 for salaried workers—see reg 16.

[35] ibid, regs 27–28.

[36] *Scottbridge Construction Ltd v Wright* 2003 SC 520, [2003] IRLR 21, 2002 SLT 1356, 2002 GWD 34-1150, [2002] ScotCS 285. This judgment was based on the original regulations, but the amendment of 2000 did not change significantly the rules concerning sleeping *at work* (see *Burrow Down Support Services Ltd v Rossiter* [2008] UKEAT 0592_07_2506, [2008] ICR 1172).

[37] *MacCartney v Oversley House Management* [2006] UKEAT 0500_05_3101, [2006] IRLR 514, [2006] ICR 510. This case dealt with a 'salaried hours work', i.e. the relevant regulation that was avoided is reg 16 rather than reg 15.

[38] *Anderson v Jarvis Hotels Plc* [2006] UKEAT 0062_05_3005.

[39] *Landeshaupstadt Kiel v Jaeger* [2003] 3 CMLR 16, [2003] IRLR 804, [2003] EUECJ C-151/02, ECLI:EU:C:2003:437.

[40] *Walton v The Independent Living Organisation* [2003] ICR 688, [2003] IRLR 469, [2003] EWCA Civ 199.

[41] *South Holland District Council v Stamp* [2003] UKEAT 1097_02_0306.

[42] Regulation 15 has so far been applied mostly in cases that involved workers who were supplied with a place of residence by the employer, near the place of work, and were required to be on-call during nights, without being called much. See *Hughes v Jones (t/a Graylyns Residential Home)* [2008] UKEAT 0159_08_0310; *South Manchester Abbeyfield Society Ltd v Hopkins* [2010] UKEAT 0079_10_3011, [2011] IRLR 300, [2011] ICR 254.

someone is working for others, even if the worker is inactive for certain periods of time. The fact that a person relinquishes his freedom to control his own time should be sufficient for these purposes. Nonetheless, there is undeniably a difference between sleeping at work and actively working. A more appropriate solution, therefore—and one which conforms better with regulation 15—is based on the idea of 'unmeasured work'. Regulations 27 and 28 offer some flexibility to reach intermediate solutions. First, regulation 28 allows an agreement between the parties 'determining the average daily number of hours the worker is likely to spend in carrying out the duties required of him'.[43] Such an agreement will be valid only if the employer can show that the average agreed upon is 'realistic'.[44] In the absence of an agreement, regulation 27 requires payment for 'the total of the number of hours spent by [the worker] during the pay reference period in carrying out the contractual duties'. Both the term 'realistic' and the question of what hours are spent 'in carrying out the contractual duties' allow ample room to manoeuvre. To best achieve the goals of the Act without placing an unreasonable burden on employers, courts could require compensation for hours in which the worker's freedom is significantly interrupted (e.g. having to spend the evening at the workplace rather than at home), and eschew compensation for actual sleeping time (based on the assumption that the interruption is relatively minimal during this time).

A purposive approach would therefore support the line of thinking adopted by the Court of Appeal in *Walton v The Independent Living Organisation*[45] in terms of considering a work-sleep combination as 'unmeasured work'—but would view a much larger number of hours as 'work' for this purpose. In *Walton* the Court approved an agreement determining the average daily working time as six hours and fifty minutes, out of the full twenty-four-hour days in which the carer had to be with the patient and attend to her needs. This figure was based on calculations of activities, with only the actual minutes of activity being counted. However, given the fact that the carer was required to stay with the patient twenty-four hours a day, her freedom to do whatever she chooses was significantly impaired. A preferred starting point is therefore to consider *all* the hours as working hours—as the approach adopted in *Scottbridge, MacCartney* and *Anderson*[46]—and then detract some hours (such as actual sleeping) in which the interruption is presumed to be minimal.

Payment for pre-work or post-work activities

A related interesting and timely question is whether time spent before or after a work shift should also be considered compensable work in some circumstances. The time spent commuting to and from work is, in some sense, for the benefit of the employer—it is needed to allow one to get to work—but the employer does

[43] National Minimum Wage Regulations 1999 reg 28(1). [44] ibid reg 28(2).
[45] n 40 above. [46] nn 36–38 above.

not enjoy this time and does not control it. In principle, at least, the worker can choose to reside right next to the workplace, thus minimizing commuting time to an insignificant amount. But what about other activities which the employer *requires* before or after the work shift? In a recent case before the US Supreme Court, workers at Amazon warehouses demanded compensation for time spent standing in line for 'security' checks after each shift.[47] The employer required all employees to remove wallets, keys, and even belts and pass through metal detectors on the way out from work—not for security reasons, obviously, but to prevent theft. This took approximately twenty-five minutes of wait time each day. The workers argued that this time could be reduced significantly (to a *de minimis* amount) either by adding more security screeners or by organizing the shifts so that they end at different times during the day. But the employer refused to introduce such changes or invest in more screeners, and refused to pay for this time as well.

From a general purposive point of view—looking at the goals of the minimum wage—it seems like an easy case. This is time spent at the workplace, at the request of the employer, controlled by the employer. The goals of the minimum wage—redistribution and protecting human dignity—apply equally if the time spent for the benefit of the employer involves the 'main' work activities or 'incidental' activities. From the workers' point of view—and from society's point of view—there is no difference between these activities. The goals of the minimum wage apply just the same.

Nonetheless, the Fair Labor Standards Act of 1938—which regulates the right to minimum wage and working time in the US—has included since 1947 an exception: there is no right to a minimum wage with regard to 'activities which are preliminary to or postliminary to' the 'principal activity or activities' which the employee is employed to perform.[48] This exception comes on top of another exception for travel/commuting time, so Congress obviously intended to exclude from the scope of the law activities such as security checks. This seems to contradict the general goals of the minimum wage. What do we do if there is a conflict between the goals of the law as a whole and the goals of the specific section under consideration? In principle, according to regular interpretation rules, the specific section should take precedence. However, to the extent possible it should be interpreted in line with the general goals of the law, to avoid the conflict.

Is it possible, in the current context, to understand the anti-theft screening as *not* being postliminary to the principal activity the workers were employed to perform? Taking a literal approach this would be difficult. Taking an 'original intent' approach—by focusing on the goals of Congress in 1947—this would be very difficult, as well. This is usually the approach of US Supreme Court judges,

[47] *Integrity Staffing Solutions v Busk* 574 US ____ (2014). The actual employer was not Amazon but another company operating the warehouse on its behalf.

[48] Fair Labor Standard Act, 29 US Code § 254. For an overview and discussion of US law in this context, see Jeffrey M Hirsch and Samuel Estreicher (eds), *Compensation, Work Hours and Benefits* (Kluwer 2009), especially chs 8 and 9.

so it is hardly surprising that they unanimously rejected the workers' arguments. In contrast, from a purposive point of view, the thoughts and subjective intentions of some members of Congress back in 1947 cannot determine the results of the case.[49] The question is rather, can we interpret the section in a way that will make sense and will not undercut the objective goals of the law? The Court of Appeals (9th Circuit) apparently thought so—albeit without making any reference to a purposive approach—relying on the fact that the screening was (a) necessary for the primary work and (b) done for the employer's benefit.[50] For these reasons it is 'integral and indispensable' to the primary activity, which is the test adopted in previous Supreme Court precedents to warrant compensation.[51]

The Supreme Court rejected this view, and added an explicit objection to another possible criterion, that appeared in the 9th Circuit's judgment implicitly: the fact that the workers were *required* by the employer to undergo the anti-theft screening. During these twenty-five minutes, every day, they were (still) under the control of the employer, not free to do as they please with their time. This should be enough to require compensation, given the goals of the minimum wage. For reasons of human dignity and redistribution, people should not have to work for the benefit of others and under their control without getting paid—any time in which an employee is not free, but rather under the effective control of the employer, should be understood as a 'principal' activity for purpose of the Act. In contrast, if you have to take a shower because of the work (for example), but it is up to you whether, when, and where to take it, this would be a 'postliminary' activity that can be excluded from the Act, given section 254, without undercutting its goals.

The Supreme Court rejected the relevance of the fact that screening was required by the employer, by noting that this will sweep into 'principal activity' the very activities that Congress intended in 1947 to exclude. This may be so, but it only serves to show the illogical and regressive nature of the 'original intent' method of interpretation. What if the contemporary Congress—sixty-nine years later—has a different understanding of the reasons behind the Act, and different reasons for keeping this section on the books? And what if, among the members of Congress, then and now, there are many different views, political and ideological, and many different 'intentions' concerning the Act and this specific section? The purposive approach avoids these problems by focusing on a different level of abstraction. The preferred interpretation of the Act is not the one that some members of Congress in 1947 would have preferred, but rather the one that fits best with the goals of the Act from a broader perspective—its objective justifications.[52]

[49] See Chapter 2. [50] *Busk v Integrity Staffing Solutions* 713 F 3d 525 (9th Cir 2013).

[51] *Steiner v Mitchell* 350 US 247, 332 (1956). The same test was applied, albeit differently, by the Supreme Court.

[52] In another relatively recent case, the Supreme Court rightly refused to allow an employer to eschew compensation for time spent walking from a changing area (used for putting on protective gear) to a production area. See *IBP v Alvarez* 546 US 21 (2005). In the same case, however, the Court refused to consider compensable the time spent putting on protective gear at the *beginning* of the day, because it was 'two steps removed' from the principal activity. This hardly seems relevant

Part II—Rights Related to Dismissals

Change of employers and severance payments

The next topic was chosen to show that purposive interpretation should also include consideration of *context*. If we are to advance the goals of the legislation, this may require different steps depending on the context (time, place, sector, and so on). Consider, as an example, the question of whether workers have a right to severance pay when employers change, even though they continue to work in the same workplace. Below I argue that a unique interpretation is justified in the context of cleaners, even though a separate treatment does not appear in legislation.[53]

According to the Israeli Severance Pay Act of 1963, employees dismissed from their job are entitled to severance payments in an amount equal to one monthly salary per each year of work. As in many other employment regulations, the Israeli legislature recognized the connection between employees and their place of work, alongside the connection with the specific employer. Accordingly, severance payments are calculated based on the entire period of tenure at the same workplace—even if the identity of the employer has changed during this period. The law explicitly stipulates (in Article 1) that the duty to pay the severance payment *for the entire period of work at the same workplace* is on the employer dismissing the employee. If company A is selling its business to company B, the latter must take into account a future obligation to pay severance payments for dismissed workers, calculated based on their work at the same workplace for company A as well. This part of the legislation was designed to ensure that employees retain their tenure-related rights in case of ownership transfer. In practice this was also understood by the labour courts to mean that severance payments do not have to be paid during the transfer of ownership, if the employee continues to work in the same workplace. The rights are retained until the time of actual dismissal.

To understand this rule, and confront interpretive questions, we should start by considering the goals of severance pay laws. Very briefly, there are four main goals. First, to discourage unjust dismissals, for the same reasons justifying unjust dismissal laws, as discussed in Chapter 5 (mainly, providing security). Although severance payments do not prevent unjust dismissals, and are paid (at least in Israel) in any case of dismissal including for just cause, the existence of significant costs is likely to deter employers from dismissing someone without a good reason. Second, to discourage employees from leaving too easily and inflicting losses on the employer who invested in them. Knowing that by leaving voluntarily she will lose the severance payment, an employee is likely to think twice before doing so.

from the point of view of the employees, which the Act was ultimately designed to protect. They are already at work, doing what the employer requires from them—but are not getting paid. This is difficult to justify.

[53] This section reproduces some parts from Guy Davidov, 'Special Protection for Cleaners: A Case of Justified Selectivity?' (2015) 36 CLLPJ 217.

There is some debate about whether this is beneficial or rather detrimental to efficiency, but legislatures have probably assumed the former. Third, severance pay is needed to provide the worker with income in the period of looking for another job. In a sense, it supplements unemployment insurance, to ensure that the worker can go through this period without being forced to take the first offer (which could be bad for her and for the economy and society as a whole). Fourth and finally, it is often considered to be a contribution towards pension—a payment reflecting the years of service, that can be saved by the employee and used for income after the age of retirement.

With this background in mind, the rule placing the duty with the last employer (at the same workplace) can be justified for three reasons. First, employees will get the payment at the time when it is most needed, in line with the third goal above. Second, the sum will continue to accumulate, preserving a disincentive for dismissals from the first day of employment with the second employer—a large enough disincentive that takes into account the entire period of work at the same workplace. Admittedly, some employees might prefer to get the payment earlier, at the time ownership is transferred, because if eventually they leave of their own choice (without being dismissed) they will get no severance pay at all. Notwithstanding, in this respect they are not different from any other employee—they are not 'losing' anything by not getting severance payment from company A, because workers in general only get this payment as compensation for losing a job, which in the current situation did not happen.[54] Third, deferring the payment until actual dismissal is also more just from the point of view of the employers. The law is based on the assumption that in transfer of ownership situations, the tenure rights of employees will be factored into the price of the deal; the future obligation to pay severance payment can be estimated based on the average number of people being dismissed. The fact that company B will not have to pay severance payments to *all* the employees, but rather only to employees it chooses to dismiss, reduces the obligation and makes the transfer of ownership more feasible.

The understanding that the first employer does not have to pay severance payments for employees continuing to work in the same workplace has been uncontroversial in Israel for a number of decades, since the adoption of the Act. However, in recent years it became clear that the same rule—originally adopted to protect employees from losing tenure-related rights—could become detrimental for them. This is especially the case in the cleaning sector, where a large majority of workers are now employed through contractors, which tend to change frequently. Assume a person working as a cleaner at a university (or any other establishment/firm) for twenty years. It is quite possible that during this time the identity of his or her employer has changed many times. Every few years (and in some cases even every year) the university is likely to issue a new tender, and

[54] I am assuming that the employee wants to stay in the job under company B; otherwise, if he wants to leave because of the transfer, he will likely be entitled to severance payment according to Israeli case-law. See *The Histadrut v Israel Aerospace Industries* 58(6) PDA 481 (2004) (Supreme Court of Israel); *Emi Matom v Avraham*, judgment of 10 February 2004 (Israeli National Labour Court).

choose a new cleaning contractor. When contractor B is replacing contractor A it is not 'buying' the business of the previous contractor, but rather replacing it due to the university's decision. But Article 1 of the Severance Pay Act seems to apply in such situations as well.

Three problematic results follow once the regular rules are applied. First, contractor B will be reluctant to hire the same workers employed by contractor A, because they come with tenure-related obligations. In most cases they are thus likely to lose their job at the university. Second, assuming the workers are not offered the opportunity to continue with the new contractor, contractor A is likely to try to avoid paying them severance payments by offering them alternative placements (cleaning at another establishment under contractor A). According to Article 11 of the Act, employees are entitled to severance payment if resigning due to changes that significantly worsen their working conditions (a form of constructive dismissal). Thus, if the offer is not comparable to the previous placement, workers can be entitled to severance payments. However, an assessment of the new offer requires judicial discretion based on the concrete facts, so the right is difficult and costly to enforce. Furthermore, because cleaners are not likely to always have alternative options, they can be forced to accept the inferior offer to avoid unemployment, thus also waiving their right to severance payments. Third (and finally), if contractor B has decided to hire the same employees after all—whether because of demands from the client or because of the advantages of continuing with experienced workers (who are familiar with the workplace and the demands of the client)—there is a risk that, at the end of the day, severance payments for previous periods of employment will not be paid.[55] While non-compliance with labour and employment laws is always a possibility, especially in low-wage sectors such as the cleaning sector, the risk seems higher when contractor B is required to assume tenure-related duties accumulated during the period of employment with contractor A, without being compensated for this cost (compensation which can be expected in regular transfer of ownership situations). Alternatively, if contractor B is planning to comply with this duty and assume the workers' tenure-related rights, as required by law, at the very least it can be expected to demand concessions from them in return.[56]

[55] See, e.g., *Hezin v Tenufa HR Service and Maintenance 1991 Ltd*, judgment of 25 November 2006 (Israeli National Labour Court); *Mniyesko v The State of Israel—Ministry of Defense*, judgment of 29 August 2011 (Regional Labour Court Tel Aviv); *Liubov v Sheleg Lavan Cleaning Security and Guard Service Ltd*, judgment of 29 December 2005 (Regional Labour Court Haifa); *Kozentzov v Maof Human Resources Ltd*, judgment of 20 February 2013 (Regional Labour Court Haifa).

[56] The magnitude of the problem has somewhat diminished since 2008, when a general extension order created a universal right to a pension plan for Israeli workers. Employers' mandatory payments to the pension fund include two components; one of them is a payment towards severance payment (a sum equal to 6% of the salary), which became part of the pension savings. Barring exceptional circumstances, the employer will not get this money back if the employee leaves without being dismissed. As a result, much of the sum that used to be paid as severance payment—until 2008 only in case of dismissal and only at the time of dismissal—is now transferred by the employer each month to the pension fund. Still, an additional 2.33 per cent of the salary is paid according to the previous rules. And in the cleaning sector, which is based on low profit margins, this is significant enough to lead to the same incentives and same problematic results.

By refraining from employing the cleaning staff directly, the 'client' is surely responsible for these problems. But let us assume for current purposes that such indirect employment is legitimate and legally acceptable (which has generally been the approach of Israeli law).[57] Is there a way to avoid these problematic results, and ensure that the general right to severance payment does not cause the workers to lose their jobs, or move to another workplace against their preference? Also, is there a way to ensure a realistic prospect for them to receive severance payment for the entire period of work at the same workplace, as required by the Act?

The National Labour Court responded to these challenges in 2005 by deciding that when cleaning contractors change, employees are entitled to severance payment from contractor A even if they stay at the same workplace under contractor B (thus relieving contractor B from its future obligation for this period).[58] Moreover, another judgment adds that cleaners are entitled to this payment even if they are offered a comparable placement by contractor A.[59] In other words, even if they are not actually dismissed by contractor A but simply ordered to move to a new workplace, according to this ruling workers have the right to refuse and stay at the same workplace under contractor B, without losing their right for severance payment from contractor A. These rules provide solutions (at least partial solutions) to all the problems mentioned above. Contractor B will not have to assume the costs of severance payment for periods of work under contractor A, and thus will be less reluctant to hire the same workers and allow them to continue to work at the workplace. The workers are also more likely to receive their severance pay—first from contractor A and later (if dismissed) from contractor B, for the later period.

The same two rights were later also included (codified) in a collective agreement for the cleaning sector, signed in 2013 and extended in February 2014 by the Minister of Economy to all cleaning contractors. However, the interesting point is the regulation of the cleaning sector by the National Labour Court, *before* the adoption of the same solutions by the collective parties. Sector-specific rules are common in collective agreements; indeed, one of the justifications for collective agreements is their ability to create rules tailored for specific workplaces or sectors. But this is much less common when initiated by courts. The Severance Pay Act is universal; it appears to apply equally to all sectors. Until recently, for many years unions were not able to achieve specific solutions for cleaners (a sector especially difficult to unionize). Faced with this reality, and realizing the difficult implications for the workers, the Court created a sector-specific solution—in effect, a *selective* regulation applicable only for cleaners—through the process of purposive interpretation.

[57] For a discussion of 'who is the employer' see Chapter 6. For a recent example of a cleaner who worked seventeen years for the same user, and the Tel-Aviv Regional Labour Court still refused to consider her an employee of this user, see *Clodette Tsagir v Bank Leumi*, judgment of 7 April 2014.

[58] *A Dinamica Services (1990) Ltd v Veronin*, judgment of 21 August 2005 (Israeli National Labour Court).

[59] *Achildave v Amishav Services Ltd*, judgment of 27 March 2006 (Israeli National Labour Court); *Ofek MB Management and Maintenance Ltd v Bliuzer*, judgment of 8 July 2013 (Israeli National Labour Court).

When reaching the decision to create separate severance pay rules for cleaners, the Court relied on the characteristics of the sector. Harsh competition, together with the special vulnerabilities of employees, created a high risk that the full severance payment (for the entire period of work) will not be paid *in practice* by the last contractor. Even more importantly, the frequent replacement of contractors meant that contractors were at the same workplace for relatively short terms, but workers naturally wanted to stay for longer periods. The universal rules created by the Act were not designed for such situations, and created an incentive to replace the workers—which was highly detrimental for them. The (selective) new rules created by the Court can correct the shortcomings and problematic incentives created by the (universal) general rules, when applied to the cleaning sector.

Procedural rules: The effective date of dismissals

The next example was chosen to show the importance of purposive interpretation in procedural questions as well. In the UK, unfair dismissal claims can only be submitted within a short period of three months following the 'effective date of termination'.[60] In addition, if the plaintiff wishes to apply for interim relief—which is to be expected when people argue that they have been unjustly dismissed, and can ask for an injunction against the dismissals—this application must be submitted within seven (!) days of the effective date of termination. These are very tight timeframes, given that one needs some time to 'process' the dismissal (which could be difficult to accept on a personal level), perhaps consult with family and friends, then find a lawyer, and the lawyer needs time to prepare the legal documents.

The tight deadlines are stipulated explicitly in the legislation, so they are obviously binding. Notwithstanding, courts have some discretion when they are asked to interpret the term 'effective date of termination'. The issue has recently reached the UK Supreme Court in the case of Lauren Barratt, who was terminated without notice from her employment at a small charitable organization because of alleged inappropriate behaviour at a private party.[61] The employer held a disciplinary hearing, and then she was told to expect to receive the outcome of the hearing by mail. When the letter arrived (by recorded delivery) Barratt was away for a few days, helping her sister who had just had a baby. The letter was received by the son of her boyfriend, but she only found out about it after she returned home, four days later. As it happened, her unfair dismissal claim was submitted after the deadline if counting from the day the letter was delivered to her home, but within the deadline if counting from the day she actually had an opportunity to read the letter. In the specific case, her ability to bring the case before the Employment Tribunal depended on how 'effective date of termination' is to be interpreted.

[60] Employment Rights Act 1996 s 111(2).

[61] *Gisda Cyf v Barratt* [2010] IRLR 1073, [2010] 4 All ER 851, [2010] ICR 1475, [2010] UKSC 41.

In situations of dismissals without notice, the legislation states simply that the effective date of termination is 'the date on which the termination takes effect'.[62] The employer argued that the termination took effect on the day the letter of dismissal was formally received at the employee's place of residence. The Court in contrast concluded that the termination took effect only when she had a reasonable opportunity to learn about it, and that in considering 'reasonable opportunity' the specific circumstances should be taken into account. Here, it was clear that Barratt did not avoid receiving the letter on purpose; and although in theory she could have asked someone to read the letter for her, the judges thought it was reasonable not to do so, both because she was preoccupied with helping her sister, and because a harsh dismissal letter is something a person usually prefers to read in person. More generally, the Court emphasized that expectations from the employee should be 'mindful of the human dimension'[63]—meaning that a formalist reading of the legislation (which might lead one to expect everything that is practically feasible, even if it is unrealistic or unfair in the circumstances) must be avoided. The Court went on to add that the legislation has to be interpreted with the inequality between the parties and the employees' need of protection in mind.[64]

What are the goals behind the tight deadlines? Presumably, the main goal is to ensure finiteness for employers, so that they are not exposed to legal suits for long periods after the end of the relationship. A related consideration is to protect employers from delayed legal proceedings, when the evidence to refute allegations may not be easily available anymore. The very strict limitation concerning interim relief is probably designed to prevent the possibility of reinstatement after the relations have been severed in practice for a significant period—presumably based on the assumption that this could disrupt labour relations in the workplace, and is likely to harm third parties (a new employee hired to replace the discharged one). In contrast, the goals of the Act as a whole, and the part concerning unjust dismissals more specifically, are designed to protect employees from arbitrary, discriminatory, or otherwise unjust termination. To achieve this goal it is obviously necessary to give them sufficient time to file their claims. A formalistic rule based on the date of delivering the letter of termination would ensure more certainty to employers, but the uncertainty created by the relative flexibility of the rule adopted by the Court is very minimal.[65]

From a purposive point of view, paying a small price in terms of certainty is justified, indeed necessary, in order to protect the broader goals of the legislation as a whole: allowing people sufficient time to legally challenge unfair dismissals. This requires that we consider the *actual* time that they have, not the *theoretical* time counted from the day they could have read the letter but did not—subject of course to the condition that their actions are reasonable and in good faith. The

[62] Employment Rights Act 1996 s 97(1).
[63] *Gisda Cyf v Barratt* (n 61) para 30.
[64] ibid para 35.
[65] As the Court itself noted in para 43.

UK Supreme Court did not explicitly use the purposive approach in this case, but implicitly the decision is clearly based on the goals of the Act. With the periods for filing claims being so short to begin with, a liberal interpretation of the term 'effective date of termination' becomes necessary, to ensure that employees will have a realistic option of legal recourse.

Part III—Freedom of Association Rights

Freedom of association and derived rights

Purposive interpretation is also required when considering the scope of constitutional rights. A prominent timely example concerns the question of which rights should be derived from freedom of association. Is the right to bargain collectively, for example, constitutionally protected? Is the right to strike also constitutionally protected? These questions have important practical implications when governments and legislatures limit the ability of workers to engage in collective bargaining or strike. In Ontario, for example, for many years the law prevented collective bargaining by farm workers. In British Columbia, faced with the need to cut health care costs, the legislature decided on wage cuts and other measures which contradicted the rights secured in collective agreements. If these are considered infringements of freedom of association—which in many legal systems (including Canada) is constitutionally protected—then the infringement has to be justified in accordance with constitutional demands (specifically, the principle of proportionality). If workers have a constitutional *right* to bargain collectively, and a constitutional *right* to strike, this is obviously a strong protection. It does not mean that governments and legislatures cannot limit these rights, but they have an obligation to respect them, for example by minimizing any limitation to the extent necessary for the achievement of a legitimate goal.[66]

In recent years the Supreme Court of Canada reversed previous precedents to conclude that a right to bargain collectively is constitutionally entrenched—thus offering protection to both farm workers in Ontario and health care workers in British Columbia.[67] A constitutional right to strike was recognized by the same Court a few years later.[68] Both rights were derived from the freedom of association protected by the *Canadian Charter of Rights and Freedoms*. This was justified, indeed necessary, from a purposive point of view. When considering the appropriate

[66] The following paragraphs rely on (and sometimes reproduce parts from) Pnina Alon-Shenker and Guy Davidov, 'Organizing: Should the Employer Have a Say?' (2016) 17 Theoretical Inquiries in Law 63, and Guy Davidov, 'Judicial Development of Collective Labour Rights—Contextually' (2010) 15 CLELJ 235.

[67] *Dunmore v Ontario (Attorney General)* [2001] 3 SCR 1016; *Health Services and Support-Facilities Subsector Bargaining Association v British Columbia* [2007] 2 SCR 391. For a similar conclusion by the European Court of Human Rights, also reversing a contradictory previous precedent, see *Demir and Baykara v Turkey* App no 34503/97 (ECtHR, 12 November 2008).

[68] *Saskatchewan Federation of Labour v Saskatchewan* [2015] 1 SCR 245.

scope of freedom of association, courts should ask themselves what is needed given the purpose of this freedom. In this respect, changes in the labour market and in labour relations have to be taken into account. The right to organize does not have much meaning in the current labour context if workers are prohibited from bargaining collectively through their union, and there is little point in allowing them to bargain collectively if they are not allowed to strike. This was probably true in the 1980s, although the Canadian Court rejected the idea at that time.[69] It is certainly true today, when unions are weaker, governments are more often hostile, outsourcing and subcontracting are widespread, global competition is fierce, and workers are frequently employed by small, less well-established enterprises that are not as likely to provide decent conditions and are more difficult to organize.[70]

It may be ironic that unions are winning the day at the Supreme Court of Canada only after becoming weaker (and therefore less feared).[71] There are surely many explanations for this irony that are unflattering to the Court. But there is also a benign reason that should not be ignored: as unions become weaker, they *need* constitutional protection more, and a purposive/contextual interpretation of *Charter* rights must take into account the fact that new rights are needed in order to protect the same basic freedoms.

Admittedly, in theory there could be different ways to make freedom of association effective. Constitutional protection cannot mean that the legislature is obligated to apply the current model.[72] So if a legislature can come up with another system, instead of collective bargaining, that will achieve the goals discussed in Chapter 5 (democracy in the workplace (including, specifically, voice), redistribution, and efficiency), this could lead to a new interpretation. In practice, though, for the past century collective bargaining has been the main system used in democratic societies for these purposes. So the fact that it is theoretically possible to come up with another system cannot be used as an excuse to withhold constitutional protection based on the current system.

Interpreting freedom of association is not always a constitutional issue. In Israel, the right to organize is protected in legislation (the Collective Agreement Act of 1957, as amended), and the National Labour Court recently faced a similar need to decide which rights and duties can be derived from it. Specifically, the question was whether an employer should be allowed to voice its opposition to unionization

[69] The previous precedents, known as the 'labour trilogy', were *Reference Re Public Service Employee Relations Act (Alberta)* [1987] 1 SCR 313; *PSAC v Canada* [1987] 1 SCR 424; *RWDSU v Saskatchewan* [1987] 1 SCR 460. For early critiques of this trilogy, see Geoffrey England, 'Some Thoughts on Constitutionalizing the Right to Strike' (1988) 12 Queen's LJ 168; David Beatty and Steve Kennett, 'Striking Back: Fighting Words, Social Protest and Political Participation in Free and Democratic Societies' (1988) 12 Queen's LJ 214.

[70] For a succinct review of these changes and the resulting need to update employment laws, see Harry Arthurs, *Fairness at Work: Federal Labour Standards for the 21st Century* (Human Resources and Skill Development Canada, 2006).

[71] Eric Tucker, 'The Constitutional Right to Bargain Collectively: The Ironies of Labour History in The Supreme Court of Canada' (2008) 61 Labour/Le Travail 151.

[72] Brian Langille, 'Why Are Canadian Judges Drafting Labour Codes—And Constitutionalizing The Wagner Model?' (2009–2010) 15 CLELJ 101.

during an organizing campaign. The question has no answer in Israeli legislation, where collective labour law is almost entirely judge-made. For historical reasons—especially the strong political stance of the *Histadrut* (Israel's major labour union) during the 1950s, when labour legislation was introduced—legislatures left much autonomy to the parties to settle their own disputes. However, this proved insufficient in recent years. Quite often, the *Histadrut* no longer has the power to protect its interests through strikes (or the threat thereof), so it seeks help from the courts. The legislature has mostly remained silent, leaving labour courts with the task of developing the law and finding solutions to the many new problems that emerged.[73] On the specific issue mentioned above there was a lacuna which the National Labour Court was asked to address. In a dramatic, innovative decision, employers have been prohibited from any speech during a union organizing drive.[74] This controversial judgment places significant limit on employers. Is it justified?

A purposive analysis of this question requires us to articulate the goals of freedom of association. Briefly stated, unionization is needed to protect the dignity of workers (or: ensure decent work); to achieve a degree of workplace democracy; to promote equality between different workers; and to advance distributive justice between capital and labour.[75] At a more concrete level, the protection and advancement of unions is justified because through collective bargaining it leads to the redistribution of resources from employers to employees; it creates a mechanism for workers to voice their views and concerns, as well as a structure of (relatively) democratic co-governance in the workplace; it prevents arbitrary decisions and ensures an internal 'rule of law' in the workplace; and it can also (more controversially) promote efficiency.[76] Overall, unions are good for us (as a society). Admittedly, real life is not always the same as the ideal just described; unions have their own problems. But these can (and should) be solved through targeted legislation and other means, without losing the crucial benefits.

For freedom of association, and the right to organize, to be effective—which is important for all of the reasons just mentioned—workers must have a free choice about joining a union. If this is possible to achieve without limiting the employers' freedom of speech, then we should not limit the employers' rights gratuitously. But if free choice cannot be assured without limiting the employers' speech, then it seems quite obvious that freedom of association should trump. For the workers, this is crucial; and society supports their organizing. The speech, in contrast, is

[73] Some of the judicial developments in the context of collective labour law are described in Davidov (n 66). See also Guy Mundlak, *Fading Corporatism: Israel's Labour Law and Industrial Relations in Transition* (Cornell UP 2007).

[74] *The Histadrut v Pelephone Communications Ltd*, judgment of 2 January 2013 (Israeli National Labour Court). The decision was later upheld by the Supreme Court; see *Coordinating Chamber of Economic Organizations v National Labour Court*, judgment of 7 July 2014.

[75] See Chapter 4, dealing with the goals of labour law in general. Noted here are only some of the goals most relevant to unionization.

[76] See Chapter 5.

protected but has very limited value in the particular context.[77] A purposive and contextual analysis of the two conflicting freedoms therefore leads to this conclusion: If organizing is not truly free, because of the employer's speech, then the speech should be prohibited.

The question thus becomes an empirical one: Is it possible to ensure free choice by employees even when they are advised by the employer not to join a union? From a formalistic point of view, the problem can be 'solved' with a legal rule preventing coercion. If the goal is to ensure free choice, on the face of it a rule preventing the employer from intervening in the free choice of employees (but allowing the mere voicing of an opinion) might seem sufficient. Such an analysis, however, entirely ignores the context: it ignores the inherent vulnerability of employees in the relationship, the inequality of power, the difficulties of enforcement, the significant (and growing) barriers to unionization, and the reality of aggressive union-busting tactics.

Assume that a worker has been intimidated not to join a union. There are several possible scenarios: (a) she will be afraid to disobey the employer and avoid joining the union; (b) she will ignore the employer and join the union or otherwise make a free choice; (c) she will notify the union about the intimidation, and the union will take this to court and ask for an injunction. In this last scenario, there are several ways in which the story can unfold: (c1) The union cannot prove the intimidation (even though it has occurred) and fails; (c2) the union gets an injunction, but the damage is already done, workers have been intimidated; (c3) the union gets an injunction and sufficient protection for individual workers to feel secure to make an entirely free choice. A rule against coercion by employers will suffice, by itself, only if scenarios (b) and (c3) are the ones expected to materialize in the large majority of cases.

Is this a realistic expectation? That depends on the additional/supporting legal mechanisms to protect organizing, including mechanisms of enforcement. Absent any other mechanisms to protect the right to organize, options (a), (c1),

[77] There are three main purposes/justifications behind freedom of speech (see, e.g., Kent Greenawalt, 'Free Speech Justifications' (1989) 89 Colum LR 119, 122). First, self-fulfilment; but this is less relevant for profit-motivated commercial speech by corporations. The importance of this justification is stronger in the small number of cases when the organizing attempt is made within a small business and the owner is a specific person who is attached to the business and has strong feelings against union involvement in it. In such cases it could certainly be the case that the ability to express these feelings is important to the autonomy and personality development of the owner. However, given the various barriers to unionization, especially in small businesses, this scenario is likely to be rare. Second, truth discovery and the advancement of a 'marketplace of ideas'; but this idea attaches an instrumental or societal value to speech and justifies free speech for its benefits to the *listeners* rather than to the *speaker*. Given the inherent imbalance of bargaining power between the parties, it seems more justifiable to *limit* the speech by the stronger party to guarantee a meaningful 'marketplace of ideas'. Moreover, presumably some of the workers are against unionization and will engage in discussion and debates with co-workers about whether or not to vote for a union. There is therefore no reason to assume that employer speech would be necessary to the listeners for discovering the 'truth'. Third and finally, the self-governance and democracy justification; but protecting employer speech might actually *impede* democracy in the workplace because it may allow employers to unduly influence the true wishes of employees.

and (c2) are just as likely, to say the least. I do not have direct empirical evidence to support this claim, only logic, based on the understanding of the context; and there is plenty of evidence from the United States (and anecdotal evidence from Israel) showing that joining a union could be risky for employees and lead to reprisals.[78] A court of law cannot assume, in these circumstances, that the choice about unionization can be free in the face of anti-union speech by the employer.[79] This indeed is the situation in Israel. There are no significant tools or legislated mechanisms to ensure that scenarios (b) and (c3) will be the dominant ones in real life. The National Labour Court was therefore right to conclude that coercion is quite possible, indeed likely, even with a rule against coercion in place. The solution of the Court—a sweeping ban on employer speech against unionization during an organizing campaign—does not ensure 100 per cent free choice. It does, nevertheless, create a rule that is much easier to enforce. Violations are easier to catch and easier to prove; there are no grey areas. This can certainly be expected to minimize coercion significantly.

The conclusion advanced here (supporting the conclusion of the Israeli courts) is based on a purposive analysis. First, it asks what legal rules are needed to advance the goals of the legislation (the Collective Agreements Act) and the goals of labour law more generally. Second, it takes into account two crucial contextual factors: the real-life current experience concerning the struggles of organizing, and the surrounding legal rules designed to make such organizing possible. It should be clear, therefore, that the conclusion is sensitive to time and place. A sweeping ban on employer speech may not have been necessary in Israel a few decades ago, when the barriers to organizing were much less daunting. Similarly, such a ban might not be necessary in other legal systems, if they have alternative legal measures designed to protect organizing that are sufficiently successful. In Canada, for example, other mechanisms such as reverse onus of proof and remedial certification have proved to be somewhat effective (though only to a certain extent given the increasing use of union-busting tactics by large and resourceful employers).[80] Such detailed arrangements can be adopted in legislation, but not by courts.

Another way to put the dilemma is by asking whether it is possible—and realistic—to achieve 'laboratory conditions' for the decision-making process of

[78] In the US see, e.g., Benjamin I Sachs, 'Enabling Employee Choice: A Structural Approach to the Rules of Union Organizing' (2010) 123 Harv LR 655, 681–87. In Israel, see, e.g., *Mif'aley Tachanot Ltd v Israel Yaniv* 33 PDA 389 (1996) (Israeli National Labour Court); *The Histadrut v Pelephone Communication Ltd*, judgment of 7 January 2013 (Israeli National Labour Court).

[79] Another way to make this point is by reference to the difficulty of changing the default: in practice, it is much more difficult to opt-in (when the default rule is no union) than to opt-out (if the default rule would have been the existence of a union). Therefore, if we want to maximize free choice, the solution could be to change the default to opt-out, or alternatively to correct this asymmetry by other means, removing as much as possible impediments to opt-in. See Sachs, ibid.

[80] David J Doorey, 'The Medium and the "Anti-Union" Message: "Forced Listening" and Captive Audience Meetings in Canadian Labor Law' (2008) 29 CLLPJ 79. And see additional discussion in Alon-Shenker and Davidov (n 66).

employees (whether it culminates in an election, as in some countries, or simply signing-up of new members as in Israel). Such 'laboratory conditions'—free of any employer coercion—have been required by the National Labour Relations Board in the US, at least in theory.[81] There seems to be a broad consensus among American commentators that such conditions have not been secured in practice, leading to (or at least significantly contributing to) the decline in union density.[82] Given the contextual factors just described, the prospects of 'laboratory conditions' in organizing drives in present-day Israel are not high—hence the necessity of ostensibly extreme measures to give organizing a chance. This is not to suggest that the wholesale ban is the only possible or acceptable solution. Many other solutions have been proposed for the same problem;[83] but they all require legislative intervention. The Court, in contrast, is not in a position to create a detailed arrangement. The ban on employer speech was therefore necessary.

Compulsory union agency fees

In legal systems that created a model of exclusive representation by unions, a duty to pay agency fees is common. If there is one union that has the power to represent all the employees in the workplace (or at least in the same 'bargaining unit')—including bargaining on their behalf or making decisions on strikes—then by law all the employees enjoy the work and efforts of this union, whether they are members or not. It is therefore considered justified to allow the union to take agency fees from workers who are represented by it. Those who choose to become members pay union dues; those who prefer not to become members have to pay the agency fees. This is usually secured by the union as part of the collective agreement: the employer agrees to deduct the agency fees from non-members and transfer them directly to the union. However, in the US as many as twenty-four states enacted so-called 'right to work' laws that prohibit this 'agency shop' arrangement.[84]

A law prohibiting agency shop obviously makes it very difficult to unionize and bargain collectively. If workers can enjoy the same benefits whether they pay

[81] *General Shoe Corp* 77 NLRB 124, 127 (1948), *enforced*, 192 F 2d 504 (6th Cir 1951), *cert denied*, 343 US 904 (1952).

[82] See, e.g., Paul Weiler, 'Promises to Keep: Securing Workers' Rights Under the NLRA' (1983) 96 Harv LR 1769; Kate E Andrias, 'A Robust Public Debate: Realizing Free Speech in Workplace Representation Elections' (2003) 112 Yale LJ 2415, 2418; Paul M Secunda, 'Toward the Viability of State-based Legislation To Address Workplace Captive Audience Meetings in the United States' (2008) 29 CLLPJ 209; Sachs (n 78).

[83] See, e.g., the various contributions in n 82. See also Mark Barenberg, 'Democracy and Domination in the Law of Workplace Cooperation: From Bureaucratic to Flexible Production' (1994) 94 Colum LR 753.

[84] A list of these states is available at the National Conference of State Legislatures website at <http://www.ncsl.org/research/labor-and-employment/right-to-work-laws-and-bills.aspx> accessed 15 October 2015.

union dues or not, many could be tempted to save the money and enjoy the benefits as 'free riders'. This is a classic collective action problem; even though everyone would benefit from unionizing, it might not happen if people rely on others to pay the dues. In other words, 'right to work' laws infringe freedom of association by preventing the collective parties from agreeing on agency fees even though the union must represent *all* the workers.[85]

Given that freedom of association is constitutionally entrenched,[86] one would expect the legal debates to revolve around whether 'right to work' laws that prohibit agency shop arrangements are constitutional. Nevertheless, in the current US climate, it is the agency shop model itself that is being challenged. Although the union is only allowed to impose agency fees corresponding to expenses related to collective bargaining etc., and must exempt the non-members from dues that are used to cover 'political' expenses (such as supporting political candidates that would further the union's goals),[87] this is still insufficient for anti-union activists. In a recent case, a number of in-home care providers have challenged an Illinois law that deemed them to be 'public employees' for purposes of collective bargaining, which resulted in representation by a public employees union and the payment of agency fees. The care providers are 'controlled' by the customer but paid by the state.

In a 5–4 decision of the US Supreme Court, the majority criticized previous precedents that allowed agency shop arrangements, and although not going so far as to overturn them, it construed them narrowly, refusing to apply them in the current case.[88] The result is that care providers in Illinois can enjoy the benefits of collective bargaining without paying any fees. The union will be weakened and in the long run is very likely to disappear altogether, as a result of collective action problems.[89]

It is remarkable, and unfortunate, that the Court completely ignored the impact of its decision on freedom of association.[90] The problem of 'free riders' is mentioned, but the Court failed to realize (or acknowledge) the fact that it is crucial mainly because of the broader concerns affected. A purposive approach requires that we analyse the issue through the lenses of freedom of association, taking into account the normative justifications behind collective bargaining regimes (and ultimately, agency shop arrangements). Any limitation on agency fees clearly undercuts freedom of association and the actual ability to engage in collective bargaining. This could still be justified if there are very strong conflicting rights.

[85] For a proposal to solve this problem by excluding those who refuse to pay dues from the scope of bargaining and protection, see Catherine Fisk and Benjamin Sachs, 'Restoring Equity in Right-to-Work Law' (2014) 4 UC Irvine LR 859.

[86] In the US it has been inferred from the First Amendment, which protects the freedom of speech and assembly. See *NAACP v Alabama* 357 US 449 (1958).

[87] *Abood v Detroit Board of Education* 431 US 209 (1977).

[88] *Harris v Quinn* 573 US ___ (2014).

[89] And see Daphne Gottlieb Taras and Allen Ponak, 'Mandatory Agency Shop Laws as an Explanation of Canada–U.S. Union Density Divergence' (2001) 22 JLR 541.

[90] See also Catherine L Fisk and Margaux Poueymirou, 'Harris v. Quinn and the Contradictions of Compelled Speech' (2014) 48 Loyola of LA LR 439.

For example, it seems entirely justified to prohibit arrangements that force membership in the union ('closed shop'). But the mere duty to pay agency fees, when the economic benefits of the union far outweigh these fees, is a very minimal infringement of the rights of the few anti-union workers. It cannot justify a ruling that will end up harming many more employees and their ability to effectively organizc.

9

Addressing the Compliance/ Enforcement Crisis

It is widely acknowledged that lack of compliance and enforcement is a major component of the much-discussed 'crisis of labour law'. This is part of the broader 'coverage crisis'—the fact that many workers who need the protection of labour law do not in fact enjoy such protection. In some cases, this is because the laws themselves are outdated and irrelevant; in other cases it is because they are excluded from the definition of 'employee'. Both of these problems have been addressed in previous chapters. A third and perhaps the most dramatic problem leading to the coverage crisis is the wide-spread non-compliance with labour law and the lack of sufficient enforcement. Addressing this problem is crucial for the purposive project. When employers fail to comply with labour laws, and society fails to enforce them, the goals behind these laws are frustrated. We must constantly remind ourselves of the obvious: the goals of a minimum wage act, for example, are not achieved simply by the enactment of this act. They are only achieved once the words written on paper translate into real-life action and this requires compliance, which requires enforcement. To put it bluntly, there is not much point in the discussion of the previous chapters if the conclusions remain on paper and are not enforced.

This chapter starts by explaining the reasons for the current enforcement crisis. I then move to discuss possible solutions to address it, first by considering whether there are ways to redesign labour regulations so as to improve/encourage better rates of compliance (Part II) and then by examining new ideas concerning enforcement (Part III). The line between inducing compliance and improving enforcement is not always clear and some ideas could be classified in either group or both. This is not important in itself. Still, the distinction (even if not a sharp one) is helpful in organizing our thinking about this problem.

Part I—The Enforcement Crisis

Labour laws have never been entirely successful in terms of compliance and enforcement records.[1] While they usually combine the possibility of both self-enforcement and State enforcement—civil, criminal, and administrative—they

[1] This part is based on Guy Davidov, 'The Enforcement Crisis in Labour Law and the Fallacy of Voluntarist Solutions' (2010) 26 IJCLLIR 61, reproducing and updating some paragraphs from there.

also suffer from some inherent difficulties that hinder both compliance and enforcement: employers often have strong incentives for non-compliance; employees usually face various barriers that prevent self-enforcement; and effective enforcement by the State is costly and complicated. All of these difficulties have been exacerbated in recent years, as a result of globalization as well as domestic developments in management techniques, industrial relations and employment practices.

For most employers, labour standards are usually directly associated with more costs. Therefore some degree of non-compliance is hardly surprising—and it can be expected to remain with us.[2] It is a given that society must devote efforts and resources to the enforcement of labour laws. It appears, though, that in recent years the problem has become much more acute. In Israel, for example, non-compliance with the Minimum Wage Act has been measured at 14.1 per cent and is constantly on the rise—with the percentage of employees earning less than the minimum required by law much higher among new immigrants (22.5%), young workers (33.2%), workers without high-school education (29.3%) or without university education (20%), minority Arab workers (22.6%), and part-time workers (16.7%).[3] The enforcement crisis has been especially apparent in some specific sectors, such as cleaning and security.[4] Other countries are struggling with similar problems. In the United States, the garment industry has seen notoriously low compliance levels,[5] and a comprehensive study which focused on the three largest cities in the US found widespread violations of labour and employment laws in many other sectors as well.[6] In the United Kingdom there have been calls to create a new enforcement agency, in response to increased enforcement problems affecting vulnerable workers.[7] In Canada a detailed report for the Federal government revealed widespread violations of employment laws,[8] and a comprehensive study of precarious workers in Ontario confirmed that their rights are not enforced.[9]

[2] Orley Ashenfelter and Robert S Smith, 'Compliance with the Minimum Wage Law' (1979) 87 J of Political Economy 333.

[3] Tammy Eliav, Miri Endweld, Daniel Gottlieb, and Israel Kachanovski, *Trends in Minimum Wage Compliance: The Case of Israel* (Israel National Insurance Institute Working Paper 2009) (Hebrew).

[4] Guy Davidov, 'Enforcement Problems in "Informal" Labor Markets: A View from Israel' (2005) 27 CLLPJ 3, 7 and references therein.

[5] See, e.g., David Weil, 'Public Enforcement/Private Monitoring: Evaluating a New Approach to Regulating the Minimum Wage' (2005) 58 ILRR 238.

[6] Annette Bernhardt and others, *Broken Laws, Unprotected Workers: Violations of Employment and Labor Laws in America's Cities* (National Employment Law Project, 2009) <www.nelp.org/content/uploads/2015/03/BrokenLawsReport2009.pdf?nocdn=1> accessed 9 October 2015.

[7] TUC Commission on Vulnerable Employment, *Hard Work, Hidden Lives* (2008) <www.vulnerableworkers.org.uk/files/CoVE_full_report.pdf> accessed 9 October 2015; Citizen's Advice Bureau, *Give Us a Break! The CAB Service's Case for a Fair Employment Agency* (April 2011) <www.citizensadvice.org.uk/global/migrated_documents/corporate/give-us-a-break.pdf> accessed 9 October 2015 10–11.

[8] Harry W Arthurs, *Fairness at Work: Federal Labour Standards for the 21st Century* (Human Resources and Skills Development Canada 2006) 190–95.

[9] Leah F Vosko, Eric Tucker, Mark P Thomas, and Mary Gellatly, *New Approaches to Enforcement and Compliance with Labour Regulatory Standards: The Case of Ontario, Canada* (A Report for the

What are the reasons for these difficulties? Below are some possible explanations, starting with the basic inherent difficulty and moving to several explanations for the apparent intensification of the problem.

The inherent difficulty with self-enforcement. Employment laws usually have a dual enforcement mechanism, allowing employees to sue for their own rights (a civil suit) while at the same time allowing the State to use criminal and/or administrative sanctions in the case of non-compliance.[10] Consistent with market norms—the understanding that an employee has the most interest in enforcing his own rights and the strongest incentives for doing so—there is a significant reliance on self-enforcement. But there are also some well-known and crucial difficulties that often prevent such self-enforcement: lack of knowledge or understanding that employment rights have been infringed; lack of resources to hire a lawyer and sue; and fear of retaliation by the employer.[11] Attempts to tackle all three difficulties—by disseminating 'user-friendly' information about employment laws, by providing some legal assistance to employees or making it possible to file a suit without a lawyer, and by making it illegal to dismiss an employee because he sued—are important, but have very limited impact. It is the fear of retaliation in particular that inhibits self-enforcement. The well-informed employee will know that although retaliation is illegal, the employer will make every effort to show that there were other reasons for dismissing the employee. This means that lengthy and highly costly legal proceedings will be unavoidable.[12] Not to mention the fear of having a 'trouble-maker' reputation when facing potential employers in the future.

Increased pressure to cut costs. Employers facing increased global competition are under pressure to cut costs and may even feel more justified in evading some labour laws. More specifically, the low wages paid by employers in the developing world are pressuring competitors in developed economies to lower wages, thus widening the difference between the market wage (and benefits) and the minimum wage (and benefits) provided by law—at least in some problematic sectors. There is evidence showing a correlation between this higher differential and the level of non-compliance.[13]

The diminution of unionism. The existence of a labour union and a collective agreement in the workplace has proved to be highly instrumental for the

Law Commission of Ontario, November 2011) <http://papers.ssrn.com/sol3/papers.cfm?abstract_id=1975867> accessed 9 October 2015.

[10] See, e.g., Federal Labor Standards Act, 29 US Code § 216.

[11] See generally William LF Felstiner, Richard L Abel, and Austin Sarat, 'The Emergence and Transformation of Disputes: Naming, Blaming, Claiming' (1980) 15 Law & Society Review 631; David Weil and Amanda Pyles, 'Why Complain? Complaints, Compliance and the Problem of Enforcement in the U.S. Workplace' (2007) 27 CLLPJ 59, 63–65; Bernhardt and others (n 6); Charlotte S Alexander and Arthi Prasad, 'Bottom-Up Workplace Law Enforcement' (2014) 89 Indiana LJ 1069. For a more detailed analysis of barriers see Vosko and others (n 9).

[12] Empirical studies from the US show that retaliation is common and the protections against it ineffective; see Bernhardt and others (n 6) 24–25; Alexander and Prasad (n 11).

[13] Chang Yang-Ming and Isaac Ehrlich, 'On the Economics of Compliance with the Minimum Wage Law' (1985) 93 J of Political Econ 84.

enforcement of employment standards.[14] Unions are obviously in a much better position (compared with the individual employee) to self-enforce their agreements; and since collective agreements often cover many of the same issues covered by legislation—adding additional benefits *beyond* the legislated minimum—enforcing those agreements ensures compliance with the minimum provided by law as well. Furthermore, even with regard to employment standards not covered by a collective agreement, the union may provide the necessary resources (knowledge, legal assistance) as well as the job security needed to allow the individual employee to sue. It is thus clear why diminished union density and influence has been devastating for employees not only with regard to the chance of getting *additional* benefits, but also with regard to minimum employment standards, which are now much more difficult to self-enforce.

The proliferation of migrant workers. As part of the processes of globalization, an increasing number of migrant workers are working in foreign countries. For migrant workers, the inherent difficulties preventing self-enforcement are all exacerbated.[15] Less familiar with the local language, legal system, and customs, they are less likely to know their rights. Having migrated from developing countries they are less likely to have the resources to hire a lawyer and sue. Finally, working (usually) in the lowest-paid jobs they are easily replaceable and thus more likely to be fearful of reprisals.

There are also additional worries stemming from lack of a work permit. Elsewhere I distinguished between three types of enforcement problems in labour markets: violations of specific legal requirements (partial exclusion of employees from the application of certain regulations); sweeping exclusion by 'legal' employing entities, i.e. evading *all* labour regulations with regard to certain workers, for example by disguising employees as independent contractors, or by concealing the employment of certain employees; and finally, sweeping exclusion in non-declared employing entities, i.e. when the business as a whole is not declared to the tax and other relevant authorities, and the violation of labour laws is only part of a bigger picture of illegality.[16] Migrant workers often enter the country without permit, and are then likely to fall into the second group. Once their employment is not declared to the relevant authorities, enforcement of labour laws is very unlikely. Workers without permit are not likely to initiate any formal complaints or sue, for fear of being deported.

Outsourcing and subcontracting. As part of a continuing trend throughout the world in recent years, bigger organizations outsource some of their tasks to others (usually smaller corporations). Sometimes this is done with the direct goal of evading employer responsibilities. But there are also legitimate business reasons for choosing to outsource, like a preference for concentrating on core

[14] For a summary of the studies see David Weil, 'Individual Rights and Collective Agents: The Role of Old and New Workplace Institutions in the Regulation of Labor Markets' in Richard B Freeman, Joni Hersch, and Lawrence Mishel (eds), *Emerging Labor Market Institutions for the Twenty-First Century* (U of Chicago Press 2005) 13.

[15] See Bernhardt and others (n 6) 41–48.

[16] Davidov (n 4) 13.

competencies—having tasks that are more peripheral to the business done by others, who specialize in such tasks. A similar trend is dominant in the public sector, where neo-liberal governments attempt to become smaller and more flexible. Public employers are accordingly making every effort to avoid direct employment, preferring instead to engage with contractors.

As a result, fewer workers are employed by big and established organizations, with human resources and legal departments that usually ensure compliance with labour laws, and more workers are employed by small firms who specialize in specific tasks but lack such organizational advantages, and thus have a higher propensity for non-compliance.[17] The increased number of small (and less established) employers means that enforcement becomes more difficult as well. First, the fear of retaliation is higher in smaller workplaces, and so the probability of self-enforcement is lower.[18] And second, the ability of labour inspectors to enforce the law is much more limited when facing a larger number of businesses with less inclination to maintain formal documentation.

New employment practices. The proliferation of 'non-traditional' employment relations is yet another reason for the deterioration in labour laws' enforcement record. Working part-time, from home, on irregular hours, on a 'zero-hours contract', or otherwise in an 'atypical' arrangement has two important implications in terms of enforcement. First, there is less contact (social networks) between workers working for the same employer, and as a result workers are less likely to know their rights and pursue self-enforcement.[19] Second, the ability of labour inspectors to enforce the law is much more limited when facing such a dispersed workforce.[20]

An extreme example of an 'atypical' employment relationship associated with less enforcement is employment for lengthy periods of time through a temporary employment agency. Such a sham arrangement, in which the role of the agency is limited to 'payrolling', is akin to outsourcing the 'employer' legal status.[21] In such cases, workers may be part of a social network within the user enterprise, but this will be unhelpful for knowing their rights, as they have a different formal employer and a different (inferior) set of rights. Or they may even be excluded from the social network, considered by their own peers as inferior. Ever hoping to get accepted into a 'normal' position, they are especially unlikely to sue when labour laws are infringed. And enforcement by the State is more difficult when dealing with employment agencies that have a dispersed workforce. In addition, such agencies are often small and not established (given that hardly any resources are needed to set up such a business).

[17] See Arthurs (n 8) 193; Janice Fine and Jennifer Gordon, 'Strengthening Labor Standards Enforcement through Partnerships with Workers' Organizations' (2010) 38 Politics & Society 552.

[18] Arthurs (n 8) 194.

[19] For the example of Canadian truckers see ibid 194.

[20] See also Glenda Maconachie and Miles Goodwin, 'Recouping Wage Underpayment: Increasingly Less Likely?' (2006) 41 Aust J of Social Issues 327.

[21] Guy Davidov, 'Joint Employer Status in Triangular Employment Relationships' (2004) 42 BJIR 727.

Dwindling government budgets. Lastly, governmental budget cuts can be seen as yet another explanation for poor enforcement records. In many countries, even when centre-right governments were replaced by centre-left ones, social spending has not been returned to its original (real value) levels. That includes spending on the enforcement of labour laws—in particular the allocation of sufficient resources for inspectors,[22] prosecutors and judges, as well as campaigns to educate employers and employees about their duties and rights. Considering the difficulties with enforcement as detailed above, there is a need to devote significantly *more* resources than before just to maintain the same level of enforcement. Overcoming the inherent barriers and difficulties—i.e. seeking an *improvement* of those levels—will require a complete re-evaluation of the role of State-enforcement vs self-enforcement in this context, and a dramatic increase in resources as a result.

Part II—Improving Compliance

Given the recognized importance of labour laws—for the various reasons discussed in the first part of this book—society cannot accept this enforcement crisis. Before we turn to new enforcement ideas (in Part III below), it is pertinent to consider possibilities that will improve compliance without investing resources in enforcement. Obviously this will be ideal to the extent it is possible. How do we convince employers to comply with labour laws, without having to resort to enforcement mechanisms? Can we structure our laws in a way that will be more conducive to compliance, without having to constantly rely on self-enforcement or State-enforcement, both of which often prove very difficult to achieve?

It is likely that some employers (especially small employers) are violating labour laws unknowingly, so for them better education and dissemination of information about their duties could be sufficient. Others might not realize the severity of their actions; after all, we all violate some laws occasionally (such as crossing a street on a red light as a pedestrian). There are perhaps employers who think that some labour law violations are considered acceptable by society, perhaps because 'everyone is doing it', or they may even tell themselves that it is a 'victimless crime' (their logic could go like this: if I had to obey all labour laws, the costs would have been too high and I would not have been able to employ this worker, so he is better off not getting this legal right). For some of these employers, it could be helpful to 'put a mirror in front of them' through public campaigns infiltrating the understanding that labour law violations are 'wage theft',[23] socially

[22] See International Labour Office, 'Strategies and Practice for Labour Inspection' (Report of the Committee on Employment and Social Policy to the Governing Body, 297th Session, 2006) 4. See also Leah F Vosko, John Grundy, and Mark P Thomas, 'Challenging New Governance: Evaluating New Approaches to Employment Standards Enforcement in Common Law Jurisdictions' (forthcoming) Economic and Industrial Democracy, fn 2 and accompanying text.

[23] See, e.g., Matthew W Finkin, 'From Weight Checking to Wage Checking: Arming Workers to Combat Wage Theft' (2015) 90 Indiana LJ 851.

unacceptable and extremely harmful for the workers.[24] Publicizing the names of offenders and shaming them is also instrumental in deterring violations.[25] These steps are important; there is ample empirical evidence to show that social and moral considerations can motivate compliance.[26] But it is fair to assume that for many other non-complying employers they will not suffice.

This part focuses on three other ideas: creating (economic) incentives for compliance; inducing compliance through pressure on 'lead companies'; and promoting unionization (or alternative forms of worker representation). It is not suggested that these are the only or necessarily the best methods, but they have attracted a lot of attention and are especially worthy of discussion.

Creating incentives for compliance

A promising route is to build positive incentives for compliance as an inherent part of regulations. Consider the following example: until recently there was no legal duty in Israel to provide a wage slip to employees (even though it was common practice, at least among large employers, to provide them). For tax purposes, there were duties to maintain written documentations regarding the wages paid etc., but there was no duty to present the worker with a document detailing and explaining the payments. In 2008 the Israeli legislature instituted a duty to issue monthly wage slips to each employee, which include information about the payments made, as well as the hours worked, the vacation days taken and those remaining, and so on. This was an important step to help workers understand what they are getting, and by that assist them in monitoring and if needed self-enforcing their rights. However, how do we ensure that employers actually comply with this new duty? The legislation includes a multitude of methods; for example, failing to provide a wage slip is a criminal offence, and it is also a civil harm that can lead to an award of punitive damages without proof of actual damage. More importantly for current purposes, the legislation also includes an important incentive for the employer to comply and issue a wage slip: in case of disputes about overtime payments, vacation rights, and so on, in the absence of a wage slip there is a presumption in favour of the employee that the wages did not include those rights. In other words, even if the employer actually paid overtime,

[24] It has even been suggested that labour law violations should be conceptualized as a public health problem; see Meredith Minkler and others, 'Wage Theft as a Neglected Public Health Problem: An Overview and Case Study From San Francisco's Chinatown District' (2014) 104 Amer J of Public Health 1010.

[25] This has been used in some countries and has a growing potential in the era of social media. The enforcement agency does not necessarily have to communicate the information directly to the public—it is possible that non-governmental organizations (NGOs) could be more effective in doing this; see Judith van Erp, 'Naming and Shaming in Regulatory Enforcement' in Christine Parker and Vibeke Lehmann Nielsen (eds), *Explaining Compliance: Business Responses to Regulation* (Edward Elgar 2011) 322. And see more generally Oona Hathaway and Scott J Shapiro, 'Outcasting: Enforcement in Domestic and International Law' (2011) 121 Yale LJ 252.

[26] Robert A Kagan, Neil Gunningham, and Dorothy Thornton, 'Fear, Duty, and Regulatory Compliance: Lessons from Three Research Projects' in Parker and Lehmann Nielsen (n 25) 37.

or vacation rights (etc.), the burden will be on him to prove so and refute the presumption that these sums were not paid.

It is not clear if this method creates a stronger reason to comply compared with the threat of criminal sanctions and civil punitive damages. Nevertheless, it certainly adds another layer which in some cases could make the difference and lead to compliance.

In theory, the legislature could have settled for the legal presumption, using it *instead* of the other methods designed to ensure compliance, rather than on top of them. Such a 'soft' version of the law would have avoided the threat of stronger sanctions and limit itself to creating an incentive to comply, by making it beneficial to the employer to be able to present the wage slips in the event it is sued (and suffer some consequences otherwise). In some cases, if the societal interest is not very strong, and all we want is to 'nudge' people in some direction, perhaps we can use such soft law.[27] But this is likely to be quite rare in the context of labour law. For reasons discussed in the first part of the book, we generally cannot leave employers with the freedom to choose how to act. But could it be the case that a soft version of the law would be more conducive to compliance than the full package of hard and soft sanctions?

In the specific context of a law mandating the issuance of wage slips, the answer is obviously negative. Whatever the merits of creating an incentive through the legal presumption, the additional threat of criminal and civil sanctions does not *detract* from it. There is no reason to think that the full package of methods would be less effective than the single soft method; quite the contrary.[28] The same is true for most other labour laws.[29] Take the minimum wage as a simple example. If the UK legislature wants to ensure that each worker is paid at least £6.70 per hour, this is a very clear requirement which the threat of sanctions can support. Additional (softer) methods can be useful as complementary methods, but they cannot be more effective by themselves. For those employers who wish to save money by paying less than the minimum wage, the lack of direct ('hard') sanctions would make the evasion much easier. In fact, if we settle only for positive

[27] For such techniques see generally Richard H Thaler and Cass R Sunstein, *Nudge: Improving Decisions about Health, Wealth, and Happiness* (Yale UP 2008).

[28] One might argue that a soft law could be more helpful for retaining—or improving—internal motivation to comply with the law, and the hard sanctions could be detrimental to such motivation. It is far from clear that traditional sanctions are harmful for internal motivation; the literature shows complex interactions (see Yuval Feldman, 'The Complexity of Disentangling Intrinsic and Extrinsic Compliance Motivations: Theoretical and Empirical Insights from the Behavioral Analysis of Law' (2011) 35 Wash U J of L & Pol'y 11). Moreover, our ultimate goal is compliance, whether coming from internal motivation or not. In any case, the soft law discussed in the above example is designed to create *external* motivation, rather than internal—just like traditional sanctions.

[29] And see Finkin (n 23) 856 (arguing that self-regulation solutions are ill-fitted to deal with wage theft); Fine and Gordon (n 17) 558 ('Without a consistently enforced public regime of penalties for noncompliance, self-regulation would likely contribute to the further degeneration of standards in low-wage sectors'); Vosko, Grundy, and Thomas (n 22) (arguing that a prominent role must be maintained for 'hard' enforcement mechanisms).

incentives, it would mean giving those employers a legal licence to pay less than the minimum wage.[30] For basic minimum standards that would be untenable.[31]

Would the answer be different if our goal is to encourage the employer to go 'beyond compliance'? Imagine, for example, the societal goal of advancing equal employment opportunities. A regular move is to prohibit discrimination based on gender (for example). But there is a big difference between avoiding discrimination and actively promoting equal opportunities. If we want employers to be pro-active, for example by giving priority to women, we can demand such action in traditional 'command and control' regulations, such as by requiring affirmative action. But this would be very difficult to enforce; if the idea is that employers must give some advantage to women during a selection process, it is practically impossible to review the judgment call of the employer. A more enforceable solution is to create a system of quotas—a minimum percentage of women in certain levels of the organization. But this is likely to be seen as too much intervention in the context of the private sector. So let us assume that society wants to encourage employers to be pro-active about equality, and perform some affirmative action, but without legally mandating quotas. The question then becomes, would a soft law be able to do that?

Several proponents of 'new governance' seem to believe so.[32] But it involves a cost: to encourage employers to be pro-active about equality, we have to give them an incentive in the form of (some) immunity from legal action against discrimination.[33] The idea is that in order to promote equal opportunities, they have to study their own internal processes and understand the barriers they may

[30] See also Robert Baldwin, 'Regulation: After "Command and Control"' in Keith Hawkins (ed.), *The Human Face of Law: Essays in Honour of Donald Harris* (Clarendon 1997) 65, 70.

[31] David Doorey has proposed to subject employers who violate basic labour laws to more stringent rules concerning their ability to object to unionization (David J Doorey, 'A Model of Responsive Workplace Law' (2012) 50 Osgoode Hall LJ 57; for support of this proposal, see Cynthia Estlund, 'Labor Law Reform Again? Reframing Labor Law as a Regulatory Project' (2013) 16 NYU J Legis & Pub Pol'y 383). In effect this means that the freedom of association is traded against the willingness to obey the law; if you obey the law, the 'prize' is that you are allowed to use different means to topple organizing drives. Admittedly, much depends on the baseline: Doorey proposes to make unionizing *easier* for workers when the employer is an offender of labour laws, and keep the legal situation much the same for the complying employers. Still, given that freedom of association is not protected only (or even mainly) for reasons of ensuring compliance, if we believe it is justified to change the law so as to make organizing easier, why exclude some workers from those rights only because their employers are doing what they have to do anyway? The answer might be political feasibility, if better laws are considered unrealistic. However, as a matter of principle I find it difficult to trade one (substantive) right in return for compliance with another.

[32] See, e.g., Susan P Sturm, 'Second Generation Employment Discrimination: A Structural Approach' (2001) 101 Colum LR 458; Orly Lobel, 'The Renew Deal: The Fall of Regulation and the Rise of Governance in Contemporary Legal Thought' (2004) 89 Minn LR 342; Cynthia Estlund, 'Rebuilding the Law of the Workplace in an Era of Self-Regulation' (2005) 105 Colum LR 319. The theory of reflexive law similarly supports incentives for self-regulation; see generally Ralf Rogowski, *Reflexive Labour Law in the World Society* (Edward Elgar 2013).

[33] Such an incentive could be set in legislation, or—as developed in practice in the US—by courts deciding that self-assessment and monitoring by employers is a good defence ('liability shield') against discrimination suits. For a review of these cases see Cynthia Estlund, *Regoverning the Workplace: From Self-Regulation to Co-Regulation* (Yale 2010) 83–88.

have for the advancement of women (for example). Employers have no interest in doing such a study if it creates a risk of exposing information that could be used against them in legal suits alleging discrimination. By providing immunity against such suits, we can encourage pro-active steps on the part of employers, which could eventually promote equality. The problem, though, is that such a system relies on a number of questionable assumptions. For the gains to outweigh the cost, the employer must be well-intentioned and with high capacity.[34] Without the ability to make distinctions between employers based on these characteristics, we could very well end up giving a 'bonus' for ill-intentioned and/or low-capacity employers, who will get immunity for discrimination without doing anything in return.[35]

Implicitly, proponents of 'new governance' solutions in this context perhaps assume as a starting point that enforcement is impossible or at least non-existent. If in practice employers can discriminate as they wish without being sued, the cost of giving them immunity is theoretical rather than real. Under these assumptions, it is easy to conclude that even meagre or questionable gains outweigh the cost. Yet it would be a gross exaggeration to say that anti-discrimination laws are entirely unenforceable. There have been many successful suits against discrimination, and there are many ways in which we can still attempt to improve enforcement in this area (some of which are discussed in the next part). These can also be 'soft': for example, instead of setting quotas, we can impose on employers duties to submit reports with data on the number of workers, applicants etc. at each level—which can then be used as a basis for further investigation by the State enforcement agency.[36]

It is, however, possible to conceive of positive incentives that will encourage employers to go 'beyond compliance' without giving them immunity. Reut Shemer-Begas has recently proposed such a scheme in the context of equal employment opportunities for minority Arab workers in Israel.[37] As in the previous example, while it is illegal to discriminate against Arabs in the workplace, there is no legal duty of affirmative action in their favour in the private sector. Shemer-Begas used another law, the Hours of Work and Rest Act of 1951, to create the positive

[34] On these distinctions see Robert Baldwin, 'From Regulation to Behaviour Change: Giving Nudge the Third Degree' (2014) 77 MLR 831.

[35] In theory, in the US courts should apply the 'liability shield' only when the internal programme is 'reasonable' and has been applied in good faith (see Estlund (n 33) 88). In practice, research reveals that courts have failed in making these distinctions, and have been quick to insulate employers from liability even though internal programmes tend to be merely cosmetic (symbolic) and ineffective. See Lauren B Edelman and others, 'When Organizations Rule: Judicial Deference to Institutionalized Employment Structures' (2011) 117 Amer J of Soc 888. For critiques of the US precedents, see Susan Bisom-Rapp, 'An Ounce of Prevention is a Poor Substitute for a Pound of Cure: Confronting the Developing Jurisprudence of Education and Prevention in Employment Discrimination Law' (2001) 22 BJELL 1; Kimberly D Krawiec, 'Cosmetic Compliance and the Failure of Negotiated Governance' (2003) 81 Wash U Law Quarterly 487.

[36] This has been successfully used in Northern Ireland. See Bob Hepple, 'Agency Enforcement of Workplace Equality' in Linda Dickens (ed), *Making Employment Rights Effective* (Hart 2012) 49, 57.

[37] Reut Shemer-Begas, *Employees' Rights in the Era of Corporate Governance* (PhD Dissertation submitted to the Hebrew University, September 2015).

incentive for affirmative action. According to this law, the employer is not allowed to employ Jews on Saturdays (subject to some exceptions for specific sectors). Arab workers have another mandatory rest day, based on their religion (whether Muslim or Christian). The proposal is to give employers a permit to operate on Saturdays if at least one seventh of their workers are Arab. An employer will thus have an incentive to hire more Arab workers, in order to get the coveted permit to open the business on Saturday as well. This proposal makes sense conceptually, because one can presume that the Arab workers are the ones operating the workplace on Saturdays. It also makes sense given the percentage of Arabs in Israel (approximately one-fifth of the population).

Again this is not a problem-free solution. The goals of the Hours of Work and Rest Act will be frustrated to some extent. But it seems more likely that the gains will outweigh the costs in this case. Overall, while we should be sceptical about 'soft law' solutions designed to improve compliance, this example shows that in some specific contexts they could be highly advisable.[38]

Using 'lead company' liability to improve compliance among contractors

Pushing employers to comply with labour laws can sometimes be more effective when done indirectly. Consider, for example, a cleaning company that employs a small number of cleaners and pays them less than the minimum wage. Given the barriers described in the previous part, the workers might not complain, and the State might not know about this violation. An effective way to insert pressure could be indirectly through the clients, especially if those are large organizations that are easier to reach and more sensitive to reputation harms. Assume that the cleaners work at a university, for example, and the law requires the university to guarantee that the contractor pays the cleaners what they are owed according to labour laws. With such a legal rule in place, the university can be expected to prevent violations by the contractor, by choosing reliable contractors (with a good labour law record), by insisting on collaterals, and to some extent by monitoring the contractor.

The client obviously has the power to prevent violations in such cases, but doing so involves some costs. Is it justified to impose these costs on the client? Or more generally to impose liability on the client if its efforts have somehow failed and the workers were paid less than what was due? We should make a clear distinction between cases of *real* outsourcing/subcontracting and cases of *sham* indirect relations, i.e. when the user/client should actually be considered the legal employer (or at least a joint employer). In Chapter 6 I discussed the tests that are used (or

[38] Another interesting idea proposed by Estlund (n 33) 219 is to raise the sanction tied to a specific violation, but then forgo the higher sanction and keep the lower one for employers who have a system of self-regulation and monitoring. But if the higher sanction is justified, why forgo it so easily in case of violations?

should be used) to decide who is the employer. If the client should be considered an employer, then the issue does not arise—the 'client'-employer is obviously liable towards the employees (directly and not indirectly). But assume for current purposes that the university—to continue with the above example—has no characteristics of an employer vis-à-vis the cleaning workers. Consider also the relationship between a franchisor (say, McDonald's) and workers of its franchisees, or a brand using a supply/production chain (say, Nike) and the workers of subcontractors at the bottom of that chain. In all of those cases we have a 'lead company' (or lead organization) that has the power to significantly improve compliance with labour laws by other firms. Should we impose on it a 'residual' (guarantor) liability in these situations?

Several possible justifications can be advanced.[39] First, it could be argued that the lead company has *caused* the infringement of employment rights by the direct employer. Using tort law doctrines that are widely considered justified, the tests of causation can lead to liability when it can be shown that the violation would not have occurred 'but for' the acts of the lead company, and the harm to the workers was foreseeable.[40] This is perhaps the case in situations of a 'losing contract'—when the lead company pays the contractor a per-hour fee which is less than the minimum required to pay the workers their basic legislated rights.[41] In such cases the lead company is not only causing the harm, it is also *benefiting* from it, which is akin to unjust enrichment.[42]

Second, the lead company should arguably be liable because it has the *power to prevent* the infringements, and if the harm (infringement) has occurred, to *spread the loss* among many clients/consumers. Notwithstanding, unlike other commentators, who seem to assume that the power to prevent the harm is sufficient to justify lead company liability,[43] I find this difficult to accept without an

[39] For a fuller discussion of these arguments see Guy Davidov, 'Indirect Employment: Should Lead Companies Be Liable?' (2015) 37 CLLPJ 5. See also Yossi Dahan, Hanna Lerner, and Faina Milman-Sivan, 'Global Justice, Labor Standards and Responsibility' (2011) 12 Theoretical Inquiries in Law 117.

[40] For previous contributions relying on tort law to examine 'lead company' liability, see Brishen Rogers, 'Towards Third-Party Liability for Wage Theft' (2010) 31 BJELL 1; Debra Cohen Maiyanov, 'Sweatshop Liability: Corporate Codes of Conduct and the Governance of Labor Standards in the International Supply Chain' (2010) 14 Lewis & Clark LR 397; Radu Mares, 'Responsibility to Respect: Why the Core Company Should Act When Affiliates Infringe Human Rights' in Radu Mares (ed), *The UN Guiding Principles on Business and Human Rights–Foundations and Implementation* (2012) 169.

[41] On the losing contracts phenomenon see also David Weil, *The Fissured Workplace: Why Work Became So Bad for So Many and What Can Be Done to Improve It* (HUP 2014) 137.

[42] For a moral discussion, see Robert E Goodin and Christian Barry, 'Benefiting from the Wrong-doing of Others' (2014) 31 J of Applied Phil 363.

[43] See Rogers (n 40) 36–38; Alan Hyde, 'Legal Responsibility for Labor Conditions Down the Production Chain' in Judy Fudge, Shae McCrystal, and Kamala Sankaran (eds), *Challenging the Legal Boundaries of Work Regulation* (2012) 83 (arguing in favour of legal responsibility down the production chain, but only for core labour rights); Brian Langille, '"Take These Chains From My Heart and Set Me Free": How Labor Law Theory Drives Segmentation of Workers' Rights' (2015) 36 CLLPJ 257; Mark Anner, Jennifer Bair, and Jeremy Blasi, 'Toward Joint Liability in Global Supply Chains: Addressing the Root Causes of Labor Violations in International Subcontracting

additional justification. In a modern market economy, every firm is connected with numerous other firms which it can influence. This ability cannot in itself be sufficient to create legal liability towards the workers of other firms. Such liability is justified only when there is some special connection between the lead company and the workers. Relying again on tort law doctrines, such a special connection is needed to impose liability for omissions rather than actions,[44] and also in situations analogous to vicarious liability.[45]

Such a special connection exists, in my view, in two situations. The first is when the lead company makes representations to the public (or to the workers)—even implicitly—suggesting that the workers are working for it and it has control over their rights.[46] Arguably, this can also be seen as an independent justification, but in such a case, by inference from tort law doctrines, liability will be justified only if the workers can show *reliance* on this representation when making their decision to work for the contractor.[47] This will be difficult to prove. Nonetheless, the representation itself (which is sometimes implicit in the brand name) is sufficient, in my view, to create a special connection justifying liability for failure to prevent the harm, as noted above.

The other situation in which we can see some direct connection between the lead company and the workers is when the work is performed on the lead company's premises. In this scenario, the workers are part of the same community, and should be seen as 'citizens' in this community.[48] Again this can be seen as an independent justification as well, but it will have to be balanced against considerations of efficiency: companies have a legitimate interest in concentrating on their core competencies and outsourcing other tasks to contractors. Assuming this is real (rather than sham) outsourcing, and the lead company has no characteristics of an employer—which is possible theoretically even for workers performing work on its premises—the imposition of liability will in practice prohibit this legitimate

Networks' (2013) 35 CLLPJ 1, 21; David Weil (n 41) 205–06; Cynthia Estlund, *Regoverning the Workplace: From Self-Regulation to Co-Regulation* (Yale UP 2010) 199; Dahan, Lerner, and Milman-Sivan (n 39).

[44] See generally Simon Deakin, Angus Johnston, and Basil Markesinis, *Tort Law* (7th edn, Clarendon Press 2013) 178; *Chandler v Cape Plc* [2012] EWCA Civ 525, [2012] 3 All ER 640.

[45] Although the doctrine of vicarious liability itself applies only in cases of employer–employee and principal–agent relations, courts sometimes place liability on other third parties when the same underlying rationales exist. See, e.g., *John Doe v Bennett*, [2004] 1 SCR 436 (Supreme Court of Canada); Ewan McKendrick, 'Vicarious Liability and Independent Contractors: A Re-Examination' (1990) 53 Modern LR 770 (reviewing UK cases); Rogers (n 40) 42–47 (reviewing US cases). The requirements seem to be a degree of control (here: of the lead company over the contractor), alongside some connection/proximity with the injured party (here: the employees).

[46] The doctrines of 'apparent manufacturer' and 'apparent agent' support this idea. I discuss them in Davidov (n 39) 26–29.

[47] See Alan O Sykes, 'The Economics of Vicarious Liability' (1984) 93 Yale LJ 1231, 1276–77; John L Hanks, 'Franchisor Liability for the Torts of Its Franchisees: The Case for Substituting Liability as a Guarantor for the Current Vicarious Liability' (1999) 24 Okla City U LR 1, 13.

[48] On the ideas of citizenship/community at work see Linda Bosniak, 'Citizenship and Work' (2002) 27 North Carolina J Int'l L & Com Reg 497; Cynthia Estlund, *Working Together: How Workplace Bonds Strengthen a Diverse Democracy* (OUP 2003). And see Chapter 4.

business choice. So relying on the citizenship argument as an independent justification for imposing liability is difficult. Nonetheless, the idea of community/citizenship can certainly be used to provide the connection/proximity needed to place an obligation on the lead company for failing to prevent violations when it could have.

Overall, it seems justified to place liability on the indirect employer (lead company) in the following situations: in cases of 'losing contracts'; when the work is performed on the lead company premises and it has failed to take action to prevent the violation; and when the lead company has made representations (even implicitly) that it has control over the workers' rights, again assuming it could have prevented the harm. Imposing liability in such cases can go a long way towards preventing labour law violations by contractors.

The issue of 'losing contracts' is relatively straightforward. The law can include an explicit prohibition on such contracts, whether in general or in specific sectors known to be problematic.[49] Alongside a prohibition, the law should also make clear that the client will be liable directly towards the employee in case of violations.[50] This should give the client an additional incentive to make the effort to prevent such violations. With regard to workers on the premises of the lead company, it is again possible to place liability on the client; this was recently adopted in California, subject to certain exceptions.[51] A more moderate solution could be to limit such liability to specific sectors (such as cleaning and security), or alternatively to create a legal presumption of liability for workers employed on the client's premises, that can be refuted if the lead company shows that it could not have reasonably prevented the harm. The same is true for production/supply chains and franchising. It is proposed to create a presumption of liability by the lead company towards those working down the chain, which can be refuted if the company proves that there was no representation suggesting (even implicitly) control over work conditions, or no practical ability to prevent the harm.

If solutions are focused on specific sectors, the choice of sectors should be based on the known frequency and severity of labour law violations, but also, arguably, on the degree to which contractors are dependent on the lead company in this sector. Thus, for example, if the apparel industry is known for prevalent labour law violations, and also for a structure in which subcontractors have very little power over the terms of employment (because they are heavily dependent on their clients), this provides further justification for 'guarantor' client responsibility.[52]

[49] See, e.g., Cal Labor Code § 2810 (2004), and the Act to Improve the Enforcement of Labour Law § 28 (2011) (Isr), both dealing with losing contracts, albeit only in specific problematic sectors.

[50] This is indeed the case in both California and Israel (ibid).

[51] See Cal Labor Code § 2810.3 (2014). According to this new section, a client employer shall share with a labour contractor civil liability for employment law violations, under certain conditions, among them that the work is performed on the client's premises. Small employers have been excluded, as well as executive, administrative, and professional employees exempted from overtime rights, and some specific sectors.

[52] See Anner, Bair, and Blasi (n 43) 16 (describing agreements in the first half of the twentieth century for buyers' liability in the US apparel industry, which relied on the idea that the industry was based on an 'integrated process of production').

Such thinking can perhaps explain the legislation adopted in Australia, imposing liability on lead companies in apparel supply chains, without limiting itself to 'losing contracts' or those working on the lead company premises.[53]

Promoting unionization (or alternative worker representation)

So far my discussion has concentrated on creating incentives for employers to comply (or to push their contractors to comply). But another way to improve compliance could be based on creating monitoring mechanisms. While we cannot rely on employers to monitor their own compliance with labour legislation, arguably it is possible to rely on systems that involve a third party. This could be an external independent monitoring body—an option that will be discussed in the next part (as it would more appropriately be characterized as a method of enforcement). Yet another monitoring mechanism is very familiar to labour lawyers and will be discussed here: unions.

In many ways, the traditional, 'old' system of labour law already has a built-in mechanism designed to ensure compliance: with employment standards set only at a minimal level, employees have an incentive to unionize in order to bargain collectively and secure better wages and other work conditions. Their union, in turn, by its very presence helps to ensure compliance with labour standards. Sometimes unions actively help their members in enforcing their rights, but more often, it is the constant presence of a union in the workplace that makes it clear to employers that they must comply with labour laws. The inherent difficulties of not knowing your rights, not having the resources to sue, and fearing retaliation, are all solved when there is a functioning union representing the employees. Employers will generally realize that, and as a result compliance levels can be expected to improve significantly.

The problem, of course, is with the difficulty of getting there: the stage of unionizing. This was a great solution for many workers in the past, but with the sharp decline in union density around the world it is not possible to rely on the existence of unions anymore. Having an incentive to organize is not enough; workers must be able to act on this incentive and join a union. In reality they have to face mounting employer resistance, as well as other barriers (such as the difficulty of organizing employees in atypical, precarious arrangements).[54]

[53] See Michael Rawling and John Howe, 'The Regulation of Supply Chains: An Australian Contribution to Cross-National Legal Learning' in Katherine VW Stone and Harry Arthurs (eds), *Rethinking Workplace Regulation: Beyond the Standard Contract of Employment* (Russell Sage Foundation 2013) 233; Shelley Marshall, 'Regulating Work in Complex Apparel Supply Chains: New Models', <http://papers.ssrn.com/sol3/papers.cfm?abstract_id=2524253> accessed 10 October 2015. See also the Posted Workers Enforcement Directive (2014/67/EU), which imposed similar liability in the construction sector within the European Union.

[54] It is not at all clear that resisting unions is a rational move for employers. As noted in Chapter 5, research shows that unions can actually help increase efficiency, as long as the employer decides to adopt a cooperative (rather than adversarial) stance. However, the attitudes of employers towards unions are embedded in country-specific contexts, based on cultural, historical, and political factors. Changing a hostile attitude towards unions, even if theoretically possible, is necessarily

A possible route could be to look for ways to strengthen the freedom of association—the actual ability of workers to unionize—thereby restoring the system that relied on the existence of unions to ensure compliance with labour laws. In many ways this would be a preferred route, given that it would also promote worker voice, and generally advance the other goals of unionization and collective bargaining (as discussed in Chapter 5). Many ideas have been proposed in recent years to restore the power of unions,[55] and some have even been adopted: in Israel, for example, the National Labour Court has recently stripped employers from their freedom of speech during an organizing drive, ruling that they cannot voice any view concerning unionization. This far-reaching prohibition came on top of the more 'regular' rules prohibiting threat, intimidation etc. that have proved insufficient to protect workers during this sensitive stage.[56] Although it has succeeded in supporting some invigoration of the labour movement in Israel, and has stopped the steep decline in union density, it is unlikely—at least in the foreseeable future—that we will see unions protecting a majority of the workers in Israel as a result of this new rule.

One can suggest more radical solutions to promote unionization; for example, making membership in a union the default rule. Together with a strict prohibition on employer interference, this could be revolutionary, but it seems to be politically unfeasible in current times. Perhaps a more realistic route would be to create a structure of positive incentives for employers to willingly accept unions. Arguably, this idea already exists in some countries, where labour laws include 'derogation clauses' allowing an employer to derogate from specific standards subject to an agreement with a union. In Israel, for example, the Hours of Work and Rest Act of 1951 sets the regular day of work at eight hours—with any additional hour requiring overtime payment—but allows the employer to lengthen the regular day in a collective agreement approved by the Minister. Similarly, the Employment through Temporary Employment Agencies Act of 1996 (as amended in 2000) gives temporary employment agency employees a right to equality with employees of the user firm in terms of pay and conditions, unless these employees are subject to a collective agreement extended by the Minister. In both contexts, then, there is a default rule in the legislation, which the employer can opt-out of by way of a collective agreement setting alternative (even if inferior) rights for the employees. The union and the employees might want to settle for less than

a difficult and lengthy process. I will assume, therefore, some level of employer resistance—and a corresponding difficulty of organizing.

[55] See, e.g., Benjamin I Sachs, 'Enabling Employee Choice: A Structural Approach to the Rules of Union Organizing' (2010) 123 Harv LR 655; Catherine L Fisk, 'Reimagining Collective Rights in the Workplace' (2014) 4 UC Irvine LR 523 (an opening article for a special issue on this topic).

[56] *The Histadrut v Pelephone Communications Ltd*, judgment of 2 January 2013 (Israeli National Labour Court). The decision was later upheld by the Supreme Court; see *Coordinating Chamber of Economic Organizations v National Labour Court*, judgment of 7 July 2014. For a brief discussion of this case see Chapter 8. For an extensive discussion see Pnina Alon-Shenker and Guy Davidov, 'Organizing: Should the Employer Have a Say?' (2016) 17 Theoretical Inquiries in Law 63.

what the legislation gives them, because of other advantages unrelated to the specific piece of legislation, including the ongoing presence of a union that is instrumental for ensuring compliance with labour law—but also, presumably, to secure other gains. The employer might prefer these alternative arrangements over the statutory one and in such cases will have an incentive to allow the organizing and cooperate with a union.

Another example could be a legal rule prohibiting dismissals without 'just cause', together with a relatively strict process for the employer to prove cause before dismissals can take effect. If this process is created as a default, which can be changed to an easier process in cooperation with a union, the employer would again have an incentive to cooperate with a union in order to create an alternative regime.[57]

These models seem very promising, because (once again) they are not only good for improving compliance, but also advance the other goals of unionization. Nonetheless, there are several difficulties. First, there is a risk that the employer will try to set up a 'company union', or otherwise choose to work with a union that is not truly independent. If we try to trigger unionization through incentivizing the employer, this is a likely scenario—absent a bottom-up attempt to unionize we can expect to see a union appearing behind the backs of the employees and negotiating over their heads. Second, even if the union is independent, there is a risk that it will act opportunistically in the interest of easily securing union dues, by reaching a quick deal with the employer and disappearing. Again this is a risk inherent in the fact that the initiative for unionizing (or working with a union) is expected to come from the employer and not in a 'natural' process of bottom-up organizing, which includes the building of solidarity, grass-roots support for a union, building of ties with the union, and the development of local worker-leaders. Finally there is the more fundamental dilemma of which 'discounts' should be offered to the employer in return for welcoming unionization. These should be significant enough for the employer to create a positive incentive (even after factoring-in the downsides of unions, from the point of view of the employer). But at the same time we would not want to risk too much in terms of allowing derogations from basic employment rights.

The first two difficulties can be addressed, to some extent, by inserting into the law specific conditions to ensure that the union is independent, has an ongoing connection with the workers and support from them, and remains active and 'present' in the specific workplace. None of this is easy to achieve, but I will refrain here from getting into the fine details and assume that it is possible—at least to minimize the risks. The third concern is more general and casts doubts on the very idea. Do we have enough to 'sell' by way of incentives to employers, assuming we want to insist on non-waivable basic employment rights?

[57] Guy Mundlak, 'Information-Forcing and Cooperation-Inducing Rules: Rethinking the Building Blocks of Labour Law' in Gerrit de Geest, Jacques Siegers, and Roger van den Bergh (eds), *Law and Economics and the Labour Market* (Edward Elgar 1999) 55.

In theory this should not be too difficult; we would just have to create two levels of standards, one mandatory, and the other adding additional rights that can be waived as part of a collective agreement. Presumably, even if the overall cost to the employer is the same, it should be attractive to the employer to gain more flexibility this way (adapting the general-universal rules to the needs of the specific firm). In practice, though, given a status quo of a specified bundle of labour regulations, we can either carve the second level from within the current rights, or add it on top of the existing rights. Either way, to create a meaningful package (a sufficiently attractive incentive) for employers, we will need to shake the status quo quite dramatically: either by lowering the mandatory standards (in effect, deregulating) or by adding a substantial set of new higher-level standards. Another (and less radical) solution could be to 'sweeten' the deal to employers by lowering the 'price' they envision. It has been proposed to do so by way of replacing the spectre of a union with some lesser form of representation.

Cynthia Estlund has offered such a solution, which she terms 'co-regulation'.[58] The idea is to allow employers some degree of self-regulation, on the condition that representatives of the employees will be given power to monitor compliance with it. Estlund argues that some form of worker representation is necessary to ensure that self-regulation is effective, rather than merely cosmetic. Absent an ability to bargain collectively and strike, this system does not give the workers (through their proposed new body) power to improve wages and work conditions. Nevertheless, Estlund sees some potential for the monitoring to turn into a degree of shared governance later on. More importantly for current purposes, can the workers' body ensure compliance with labour laws? Can a workers' committee (or even a 'work council') be strong enough, absent the backing of a union, to demand compliance from the employer? To some extent, at least in some firms, this could work. But obviously the lack of actual power—which comes from the backing of a large union with resources, and the right to strike—the ability of such an alternative body to secure high levels of compliance will be limited. The idea could certainly be justified, as the creation of a work council (or some other collective body) obviously has other advantages. But as far as compliance is concerned, the advantages are likely to be minimal, so it would not be justified in my view to offer concessions to employers in return for allowing such work councils to form.

Part III—Improving Enforcement

Now assume that our efforts to induce compliance have failed, and we need to use enforcement. This is bound to be costly, so society should not necessarily aim at achieving 'complete' enforcement;[59] but we cannot accept a reality of massive non-compliance either. One obvious solution is to allocate significantly more resources

[58] Estlund (n 33).

[59] George J Stigler, 'The Optimum Enforcement of Laws' (1970) 78 J of Political Econ 526.

for enforcement, but this is often unrealistic and always insufficient. There are also proposals for better utilizing existing labour inspection resources,[60] the importance of which is emphasized by reports on the inefficient and untargeted use of such resources.[61] However, while essential, such solutions cannot by themselves respond to the crisis in enforcement, which has developed in recent years for reasons (outlined above) unrelated to the shortcomings of inspection bodies.

At the other extreme it is tempting to rely on self-enforcement and try to enhance it, but as long as the power imbalance that characterizes the employment relationship exists, self-enforcement will remain unrealistic for many employees.[62] Again, this is not to say that enhancing the realistic ability to sue is not essential. Punitive damages are an important way to raise the incentive for employees to complain and bring their claims to court, and at the same time raise the cost of non-compliance for the employer. Class action suits are a crucial mechanism that combines an incentive to the worker bringing the suit (and his lawyers), remedies for a large number of workers, and again a high cost for non-complying employers.[63] Independent labour courts are a further important factor as they are much more accessible to individual employees—even those without legal representation—compared with regular civil courts. Legal systems that have such courts are likely to offer a more realistic option of self-enforcement.[64] Transparency

[60] See, e.g., Robert Baldwin and Julia Black, 'Really Responsive Regulation' (2008) 71 MLR 59; Patrice A Dutil and Ron Saunders, *New Approaches in Achieving Compliance with Statutory Employment Standards* (2005) <http://www.cprn.org/documents/37835_en.pdf> accessed 10 October 2015; David Weil, 'Crafting a Progressive Workplace Regulatory Policy: Why Enforcement Matters' (2007) 28 CLLPJ 125.

[61] See, e.g., State Comptroller of Israel, *Annual Report 58B for the Year 2007* (2008) 1105–42, <http://www.mevaker.gov.il> accessed 10 October 2015 (Hebrew); United States Government Accountability Office, *Fair Labor Standards Act: Better Use of Available Resources and Consistent Reporting Could Improve Compliance* (2008), <www.gao.gov/new.items/d08962t.pdf> accessed 10 October 2015; United States Government Accountability Office, *Wage and Hour Division's Complaint Intake and Investigative Processes Leave Low Wage Workers Vulnerable to Wage Theft* (2009), <www.gao.gov/new.items/d09458t.pdf> accessed 10 October 2015.

[62] On the limits of private enforcement see also Mitchell A Polinsky, 'Private versus Public Enforcement of Fines' (1980) 9 JLS 105.

[63] On raising the cost of non-compliance through punitive damages, class action, or other methods see Hugh Collins, 'Justifications and Techniques of Legal Regulation of the Employment Relation' in Hugh Collins, Paul Davies, and Roger Rideout (eds), *Legal Regulation of the Employment Relation* (Kluwer 2000) 3, 23; Pamela H Bucy, 'Private Justice' (2002) 76 Southern Cal LR 1; John Braithwaite, *Regulatory Capitalism: How It Works, Ideas For Making It Work Better* (Edward Elgar 2008) ch 3. In Israel, the National Labour Court struggled in recent years to find the right balance between allowing class action suits and avoiding harm to unions as a result. At first, class actions were not approved where the workers were part of a collective agreement and a union could in principle represent them (see, e.g., *Oren v Bank Hapoalim*, judgment of 18 January 2009). Later, realizing that this is an important method to tackle the enforcement crisis, the National Labour Court started to approve class actions whenever the union was not sufficiently active in enforcing the rights (see, e.g., *Yigal Viron v Tevel Security Cleaning and Services*, judgment of 3 January 2011). This approach has recently been approved by the Israeli Supreme Court; see *Israeli Organization of Security Companies v The National Labour Court*, judgment of 30 August 2015.

[64] For evidence supporting the superiority of specialized courts in enforcing labour laws, see Danielle Venn, 'Legislation, Collective Bargaining and Enforcement: Updating the OECD Employment Protection Indicators' (OECD Social, Employment and Migration Working Papers, No. 89, July 2009) 33.

of information can help employees know their rights and expose violations.[65] All of these elements are crucial parts of the solution, but given the inherent difficulties of self-enforcement considered above, they are bound to remain insufficient.

Without detracting from these solutions, I will focus in this part on three other ideas, which received much attention in recent years: 'responsive' enforcement, withholding privileges (e.g. in procurement), and independent monitoring. Ultimately there is no single solution; we must use a multitude of different means concurrently in order to address a compliance/enforcement crisis.

Responsive enforcement

A major component of 'responsive law' theories concerns enforcement practices. It has been shown that communicating with the subjects of a law could be more effective than simply hitting them with sanctions. In a responsive environment, violators are treated differently depending on the context. An employer who failed to understand the law, or 'slipped' once, could be given a warning, alongside education, guidance, and support. A repeat offender, in contrast, should attract much harsher sanctions. The main idea is to push towards compliance in a forward-looking way rather than focus on punishing. Inspectors should start with persuasion, with gradual escalation to sanctions depending on the level of cooperation from the offender.[66] Obviously this requires the law to grant broad discretion and powers to inspectors, a system that has been common in Southern Europe and Latin America[67] and to some extent has recently been adopted in other countries (notably Australia[68]).

These ideas should be applied with some caution in the context of employment law: when dealing with minimum wage violations, for example, where the law is usually clear and the harm is severe, persuasion or warnings are hardly sufficient.[69] Moreover, the responsive approach is more suitable for ongoing relations between an inspector and the subject of the regulation, while in our context inspectors reach a specific employer only rarely, if at all.[70] For the same reason

[65] Cynthia Estlund, 'Just the Facts: The Case for Workplace Transparency' (2010) 63 Stan LR 351.

[66] See generally Ian Ayres and John Braithwaite, *Responsive Regulation: Transcending the Deregulation Debate* (OUP 1992) ch 2; John Braithwaite, 'The Essence of Responsive Regulation' (2011) 44 UBC LR 475. For further development of these ideas (and additional nuances required in their application) see Baldwin and Black (n 60).

[67] See Michael J Piore and Andrew Schrank, 'Toward Managed Flexibility: The Revival of Labour Inspection in the Latin World' (2008) 147 ILR 1; Michael Piore, 'Flexible Bureaucracies in Labour Market Regulation' in Guy Davidov and Brian Langille (eds), *The Idea of Labour Law* (OUP 2011) 385.

[68] John Howe, Tess Hardy, and Sean Cooney, 'Mandate, Discretion, and Professionalisation in an Employment Standards Enforcement Agency: An Antipodean Experience' (2012) 35 Law & Policy 81.

[69] The theory of responsive regulation strives to build capacity among the regulated and enhance their internal motivation. This is more difficult to achieve with regard to regulations that have a distributive aspect. Some employers will always be reluctant to pay more to their employees.

[70] See also Fine and Gordon (n 17) 562.

I am quite sceptical about the idea of exempting employers from routine inspection if they have a good record.[71] Regular inspections in themselves are hardly a major burden on employers, so such an exemption could do more harm (sending a signal of immunity) than good.

Nonetheless, the responsive approach could be effective if the enforcing agency uses the threat of 'hard' sanctions to reach an agreement with the offender regarding future actions. For example, from a future-looking perspective, it could be justified to forgo some sanctions in return for an employer's agreement to subject itself to measures that are not required by law (e.g. independent monitoring, training, payments to worker centres).[72] There have been some positive experiments with such agreements in the US,[73] Northern Ireland,[74] and Australia.[75]

Further, the basic idea of maintaining an arsenal of different legal responses to violations is itself highly important. While it is crucial to have the option of severe sanctions for severe violations, the ultimate sanction (usually a criminal one in employment legislation) requires a long and difficult process. Although it could be possible to improve the process and make it somewhat faster and easier, at some level the difficulties are inherent and unavoidable: severe sanctions require more safeguards. A criminal conviction, and the sanctions that follow it, are only possible after the findings are transferred from the inspector to a prosecutor, who prepares the legal documents, and only after a court hearing. We would not want to forgo these safeguards, but they take a lot of time and as a result are only rarely used (relatively). It is in this context that, in recent years, many legal systems have adopted the option of *administrative sanctions* that can be imposed directly by an inspector.[76]

In Israel, for example, the Act to Improve the Enforcement of Labour Laws of 2011 gives the enforcing agency broad powers to impose fines for violations of labour laws, without the need for lengthy legal proceedings. There is still a process that requires a hearing before the decision, and the employer has the right to appeal it, but these (necessary) safeguards are much less onerous compared with criminal proceedings, which are now reserved only for extreme cases. The

[71] This has been used, for example, in the US in the context of health and safety regulations. See Estlund (n 33) 79.

[72] Bob Hepple (n 36), for example, has argued that this could be more effective than traditional enforcement.

[73] The 'hot goods' provision of the Fair Labor Standards Act was used as background to impose agreements by which employers in some sectors committed to monitoring contractors. Similarly, greengrocers in New York City were given provisional amnesty for past violations in return for agreeing to a code of conduct with monitoring. See Estlund (n 33) 110 ff.

[74] In the context of employment equality, agreements were reached with employers following reports that they had to submit. See Hepple (n 36) 54–57.

[75] The relatively new Fair Work Ombudsman was given the power to sign 'enforceable undertakings' with employers, even with regard to violations of employment standards. See discussions in Tess Hardy and John Howe, 'Too Soft or too Severe? Enforceable Undertakings and the Regulatory Dilemma Facing the Fair Work Ombudsman' (2013) 41 Federal LR 1; Vosko, Grundy and Thomas (n 22).

[76] Maria Luz Vega and René Robert, 'Labour Inspection Sanctions: Law and Practice of National Labour Inspection Systems' (ILO LAB/ADMIN working document no. 26, 2013).

initial experience with these new measures is positive; the number of labour law violations that were met with sanctions rose dramatically and the timeframe for imposing a sanction has shortened significantly.[77]

Withholding privileges

Alongside the arsenal of sanctions available to the enforcement agency itself, there are also actions that can be taken by other governmental agencies. There are two main privileges that the government can withhold from firms that violate labour laws: licences and the right to do business with it.

Where a licence is required to operate a business in a specific sector, is it justified to refuse to grant it (or refuse to extend an existing licence that has expired) because of a record of labour law violations? If the service is mostly human resources, i.e. the main activity of the business is employing people, it seems only appropriate to put an emphasis on doing so in line with legal requirements. Temporary employment agencies are an obvious example; but the same idea can apply to cleaning and security companies, because a large part of their service is recruiting workers, employing them and sending them to work for others.[78] If this service is used in practice as a vehicle for systematically violating labour laws, there is every reason to prevent this activity. People who have repeatedly violated labour laws should not be given a licence to operate a business when the main function of the business is employing people (which requires adherence to labour laws).

What if a licence is required for other reasons, unrelated to labour law? Imagine for example that one needs a licence in order to operate a transport company, or open a kindergarten, or buy a radio station. The goal of the licensing requirement in such cases is to protect societal interests unrelated to labour law; the government will check first and foremost the record of the applicants in other areas. But assume that the applicants, who also plan to employ some people as part of their new business, have a record of not respecting labour laws. Is this a consideration that the government should take into account? If the licensing agency only ensures that applicants pass some level of minimal requirement, then probably considerations of freedom of occupation prevent such a sanction. We cannot punish people and limit their freedom to open a business because of violations that happened in the past and can be treated separately. The conclusion may be different, however, when the licence is only given to a small number of applicants (for whatever reason), based on multiple criteria designed to identify the best candidates. In such cases—when the

[77] Michael Atlan and Deborah Sapir Eliezer, 'Notes on the Act to Improve the Enforcement of Labour Laws–Really Responsive Regulation', (forthcoming) Hukim – Journal on Legislation (Hebrew).

[78] In Israel, the Employment through Temporary Employment Agencies Act of 1996 requires agencies to have a licence in order to operate in the Israeli labour market. In 2009 the Act was amended to require a licence from cleaning and security companies as well.

licensing agency has to use its discretion to award the licence to the most suitable people—it seems perfectly legitimate and justified to take the labour law record into account as one of the considerations.

Probably more influential, as a matter of practice, is giving weight to labour law violations during procurement decisions. Governments have enormous power as purchasers of products and services. Should they use this power as 'ethical consumers' and refrain from contracting with repeat offenders of labour laws? This seems perfectly justified in principle;[79] the difficulty is to find the right balance in defining who should count as a repeat offender.[80] We should not impose this sanction too easily, based on a one-time 'slip', given its implications for the livelihood of the contractor and its workers. But at the same time it has to be effective. The Israeli experience is useful to illustrate these challenges. According to the Public Entities' Transactions Act of 1976, as amended in 2004, the government and all entities funded by it cannot contract with firms with a record of labour law violations. However, originally the law was so restrictive in its definitions as to become entirely meaningless. First, it referred only to violations of the Minimum Wage Act and the Foreign Workers Act, ignoring numerous other employment rights included in separate pieces of legislation. Second, the group of repeat offenders was defined based on more than two criminal convictions, the last one being during the twelve months prior to signing the contract. Given the small number of criminal indictments—and as a result convictions—this was virtually an empty group.

More recently the definitions were relaxed, but only with regard to the cleaning and security sectors: engaging a contractor in these specific sectors is prohibited if there were more than two criminal convictions and the last one was in the past three years, or alternatively if the contractor received more than six administrative labour-related fines during the last three years. Moreover, for these two sectors, other labour law violations (not related to the above two Acts) are also counted. Even with these changes, contractors with a record of repeated labour law violations can still be hired by the government; imagine, for example, a contractor with several criminal convictions (one of them in the last three years), several administrative fines (five of them in the last three years), and numerous civil suits, including class actions, that have been litigated successfully against it. The current Israeli law fails to recognize such a cumulative record as indicative of systematic violations. A possible solution is to appoint a committee within the government that will have discretion to disqualify some companies from doing business with the government, based on the cumulative evidence from all sources, on top of those disqualified based on a set number of convictions and/or administrative fines.

[79] For an extensive discussion see Christopher McCrudden, *Buying Social Justice: Equality, Government Procurement, and Legal Change* (OUP 2007) ch 5.

[80] For a discussion of EU law, exposing some legal difficulties in using 'social' considerations in tenders, see Catherine Barnard, 'Using Procurement Law to Enforce Labour Standards' in Davidov and Langille (n 67) 256.

Independent monitoring

Perhaps the most far-reaching solution—in terms of its ability to reach a large number of workers and transform the reality of widespread non-compliance—is the introduction of independent monitors. Imagine having an inspector to examine the compliance of a specific employer, with access to all documents and the workers in-house, on an ongoing basis. While it is obviously impossible to achieve with State inspectors, the closest parallel is independent monitors that could have the same level of expertise and the same level of access to the workplace. What they unavoidably lack is the powers of State inspectors to initiate formal legal proceeding (or inflict sanctions) against the employer. Nevertheless, with access to all the information about hours worked, wages paid etc., as well as the ability to discuss with workers their work conditions, the monitors should be able to expose violations and report them to the employer, the workers and the State enforcement bodies. This does not in itself ensure enforcement, but it certainly takes a major step towards that goal.

There is growing evidence that independent monitoring is possible and could be successful.[81] For example, the United States government has used the 'hot goods' provision of the Fair Labor Standards Act—allowing it to embargo goods produced in violation of labour laws—to pressure manufacturers into monitoring their subcontractors. The provision was used as background for agreements with manufacturers in the apparel industry instituting monitoring mechanisms—which have proved to minimize violations of employment standards significantly.[82]

In fact, a model of independent monitoring existed in the US already at the beginning of the twentieth century.[83] It originated in the coal-mining sector, where payments to workers were commonly made based on the weight of the coal mined, and employers could use their control over the weighing process to cheat. In response, legislatures in various states introduced a right to workers to appoint a 'checkweighman' to monitor the process on their behalf. The workers had to choose to use this right, elect their checkweighman, and pay him. In some states the right was extended to any sector where wages are paid on a piece-rate basis.[84] Some of these laws are still in force, although apparently they have not been used for many years.

[81] For discussions of different forms of private monitoring see Dara O'Rourke, 'Outsourcing Regulation: Analyzing Nongovernmental Systems of Labor Standards and Monitoring' (2003) 31 The Policy Studies J 1; Fine and Gordon (n 17). On successful independent monitoring in developing countries see Drusilla Brown, Rajeev Dehejia, and Raymond Robertson, 'Regulations, Monitoring and Working Conditions: Evidence from Better Factories Cambodia and Better Work Vietnam' in Deirdre McCann and others (eds), *Creative Labour Regulation: Indeterminacy and Protection in an Uncertain World* (ILO 2014) 185.

[82] David Weil and Carlos Mallo, 'Regulating Labour Standards via Supply Chains: Combining Public/Private Interventions to Improve Workplace Compliance' (2007) 45 BJIR 791. See also Estlund (n 33) 111.

[83] See Finkin (n 23).

[84] See the West Virginia Code Ann § 21-5-8.

Matt Finkin has suggested resurrecting this system, noting that it appears to have been effective at the time.[85] He proposes to allow employees at any workplace to decide if they wish to appoint a 'wage-checker', giving this monitoring body—which could be for example a law firm, an accounting firm, a legal clinic, a worker centre, or a union—authority to get information on the workers, get records from the employer, enter the workplace as needed, and pursue any legal avenue for redress of violations when found. This seems promising; but there are also two problematic elements of the original model that he proposes to maintain: a majority of the workers will have to decide to use this right, and the workers themselves will have to pay for it.

Why should employees pay for these monitors? We all pay as taxpayers for the State to make sure that laws are enforced; if extra steps are necessary, it would not be justified to ask the victims of the violations to pay for them. Moreover, given that the workers most in need of these monitors are low-wage workers, they are unlikely to pay from their meagre wages—which means that the whole project will fail. Finkin realizes this difficulty, of course, but hopes that unions would cover the cost, in the interest of gaining access to new workplaces and eventually organizing them.[86] This may be ideal in theory, but reliance on the ability of unions to re-invent themselves as part of this model means that its reach would remain quite limited.

Janice Fine and Jennifer Gordon have also proposed a private-public partnership that faces the same challenge. They would give 'public interest groups like unions and worker centers a formal, ongoing role in the detection of violations'.[87] Relying on three somewhat successful examples from the US, Fine and Gordon argue that unions and worker centres should in effect become independent monitors, working in collaboration with the government. Nevertheless, they give only little attention to the crucial issue of funding, simply suggesting that the State should cover the costs of these partnerships.[88] It is certainly untenable to rely on the civil society organizations themselves to foot the bill.[89] However, if the idea is to use independent monitoring on a large scale, the cost for the State would be enormous. It is doubtful whether imposing these costs on tax-payers at large would be realistic or fair.

Why not require *employers* to pay for the monitoring? If this is done only in sectors that are prone to violations, it is certainly justified to expect employers to shoulder the burden. Even if they shift some (or all) of these costs to their clients/consumers, it is more justified to internalize these costs as part of the product/service price than shift them to society at large. Moreover, as long as the cost is imposed consistently on all employers in the same sector, it should not disturb their competitive stance, at least within the same jurisdiction; and if the

[85] Finkin (n 23) 862. [86] ibid 867. [87] Fine and Gordon (n 17) 559.

[88] ibid 561, 573.

[89] NGOs rely on donations for their existence, so it is not possible (nor justified) to rely on funding from them. Unions rely on dues from their members, which cannot be used on a regular basis to enforce the rights of other workers.

sector is responding to competition from other countries by systematic violations of labour laws, interfering with this system by imposing the cost of monitoring would only be an advantage. Admittedly, it seems problematic to treat the 'good' employers who comply with labour laws in the same way, making them pay for the sins of their competitors. Notwithstanding, the law-abiding employers will greatly benefit from this system, which would undercut the ability to use labour law violations as a competitive advantage.

There remains a crucial question: can we ensure that monitors paid by employers are truly independent and are able to confront employers about violations? The Israeli Act to Improve the Enforcement of Labour Laws of 2011 attempts to solve this by relying on professional ethics. The Act introduces a new profession of 'certified wage checkers': people with a relevant professional background (lawyers, accountants etc.) who will go through some training to be certified as wage checkers.[90] The Act does not *require* employers to hire wage checkers, but rather uses a 'soft law' approach: in the cleaning and security sectors, relying on monitoring by a wage checker provides a defence against direct liability towards the workers in case of labour law violations by the contractor.[91] Apparently, it is presumed that wage checkers will feel obligated by their professional responsibility to report all violations. This may certainly be the case when confronted with severe violations; however, it is likely that some violations are more doubtful, or require an extra effort to 'dig deep' and uncover. In such cases, as long as employers are the ones making the decision about the identity of the wage checker (which is the case in Israel), the incentive structure is problematic. If the wage checkers rely on being hired by employers to make their living, this might tilt them (at the very least unconsciously) towards adopting the view more favourable to the employer. There is still no experience with this new law to allow for an empirical examination of these concerns.[92] In any case, since the wage checkers envisioned by the Act will examine the contractors and not the 'clients' who pay for them, the incentive structure could be different. It is yet to be seen whether a monitor's independence can be secured when an employer is required to pay for it to monitor the employer itself.[93]

A possible solution is to take the decision out of the hands of employers. That is, although employers will have to pay the fees of the wage checkers, the identity of these monitors will be determined by others. Yet it must be admitted that creating a process by which non-unionized low-wage workers will choose a professional wage checker from several candidates, while avoiding employer interference, is bound to be complicated and difficult to implement.[94] Perhaps another route to

[90] s 40. [91] s 27.

[92] In practice, this part of the law has not been applied yet; although a number of years have passed, it still awaits the adoption of detailed regulations. In the meantime, a temporary measure designates all certified accountants as wage checkers for the purpose of the above-mentioned defence.

[93] And see Estlund (n 33) 205 (arguing that independence is possible even when the employer is paying the monitors).

[94] Cynthia Estlund has rightly stressed the need to adopt safeguards to prevent the 'capture of monitors by the monitored firms' (n 33 159). She eventually concludes that some form of worker representation is necessary (205, 216).

minimize (although not entirely eliminate) the potential conflict is by legislating a code of ethics for wage checkers (with sanctions for violations) as well as detailed regulations about the way they should perform their duties.

Either way, to be effective, it seems crucial that the duty to hire a wage checker should apply without the need for employee action. Low-wage workers who are most in need of this protection are not likely to demand a wage checker from their employer. Requiring all employers in some specific sectors to hire a certified wage checker could be done by 'command and control' regulations—as a duty with sanctions for violations—or by way of 'soft' incentives. The former is obviously stronger and will secure better results, albeit at a higher cost.

Conclusion

It was not possible to cover all conceivable solutions to the compliance/enforcement crisis in this chapter, or even to do justice to the specific solutions chosen for discussion. Many of them raise additional challenges or promises that have been examined more fully by others. The goal of the chapter was not to offer comprehensive solutions or discussions, but rather to explore relatively briefly several possible ways to address compliance and enforcement problems. As elsewhere in this book, the basic point I wanted to advance is that we must examine our labour laws through the purposive lenses: we should always think about our goals and about the best ways to advance them. The current chapter used this point of view to rethink the challenges of compliance and enforcement.

10

Conclusion

This book was about labour law as it should (and could) be. I did not set out to explain the current difficulties of labour law or the reasons behind them. The book was about the *future* of labour law. It started from a very simple, common-sense point: any discussion of labour law—whether it is about grand reforms or small adaptations, whether in legislation or in judicial interpretation—has to start from understanding what we are trying to achieve. We have to articulate to ourselves, and to others, the goals of what we want to do: the goals of the 'project' of labour law as a whole and the goals of any specific regulation under discussion.

The first part of the book was dedicated to this task. It started (in Chapter 2) by explaining the importance of purpose and inquiring into several methodological questions about the best way to articulate purposes. I then moved to a study of the general goals of labour law, divided into two levels of abstraction/generality. First (in Chapter 3) labour laws were explained as a solution to the 'labour problem'—a response to the existence of inherent vulnerabilities in employment relationships. My discussion of the unique characteristics of employment relations, which justify regulatory intervention, has led me to two vulnerabilities that are very familiar to labour lawyers: subordination and dependency. However, I have argued that these ideas should be understood somewhat differently, pointing attention to democratic deficits (subordination in a broad sense), inability to spread risks (a specific understanding of dependency), and also the importance of work for the individual (dependency for the fulfilment of social and psychological needs rather than only economic). In the remainder of the chapter I also considered two other common articulations: that labour laws are needed to correct market failures and that they are a response to the 'inequality of bargaining power'—and showed that both ideas could be useful but only to a limited extent.

Next (in Chapter 4) labour law was explained at a higher level of generality and in a more positive way: not as a solution to a 'problem' but as an attempt to advance various important values. I focused on workplace democracy, redistribution, dignity (examining also whether a human rights approach would be useful), social inclusion/citizenship, stability/security, efficiency, human freedom and capabilities, and emancipation/social equality. This list is surely not exhaustive, and also some of the goals share similarities with others. The idea was not to present a closed group of goals that are entirely distinguishable from each other, but rather to discuss the main goals that have been presented in the literature as explaining and informing labour laws. Together they put forward a coherent and broad explanation of why labour laws are needed. The chapter also made some cautionary comments about the recent shift in emphasis towards 'universal' goals that are good for everyone. At the end of the day labour laws are redistributive and are needed to protect employees in a market economy. Ignoring or downplaying these aspects would not be productive for the future of labour law.

The general idea of labour law is important for broad reforms, when interpreting general concepts (such as 'employer' and 'employee') and also it is relevant for the understanding of specific regulations. At the same time it is not sufficient in itself. Different labour laws have different goals, so before reforming or interpreting them we must articulate the goals of these specific regulations. The first part of the book concluded (in Chapter 5) with an examination of three basic labour laws that exist in many legal systems (although not all): a minimum wage law, a collective bargaining law (allowing and often encouraging workers to join unions and bargain collectively), and an unfair dismissal law (prohibiting dismissals without 'just cause'). For each of the three laws, the chapter considered possible goals, discussed advantages as well as critiques, and attempted to offer a clear and coherent articulation of the idea behind these laws. While this is intended, first and foremost, to be helpful for those thinking about these specific laws, my goal was also to show how a 'rich' purposive analysis should be performed, for other labour laws as well.

Obviously different legislatures, at different countries and at different times, have their own ideas about labour laws. Accordingly some might question whether it is at all possible to discuss goals in the abstract, without the context of a specific time and place. I answer this concern in Chapter 2 (alongside other methodological issues), explaining that a purposive analysis is not focused on legislative intent, but rather on more general justifications. The general goals of a minimum wage law, for example, are the same in every country that has such a law with the same general structure. At the same time, when referring to the laws of a specific legal system, clearly one has to be mindful to the unique features of this system and possibly adapt the conclusions accordingly.

Once we are clear about what exactly we are trying to achieve, the next problem is *how* to achieve it. The second part of the book was dedicated to this task. It started (in Chapter 6) with the 'building blocks' of labour law—the concepts of 'employer' and 'employee' setting the scope of the field. When interpreting these terms—that in most countries appear in labour legislation without any definition—courts decide who will enjoy the protection of labour laws and who will be left outside, as well as who will bear responsibility as the legal employer. This is obviously a crucial question for both employees and employers (who often try to evade the costs associated with labour laws), so it is not surprising that these questions received enormous attention in the case-law and in the academic literature. Encouragingly, it is quite widely agreed, in recent years, that the interpretation of these terms has to be purposive. However, surprisingly little work has been done in an attempt to re-examine the various indicia used to identify 'employees' in light of the goals of labour laws. I have attempted to fill this gap, relying on the vulnerabilities of democratic deficits and dependency that explain the need for labour laws. I have also reviewed some legal techniques (e.g. presumptions) that can be used to help address common misclassification problems.

The chapter further discussed (favourably) the introduction of a third intermediate category of 'dependent contractors', proposing to capture with this category workers that are dependent on one employer but (unlike employees) are not in a situation of subordination. I argued that large parts of labour law—although not all—should be extended to dependent contractors as well. Although in theory, the purpose would best be advanced if we interpret the term 'employee' differently for each law, in practice it is useful to maintain some clear categories, to make it easier for workers to know their rights, and generally for the law to be more predictable. Earlier in the chapter I explained the pros and cons of universalism versus selectivity, and the need to find the right balance between them. There is certainly no reason to use an 'all or nothing' approach to the regulation of labour law; a more nuanced and selective application of specific laws is sometimes justified. At the same time, we always have to think about the best methods to advance the goals. An intermediate category is a good legal tool to help us achieve the balance between universalism and selectivity.

Finally, the chapter delved into the timely problem of indirect employment, i.e. employment through temporary employment agencies or subcontractors. To achieve the goals of labour law we have to identify sham arrangements designed to frustrate these goals and look beyond them. Here as well I have argued that the level of generality most useful is the one focusing on democratic deficits (subordination, broadly conceived) and dependency. If the worker is dependent on and subordinate to a specific entity, this entity should bear responsibility as the legal employer, notwithstanding any presentation to the contrary by some intermediary. The more difficult problem is to decide who should be the employer when two or more entities both have *some* of the characteristics of an employer. I concluded that the solution of 'joint employer' would best advance the goals of labour law.

After discussing the 'building blocks', the book moved to consider another issue of regulatory design, arguing (in Chapter 7) that open-ended standards are a useful method to advance our goals. Considering the general pros and cons of (concrete) rules versus (open-ended) standards, the chapter showed that standards are especially appropriate for regulating employment relationships which are constantly changing. It was not argued that standards should replace rules, of course, but rather that standards should *supplement* rules and add an open-ended obligation on top of them. The standards can then be filled with content in a way responsive to changing realities and new challenges. Focusing on three standards that have been used in different legal systems—good faith, the managerial prerogative, and proportionality—I showed how they have already been useful in practice, and can be even more useful potentially.

Next, the book moved from general 'structural' issues to more concrete problems that have been raised before the courts, showing (in Chapter 8) how such problems can be addressed by way of purposive interpretation. Examples were brought from several different legal systems, concerning different pieces of legislation, and dealing with diverse 'levels' of law: constitutional and statutory, substantive and procedural. The point was to show that by 'keeping our eyes on the ball'—i.e. remembering our goals at all times—we are directed towards certain solutions. It is not argued, of course, that a purposive approach necessarily leads to one solution. There is surely room for discretion in performing this analysis. Nevertheless, by adopting a purposive approach we are more likely to avoid formalistic applications of the law based on pre-conceived assumptions. Instead, the idea is to always focus on justifications, and adopt the interpretation that best advances the goals of the law (in line with the justifications behind it). Some may wonder whether it is realistic to expect lawyers and judges to perform such an analysis in each case. But note that it is not required in each and every case, only when faced with a new problem. Once we adopt a purposive interpretation for a specific provision, we can apply the same interpretation in future cases as well (subject to the need to reconsider it when circumstances change or after several years). Moreover, the difficulty of performing a 'rich' purposive analysis is exactly where this book comes in. It is intended (together with other academic works) to assist judges and lawyers in this task.

In discussing how to achieve the goals of labour law the book focused for the most part on 'traditional' legal means. Large parts of the book were devoted to interpretation by judges (most of Chapter 6 and all of Chapter 8). Another part was concerned with the legislative design of legal commands (Chapter 7), with some focus again on how these commands (open-ended standards) should be interpreted by courts. In Chapter 6 a few proposals were also made for concrete legislative amendments. Some might say that it is naïve to make proposals that rely on judges, and to some extent on legislatures, for implementation. In many countries both the courts and the legislatures have consistently failed to protect workers. This has led many scholars in recent years to abandon discussion of 'traditional' legal means and focus instead on alternative approaches to regulation—such as 'reflexive labour law' or 'new governance'—that rely to one extent or another on the hope of enlisting employers to advance our goals through self-regulation.

I decided to concentrate on 'traditional' modes of regulation in this book, for several reasons. First, it would be a gross exaggeration to suggest that courts and legislatures never try to advance the goals of labour law discussed in the book. Notwithstanding justified criticism, quite often at least some courts and some legislatures *do* want to advance these goals—there are many examples for that throughout the book—and when they do, the discussion in this book can help to guide them. Second, while it is good to think about entirely new methods—such as 'soft' and 'reflexive' methods—we should not abandon the continuing development of 'traditional' legal methods as well. Our current labour laws are mostly of the 'command and control' type and can be expected to remain so (in whole or at least in a significant part) for the foreseeable future. It is crucial to continue to think about how they should be interpreted and how they can be adapted to changing realities. Third, while I do not offer a detailed discussion of this topic, I admit to being somewhat sceptical about the 'reflexive' methods. It may be naïve to expect judges to develop the law so as to ensure the necessary protection for workers, but it is even more naïve to expect employers to do so on their own. Finally, as explained throughout the book, the purposive approach aims to ensure responsivity to context and the ability to reach nuanced, adaptive and changing solutions. These are some of the same advantages sought by 'reflexive law' proponents. If we can achieve these advantages by way of 'traditional' regulations, this should be preferable over an uncertain regime which relies on self-regulation.

While the book focused for the most part on 'traditional' legal methods, the issue of 'alternative' methods was nonetheless considered as part of the discussion on compliance and enforcement (in Chapter 9). Various solutions were examined under two headings: improving compliance and improving enforcement. In the context of possible routes to improve compliance by employers, I considered ideas to build positive incentives for compliance into regulations. While recognizing the potential usefulness of such techniques, I argued that in the large majority of cases they should come *on top* of traditional methods and cannot replace 'hard' regulations of the 'command and control' type. 'Soft' laws can nonetheless be very useful even on their own in specific areas that are inherently difficult to enforce (such as advancing equality). I also considered the justifications for using 'lead company' liability to improve compliance among contractors, arguing that this is justified but only within some boundaries; and went on to argue that unionization is one of the best ways to ensure compliance, so promoting unionization is an important strategy in this light. The next set of possible solutions, focusing on improving enforcement, was also concerned to a large extent with 'alternative' methods: responsive enforcement, withholding privileges and independent monitoring. In all of these cases, I have justified the adoption of some 'soft' solutions (based on incentives) while maintaining a healthy degree of scepticism about the idea of relying on employers to regulate or monitor themselves.

Throughout the book I made relatively few explicit references to precarious work arrangements or the need to secure 'decent work'. This is certainly not because the book does not address these problems: on the contrary, the entire project is designed to address them. The crisis of labour law which I described in the Introduction leads to precarious, non-decent work arrangements. The book sets out from the very beginning to solve such problems, while at the same time addressing other problems of less vulnerable employees. For both kinds of workers we have to secure the goals of labour law, and the way to do so is through a purposive analysis. But most of the current challenges addressed in the book are more relevant to the former (precarious) group.

The purposive approach makes intuitive sense; it is even trivial. Yet, as noted in the Introduction, too often people forget that laws are meant for a reason and that these laws must continuously be interpreted or adapted to ensure that they advance their goals. The reasons behind the laws must themselves be reconsidered periodically. Not less important, adopting a purposive approach is not enough in itself; understanding our goals, and the best ways to advance them, requires an in-depth analysis. My goal in this book was to offer a convincing analysis of labour laws' goals and means. Hopefully even those who found themselves disagreeing with some of the details would still find the methodology relying on the purposive lenses convincing.

Bibliography

[All websites accessed on 15 October 2015]

Adams Z and Deakin S, 'Institutional Solutions to Inequality and Precariousness in Labour Markets' (2014) 52 BJIR 779

Adams Z et al, 'Labour Regulation Over Time: New Leximetric Evidence' <http://www.rdw2015.org/uploads/submission/full_paper/382/labour_regulation_over_time_rdw.pdf>

Albin E, *Sectoral Disadvantage: The Case of Workers in the British Hospitality Sector* (PhD dissertation, University of Oxford, 2010)

Albin E, 'A Worker–Employer–Customer Triangle: The Case of Tips' (2011) 40 ILJ 181

Albin E, 'From Domestic Servant to Domestic Worker' in Judy Fudge, Shae McCrystal, and Kamala Sankaran (eds), *Challenging the Legal Boundaries of Work Regulation* (Hart 2012) 231

Alchian AA and Demsetz H, 'Production, Information Costs, and Economic Organization' (1972) 62 Amer Econ Rev 777

Alewell D, Schot E, and Wiegand F, 'The Impact of Dismissal Protection on Employers' Cost of Terminating Employment Relations in Germany: An Overview of Empirical Research and Its White Spots' (2008–2009) 30 CLLPJ 667

Alexander CS and Prasad A, 'Bottom-Up Workplace Law Enforcement' (2014) 89 Indiana L J 1069

Alon-Shenker P and Davidov G, 'Applying the Principle of Proportionality in Employment and Labour Law Contexts' (2013) 59 McGill L J 375

Alon-Shenker P and Davidov G, 'Organizing: Should the Employer Have a Say?' (2016) 17 Theoretical Inquiries in Law 63

Alston P (ed), *Labour Rights as Human Rights* (OUP 2005)

Anderson G, 'Good Faith in the Individual Employment Relationship in New Zealand' (2011) 32 CLLPJ 685

Andrias KE, 'A Robust Public Debate: Realizing Free Speech in Workplace Representation Elections' (2003) 112 Yale L J 2415

Anner M, Bair J, and Blasi J, 'Toward Joint Liability in Global Supply Chains: Addressing the Root Causes of Labor Violations in International Subcontracting Networks' (2013) 35 CLLPJ 1

Applebaum H, *The Concept of Work: Ancient, Medieval, and Modern* (State University of New York Press 1992)

Apps KM, 'Good Faith Performance in Employment Contracts: A "Comparative Conversation" Between The U.S. and England' (2006) 8 U Pa J Lab & Emp L 883

Arneson RJ, 'Equality and Equal Opportunity for Welfare' (1989) 56 Philosophical Studies 77

Arnow-Richman R, 'From Just Cause to Just Notice in Reforming Employment Termination Law' in Estlund CL and Wachter ML (eds), *Research Handbook on the Economics of Labor and Employment Law* (Edward Elgar 2012) 296

Arrow KJ, *The Limits of Organization* (W W Norton 1974)

Arthurs H, *Fairness at Work: Federal Labour Standards for the 21st Century* (Federal Labour Standards Review 2006)

Arthurs H, 'Charting the Boundaries of Labour Law: Innis Christie and the Search for an Integrated Law of Labour Market Regulation' (2011) 34 Dalhousie L J 1

Arthurs H, 'Cross-National Legal Learning: The Uses of Comparative Labor Knowledge, Law, and Policy' in Stone KVW and Arthurs H (eds), *Rethinking Workplace Regulation: Beyond the Standard Contract of Employment* (Russell Sage Foundation 2013) 353

Arthurs H, 'Labor Law as the Law of Economic Subordination and Resistance: A Thought Experiment' (2013) 34 Comparative Labor Law & Policy J 585

Arulampalam W, Booth AL, and Bryan ML, 'Training and the New Minimum Wage' (2004) 114 Economic Journal 87

Ashenfelter O and Smith RS, 'Compliance with the Minimum Wage Law' (1979) 87 Journal of Political Economy 333

Ashiagbor D, 'Evaluating the Reflexive Turn in Labour Law' in Alan Bogg et al (eds), *The Autonomy of Labour Law* (Hart 2015) 123

Atiyah PS, *Vicarious Liability in the Law of Torts* (Butterworths 1967)

Atkinson AB, 'On Targeting Social Security: Theory and Western Experience with Family Benefits' in Walle D and Nead K (eds), *Public Spending and the Poor: Theory and Evidence* (Johns Hopkins University Press 1995) 25

Atlan M and Sapir Eliezer D, 'Notes on the Act to Improve the Enforcement of Labour Laws—Really Responsive Regulation', (forthcoming) Hukim—Journal on Legislation [Hebrew]

Atleson JB, *Values and Assumptions in American Labor Law* (U of Massachusetts Press 1983)

Autor DH, 'Outsourcing at Will: The Contribution of Unjust Dismissal Doctrine to the Growth of Employment Outsourcing' (2003) 21 Journal of Labor Economics 1

Ayotte K, Friedman E, and Smith HE, 'A Safety Valve Model of Equity as Anti-Opportunism' (2013) Northwestern Law & Econ Research Paper no 13-15 <http://ssrn.com/abstract=2245098>

Ayres I and Braithwaite J, *Responsive Regulation: Transcending the Deregulation Debate* (OUP 1992)

Azariadis C and Stiglitz JE, 'Implicit Contracts and Fixed Price Equilibria' (1983) 98 (Supp) The Quarterly Journal of Economics 1

Babbage C, *On the Economy of Machinery and Manufacturers* (first published 1832, 4th edn, Augustus M Kelley 1963) 175–76

Bagchi A, 'Unions and the Duty of Good Faith in Employment Contracts' (2003) 112 Yale L J 1881

Bagenstos SR, 'Employment Law and Social Equality' (2013) 112 Mich L Rev 225

Baker A, 'Proportionality and Employment Discrimination in the UK' (2008) 37 ILJ 305

Baker M, Benjamin D, and Stanger S, 'The Highs and Lows of the Minimum Wage Effect: A Time-Series Cross-Section Study of the Canadian Law' (1999) 17 Journal of Labor Economics 318

Baldwin R, 'Regulation: After "Command and Control"' in Keith Hawkins (ed), *The Human Face of Law: Essays in Honour of Donald Harris* (Clarendon 1997) 65

Baldwin R, 'From Regulation to Behaviour Change: Giving Nudge the Third Degree' (2014) 77 MLR 831

Baldwin R and Black J, 'Really Responsive Regulation' (2008) 71 Modern Law Review 59

Banks K, 'Progress and Paradox: The Remarkable yet Limited Advance of Employer Good Faith Duties in Canadian Common Law' (2011) 32 CLLPJ 547

Barak A, *Purposive Interpretation in Law* (Princeton UP 2005)

Barenberg M, 'Democracy and Domination in the Law of Workplace Cooperation: From Bureaucratic to Flexible Production' (1994) 94 Colum L Rev 753

Barmes L, 'Common Law Implied Terms and Behavioural Standards at Work' (2007) 36 ILJ 35

Barnard C, 'The Future of Equality Law: Equality and Beyond' in Barnard C, Deakin S, and Morris GS (eds), *The Future of Labour Law: Liber Amicorum Bob Hepple* (Hart 2004) 214

Barnard C, 'Using Procurement Law to Enforce Labour Standards' in Davidov G and Langille B (eds), *The Idea of Labour Law* (OUP 2011) 256

Barzilay AR, 'Labor Regulation as Family Regulation: Decent Work and Decent Families' (2012) 33 Berkeley J of Emp & Lab L 119

Bazen S and Skourias N, 'Is There a Negative Effect of Minimum Wages on Youth Employment in France?' (1997) 41 European Economic Review 723

Beatty DM, 'Labour is Not a Commodity' in Reiter BJ and Swan J (eds), *Studies in Contract Law* (Butterworths 1980)

Beatty DM, 'Ideology, Politics and Unionism' in Swan KP and Swinton KE (eds), *Studies in Labour Law* (Butterworths 1983) 313

Beatty DM, *Putting the Charter to Work: Designing a Constitutional Labour Code* (McGill UP 1987) 299

Beatty DM, *The Ultimate Rule of Law* (OUP 2004)

Beatty DM and Kennett S, 'Striking Back: Fighting Words, Social Protest and Political Participation in Free and Democratic Societies' (1988) 12 Queen's L J 214

Beck U, *Risk Society: Towards a New Modernity* (Sage 1992)

Befort SF and Budd JW, *Invisible Hands, Invisible Objectives: Bringing Workplace Law & Public Policy into Focus* (Stanford UP 2009)

Belman D, 'Unions, the Quality of Labor Relations, and Firm Performance' in Mishel L and Voos PB (eds), *Unions and Economic Competitiveness* (ME Sharpe 1992) 41

Bengtsson E, 'Do Unions Redistribute Income from Capital to Labour? Union Density and Wage Shares Since 1960' (2014) 45(5) Industrial Relations Journal 389

Bent JR, 'An Incentive-Based Approach to Regulating Workplace Chemicals' (2012) 73 Ohio St L J 1389

Bernhardt A et al, *Broken Laws, Unprotected Workers: Violations of Employment and Labor Laws in America's Cities* (National Employment Law Project, 2009) <www.nelp.org/content/uploads/2015/03/BrokenLawsReport2009.pdf?nocdn=1>

Betts JR, Odgers CW, and Wilson MK, 'The Effects of Unions on Research and Development: An Empirical Analysis Using Multi-Year Data' (2001) 34 Can J of Econ 785

Bisom-Rapp S, 'An Ounce of Prevention is a Poor Substitute for a Pound of Cure: Confronting the Developing Jurisprudence of Education and Prevention in Employment Discrimination Law' (2001) 22 Berkeley J Emp & Lab L 1

Blackett A, 'Situated Reflections on International Labour Law, Capabilities, and Decent Work' (2007) 20(suppl) hors série RQDI 223

Blackett A, 'Emancipation in the Idea of Labour Law' in Davidov G and Langille B (eds), *The Idea of Labour Law* (OUP 2011) 420

Blackett A and Sheppard C, 'The Links between Collective Bargaining and Equality' (2002) ILO Working Paper <http://www.ilo.org/wcmsp5/groups/public/---ed_norm/---declaration/documents/publication/wcms_decl_wp_12_en.pdf>

Blades LE, 'Employment at Will vs. Individual Freedom: On Limiting the Abusive Exercise of Employer Power' (1967) 67 Colum L Rev 1404

Blanchflower DG and Bryson A, 'Changes over Time in Union Relative Wage Effects in the UK and the US Revisited' (2002) National Bureau of Economic Research Working Paper 9395 <http://www.nber.org/papers/w9395.pdf>

Block RN, 'Rethinking the National Labor Relations Act and Zero-Sum Labor Law: An Industrial Relations View' (1997) 18 Berk J of Emp and Lab L 30

Boal WM and Pencavel J, 'The Effects of Labor Unions on Employment, Wages and Days of Operation: Coal Mining in West Virginia' (1994) 109 The Quarterly J of Econ 267

Boal WM and Ransom MR, 'Monopsony in the Labor Market' (1997) 35 J of Economic Literature 86

Bodie MT, 'Participation as a Theory of Employment' (2013) 89 Notre Dame L Rev 661

Bogg AL, *The Democratic Aspects of Trade Union Recognition* (Hart Publishing 2009)

Bogg AL, 'Good Faith in the Contract of Employment: A Case of the English Reserve?' (2011) 32 CLLPJ 729

Bogg AL, 'Sham Self-Employment in the Supreme Court' (2012) 41 ILJ 328

Bogg AL, 'Labour Law and the Trade Unions: Autonomy and Betrayal' in Bogg A et al (eds), *The Autonomy of Labour Law* (Hart 2015) 73

Bogg AL and Estlund C, 'Freedom of Association and the Right to Contest: Getting Back to Basics' in Novitz T and Bogg A (eds), *Voices at Work: Continuity and Change in the Common Law World* (OUP 2014) 141

Bogg AL and Ewing K, 'A (Muted) Voice at Work? Collective Bargaining in the Supreme Court of Canada' (2012) 33 Comparative Labour Law and Policy Journal 379

Bogg AL and Novitz T, 'Investigating Voice at Work' (2011) 33 CLLPJ 323

Böheim R and Mühlberger U, 'Dependent Self-employment: Workers between Employment and Self-employment in the UK' (2009) 42 J Labour Market Res 185

Booth AL and Chatterji M, 'Unions and Efficient Training' (1998) 108 The Economic 328

Booth AL, Chatterji M, Francesconi M, and Zoega G, 'Unions, Work Related Training and Wages: Evidence from British Men' (2003–2004) 57 Indus & Lab Rel Rev 68

Bosniak L, 'Citizenship and Work' (2002) 27 NCJ Int'l L & Com Reg 497

Bowles S, 'The Production Process in a Competitive Economy: Walrasian, Neo-Hobbesian, and Marxian Models' (1985) 75(1) Amer Econ Rev 16

Bowles S, 'Policies Designed for Self-Interested Citizens May Undermine "The Moral Sentiments": Evidence from Economic Experiments' (2008) 320 Science 1605

Bowles S and Gintis H, 'Is the Demand for Workplace Democracy Redundant in a Liberal Economy?' in Pagano U and Rowthorn R (eds), *Democracy and Efficiency in the Economic Enterprise* (Routledge 1996) 64

Braithwaite J, 'Rules and Principles: A Theory of Legal Certainty' (2002) 27 Australian Journal of Legal Philosophy 47

Braithwaite J, *Regulatory Capitalism: How it Works, Ideas for Making it Work Better* (Edward Elgar 2008)

Braithwaite J, 'The Essence of Responsive Regulation' (2011) 44 UBC L Rev 475

Breen R, 'Risk, Recommodification and Stratification' (1997) 31 Sociology 473

Breyer S, *Active Liberty* (OUP 2008)

Brodie D, 'The Heart of the Matter: Mutual Trust and Confidence' (1996) 25 ILJ 121

Brodie D, 'Beyond Exchange: The New Contract of Employment' (1998) 27 ILJ 79

Brodie D, 'Mutual Trust and the Values of the Employment Contract' (2001) 30 ILJ 84

Brodie D, 'Employees, Workers and the Self-Employed' (2005) 34 ILJ 253

Brodie D, 'Fair Dealing and the World of Work' (2014) 43 ILJ 29

Brooks A, 'Myth and Muddle—an Examination of Contracts for the Performance of Work' (1988) 11 UNSWLJ 48

Brown C, Gilroy C, and Kohen A, 'The Effect of the Minimum Wage on Employment and Unemployment' (1982) 20 J of Economic Literature 487

Brown D, Dehejia R, and Robertson R, 'Regulations, Monitoring and Working Conditions: Evidence from Better Factories Cambodia and Better Work Vietnam' in McCann D et al (eds), *Creative Labour Regulation: Indeterminacy and Protection in an Uncertain World* (ILO 2014) 185

Brudney JJ, 'Reluctance and Remorse: The Covenant of Good Faith and Fair Dealing in American Employment Law' (2011) 32 Comp Lab Law & Pol'y J 773
Bucy PH 'Private Justice' (2002) 76 Southern California L Rev 1
Budd JW, *Employment with a Human Face: Balancing Efficiency, Equity and Voice* (Cornell UP 2004)
Buechtemann CF, 'Introduction: Employment Security and Labor Markets' in Buechtemann CF (ed), *Employment Security and Labor Market Behavior: Interdisciplinary Approaches and International Evidence* (ILR Press 1993) 3
Burkhauser RV, Couch KA, and Wittenburg DC, 'Who Minimum Wage Increases Bite: An Analysis Using Monthly Data from the SIPP and the CPS' (2000) 67 Southern Economic Journal 16
Burkhauser RV, Couch KA, and Wittenburg DC, 'A Reassessment of the New Economics of the Minimum Wage Literature with Monthly Data from the Current Population Survey' (2000) 18 Journal of Labor Economics 653
Buttler F and Walwei U, 'Employment Security and Efficiency: Assumptions in the Current Debate and Empirical Evidence for West Germany' in Buechtemann CF (ed), *Employment Security and Labor Market Behavior: Interdisciplinary Approaches and International Evidence* (ILR Press 1993) 255
Cabrelli D, 'The Hierarchy of Differing Behavioural Standards of Review in Labour Law' (2011) 40 ILJ 146
Cabrelli D, *Employment Law in Context: Text and Materials* (OUP 2014)
Cameron CDR, 'The Rule of Law Goes to Work: How Collective Bargaining May Promote Access to Justice in the United States, Canada, and the Rest of the World' (2014) 20 UC Davis Journal of International Law & Policy 211
Campbell D, 'Good Faith and the Ubiquity of the Relational Contract' (2014) 77 Modern Law Review 460
Cappelli P et al, *Change at Work* (OUP 1997)
Card D, 'The Effect of Unions on Wage Inequality in the U.S. Labor Market' (2001) 54 Indus & Lab Rel Rev 296
Card D and Krueger AB, *Myth and Measurement: The New Economics of the Minimum Wage* (Princeton UP 1995)
Carlson RR, 'Why the Law Still Can't Tell an Employee When It Sees One and How It Ought to Stop Trying' (2001) 22 Berkeley J Emp and Lab L 295
Carrigan F, 'The Implications of Implied Terms in Law in the Common Law Contract of Employment' (2009) 9 Oxford University Commonwealth L J 73
Carter TJ and De Lancey PR, 'Just, Unjust, and Just-Cause Dismissals' (1997) 19 Journal of Macroeconomics 619
Caruso B, 'New Trajectories of Labor Law in the European Crisis: The Italian Case' (2015) 36 CLLPJ 181
Casale G (ed), *The Employment Relationship: A Comparative Overview* (Hart 2011)
Castel R, 'Work and Usefulness to the World' (1996) 135 Int'l Lab Rev 615
Chang Y and Ehrlich I, 'On the Economics of Compliance with the Minimum Wage Law' (1985) 93 Journal of Political Economy 84
Ciulla JB, *The Working Life: The Promise and Betrayal of Modern Work* (Times Books 2000)
Clark KB, 'The Impact of Unionization on Productivity: A Case Study' (1980) 33 Indus & Lab Rel Rev 451
Clarke JA, 'Beyond Equality? Against the Universal Turn in Workplace Protections' (2011) 86 Indiana L J 1219
Coase RH, 'The Nature of the Firm' (1937) 4 Economica 386
Cohen GA, *Self-Ownership, Freedom, and Equality* (Cambridge UP 1995)

Cohen Maiyanov D, 'Sweatshop Liability: Corporate Codes of Conduct and the Governance of Labor Standards in the International Supply Chain' (2010) 14 Lewis & Clark L Rev 397
Cohen Y et al, 'Unpacking Union Density: Union Membership and Coverage in the Transformation of the Israeli Industrial Relations System' (2003) 42 Industrial Relations 692
Collins H, 'Market Power, Bureaucratic Power, and the Contract of Employment' (1986) 15 ILJ 1
Collins H, 'Labour Law as a Vocation' (1989) 105 LQR 468
Collins H, 'Independent Contractors and the Challenge of Vertical Disintegration to Employment Protection Laws' (1990) 10 OJLS 353
Collins H, 'The Meaning of Job Security' (1991) 20 ILJ 227
Collins H, *Justice in Dismissal: The Law of Termination of Employment* (Clarendon 1992)
Collins H, *Regulating Contracts* (OUP 1999)
Collins H, 'Employment Rights of Casual Workers' (2000) 29 ILJ 73
Collins H, 'Justifications and Techniques of Legal Regulation of the Employment Relation' in Collins H, Davies P, and Rideout R (eds), *Legal Regulation of the Employment Relation* (Kluwer 2000) 3
Collins H, 'Regulating the Employment Relationship for Competitiveness' (2001) 31 ILJ 17
Collins H, 'Is There a Third Way in Labour Law?' in Conaghan J, Fischl RM, and Klare K (eds), *Labour Law in an Era of Globalization: Transformative Practices and Possibilities* (OUP 2002) 449
Collins H, *Employment Law* (2nd edn, OUP 2010)
Collins H, 'Theories of Rights as Justifications for Labour Law' in Davidov G and Langille B (eds), *The Idea of Labour Law* (OUP 2011) 144
Collins H, 'Implied Terms: The Foundation in Good Faith and Fair Dealing' (2014) 67 Current Legal Problems 297
Collins H, 'Is There A Human Right to Work?' in Mantouvalou V (ed), *The Right to Work: Legal and Philosophical Perspectives* (Hart 2015) 32
Commons JR and Andrews JB, *Principles of Labor Legislation* (rev edn, Harper & Brothers 1927)
Corazza L and Razzolini O, 'Who is an Employer?' in Finkin MW and Mundlak G, *Comparative Labor Law* (Edward Elgar 2015) 132
Corneo G and Lucifora C, 'Wage Formation under Union Threat Effects: Theory and Empirical Evidence' (1997) 4 Labour Economics 265
Countouris N, 'The Employment Relationship: A Comparative Analysis of National Judicial Approached' in Casale G (ed), *The Employment Relationship: A Comparative Overview* (Hart 2011) 35
Countouris N, *The Changing Law of the Employment Relationship: Comparative Analyses in the European Context* (Ashgate 2013)
Countouris N, 'Uses and Misuses of "Mutuality of Obligations" and the Autonomy of Labour Law' in Bogg A and others (eds), *The Autonomy of Labour Law* (Hart 2015) 169
Coutu M, 'With Hugo Sinzheimer and Max Weber in Mind: The Current Crisis and the Future of Labor Law' (2013) 34 CLLPJ 605
Coutu M, Le Friant M, and Murray G, 'Broken Paradigms: Labor Law in the Wake of Globalization and the Economic Crisis' (2013) 34 CLLPJ 565
Cox A, *Law and the National Labor Policy* (first published 1960, Greenwood Press 1983) 12
Crain M, 'Building Solidarity through Expansion of NLRA Coverage: A Blueprint for Worker Empowerment' (1990) 74 Minn L Rev 953
Crotty M et al (eds), *Termination of Employment Digest* (ILO 2000)

Currie DP, *The Constitution of the Federal Republic of Germany* (University of Chicago 1994) 30
Dagan H, 'Lawmaking for Legal Realists' (2013) 1 Theory and Practice of Legislation 187
Dahan Y, Lerner H, and Milman-Sivan F, 'Global Justice, Labor Standards and Responsibility' (2011) 12 Theoretical Inquiries in Law 117
Dahl RA, *After the Revolution? Authority in a Good Society* (Yale UP 1970)
Dahl RA, *A Preface to Economic Democracy* (University of California 1985)
Dau-Schmidt KG, 'A Bargaining Analysis of American Labor Law and the Search for Bargaining Equity and Industrial Peace' (1992) 91 Mich L Rev 419
Davidov G, 'The Three Axes of Employment Relationships: A Characterization of Workers in Need of Protection' (2002) 52 U Toronto L J 357
Davidov G, 'Joint Employer Status in Triangular Employment Relationships' (2004) 42 British Journal of Industrial Relations 727
Davidov G, 'Collective Bargaining Law: Purpose and Scope' (2004) 20 Inter J Comp Lab L & Ind Rel 81
Davidov G, 'Enforcement Problems in "Informal" Labor Markets: A View from Israel' (2005) 27 Comparative Labor Law and Policy Journal 3
Davidov G, 'Who is a Worker?' (2005) 34 ILJ 57
Davidov G, 'The Reports of My Death are Greatly Exaggerated: "Employee" as a Viable (Though Overly-Used) Legal Concept' in Davidov G and Langille B (eds), *Boundaries and Frontiers of Labour Law: Goals and Means in the Regulation of Work* (Hart 2006) 133
Davidov G, 'The (Changing?) Idea of Labour Law' (2007) 146 Int'l Lab Rev 311
Davidov G, 'In Defence of (Efficiently Administered) "Just Cause" Dismissal Laws' (2007) 23 IJCCLIR 117
Davidov G, 'Unbound: Some Comments on Israel's Judicially-Developed Labor Law' (2009) 30 CLLPJ 283
Davidov G, 'A Purposive Interpretation of the National Minimum Wage Act' (2009) 72 MLR 581
Davidov G, 'Judicial Development of Collective Labour Rights—Contextually' (2010) 15 Can Lab & Emp L J 235
Davidov G, 'The Enforcement Crisis in Labour Law and the Fallacy of Voluntarist Solutions' (2010) 26 Int J of Comp Labour Law and Ind Rel 61
Davidov G, 'Re-Matching Labour Law with Their Purpose' in Davidov G and Langille B (eds), *The Idea of Labour Law* (OUP 2011) 179
Davidov G, 'The Principle of Proportionality in Labor Law and Its Impact on Precarious Workers' (2012) 34 CLLPJ 63
Davidov G, 'Freelancers: An Intermediate Group in Labour Law?' in Fudge J, McCrystal S, and Sankaran K (eds), *Challenging the Legal Boundaries of Work Regulation* (Hart 2012) 171
Davidov G, 'The (Incomplete) Purposive Revolution: A Review of Freedland & Kountouris' (2013) 7 Jerusalem Rev of Leg Stud 87
Davidov G, 'The Goals of Regulating Work: Between Universalism and Selectivity' (2014) 64 UTLJ 1
Davidov G, 'Setting Labour Law's Coverage: Between Universalism and Selectivity' (2014) 34 OJLS 543
Davidov G, 'Special Protection for Cleaners: A Case of Justified Selectivity?' (2015) 36 CLLPJ 217
Davidov G, 'Indirect Employment: Should Lead Companies Be Liable?' (2015) 37 Comp Lab Law & Pol'y J 5

Davidov G and Eshet E, 'Intermediate Approaches to Unfair Dismissal Protection' (2015) 44 ILJ 167

Davidov G, Freedland M, and Kountouris N, 'The Subjects of Labor Law: "Employees" and Other Workers' in Finkin M and Mundlak G (eds), *Research Handbook in Comparative Labor Law* (Edward Elgar 2015) 115

Davidov G and Langille B (eds), *The Idea of Labour Law* (OUP 2011)

Davidov G, Yovel J, Saban I, and Reichman A, 'State or Family? The 2003 Amendment to the Citizenship and Entrance to Israel Law' (2005) 8 Mishpat Umimshal 643 (in Hebrew)

Davies ACL, 'Casual Workers and Continuity of Employment' (2006) 35 ILJ 196

Davies ACL, 'The Contract for Intermittent Employment' (2007) 36 ILJ 102

Davies ACL, 'Judicial Self-Restraint in Labour Law' (2009) 38 ILJ 278

Davies ACL, 'Sensible Thinking about Sham Transactions: Protectacoat Firthglow Ltd v Szilagy' (2009) 38 ILJ 318

Davies ACL, 'Identifying "Exploitative Compromises": The Role of Labour Law in Resolving Disputes Between Workers' (2012) 65 CLP 269

Davies D, 'Death of a Labour Lawyer?' in Conaghan J, Fischl RM, and Klare K (eds), *Labour Law in an Era of Globalization* (OUP 2002) 159

Davies P, 'Efficiency Arguments for the Collective Representation of Workers: A Sketch' in Bogg A et al (eds), *The Autonomy of Labour Law* (Hart 2015) 367

Davies P and Freedland M, *Kahn-Freund's Labour and the Law* (3rd edn, Stevens 1983)

Davies P and Freedland M, *Towards a Flexible Labour Market: Labour Legislation and Regulation since the 1990s* (OUP 2007)

Deakin S, 'The Changing Concept of the 'Employer' in British Labour Law' (2001) 30 ILJ 72

Deakin S, '*Capacitas*: Contract Law, Capabilities and the Legal Foundations of the Market' in Deakin S and Supiot A (eds), *Capacitas: Contract Law and the Institutional Preconditions of a Market Economy* (Hart 2009) 1

Deakin S, 'The Contribution of Labour Law to Economic and Human Development' in Davidov G and Langille B (eds), *The Idea of Labour Law* (OUP 2011) 162

Deakin S, 'Conceptions of the Market in Labour Law' in Numhauser-Henning A and Rönnmar M (eds), *Normative Patterns and Legal Developments in the Social Dimension of the EU* (Hart 2013) 141

Deakin S and Morris GS, *Labour Law* (6th edn, Hart 2012)

Deakin S and Wilkinson F, 'The Law and Economics of the Minimum Wage' (1992) 19 Journal of Law and Society 379

Deakin S and Wilkinson F, 'Labour Law and Economic Theory: A Reappraisal,' in De Geest G et al, *Law and Economics and the Labour Market* (Edward Elgar 1999) 27.

Deakin S and Wilkinson F, 'Labour Law and Economic Theory: A Reappraisal' in Collins H, Davies P, and Rideout R (eds), *Legal Regulation of the Employment Relation* (Kluwer 2000) 29

Deakin S and Wilkinson F, 'Minimum Wage Legislation' in Bouckaert B and De Geest G (eds), *Encyclopedia of Law and Economics,* vol III (Edward Elgar 2000) 566

Deakin S and Wilkinson F, *The Law of the Labour Market: Industrialization, Employment and Legal Evolution* (OUP 2005)

Deakin S and Wilkinson F, 'Minimum Wage Legislation' in Dau-Schmidt KG, Harris SD and Lobel O (eds), *Encyclopedia of Labor and Employment Law and Economics* (Edward Elgar 2009) ch 5

Deakin S, Johnston A, and Markesinis B, *Tort Law* (7th edn, Clarendon 2013)

Deery SJ and Iverson RD, 'Labor–Management Cooperation: Antecedents and Impact on Organizational Performance' (2005) 58 Indus & Lab Rel Rev 588
DeFina RH, 'Unions, Relative Wages, and Economic Efficiency' (1983) 1 J of Labor Econ 408
Dickens L, 'Comparative Systems of Unjust Dismissal: The British Case' (1994) 536 Annals Am Acad Pol Soc Sci 43
Dickens R, Machin S, and Manning A, 'The Effects of Minimum Wages on Employment: Theory and Evidence from Britain' (1999) 17 J of Labor Econ 1
Dickerson A, 'Longer-Term Implications of the NMW: A Re-Examination Of Employer-Provided Training', Report presented to the Low Pay Commission (March 2007) <http://webarchive.nationalarchives.gov.uk/20130626202215/http://www.lowpay.gov.uk/lowpay/research/pdf/t0JK67V2.pdf>
Doorey D, 'Employer "Bullying": Implied Duties of Fair Dealing in Canadian Employment Contracts' (2005) 30 Queen's L J 500
Doorey D, 'The Medium and the "Anti-Union" Message: "Forced Listening" and Captive Audience Meetings in Canadian Labor Law' (2008) 29 CLLPJ 79
Doorey D, 'A Model of Responsive Workplace Law' (2012) 50 Osgoode Hall L J 57
Doucouliagos H and Laroche P, 'Unions and Profits: A Meta-Regression Analysis' (2009) 48 Industrial Relations 146
Draca M, Machin S, and Reenen JV, 'Minimum Wages and Firm Profitability' (2011) 3 American Economic Journal: Applied Economics 129
Dukes R, 'Constitutionalizing Employment Relations: Sinzheimer, Kahn-Freund, and the Role of Labour Law' (2008) 35 J L Soc'y 341
Dukes R, *The Labour Constitution: The Enduring Idea of Labour Law* (OUP 2014)
Dutil P and Saunders R, *New Approaches in Achieving Compliance with Statutory Employment Standards* (2005) <http://mattelrod.org/celarc/cppcdoc1-12/201703.pdf>
Dworkin R, *Law's Empire* (Harvard UP 1986)
Dworkin R, *Sovereign Virtue: The Theory and Practice of Equality* (Harvard UP 2000)
Edelman LB et al, 'When Organizations Rule: Judicial Deference to Institutionalized Employment Structures' (2011) 117 American J of Sociology 888
Eden G, 'Reinstatement in the Nonunion Sector: An Empirical Analysis' (1994) 49 Indus Rel 87
Edwards R, *Contested Terrain: The Transformation of the Workplace in the Twentieth Century* (Basic Books 1979)
Eger T, 'Opportunistic Termination of Employment Contracts and Legal Protection against Dismissal in Germany and the USA' (2004) 23 Int Rev of Law and Econ 381
Ehrlich I and Posner RA, 'An Economic Analysis of Legal Rulemaking' (1974) 3 J of Legal Studies 257
Eliav T, Endweld M, Gottlieb D and Kachanovski I, *Trends in Minimum Wage Compliance: The Case of Israel* (Israel National Insurance Institute Working Paper, 2009) (Hebrew)
Elvira MM and Saporta I, 'How Does Collective Bargaining Affect the Gender Gap?' (2001) 28 Work and Occupations 469
Emiliou N, *The Principle of Proportionality in European Law* (Kluwer 1996)
Engels C, 'Belgium' (Special Issue: Employed or Self-Employed) (1992) 24 Bull Com Lab Rel 29
Engels F, 'On Authority' in Karl Marx and Friedrich Engels, *Basic Writings on Politics and Philosophy* (Lewis S Feuer ed, Doubleday 1959) 481
England G, 'Some Thoughts on Constitutionalizing the Right to Strike' (1988) 12 Queen's L J 168

England G, 'Recent Developments in the Law of the Employment Contract: Continuing Tension between the Rights Paradigm and the Efficiency Paradigm' (1995) 20 Queen's L J 557

Epstein RA, 'In Defense of the Contract at Will' (1984) 51 U Chi L Rev 947

Epstein RA, 'Agency Costs, Employment Contracts, and Labor Unions' in Pratt JW and Zeckhauser RJ (eds), *Principles and Agents: The Structure of Business* (Harvard Business School 1985) 127

Eshet E, *The Social Dimension of Contract, Property and Corporate Law in Business Transfers* (PhD dissertation, Hebrew University, 2013) (Hebrew)

Eskridge WN Jr, 'Public Values in Statutory Interpretation' (1989) 137 U Pa L Rev 1007

Eskridge WN Jr, 'The New Textualism' (1990) 37 UCLA L Rev 621

Eskridge WN Jr and Frickey P P, 'Statutory Interpretation as Practical Reasoning' (1990) 43 Stan L Rev 321

Estlund C, *Working Together: How Workplace Bonds Strengthen a Diverse Democracy* (OUP 2003)

Estlund C, 'Rebuilding the Law of the Workplace in an Era of Self-Regulation' (2005) 105 Columbia Law Review 319

Estlund C, 'Just the Facts: The Case for Workplace Transparency' (2010) 63 Stan L Rev 351

Estlund C, *Regoverning the Workplace: From Self-Regulation to Co-Regulation* (Yale UP, 2010)

Estlund C, 'Labor Law Reform Again? Reframing Labor Law as a Regulatory Project' (2013) 16 NYU J Legis & Pub Pol'y 383

Estreicher S, 'Unjust Dismissal Laws: Some Cautionary Notes' (1985) 33 Am J Comp L 310

Estreicher S and Hirsch JM, 'Comparative Wrongful Dismissal Law: Reassessing American Exceptionalism' (2014) 92 N C L Rev 343

European Labour Law Network, 'Thematic Report 2011: Dismissal—Particularly for Business Reasons—and Employment Protection' (2011) <www.labourlawnetwork.eu/frontend/file.php?id=218&dl=1>

Ewing KD, 'The Death of Labour Law?' (1988) 8 OJLS 293

Ewing KD, 'Democratic Socialism and Labour Law' (1995) 24 ILJ 103

Ewing KD, 'The Function of Trade Unions' (2005) 34 ILJ 1

Fallon RH Jr and Weiler PC, 'Firefighters v. Stotts: Conflicting Models of Racial Justice' (1984) Sup Ct Rev 1

Farber HS, 'Non Union Wage Rates and the Threat of Unionization' (2005) 58 Industrial and Labor Relations 335

Feldman Y, 'The Complexity of Disentangling Intrinsic and Extrinsic Compliance Motivations: Theoretical and Empirical Insights from the Behavioral Analysis of Law' (2011) 35 Wash U J of L & Pol'y 11

Feldman Y and Smith HE, 'Behavioral Equity' (2014) 170 Journal of Institutional and Theoretical Economics 137

Felstiner WLF, Abel RL, and Sarat A, 'The Emergence and Transformation of Disputes: Naming, Blaming, Claiming' (1980) 15 Law & Society Review 631

Fenwick C and Novitz T (eds), *Human Rights at Work: Perspectives on Law and Regulation* (Hart 2010)

Fine J and Gordon J, 'Strengthening Labor Standards Enforcement through Partnerships with Workers' Organizations' (2010) 38 Politics & Society 552

Finkin MW, 'Menschenbild: The Conception of the Employee as a Person in Western Law' (2002) 23 CLLPJ 577

Finkin MW, 'The Death and Transfiguration of Labor Law' (2011) 33 CLLPJ 171
Finkin MW, 'Introduction: The Past and Future of Labor Law in Comparative Perspective' in Hepple BA and Kahn-Freund O (eds), *XV International Encyclopedia of Comparative Law* (Mohr Siebeck 2014) 3
Finkin MW, 'From Weight Checking to Wage Checking: Arming Workers To Combat Wage Theft' (2015) 90 Indiana L J 851
Fisk CL, 'Reimagining Collective Rights in the Workplace' (2014) 4 UC Irvine L Rev 523
Fisk CL and Poueymirou M, 'Harris v. Quinn and the Contradictions of Compelled Speech' (2014) 48 Loyola of LA L Rev 439
Fisk CL and Sachs B, 'Restoring Equity in Right-to-Work Law' (2014) 4 UC Irvine L Rev 859
Flanders AD, *Management and Unions: The Theory and Reform of Industrial Relations* (Faber and Faber 1970) 252
Foo LJ, 'The Vulnerable and Exploitable Immigrant Workforce and the Need for Strengthening Worker Protective Legislation' (1994) 103 Yale L J 2179
Foster N and Sule S, *German Legal System and Laws* (4th edn, OUP 2010)
Fox A, *Beyond Contract: Work, Power and Trust Relations* (Faber and Faber 1974)
Fredman S, 'The New Rights: Labour Law and Ideology in the Thatcher Years' (1992) 12 OJLS 244.
Fredman S, 'Equality: A New Generation?' (2001) 30 ILJ 145
Fredman S, 'The Ideology of New Labour Law' in Barnard C, Deakin S, and Morris GS (eds), *The Future of Labour Law: Liber Amicorum Bob Hepple* (Hart 2004) 9
Fredman S and Fudge J, 'The Legal Construction of Personal Work Relations and Gender' (2013) 7 Jerusalem Rev of Leg Studies 112
Freed MG and Polsby DD, 'Just Cause For Termination Rules and Economic Efficiency' (1989) 38 Emory L J 1097
Freedland M, 'The Segmentation of Workers' Rights and the Legal Analysis of Personal Work Relations: Redefining a Problem' (2015) 36 CLLPJ 241
Freedland M and Kountouris N, *The Legal Construction of Personal Work Relations* (OUP 2011)
Freedland M et al, *Public Employment Services and European Law* (OUP 2007)
Freeman RB, 'American Exceptionalism in the Labor Market: Union–Nonunion Differentials in the United States and Other Countries' in Kerr C and Staudohar PD (eds), *Labor Economics and Industrial Relations: Markets and Institutions* (Harvard UP 1994) 272
Freeman RB, 'Myth and Measurement: The New Economics of the Minimum Wage (Book Review)' (1995) 48 Indus & Lab Rel Rev 830
Freeman RB, 'The Minimum Wage as a Redistributive Tool' (1996) 106 The Economic Journal 639
Freeman RB and Medoff JL, *What Do Unions Do?* (Basic Books 1984)
Freyens B and Oslington P, 'Dismissal Costs and Their Impact on Employment: Evidence from Australian Small and Medium Enterprises' (2007) 83 The Economic Record 1
Friedman AL, *Industry & Labour: Class Struggle at Work and Monopoly Capitalism* (Macmillan 1977) 82
Friedman M, *Capitalism and Freedom*, (University of Chicago Press 1962)
Friedman M, 'Minimum Wage-Rates' in Samuelson PA (ed), *Readings in Economics* (6th edn, McGraw-Hill 1970) 247
Friedman M and Friedman R, *Free to Choose: A Personal Statement* (Harcourt Brace Jovanovich 1980)

Fudge J, 'Employee or Independent Contractor? Charting the Legal Significance of the Distinction in Canada' (2002) 10 Can Lab & Emp L J 193

Fudge J, 'Fragmenting Work and Fragmenting Organizations: The Contract of Employment and the Scope of Labour Regulation' (2006) 44 Osgoode Hall L J 609

Fudge J, 'The New Discourse of Labor Rights: From Social to Fundamental Rights?' (2007) 29 CLLPJ 29

Fudge J, 'A Canadian Perspective on the Scope of Employment Standards, Labor Rights, and Social Protection: The Good, the Bad, and the Ugly' (2010) 31 CLLPJ 253

Fudge J, 'Labour as a 'Fictive Commodity': Radically Reconceptualizing Labour Law' in Davidov G and Langille B (eds), *The Idea of Labour Law* (OUP 2011) 120

Fuller LL and Perdue WR Jr, 'The Reliance Interest in Contract Damages: 1' (1936) 46 Yale L J 52

Funk L, 'Survey finds that Statutory Protection against Dismissal Hurts Small Firms' 2003 EIROnline 6 <www.eiro.eurofound.eu.int/2003/06/feature/de0306108f.html>

Galanter M, 'Why the "Haves" Come Out Ahead: Speculations on the Limits of Legal Change' (1974) 9 Law and Society Review 95

Galbraith JK, *American Capitalism: The Concept of Countervailing Power* (Houghton Mifflin Co. 1956)

Gallie D et al, *Restructuring the Employment Relationship* (Clarendon 1998) 3

Gerards J, 'How to Improve the Necessity Test of the European Court of Human Rights' (2013) 11 I-CON 466

Germain CM, 'Approaches to Statutory Interpretation and Legislative History in France' (2003) 13 Duke J Comp & Int'l L 195

Glasbeek HJ, 'Voluntarism, Liberalism, and Grievance Arbitration: Holy Grail, Romance, and Real Life' in Geoffrey England (ed), *Essays in Labour Relations Law* (CCH Canadian Ltd 1986) 57

Godard J, 'The Exceptional Decline of the American Labor Movement' (2009–2010) 63 Indus & Lab Rel Rev 82

Goldin A, 'Global Conceptualizations and Local Constructions of the Idea of Labour Law' in Davidov G and Langille B (eds), *The Idea of Labour Law* (OUP 2011) 69

Goldstein B and others, 'Enforcing Fair Labor Standards in the Modern American Sweatshop: Rediscovering the Statutory Definition of Employment' (1999) 46 UCLA L Rev 983

Goodin RE, 'Enfranchising all Affected Interests, and Its Alternatives' (2007) 35 Phil & Pub Aff 41

Goodin RE and Barry C, 'Benefiting from the Wrong-doing of Others' (2014) 31 Journal of Applied Philosophy 363

Goodman J, *Employment Relations in Industrial Society* (Philip Allan 1984)

Gordon J and Lenhardt RA, 'Rethinking Work and Citizenship' (2008) 55 UCLA L Rev 1161

Gottlieb Taras D and Ponak A, 'Mandatory Agency Shop Laws as an Explanation of Canada–U.S. Union Density Divergence' (2001) 22 J of Labor Research 541

Greenawalt K, 'Free Speech Justifications' (1989) 89 Colum L Rev 119

Greenawalt K, 'Constitutional and Statutory Interpretation' in Coleman J and Shapiro S (eds), *The Oxford Handbook of Jurisprudence and Philosophy of Law* (OUP 2002) 268

Gunderson M and Hyatt D, 'Workplace Risks and Wages: Canadian Evidence from Alternative Models' (2001) 34 Canadian Journal of Economics 377

Haines F, *Corporate Regulation: Beyond 'Punish or Persuade'* (Clarendon 1997) 235

Hamermesh DS, 'Myth and Measurement: The New Economics of the Minimum Wage (Book Review)' (1995) 48 Indus & Lab Rel Rev 835
Hanks JL, 'Franchisor Liability for the Torts of Its Franchisees: The Case for Substituting Liability as a Guarantor for the Current Vicarious Liability' (1999) 24 Okla City U L Rev 1
Hansmann H, 'When Does Worker Ownership Work? ESOPs, Law Firms, Codetermination, and Economic Democracy' (1990) 99 Yale L J 1749
Hardy T and Howe J, 'Too Soft or too Severe? Enforceable Undertakings and the Regulatory Dilemma Facing the Fair Work Ombudsman' (2013) 41 Federal Law Review 1
Harpaz I, *The Meaning of Work in Israel: Its Nature and Consequences* (Praeger 1990)
Harper MC, 'Defining the Economic Relationship Appropriate for Collective Bargaining' (1998) 39 Boston College L Rev 329
Harrison JL, 'The "New" Terminable-at-Will Employment Contract: An Interest and Cost Incidence Analysis' (1984) 69 Iowa L Rev 327
Hart HM Jr and Sacks AM, *The Legal Process: Basic Problems in the Making and Application of Law* (Foundation Press 1994)
Hathaway O and Shapiro SJ, 'Outcasting: Enforcement in Domestic and International Law' (2011) 121 Yale L J 252
Hatton TJ, 'Trade Boards and Minimum Wages, 1909–39' (1997) 17 Economic Affairs 22
Hayter S, 'Introduction' in Hayter S (ed), *The Role of Collective Bargaining in the Global Economy* (Edward Elgar 2011) 1
Hendrickx F, 'Foundations and Functions of Contemporary Labour Law' (2012) 3 ELLJ 108
Hepple B, 'Agency Enforcement of Workplace Equality' in Dickens L (ed), *Making Employment Rights Effective* (Hart 2012) 49
Hirsch BT, 'Firm Investment Behavior and Collective Bargaining Strategy' (1992) 31 Industrial Relations 95
Hirsch BT, 'What Do Unions Do For Economic Performance?' (2004) 25 Journal of Labor Research 415
Hirsch BT and Addison JT, *The Economic Analysis of Unions: New Approaches and Evidence* (Allen & Unwin 1986)
Hirsch BT and Link AN, 'Labor Union Effects on Innovative Activity' (1987) 8 Journal of Labor Research 323
Hirsch BT, Kaufman BE, and Zelenska T, 'Minimum Wage Channels of Adjustment' (2011) IZA Discussion Paper No 6132 <http://www.econstor.eu/bitstream/10419/58927/1/690181728.pdf>
Hirsch JM, 'The Law of Termination: Doing More with Less' (2008) 68 Md L Rev 89
Hirsch JM and Estreicher S (eds), *Compensation, Work Hours and Benefits* (Kluwer 2009)
Hirschman AO, *Exit, Voice, and Loyalty* (Harvard UP 1971)
Holcombe AN, 'The Legal Minimum Wage in the US' (1912) 2 Am Econ Rev 21
Horvart B, *The Political Economy of Socialism: A Marxist Social Theory* (ME Sharpe 1982) 447
Houseman SN, 'Why Employers Use Flexible Staffing Arrangements: Evidence from an Establishment Survey' (2000) Upjohn Institute Staff Working Paper <http://research.upjohn.org/cgi/viewcontent.cgi?article=1084&context=up_workingpapers>
Howe John, 'The Broad Idea of Labour Law: Industrial Policy, Labour Market Regulation, and Decent Work' in Davidov G and Langille B (eds), *The Idea of Labour Law* (OUP 2011) 295

Howe John, Hardy T, and Cooney S, 'Mandate, Discretion, and Professionalisation in an Employment Standards Enforcement Agency: An Antipodean Experience' (2012) 35 Law & Policy 81

Howe Joanna, 'Poles Apart? The Contestation between the Ideas of No Fault Dismissal and Unfair Dismissal for Protecting Job Security' (2013) 42 ILJ 122

Hutchinson H, 'Toward a Critical Race Reformist Conception of Minimum Wage Regimes: Exploding the Power of Myth, Fantasy, and Hierarchy' (1997) 34 Harv J on Legis 93

Hutt WH, *The Strike-Threat System: The Economic Consequences of Collective Bargaining* (Arlington House 1973)

Hyde A, 'What is Labour Law?' in Davidov G and Langille B (eds), *Boundaries and Frontiers of Labour Law: Goals and Means in the Regulation of Work* (Hart 2006) 37

Hyde A, 'The Idea of the Idea of Labour Law: A Parable' in Davidov G and Langille B (eds), *The Idea of Labour Law* (OUP 2011) 88

Hyde A, 'Legal Responsibility for Labour Conditions down the Production Chain' in Fudge J, McCrystal S, and Sankaran K (eds), *Challenging the Legal Boundaries of Work Regulation* (Hart 2012) 83

Hyman R, *Marxism and the Sociology of Trade Unionism* (Pluto Press 1973)

Hyman R, 'A Critical View of Industrial Democracy Schemes' in England G and Lerner G (eds), *Essays in Collective Bargaining and Industrial Democracy: Papers presented at the Conference on Collective Bargaining, School of Management, University of Lethbridge, September 9–23 1982* (CCH Canadian 1983) 107

Ichino A and Riphahn RT, 'The Effect of Employment Protection on Worker Effort: A Comparison of Absenteeism During and After Probation' (2004) IZA Discussion Paper No 385 <www.iue.it/Personal/Ichino/short44.pdf>

ILO, *Minimum Wage-Fixing Machinery: An International Study of Legislation and Practice* (1927)

ILO, *World Labour Report 1997/98: Industrial Relations, Democracy and Social Stability* (1998)

ILO, International Labour Conference (86th Session) Report V (2B) Addendum: Committee on Contract Labour (Geneva June 1998)

ILO, *Your Voice At Work: Global report under the follow-up to the ILO Declaration on fundamental principles and rights at work. Report of the Director-General* (2000) <http://www.ilo.org/wcmsp5/groups/public/@dgreports/@dcomm/@publ/documents/publication/wcms_publ_9221115046_en.pdf>

ILO, International Labour Conference (91st Session) Report V: The Scope of the Employment Relationship (2003)

ILO, 'Strategies and Practice for Labour Inspection' (Report of the Committee on Employment and Social Policy to the Governing Body, 297th Session, 2006)

ILO, 'Collective Bargaining and the Decent Work Agenda' (Committee on Employment and Social Policy 300th Session GB.300/ESP/1, November 2007) <http://www.ilo.org/wcmsp5/groups/public/---ed_norm/---relconf/documents/meetingdocument/wcms_084557.pdf>

ILO, 'The Employment Relationship: An Annotated Guide to ILO Recommendation No. 198' (2007) 27 <http://www.ilo.org/wcmsp5/groups/public/@ed_dialogue/@dialogue/documents/genericdocument/wcms_172417.pdf>

ILO, 'Regulating the Employment Relationship in Europe: A Guide to Recommendation No. 198' (2013) <www.ilo.org/wcmsp5/groups/public/---ed_dialogue/---dialogue/documents/publication/wcms_209280.pdf>

Ingram JD, 'Covenants Not to Compete' (2002) 36 Akron L Rev 49

Iverson RD and Currivan DB, 'Union Participation, Job Satisfaction, and Employee Turnover' (2003) 42 Indus Rel 101

Jacoby SM, 'Are Career Jobs Headed for Distinction?' (1999) 42(1) California Management Review 123

Jonsson E, 'Labour as Risk-Bearer' (1978) 2 Camb J Econ 373, 375

Kagan RA, Gunningham N, and Thornton D, 'Fear, Duty, and Regulatory Compliance: Lessons from Three Research Projects' in Parker Cand, Lehmann Nielsen V (eds), *Explaining Compliance: Business Responses to Regulation* (Edward Elgar 2011) 37

Kahn-Freund O, 'On Uses and Misuses of Comparative Law' (1974) 37 MLR 1

Kamiat W, 'Labor and Lemons: Efficient Norms in the Internal Labor Market and the Possible Failures of Individual Contracting' (1996) 144 U Pa L Rev 1953

Kaplow L, 'Rules versus Standards: An Economic Analysis' (1992) 42 Duke L J 577

Kaplow, L and Shavell S, 'Why the Legal System is Less Efficient than the Income Tax in Redistributing Income' (1994) 23 JLS 667

Kates B, 'The Supply Chain Gang: Enforcing the Employment Rights of Subcontracted Labour in Ontario' (2012) 16 Can Lab & Emp L J 449

Kaufman BE, 'Labor's Inequality of Bargaining Power: Changes over Time and Implications for Public Policy' (1989) 10 Journal of Labour Research 285

Kaufman BE, 'Labor's Inequality of Bargaining Power: Myth or Reality?' (1991) 12 Journal of Labour Research 151

Kaufman BE, 'The Evolution of Thought on the Competitive Nature of Labor Markets' in Kerr C and Staudohar PD (eds), *Labor Economics and Industrial Relations: Markets and Institutions* (Harvard UP 1994) 145

Kaufman BE, 'The Impossibility of a Perfectly Competitive Labour Market' (2007) 31 Camb J Econ 775

Kaufman BE, 'Promoting Labour Market Efficiency and Fairness through a Legal Minimum Wage: The Webbs and the Social Cost of Labour' (2009) 47 British Journal of Industrial Relations 306

Kaufman BE, 'Institutional Economics and the Minimum Wage: Broadening the Theoretical and Policy Debate' (2010) 63 Indus & Lab Rel Rev 427

Kaufman BE, 'Economic Analysis of Labor Markets and Labour Law: An Institutional/Industrial Relations Perspective' in Estlund CL and Wachter ML (eds), *Research Handbook on the Economics of Labor and Employment Law* (Edward Elgar 2012) 52

Keefe JH, 'Do Unions Hinder Technological Change?' in Mishel L and Voos PB (eds), *Unions and Economic Competitiveness* (ME Sharpe 1992) 109

Kennedy D, 'Form and Substance in Private Law Adjudication' (1976) 89 Harv L Rev 1685

Kershaw D, 'No End in Sight for the History of Corporate Law: The Case of Employee Participation in Corporate Governance' (2002) 2 J Corporate Law Studies 34

Kim PT, 'Bargaining with Imperfect Information: A Study of Worker Perceptions of Legal Protection in an at-Will World' (1997) 83 Cornell L Rev 105

Klare KE, 'Labor Law as Ideology: Toward a New Historiography of Collective Bargaining Law' (1981) 4 IRLJ 450

Klare KE, 'Workplace Democracy and Market Reconstruction: An Agenda for Legal Reform' (1988) 38 Cath U L Rev 1

Klare KE, 'Countervailing Workers' Power as a Regulatory Strategy' in Collins H et al (eds), *Legal Regulation of the Employment Relation* (Kluwer 2000)

Knight FH, *Risk, Uncertainty and Profit* (Houghton Mifflin Co 1921)

Kohn ML and Schooler C, *Work and Personality: An Inquiry into the Impact of Social Stratification* (Ablex Pub Corp 1983)
Kolben K, 'Labor Rights as Human Rights?' (2010) 50 Va J Int'l L 449
Krawiec KD, 'Cosmetic Compliance and the Failure of Negotiated Governance' (2003) 81 Washington University Law Quarterly 487
Kronman AT, 'Contract Law and Distributive Justice' (1980) 89 Yale L J 472
Kugler AD and Saint-Paul G, 'How do Firing Costs Affect Worker Flows in a World with Adverse Selection?' (2004) 22 Journal of Labor Economics 553
Kuhn P, 'Unions and the Economy: What We Know; What We Should Know' (1998) 31 Canadian Journal of Economics 1033
Kymlicka W, *Contemporary Political Philosophy: An Introduction* (OUP 1990)
La Torre M, Pattaro E and Taruffo M, 'Statutory Interpretation in Italy' in MacCormick N and Summers R (eds), *Interpreting Statutes: A Comparative Study* (Dartmouth 1991) 213
Lambropoulos V, *Rethinking the Employer's Summary Dismissal Power in the Employment Contract* (PhD thesis, Deakin University, Australia, June 2015)
Lamont J, 'The Concept of Desert in Distributive Justice' (1994) 44 The Philosophical Quarterly 45
Lane RE, *The Market Experience* (Cambridge UP 1991)
Langille BA, 'General Reflections on the Relationship of Trade and Labor (Or: Fair Trade is Free Trade's Destiny)' in Bhagwati J and Hudec RE (eds), *Fair Trade and Harmonization (Vol. 2): Legal Analysis* (MIT Press 1996) 231
Langille BA, 'Freedom of Association and the Effective Recognition of the Right to Collective Bargaining: A Reflection upon Our Fundamental Commitments' (a paper prepared for the ILO, 1999)
Langille BA, 'Labour Law's Back Pages' in Davidov G and Langille B (eds), *Boundaries and Frontiers of Labour Law: Goals and Means in the Regulation of Work* (Hart 2006) 13
Langille BA, 'The Freedom of Association Mess: How We Got into It and How We Can Get out of It' (2009) 54 McGill L J 177
Langille BA, 'Why Are Canadian Judges Drafting Labour Codes—and Constitutionalizing The Wagner Model?' (2009–2010)' 15 Can Lab & Emp L J 101
Langille BA, 'Labour Law's Theory of Justice' in Davidov G and Langille B (eds), *The Idea of Labour Law* (OUP 2011) 101
Langille BA, 'A Question of Balance in the Legal Construction of Personal Work Relations' (2013) 7 Jerusalem Rev of Leg Studies 99
Langille BA, ' "Take These Chains from My Heart and Set Me Free": How Labor Law Theory Drives Segmentation of Workers' Rights' (2015) 36 CLLPJ 257
Langille BA and Alon-Shenker P, 'Law Firm Partners and the Scope of Labour Law' (2015) 4 Can J Hum Rts 211
Langille BA and Davidov G, 'Beyond Employee and Independent Contractors: A View from Canada' (1999) 21 CLLPJ 6
Leighton P and Wynn M, 'Classifying Employment Relationships: More Sliding Doors or a Better Regulatory Framework?' (2011) 40 ILJ 5
Lemieux T, 'Unions and Wage Inequality in Canada and the United States' in Card D and Freeman RB (eds), *Small Differences That Matter: Labor Markets and Income Maintenance in Canada and the United States* (University of Chicago Press 1993) 69
Lemieux T and Riddell CW, 'Unions and Wage Inequality' (2004) 25 Journal of Labor Research 519
Lemos S, 'A Survey of the Effects of the Minimum Wage on Prices' (2008) 22 Journal of Economic Surveys 187

Leonard AS, 'A New Common Law of Employment Termination' (1988) 66 North Carolina L Rev 631
Lester G, 'Beyond Collective Bargaining: Modern Unions as Agents of Social Solidarity' in Davidov G and Langille B (eds), *The Idea of Labour Law* (OUP 2011) 329
Lester G, 'Can Joe the Plumber Support Redistribution? Law, Social Preferences, and Sustainable Policy Design' (2011) 64 Tax L Rev 313
Lester RA, 'Shortcoming of Marginal Analysis for Wage-Employment Problems' (1946) 36 Am Econ Rev 63
Levine P, 'The Legitimacy of Labor Unions' (2001) 18 Hofstra Lab & Emp L J 529
Levitan SA and Belous RS, *More Than Subsistence: Minimum Wages for the Working Poor* (Johns Hopkins University 1979)
Lewinson-Zamir D, 'In Defense of Redistribution through Private Law' (2006) 91 Minn L Rev 326
Libenson DJ, 'Leasing Human Capital: Toward a New Foundation for Employment Termination Law' (2006) 27 Berkeley J Emp & Lab L 111
Lindbeck A and Snower DJ, *The Insider-Outsider Theory of Employment and Unemployment* (MIT Press 1988)
Linder M, *The Employment Relationship in Anglo-American Law: A Historical Perspective* (Greenwood Press 1989)
Linder M, *Farewell to the Self-Employed: Deconstructing a Socioeconomic and Legal Solipsism* (Greenwood Press 1992)
Linder M, *Migrant Workers and Minimum Wages: Regulating the Exploitation of Agricultural Labor in the US* (Westview Press 1992)
Linder M, 'Dependent and Independent Contractors in Recent U.S. Labor Law: An Ambiguous Dichotomy Rooted in Simulated Statutory Purposelessness' (1999) 21 CLLPJ 187
Lobel O, 'The Renew Deal: The Fall of Regulation and the Rise of Governance in Contemporary Legal Thought' (2004) 89 Minnesota L Rev 342
Low Pay Commission, 'The National Minimum Wage: First Report by the Low Pay Commission (1998)' <http://www.berr.gov.uk/files/file37987.pdf > accessed 28 July 2014
Low Pay Commission, 'The National Minimum Wage: The Story So Far' (2000) <http://webarchive.nationalarchives.gov.uk/20130626202215/http://www.lowpay.gov.uk/lowpay/report/pdf/complete.pdf>
Low Pay Commission, 'National Minimum Wage: Low Pay Commission Report 2006' <https://www.gov.uk/government/uploads/system/uploads/attachment_data/file/273274/6759.pdf>
Low Pay Commission, 'National Minimum Wage: Low Pay Commission Report 2015' <https://www.gov.uk/government/uploads/system/uploads/attachment_data/file/413415/The_National_Minimum_Wage_Low_Pay_Commission_Report_2015.pd>
Macaulay S, 'Non-Contractual Relations in Business: A Preliminary Study' (1963) 28 Am Soc Rev 55
Machin S and Manning A, 'The Effects of Minimum Wages on Wage Dispersion and Employment: Evidence from the U.K. Wages Councils' (1994) 47 Indus & Lab Rel Rev 319
Machin S and Manning A, 'Employment and the Introduction of a Minimum Wage in Britain' (1996) 106 The Economic Journal 667
Machin S and Manning A, 'Minimum Wages and Economic Outcomes in Europe' (1997) 41 European Economic Review 733

Machlup F, *The Political Economy of Monopoly: Business, Labor and Government Policies* (Johns Hopkins Press 1952)

Macneil IR, *The New Social Contract: An Inquiry into Modern Contractual Relations* (Yale UP 1980)

Maconachie G and Goodwin M, 'Recouping Wage Underpayment: Increasingly Less Likely?' (2006) 41 Australian Journal of Social Issues 327

Malin MH, 'The Distributive and Corrective Justice Concerns in the Debate over Employment at Will: Some Preliminary Thoughts' (1992) 68 Chi-Kent L Rev 117

Manning A, *Monopsony in Motion: Imperfect Competition in Labor Markets* (Princeton UP 2003)

Mantouvalou V, 'Human Rights and Unfair Dismissal: Private Acts in Public Spaces' (2008) 71 Modern Law Review 912

Mantouvalou V, 'Are Labour Rights Human Rights?' (2012) 3 ELLJ 151

Mantouvalou V, 'Democratic Theory and Voices at Work' in Bogg A and Novitz T (eds), *Voices at Work: Continuity and Change in the Common Law World* (OUP 2014) 214

Mares R, 'Responsibility to Respect: Why the Core Company Should Act When Affiliates Infringe Human Rights' in Mares R (ed), *The UN Guiding Principles on Business and Human Rights—Foundations and Implementation* (2012) 169

Margalioth SR, 'Regulating Individual Employment Contracts Through Good Faith Duties' (2011) 32 CLLPJ 663

Marginson P, 'Power and Efficiency in the Firm: Understanding the Employment Relationship' in Pitelis C (ed), *Transaction Costs, Markets and Hierarchies* (Blackwell 1993) 133

Marglin SA, 'What Do Bosses Do? The Origins and Functions of Hierarchy in Capitalist Production' (1974) 6(2) Review of Radical Political Economics 60

Marmor A, *Interpretation and Legal Theory* (2nd edn, Hart 2005)

Marshall S, 'Regulating Work in Complex Apparel Supply Chains: New Models' <http://papers.ssrn.com/sol3/papers.cfm?abstract_id=2524253>

Marshall TH, 'Work and Wealth' in Marshall TH, *Class, Citizenship, and Social Development* (Anchor Books 1965) 230

Marx K, *Capital: A Critical Analysis of Capitalist Production* (14th edn, William Glaisher 1912)

Marx K, *Capital: A Critique of Political Economy*, vol I (first published 1867, Penguin 1976)

McCaffrey FJ, 'The Rule in Pari Materia as an Aid to Statutory Construction' (1949) 3 Law & L Notes 11

McCallum R, 'In Defence of Labour Law' (2007) University of Sydney Legal Studies Research Paper 07/20, 8 <http://ssrn.com/abstract=985006>

McClelland J, 'A Purposive Approach to Employment Protection or a Missed Opportunity?' (2012) 75 MLR 427

McCrudden C, *Buying Social Justice: Equality, Government Procurement, and Legal Change* (OUP 2007)

McCrudden C, 'Two Views of Subordination: The Personal Scope of Employment Discrimination Law in *Jivraj v Hashwani*' (2012) 41 ILJ 30

McCrudden C (ed), *Understanding Human Dignity* (OUP 2013)

McCrystal S, 'Organising Independent Contractors: The Impact of Competition Law' in Fudge J, McCrystal S and Sankaran K (eds), *Challenging the Legal Boundaries of Work Regulation* (Hart 2012) 139

McCrystal S, 'Collective Bargaining Beyond the Boundaries of Employment: A Comparative Analysis' (2014) 37 Melbourne U L Rev 662

McKendrick E, 'Vicarious Liability and Independent Contractors: A Re-Examination' (1990) 53 MLR 770

Menezes-Filho N, Ulph D, and Van Reenen J, 'R&D and Unionism: Comparative Evidence from British Companies and Establishments' (1998) 52 Indus & Lab Rel Rev 45

Metcalf D, 'Why has the British National Minimum Wage had Little or No Impact on Employment?' (2008) 50 JIR 489

Milgrom P and Roberts J, *Economics, Organization, and Management* (Prentice-Hall 1992)

Mill JS, *Principles of Political Economy with some of their applications to social philosophy* (William J Ashley ed, first published 1848, A M Kelley 1961)

Minkler M et al, 'Wage Theft as a Neglected Public Health Problem: An Overview and Case Study from San Francisco's Chinatown District' (2014) 104 Amer J of Public Health 1010

Mishel L, 'Unions, Inequality, and Faltering Middle-Class Wages' (2012) Economic Policy Institute Issue Brief No. 342

Mitchell R, 'Where Are We Going in Labour Law? Some Thoughts on a Field of Scholarship and Policy in Process of Change' (2011) 24 Aus J of Lab Law 45

Mitchell R and Arup C, 'Labour Law and Labour Market Regulation' in Arup C et al (eds), *Labour Law and Labour Market Regulation* (Federation Press 2006) 3

Mkandawire T, 'Targeting and Universalism in Poverty Reduction' (Social Policy and Development Programme Paper No 23, UN Research Institute for Social Development 2005)

Morikawa M, 'Labor Unions and Productivity: An Empirical Analysis using Japanese Firm-Level Data' (2010) 17 Lab Econ 1030

MOW International Research Team, *The Meaning of Working* (Academic Press 1987)

Mummé Cl, '*Bhasin v. Hrynew*: A New Era For Good Faith in Canadian Employment Law, or Just Tinkering at the Margins?' (2016) 32 IJCLLIR 117

Mundlak G, 'Information-Forcing and Cooperation-Inducing Rules: Rethinking the Building Blocks of Labour Law' in De Geest G, Siegers J, and van den Bergh R (eds), *Law and Economics and the Labour Market* (Edward Elgar 1999) 55

Mundlak G, 'Human Rights and the Employment Relationship: A Look through the Prism of Juridification' in Friedmann D and Barak-Erez D (eds), *Human Rights In Private Law* (Hart 2001) 297

Mundlak G, *Fading Corporatism: Israel's Labour Law and Industrial Relations in Transition* (Cornell UP 2007)

Mundlak G, 'The Third Function of Labour Law: Distributing Labour Market Opportunities among Workers' in Davidov G and Langille B (eds), *The Idea of Labour Law* (OUP 2011) 315

Neumark D and Wascher W, 'Reconciling the Evidence on Employment Effects of Minimum Wages—A Review of Our Research Findings' in Kosters MH (ed), *The Effects of the Minimum Wage on Employment* (AEI Press 1996) 55

Neumark D and Wascher W, 'Minimum Wages And Employment: A Review Of Evidence From the New Minimum Wage Research' (2008) NBER Working Paper No 12663 <http://www.nber.org/papers/w12663.pdf>

Novitz T and Fenwick C, 'The Application of Human Rights Discourse to Labour Relations: Translation of Theory into Practice' in Fenwick C and Novitz T (eds), *Human Rights at Work: Perspectives on Law and Regulation* (Hart 2010) 1

Nozick R, *Anarchy, State, and Utopia* (Basic Books 1974)

O'Boyle EJ, 'The Need for Work as Such: Self-Expression and Belonging' in Davis JB and O'Boyle EJ (eds), *The Social Economics of Human Material Need* (Southern Illinois University 1994) 116

O'Brien GE, 'Changing Meaning of Work' in Hartley JF and Stephenson GM (eds), *Employment Relations: The Psychology of Influence and Control at Work* (Blackwell 1992) 44

OECD, *Employment Outlook June 1998* (OECD Publishing 1998)

OECD, *Employment Outlook June 1999* (OECD Publishing 1999)

OECD, *Employment Outlook 2004* (OECD Publishing 2004) <www.oecd.org/dataoecd/8/4/34846856.pdf>

OECD, *Employment Outlook 2013* <http://www.oecd-ilibrary.org/employment/oecd-employment-outlook-2013_empl_outlook-2013-en>

OECD, *Employment Outlook 2014* <http://www.oecd-ilibrary.org/employment/oecd-employment-outlook-2014_empl_outlook-2014-en;jsessionid=fo13dthqolf0p.x-oecd-live-03>

Offe C, 'The Political Economy of the Labour Market' in Offe C, *Disorganized Capitalism: Contemporary Transformations of Work and Politics* (John Keane ed, MIT Press 1985) 10

O'Higgins P, 'Labour is Not a Commodity—An Irish Contribution to International Labour Law' (1997) 26 ILJ 225

O'Higgins P, 'The End of Labour Law as We Have Known It?' in Barnard C, Deakin S, and Morris GS (eds), *The Future of Labour Law: Liber Amicorum Bob Hepple* (Hart 2004) 289

Okun AM, *Equality and Efficiency: The Big Tradeoff* (Brookings Institution 1975)

O'Rourke D, 'Outsourcing Regulation: Analyzing Nongovernmental Systems of Labor Standards and Monitoring' (2003) 31 The Policy Studies Journal 1

Parchomovsky G and Stein A, 'Catalogs' (2015) 115 Columbia L Rev 165

Parsons DO, *Poverty and the Minimum Wage* (American Enterprise Institute for Public Policy Research 1980)

Patmore G, 'Happiness as an Objective of Labour Law' (2010) CELRL working paper 48

Pedersini R and Coletto D, *Self-Employed Workers: Industrial Relations and Working Conditions* (Dublin: European Foundation for the Improvement of Living and Working Conditions 2010)

Pencavel JH, *Labor Markets under Trade Unionism: Employment, Wages, and Hours* (Blackwell 1991)

Pereiro JC, 'The Status of Self-Employed Workers in Spain' (2008) 147 ILR 91

Phillips MJ, 'Toward a Middle Way in the Polarized Debate Over Employment at Will' (1992) 30 Am Bus L J 441

Piore MJ, 'Flexible Bureaucracies in Labour Market Regulation' in Davidov G and Langille B (eds), *The Idea of Labour Law* (OUP 2011) 385

Piore MJ and Schrank A, 'Toward Managed Flexibility: The Revival of Labour Inspection in the Latin World' (2008) 147 International Labour Review 1

Pohler D and Luchak A, 'Are Unions Good or Bad for Organizations? The Moderating Role of Management's Response' (2015) 53 BJIR 423

Polanyi K, *The Great Transformation* (first published 1944, Beacon Press 1957)

Polinsky AM, 'Private versus Public Enforcement of Fines' (1980) 9 Journal of Legal Studies 105

Polinsky AM and Shavell S, 'The Theory of Public Enforcement of Law' in Polinsky AM and Shavell S (eds) *Handbook of Law and Economics: Vol 1* (Elsevier 2007) 403

Pollin R and Luce S, *The Living Wage: Building a Fair Economy* (New Press 1998)

Porter N, 'The Perfect Compromise: Bridging the Gap Between At-Will Employment and Just Cause' (2008) 87 Neb L Rev 62

Posner RA, 'Some Economics of Labor Law' (1984) 51 U Chi L Rev 988

Posner RA, 'Legal Formalism, Legal Realism, and the Interpretation of Statutes and the Constitution' (1986–87) 7 Case W Res L Rev 179

Posner RA, 'Hegel and Employment at Will: A Comment' (1989) 10 Cardozo L Rev 1625
Posner RA, *Economic Analysis of Law* (5th edn, Aspen Law & Business 1998)
Powell WW, 'Neither Market Nor Hierarchy: Network Forms of Organization' (1990) 12 Research in Organizational Behavior 295
Prasch RE and Sheth FA, 'The Economics and Ethics of Minimum Wage Legislation' (1999) 57 Review of Social Economy 466
Prassl J, 'The Notion of the Employer' (2013) 129 LQR 380
Prassl J, 'Employee Shareholder Status: Dismantling the Contract of Employment' (2013) 42 ILJ 307
Prassl J, *The Concept of the Employer* (OUP 2015)
Quinlan M, 'Contextual Factors Shaping the Purpose of Labour Law: A Comparative Historical Perspective' in Arup C et al (eds), *Labour Law and Labour Market Regulation* (Federation Press 2006) 22
Raday F, 'Individual and Collective Dismissals—a Job Security Dichotomy' (1989) 10 Comp Lab L J 121
Raday F, 'The Insider-Outsider Politics of Labor-Only Contracting' (1999) 20 CLLPJ 413
Radin MJ, *Contested Commodities* (HUP 1996) 108, ch 7
Randolph RA, 'Dictionaries, Plain Meaning, and Context in Statutory Interpretation' (1994) 17 Harv J L & Pub Pol'y 71
Rawling M and Howe J, 'The Regulation of Supply Chains: An Australian Contribution to Cross-National Legal Learning' in Stone KVW and Arthurs H (eds), *Rethinking Workplace Regulation: Beyond the Standard Contract of Employment* (Russell Sage Foundation 2013) 233
Rawls J, *A Theory of Justice* (Belknap Press of HUP 1971)
Raz J, *Between Authority and Interpretation* (OUP 2009)
Razzolini O, 'The Need to Go Beyond the Contract: "Economic" and "Bureaucratic" Dependence in Personal Work Relations' (2010) 31 CLLPJ 267
Reder MW, 'On Labor's Bargaining Disadvantage' in Kerr C and Staudohar PD (eds), *Labor Economics and Industrial Relations: Markets and Institutions* (Harvard UP 1994) 237
Reed MI, *The Sociology of Management* (Harvester Wheatsheaf 1989)
Reynold F and Hendy J, 'Reserving the Right to Change Terms and Conditions: How Far Can the Employer Go?' (2012) 41 ILJ 79
Riley J, *Employee Protection at Common Law* (Federation Press 2005)
Riley J, 'Siblings But Not Twins: Making Sense of "Mutual Trust" and "Good Faith" in Employment Contracts' (2012) 36 Melbourne University L Rev 521
Riley J, 'A Blurred Boundary between Entrepreneurship and Servitude: Regulating Business Format Franchising in Australia' in Fudge J, McCrystal S, and Sankaran K (eds), *Challenging the Legal Boundaries of Work Regulation* (Hart 2012) 101
Riley J, '"Mutual Trust and Confidence" On Trial: At Last' (2014) 36 Sydney L Rev 151
Rodgers L, 'Labour Law and Kantian Ideas of Legality and Citizenship' (2014) University of Leicester School of Law Research Paper No 14 <http://papers.ssrn.com/sol3/papers.cfm?abstract_id=2403498>
Rogers B, 'Toward Third-Party Liability for Wage Theft' (2010) 31 Berkeley J Emp & Lab L 1
Rogers B, 'Justice at Work: Minimum Wage Laws and Social Equality' (2014) 92 Texas L Rev 1543
Rogowski R, *Reflexive Labour Law in the World Society* (Edward Elgar 2013)
Rönnmar M, 'The Managerial Prerogative and the Employee's Obligation to Work: Comparative Perspectives on Functional Flexibility' (2006) 35 ILJ 56

Rosso BD, Dekas KH, and Wrzesniewski A, 'On The Meaning of Work: A Theoretical Integration and Review' (2010) 30 Research in Organizational Behavior 91
Routh S, *Enhancing Capabilities through Labour Law: Informal Workers in India* (Routledge 2014)
Rubinstein MH, 'Our Nation's Forgotten Workers: The Unprotected Volunteers' (2006) 9 U Penn J of Lab & Emp Law 1
Ryan JA, *A Living Wage: Its Ethical and Economic Aspects* (Macmillan 1906)
Sachs BI, 'Enabling Employee Choice: A Structural Approach to the Rules of Union Organizing' (2010) 123 Harv L Rev 655
Sanchirico CW, 'Taxes versus Legal Rules as Instruments for Equity: A More Equitable View' (2000) 29 JLS 797
Savarese J, 'Protecting at Will Employees Against Wrongful Discharge: The Duty to Terminate Only in Good Faith' (1980) 93 Harv L Rev 1816
Scalia A, *A Matter of Interpretation: Federal Courts and the Law* (Princeton UP 1997)
Schnabel C, 'Union Membership and Density: Some (Not So) Stylized Facts and Challenges' (2012) Diskussionspapiere No. 81, Universität Erlangen-Nürnberg, Lehrstuhl für Arbeitsmarkt- und Regionalpolitik <http://www.econstor.eu/bitstream/10419/66786/1/730117782.pdf>
Schomann K, Rogowski R, and Kruppe T, *Labour Market Efficiency in the European Union: Employment Protection and Fixed-Term Contracts* (Routledge 1998)
Schultz V, 'Life's Work' (2000) 100 Colum L Rev 1881
Schwab SJ, 'Life-Cycle Justice: Accommodating Just Cause and Employment at Will' (1993) 92 Mich L Rev 8
Schwarze J, *European Administrative Law* (Sweet & Maxwell 1992)
Secunda PM, 'Toward the Viability of State-based Legislation to Address Workplace Captive Audience Meetings in the United States' (2008) 29 CLLPJ 209
Selznick P, *Law, Society and Industrial Justice* (Russell Sage Foundation 1969)
Sen A, 'The Political Economy of Targeting' in van de Walle D and Nead K (eds), *Public Spending and the Poor: Theory and Evidence* (Johns Hopkins University Press 1995) 14
Sen A, *Development as Freedom* (OUP 1999)
Sengenberger W, 'Labour Standards: An Institutional Framework for Restructuring and Development' in Sengenberger W and Campbell D (eds), *Creating Economic Opportunities: The Role of Labour Standards in Industrial Restructuring* (International Institute for Labour Studies 1994) 5
Shamsuddin AFM, 'The Effect of Unionization on the Gender Earnings Gap in Canada: 1971–1981' (1996) 28 Applied Economics 1405
Shapiro I, *The State of Democratic Theory* (Princeton UP 2003)
Shemer-Begas R, *Employees' Rights in the Era of Corporate Governance* (PhD Dissertation submitted to the Hebrew University, September 2015)
Simpson B, 'Implementing the National Minimum Wage—the 1999 Regulations' (1999) 28 Industrial L J 171
Simpson B, 'The National Minimum Wage Five Years On: Reflection on Some General Issues' (2004) 33 ILJ 22
Skocpol T, 'Targeting within Universalism: Politically Viable Policies to Combat Poverty in the United States' in Jencks C and Peterson PE (eds), *The Urban Underclass* (Brookings Institution 1991) 411
Slater J, 'Homeland Security vs. Workers' Rights? What the Federal Government Should Learn from History and Experience, and Why' (2003–2004) 6 U Pa J Int'l Bus L 295
Smith A, *The Wealth of Nations* (Edwin Cannan ed, Methuen 1961) 169

Smith A, *An Inquiry into the Nature and Causes of the Wealth of Nations* (Kathryn Sutherland ed, first published 1776, OUP 1993)

Smith-Vidal S, 'France' (1999) 36 Bull Com Lab Rel 245

Solan LM, 'Linguistic Issues in Statutory Interpretation' in Tiersma PM and Solan LM (eds), *Oxford Handbook of Language and Law* (OUP 2012) 88

Solow RM, *The Labour Market as a Social Institution* (Blackwell Pub 1990)

Spector H, 'Philosophical Foundations of Labor Law' (2006) 33 Fla St U L Rev 1119

Sran G and Stanford J, 'Further Tests on the Link between Unionization, Unemployment and Employment: Finding from Canadian National and Provincial Data' (2009) 15 Just Labour: A Canadian Journal of Work and Society 29

St Antoine TJ, 'A Seed Germinates: Unjust Discharge Reform Heads Toward Full Flower' (1988) 67 Neb L Rev 56

St Antoine TJ, 'The Model Employment Termination Act: A Fair Compromise' (1994) 536 Annals Am Acad Pol & Soc Sci 93

Standing G, *Global Labour Flexibility: Seeking Distributive Justice* (Macmillan Press 1999)

Standing G, *The Precariat: The New Dangerous Class* (Bloomsbury Academic 2011)

Starr G, *Minimum Wage Fixing: An International Review of Practices and Problems* (ILO 1981)

State Comptroller of Israel, *Annual Report 58B for the Year 2007* (2008) <http://www.mevaker.gov.il> (Hebrew)

Stewart A, 'Good Faith: A Necessary Element in Australian Employment Law Good Faith and Fair Dealing in the Individual Employment Relationship' (2011) 32 CLLPJ 521

Stewart MB and Swaffield JK, 'The Other Margin: Do Minimum Wages Cause Working Hours Adjustments for Low-Wage Workers?' (2008) 75 Economica 148

Stigler GJ, 'The Economics of Minimum Wage Legislation' (1946) 36(3) Am Econ Rev 358

Stigler GJ, 'The Optimum Enforcement of Laws' (1970) 78 Journal of Political Economy 526

Stiglitz J, 'Democratic Development as the Fruits of Labor' (Keynote Address, Industrial Relations Research Association, Boston, January 2000) <http://www0.gsb.columbia.edu/faculty/jstiglitz/download/2000_Democratic_Development_KEYNOTE.pdf>

Stone KVW, 'Labor and the Corporate Structure: Changing Conceptions and Emerging Possibilities' (1988) 55 U Chi L Rev 73

Stone KVW, *From Widgets to Digits: Employment Regulation for the Changing Workplace* (Cambridge UP 2004)

Stone KVW, 'Revisiting the At-Will Doctrine: Imposed Terms, Implied Terms, and the Normative World of the Workplace' (2007) 36 ILJ 84

Stone KVW, 'The Decline in the Standard Employment Contract: A Review of the Evidence' in Stone KVW and Arthurs H (eds), *Rethinking Workplace Regulation: Beyond the Standard Contract of Employment* (Russell Sage Foundation 2013) 366

Stone KVW and Arthurs H (eds), *Rethinking Workplace Regulation: Beyond the Standard Contract of Employment* (Russell Sage Foundation 2013)

Storey J, 'The Means of Management Control' (1985) 19 Sociology 193

Storrie D, *Temporary Agency Work in the European Union* (European Foundation for the Improvement of Living and Working Conditions 2002)

Sturm SP, 'Second Generation Employment Discrimination: A Structural Approach' (2001) 101 Columbia L Rev 458

Sullivan KM, 'Foreword: The Justice of Rules and Standards' (1992) 106 Harv L Rev 22

Summers CW, 'Individual Protection against Unjust Dismissal: Time for a Statute' (1976) 62 Virginia L Rev 481

Summers RS, '"Good Faith" in General Contract Law and the Sales Provisions of the Uniform Commercial Code' (1968) 54 Virginia L Rev 195

Sunstein CR, 'Interpreting Statutes in the Regulation State' (1989) 103 Harv L Rev 405

Sunstein CR, *After the Rights Revolution: Reconceiving the Regulatory State* (Harvard UP 1990)

Sunstein CR, 'Problems with Rules' (1995) 83 California L Rev 953

Sunstein CR, 'Human Behavior and the Law of Work' (2001) 87 Virginia L Rev 205

Supiot A, 'Perspectives on Work: Introduction' (1996) 135 Int'l Lab Rev 603

Supiot A, *Beyond Employment: Changes in Work and the Future of Labour Law in Europe* (OUP 2001)

Sverko B and Vizek-Vidovic V, 'Studies of the Meaning of Work: Approaches, Models, and Some of the Findings' in Super DE and Sverko B, *Life Roles, Values, and Careers: International Findings of the Work Importance Study* (Jossey-Bass 1995) 3

Sykes AO, 'The Economics of Vicarious Liability' (1984) 93 Yale L J 1231

Tannenbaum AS, *Control in Organizations* (McGraw-Hill 1968)

Tausky C, 'Work is Desirable/Loathsome: Marx versus Freud' (1992) 19 Work and Occupations 3

Tawney RH, *The Establishment of Minimum Wages in the Chain Making Industry under the Trade Board Act of 1909* (Bell 1914)

Tawney RH, *The Establishment of Minimum Wages in the Tailoring Industry under the Trade Board Act of 1909* (Bell 1915)

Teichman D and Zamir E, 'Judicial Decisionmaking: A Behavioral Perspective' in Zamir E and Teichman D (eds), *The Oxford Handbook of Behavioral Economics and the Law* (OUP 2014) 664

Thaler RH and Sunstein CR, *Nudge: Improving Decisions About Health, Wealth, and Happiness* (Yale UP 2008)

Tilgher A, *Work: What it has Meant to Men through the Ages* (first published 1930, Arno Press 1977)

Torres ES, 'The Spanish Law on Dependent Self-Employed Workers: A New Evolution in Labor Law' (2010) 31 CLLPJ 231

Trebilcock MJ, *The Limits of Freedom of Contract* (Harvard UP 1993)

TUC Commission on Vulnerable Employment, *Hard Work, Hidden Lives* (2008) <www.vulnerableworkers.org.uk/files/CoVE_full_report.pdf>

Tucker E, 'The Constitutional Right to Bargain Collectively: The Ironies of Labour History in the Supreme Court of Canada' (2008) 61 Labour/Le Travail 151

Tucker E, 'Renorming Labour Law: Can We Escape Labour Law's Recurring Regulatory Dilemmas?' (2010) 39 ILJ 99

Tucker E, Fudge J, and Vosko L, 'Employee or Independent Contractor? Charting the Legal Significance of the Distinction in Canada' (2002) 10 Can Lab & Emp L J 193

Tzannatos Z and Aidt TS, 'Unions and Microeconomic Performance: A Look at what Matters for Economists (and Employers)' (2006) 145 Int'l Lab Rev 257

United States Government Accountability Office, *Fair Labor Standards Act: Better Use of Available Resources and Consistent Reporting Could Improve Compliance* (2008) <www.gao.gov/new.items/d08962t.pdf>

United States Government Accountability Office, *Wage and Hour Division's Complaint Intake and Investigative Processes Leave Low Wage Workers Vulnerable to Wage Theft* (2009) <www.gao.gov/new.items/d09458t.pdf>

Van Bever A, 'Open Norms and Employment Law's Foundations: A Legal Examination of Hidden Patterns in Employment Relationships' (2012) 2 European Labour Law Journal 173

Van Erp J, 'Naming and Shaming in Regulatory Enforcement' in Parker C and Lehmann Nielsen V (eds), *Explaining Compliance: Business Responses to Regulation* (Edward Elgar 2011) 322

Vega ML and Robert R, 'Labour Inspection Sanctions: Law and Practice of National Labour Inspection Systems' (ILO LAB/ADMIN working document no. 26, 2013)

Veneziani B, 'The Evolution of the Contract of Employment' in Hepple B (ed), *The Making of Labour Law in Europe: A Comparative Study of Nine Countries up to 1945* (Mansell 1986) 65

Venn D, 'Legislation, Collective Bargaining and Enforcement: Updating the OECD Employment Protection Indicators' (OECD Social, Employment and Migration Working Papers, No. 89, July 2009)

Verkerke JH, 'An Empirical Perspective on Indefinite Term Employment Contracts: Resolving the Just Cause Debate' (1995) 1995 Wis L Rev 837

Verkerke JH, 'Legal Ignorance and Information-Forcing Rules' (2015) 56 William & Mary L Rev 899

Vernon PV, *Mixed Jurisdictions Worldwide: The Third Legal Family* (2nd edn, Cambridge UP 2012)

Virtanen M et al, 'Temporary Employment and Health: A Review' (2005) 34 International Journal of Epidemiology 610

Vosko LF, *Temporary Work: The Gendered Rise of a Precarious Employment Relationship* (U of Toronto Press 2000)

Vosko LF, *Managing the Margins: Gender, Citizenship, and the International Regulation of Precarious Employment* (OUP 2010)

Vosko LF, Grundy J, and Thomas MP, 'Challenging New Governance: Evaluating New Approaches to Employment Standards Enforcement in Common Law Jurisdictions' (forthcoming) Economic and Industrial Democracy

Vosko LF, Tucker E, Thomas MP, and Gellatly M, *New Approaches to Enforcement and Compliance with Labour Regulatory Standards: The Case of Ontario, Canada* (A Report for the Law Commission of Ontario, November 2011) <http://papers.ssrn.com/sol3/papers.cfm?abstract_id=1975867>

Waas B, 'Good Faith in the Law of the Employment Relationship: Germany' (2011) 32 CLLPJ 603

Waltman J, *The Politics of the Minimum Wage* (U of Illinois Press 2000)

Walton RE and McKersie RB, *A Behavioral Theory of Labor Negotiations* (McGraw-Hill 1965)

Watson D, 'U.K. Wage Underpayment: Implications for the Minimum Wage' (2000) 32 Applied Economics 429

Webb S and Webb B, *Industrial Democracy* (first published 1897, Longmans, Green and Co 1926)

Weber M, *The Theory of Social and Economic Organization* (AM Henderson and Talcott Parsons tr, Talcott Parsons ed, Free Press 1964)

Weber M, *Economy and Society* (Guenther Roth and Claus Wittich eds, University of California Press 1978)

Weil D, 'Individual Rights and Collective Agents: The Role of Old and New Workplace Institutions in the Regulation of Labor Markets' in Freeman RB, Hersch J, and Mishel L (eds), *Emerging Labor Market Institutions for the Twenty-First Century* (University of Chicago Press 2005) 13

Weil D, 'Public Enforcement/Private Monitoring: Evaluating a New Approach to Regulating the Minimum Wage' (2005) 58 Industrial and Labor Relations Review 238

Weil D, 'Crafting a Progressive Workplace Regulatory Policy: Why Enforcement Matters' (2007) 28 CLLPJ 125

Weil D, *The Fissured Workplace: Why Work Became So Bad for So Many and What Can Be Done to Improve It* (Harvard UP 2014)

Weil D and Mallo C, 'Regulating Labour Standards via Supply Chains: Combining Public/Private Interventions to Improve Workplace Compliance' (2007) 45 BJIR 791

Weil D and Pyles A, 'Why Complain? Complaints, Compliance and the Problem of Enforcement in the U.S. Workplace' (2007) 27 Comp Lab Law & Pol'y J 59

Weiler PC, *Reconcilable Differences: New Directions in Canadian Labour Law* (Carswell 1980)

Weiler PC, 'Promises to Keep: Securing Workers' Rights under the NLRA' (1983) 96 Harv L Rev 1769

Weiler, PC, *Governing the Workplace: The Future of Labour and Employment Law* (Harvard UP 1990)

Weiss M, 'Industrial Action, Collective Bargaining and Trade Union Rights: Examples of Judge-made Law in Germany' (2011) paper presented at the Hebrew University

Weiss M, 'Re-Inventing Labour Law?' in Davidov G and Langille B (eds), *The Idea of Labour Law* (OUP 2011) 44

Weiss M and Schmidt M, *Labour Law and Industrial Relations in Germany* (4th revised edn, Kluwer 2008)

Wellington AJ, 'Effects of the Minimum Wage on the Employment Status of Youths: An Update' (1991) 26 Journal of Human Resources 27

Western B and Rosenfeld J, 'Unions, Norms, and the Rise in U.S. Wage Inequality' (2011) 76 American Sociological Review 513

Wilkinson TM, 'The Ethics and Economics of the Minimum Wage' (2004) 20 Econ & Phil 351

Willborn SL, 'Individual Employment Rights and the Standard Economic Objection: Theory and Empiricism' (1988) 67 Neb L Rev 101

Williams N and Mills JA, 'The Minimum Wage and Teenage Employment: Evidence from Time Series' (2001) 33 Applied Economics 285

Williamson OE, *Markets and Hierarchies: Analysis and Antitrust Implications* (Free Press 1975)

Williamson OE, 'Transaction-Cost Economics: The Governance of Contractual Relations' (1979) 22 Journal of Law and Economics 233

Williamson OE, 'Corporate Governance' (1984) 93 Yale L J 1197

Williamson OE, *The Economic Institutions of Capitalism* (Free Press 1985)

Wilson WJ, *The Truly Disadvantaged: The Inner City, the Underclass, and Public Policy* (University of Chicago Press 1987)

World Health Organization, *Closing the Gap in a Generation: Health Equity through Action on the Social Determinants of Health* (CSDH 2008) <http://whqlibdoc.who.int/publications/2008/9789241563703_eng.pdf>

Wynn M and Leighton P, 'Agency Workers, Employment Rights and the Ebb and Flow of Freedom of Contract' (2009) 72 MLR 91

Yamada DC, 'Human Dignity and American Employment Law' (2009) 43 U Rich L Rev 523

Zapirain JPL, 'Regulation of Dependent Self-Employed Workers in Spain: A Regulatory Framework for Informal Work?' in Fudge J, McCrystal S, and Sankaran K (eds), *Challenging the Legal Boundaries of Work Regulation* (Hart 2012) 155

Zatz ND, 'Working Beyond the Reach or Grasp of Employment Law' in Bernhardt A et al (eds), *The Gloves-Off Economy: Problems and Possibilities at the Bottom of America's Labor Market* (Cornell UP 2008) 31

Zatz ND, 'The Minimum Wage as a Civil Rights Protection: An Alternative to Antipoverty Arguments?' (2009) U Chi Legal F 1

Zatz ND, 'Beyond Misclassification: Tackling the Independent Contractor Problem without Redefining Employment' (2011) 26 ABA J Lab & Emp L 279

Zatz ND, 'The Impossibility of Work Law' in Davidov G and Langille B (eds), *The Idea of Labour Law* (OUP 2011) 234

Index